PATRICK FRASER TYTLER

# ENGLAND
UNDER THE REIGNS OF
## EDWARD VI. AND MARY

## VOLUME II

Elibron Classics
www.elibron.com

Elibron Classics series.

© 2005 Adamant Media Corporation.

ISBN 1-4212-2101-2 (paperback)
ISBN 1-4212-2100-4 (hardcover)

This Elibron Classics Replica Edition is an unabridged facsimile
of the edition published in 1839 by Richard Bentley,
London.

# ENGLAND

UNDER THE REIGNS OF

# EDWARD VI. AND MARY.

LONDON:

PRINTED BY SAMUEL BENTLEY,
Dorset Street, Fleet Street.

QUEEN MARY.

From the Original by Sir A. More, in the Collection
of the Duke of Bedford.

# ENGLAND

UNDER THE REIGNS OF

# EDWARD VI. AND MARY,

WITH THE

CONTEMPORARY HISTORY OF EUROPE,

ILLUSTRATED IN

# A SERIES OF ORIGINAL LETTERS

NEVER BEFORE PRINTED.

WITH HISTORICAL INTRODUCTIONS AND BIOGRAPHICAL
AND CRITICAL NOTES

BY PATRICK FRASER TYTLER, ESQ.

AUTHOR OF "THE HISTORY OF SCOTLAND," ETC.

IN TWO VOLUMES.

VOL. II.

LONDON:

RICHARD BENTLEY, NEW BURLINGTON STREET,

Publisher in Ordinary to Her Majesty.

1839.

# CONTENTS

OF

# THE SECOND VOLUME.

* Since compared with the original, which has been found.

# ORIGINAL LETTERS,

## ILLUSTRATIVE OF ENGLISH AND CONTINENTAL HISTORY.

---

### PERIOD SECOND Continued.

### 1551—1553.

#### CONTEMPORARY PRINCES.

| England. | France. | Germany. | Spain. | Scotland. | Pope. |
|---|---|---|---|---|---|
| Edward VI. | Henry II. | Charles V. | Charles V. | Mary. | Julius III. |
| Mary. | | | | | |

WE are now arrived in the course of these letters, at an event of great interest; the second fall of the Duke of Somerset, his trial and execution. It is a subject which, equally with the history of his first troubles and deposition, is involved in much obscurity, and upon which historians have formed very contrary opinions. Was he guilty or innocent of the crimes for which he was arraigned and brought to the scaffold? In reply to this question, Hume, after having consulted the best printed authorities, and evidently guided in his opinion by the narrative of Burnet and Carte, exculpates him. Dr. Lingard, on the other hand, who it is to be regret-

ted had not access, in this part of his work, to any
new sources of evidence, has condemned him; and
this historian observes, in a note, that they who
attempt his justification are compelled to make gratuitous suppositions, which are unsupported by contemporary evidence.† I propose to examine this
point, and to give some new evidence which, if I do
not overrate its weight, will set the question at rest.
It can be shown, I think, on conclusive grounds,
that Somerset was unjustly condemned; that he
was innocent of the only serious charges brought
against him; and that his ruin was the result of a
conspiracy of the Duke of Northumberland, who
felt that he might yet cross his path and bridle
his ambition.

Let us first look at the contemporary account of
the accusation as it is given by Edward himself in
his journal: I extract it as he has inserted it from
day to day.

" October 7. Sir Thomas Palmer‡ came to the
Earl of Warwick, since that time Duke of Northumberland, to deliver him his chain, being a very
fair one; * * * whereupon, in my [Lord's] garden,
he declared a conspiracy. How, at St. George's Day

† Lingard, History of England, vol. vii. p. 96.

‡ In the original Journal by Edward,§ there are here interpolated, in a minute contemporary hand, certainly not the King's,
the word, " hating the Duke, and hated of him." The words
are scored through, but so as to be perfectly legible.

§ Cotton. MSS. Nero, c. x.

last,* my Lord of Somerset, who then was going to the north, if the Master of the Horse, Sir Wm. Herbert, had not assured him on his honour that he should have no hurt, to raise the people; and the Lord Gray before, to know who were his friends. Afterwards a device was made to call the Earl of Warwick to a banquet,† with the Marquis of Northampton and divers other, and to cut off their heads. Also, if he found a bare company about them, by the way to set upon them."

Nothing more seems to have happened till the 11th of October, when Edward resumes his journal.

" 11th. He [Palmer] declared also that Mr. Vane had two thousand men in readiness. Sir Thomas Arundel had assured my Lord that the Tower was safe; Mr. Partridge should raise London, and take the great seal with the printes‡ [prentices] of London; Seymour and Hammond should wait upon him, and all the horse of the gens-d'armery should be slain."

On the 12th and 13th nothing particular occurs, but on the 14th the King writes thus :§

* April 23, 1551.

† So in the original. Edward had first written the *toure* [*Tower*]; then scoring it through, changed it to " a *banket*" [*banquet*].

‡ So in the original.

§ In the Journal, immediately after the entry on the 11th, he remarks,—" 15th. Removing to Westminster, because it was thought this matter might easelier and surelier be dispatched there, and likewise all other." Then he goes on to the 14th.

" 14th. The Duke [of Somerset] sent for the Secretary Cecil to tell him he suspected some ill.  Mr. Cecil answered that, if he were not guilty, he might be of good courage ; if he were, he had nothing to say but to lament him.  Whereupon the Duke sent him a letter of defiance, and called Palmer, who, after denial made of his declaration, was let go."

The King now passes over the events of two days, but on the 16th Oct. he thus writes :

" 16th.  This morning none was at Westminster of the conspirators.  The first was the Duke, who came later than he was wont of himself ; after dinner he was apprehended : Sir Thomas Palmer, on the terrace, walking there ; Hammond, passing by Mr. Vice-chamberlain's door, was called in by John Piers to make a match at shooting, and so taken. Newdigates was called for as from my Lord his master, and taken.  Likewise were John Seimour and Davy Seymour.  Arundel also was taken, and the Lord Grey, coming out of the country.  Vane, upon two sendings.  He said my Lord was not stout ; and, if he could get home he cared for none of them all, he was so strong.  But, after, he was found by John Piers, in a stable of his man's at Lambeth, under the straw."

" These went with the Duke to the Tower this night, saving Palmer, Arundel, and Vane, who were kept in chambers here apart.

" 17.  The Duchess, Crane and his wife, with the chamber-keeper, were sent to the Tower for devising these treasons ; James Wingfield also for casting out of bills seditiously; also Mr. Partridge was attached, and Sir James Holcroft.

" 18. Mr. Banister and Mr. Vaughan were attached and sent to the Tower, and so was Mr. Stanhope.

" 19. Sir Thomas Palmer confessed that the gens-d'armes on the muster-day should be assaulted by two thousand foot-men of Mr. Vane's, and my Lord's hundred horse; besides his friends which stood by, and the idle people which took his part. If he were overthrown, he would run through London and cry ' Liberty! Liberty!' to raise the prentices,* and if he could, he would go to the Isle of Wight or to Pool."

" On the 22nd and 23rd, the young King mentions the arrival of the Queen Dowager of Scotland, who was magnificently received and entertained. On the 24th he thus resumes the accounts of the proceedings against his uncle.

" 24. The Lords sat in the Star Chamber, and there declared the matters and accusations laid against the Duke, meaning to stay the minds of the people.

On the next day, 25th, the King's journal is occupied with an account of the proposals made to him by the confederacy of Protestant Princes; who, by their envoy, desired aid in the cause of religion

* In the Journal, as printed in Burnet's Appendix, (Oxford Edit. 1829,) the letter R has been interpolated here, so as to read, " and raise the apprentices and R," which many might be apt to construe *Romanists*. No such letter occurs in the original.

against the attacks of the Emperor, and whose petition was intrusted to the consideration of the Secretary Petre and Sir William Cecil.

The 28th, 29th, 30th, and 31st of October are occupied almost wholly with the King's account of the movements of the Queen Dowager; but, on the 31st, a notice is added, informing us that the command of the Tower had been taken from Sir John Markham, "who had suffered the Duke to walk abroad," without making any of the Council privy to it, and committed to Sir Arthur Darcy. He then corrects an omission in his journal under the date, 17th Oct. the same day on which Crane and the Duchess of Somerset had been sent to the Tower; informing us that, on this day, "there were letters sent to all parriise,* emperors, kings, ambassadors, noblemen, and chief-men, into countries, of the late conspiracy." Edward next proceeds to a minute description of the entertainments given to the Queen Dowager on the 31st Oct. and the 1st, 2nd, 3rd, 4th, 5th, and 6th of November. These appear to have been most sumptuous, and are dwelt upon by the young King with great complacency; but, in the midst of his descriptions of galas and pageants, he

---

* So in original. Edward had first meant to write that such letters were sent to all *parishes*, which appears to have been the case; but, on second thoughts, he scores it out, and only mentions the letters sent to kings and emperors. It is to these letters, in which the Council exaggerated the guilt of Somerset, that we must ascribe the inaccurate accounts of some foreign historians, De Thou, Sleidan, and others.

bethinks himself of an omission in his journal of the
26th Oct. and thus supplies it, reverting with great
equanimity to his uncle, now a prisoner in the
Tower.

" 26 Oct. Crane confessed the most part, even as
Palmer did before, and more also. How that the
place where the nobles should have been banqueted, and their heads stricken off, was the Lord
Paget's house; and how the Earl of Arundel knew
of the matter as well as he, by Stanhop, who was a
messenger between them; also some part how he
went to London to get friends, once in θ *Se* August*
last, feigning himself sick. Hammond also confessed
the watch he kept in his chamber at night. Bren
also confessed much of this matter. The Lord
Strange confessed how the Duke willed him to stir
me to marry his third daughter, the Lady Jane;
and willed him to be his spy in all matters of my
doings and sayings, and to know when some of my
Council spoke secretly with me. This he confessed
of himself."

In the month of November, Edward gives us no
additional information regarding the subject of the
Duke's alleged guilt, except a notice that on the
8th of that month the Earl of Arundel was committed to the Tower, with Stroadly and St. Alban,

---

* So in original. The King had first meant to write Oct.
and only wrote *O ;* then he meant to write September, and got
the length of *Se ;* then finally he scored both out, and wrote
August.

his men, because Crane did more and more confess
of him; he adds an intimation that, on the 23rd,
the Lord Treasurer was appointed High Steward for
the arraignment of the Duke of Somerset; that on
the 30th of the same month, " twenty-two peers and
nobles, besides the Council, heard Sir Thomas
Palmer, Mr. Hammond, Mr. Crane, and Newdigate
swear that their confession was true;" and he observes, " they did say that that was said without any
kind of compulsion, force, envy, or displeasure, but
as favourably to the Duke, as they would swear to
with safe conscience." On the 1st of December, the
King gives the following account of the trial and
condemnation of his uncle.

" 1st Decem. The Duke of Somerset came to his
trial at Westminster Hall. The Lord Treasurer
(Paulet, Marquis of Winchester,) sat as High Steward of England, under the cloth of estate, on a
bench between two posts, three degrees high.    All
the Lords to the number of twenty-six, viz.

| DUKES. | Bath. | Latimer. |
|---|---|---|
| Suffolk. | Sussex. | Burough. |
| Northumberland. | Worcester. | Souch. |
| | Pembroke. | Stafford. |
| MARQUIS. | Visct. Hereford. | Wentworth. |
| Northampton. | | Darcy. |
| EARLS. | BARONS. | Stourton. |
| Derby. | Bargavenny. | Windsor. |
| Bedford. | Audley. | Cromwell. |
| Huntingdon. | Wharton. | Cobham. |
| Rutland. | Evres. | Bray. |

These," he adds, "sat a degree under, and heard the

matter debated.  First, after the indictments read,
five in number, the learned counsel laid to my
Lord of Somerset, Palmer's confession.  To which
he answered, that he never minded to raise the
north ; and declared all ill he could devise of
Palmer: but he was afeard for bruits, and that
moved him to send to Sir William Herbert; replied it was again, that the worse Palmer was,
the more he served his purpose.

"For the banquet, first he sware it was untrue,
and required more witnesses; whence Crane's confession was read, he would have had him come
face to face.  For London, he meant nothing for
hurt of any Lord, but for his own defence.  For the
gens-d'armery, it were but a mad matter for him to
enterprise with his one hundred against nine hundred.  For having men in his chamber at Greenwich, confessed by Partridge, it seemed he meant
no harm ; because, when he could have done harm,
he did it not.  My Lord Strange's confession, he
sware it was untrue ; and the Lord Strange took
his oath it was true.  Newdigate's, Hammond's, and
Alex. Seymour's confessions he denied, because they
were his men.

"The lawyers rehearsed, how to raise men at his
house for an ill intent, as to kill the Duke of Northumberland, was treason by an Act, anno 3°. of
my reign, against unlawful assemblies; for to devise the death of the Lords was felony ; to mind
resisting his attachment, was felony ; to raise Lon-

don, was treason; and to take assault the Lords, was felony.* He answered, he did not intend to raise London, and sware that the witnesses were not there: this assembling of men was but for his own defence. He did not determine to kill the Duke of Northumberland, the Marquis, &c. but spake of it, and determined after the contrary: and yet seemed to confess he went about their death."

Such is the account of the accusation, the arguments of the crown lawyers, and the defence of the Duke, as given by the King. He next briefly states the result.

" The Lords," says he, " went together. The Duke of Northumberland would not agree that any searching of his death should be treason; so the Lords acquitted him of high treason, and condemned him of treason felonious: and so he was adjudged to be hanged. He gave thanks to the Lords for their open trial, and cried mercy of the Duke of Northumberland, the Marquis of Northampton, and the Earl of Pembroke, for his ill meaning against them, and made suit for his life, wife, children, servants, and debts, and so departed without the axe of the Tower. The people knowing not the matter, shouted half-a-dozen times so loud, that from the palace hall-door it was heard at Charing-cross plain, and rumours went that he was quit of all.'

* The King was probably about to write, " to take counsel to assault the Lords was felony;" but he had only written " *take*," which he scores out.

An interval of nearly two months now took place, for the unfortunate Duke did not suffer till the 22nd of January; on which day his royal nephew thus laconically takes leave of him.

" January 22nd. The Duke of Somerset had his head cut off on Tower Hill, between eight and nine o'clock in the morning."*

Such is the account given by King Edward of the whole " case" of the Duke of Somerset; embracing the period between the first accusation by Palmer, on the 7th Oct. 1551, to his execution on the 22nd January 1551-52. Nothing can exceed the cold heartlessness with which the story is told :† but we have already seen that, three years before, the youthful monarch had declared that he looked upon the death of his uncle the Protector as a desirable event; and increasing years do not appear to have altered his notions upon this subject.

Returning, however, to the question of Somerset's guilt or innocence, let us examine for a moment the evidence against him, as it is given in this Journal. Sir Thomas Palmer, a man, according to his own account, of a profligate and abandoned life, comes to Northumberland, then the Earl of Warwick, on the 7th of October, in his garden, and reveals a conspiracy for his assassi-

* Cotton MSS. orig.   Nero, c. x. fol. 40 to 48.

† Immediately after his notice of his uncle's decapitation, he goes on to supply an omission, under date of the 16th, thus :—

" 16th. Sir W. Pickering delivered a token to the Lady Elizabeth,—a fair diamond."

nation at the house of Lord Paget, entered into
more than five months before by the Duke of Somerset, Sir Thomas Palmer himself, Lord Paget,
Lord Grey, Sir Thomas Arundel, Sir Ralph Vane,
and many others. Upon this, what is Northumberland's conduct to Palmer? Is the informer imprisoned, and rigidly looked to? Quite the contrary. He is permitted to go at large, and four
days afterwards, on the 11th, is again examined;
again convicted by his own declaration of being
party to an abominable conspiracy to massacre
the gens-d'armerie, raise London, seize the great
seal and the Tower; and again, by Northumberland, is permitted to walk away and enjoy himself
about the court till the 16th, on which day he was
apprehended. Does not such conduct strongly
demonstrate a collusion between Northumberland
and Palmer?

But let us look to Palmer's story. He stated
that, on St. George's day last, (23rd April,) the
Duke of Somerset, being on his journey towards
the north, would have raised the people, unless
Sir William Herbert (since then created Earl of
Pembroke) had assured him that he would have received no harm. Now Palmer was notoriously an un-
principled man, and unworthy of credit; Sir William Herbert, a nobleman and an unexceptionable
witness,—a word from him would have placed the
story beyond doubt:—but *he* is *not* called, nor is
any deposition of his read, or spoken of. Indeed,

to make it impossible for him to be called, he is made to sit as one of the jury. Again, Palmer said that the Duke had sent Lord Grey before, to see who were his friends. Here was another opportunity to confirm the tale, had it been true. Care, however, is taken that Lord Grey shall neither be called nor examined. But farther, this conscientious accomplice, who had quietly kept the conspiracy in his breast for five months, asserted that Lord Paget was to have received Northumberland and the other victims into his house, where they were to have been assassinated. Here was room for another corroboration, and yet, strange to say, Paget, at the time, was neither examined nor arrested. Nay, though we find that he was afterwards sent to the Tower, he was never tried for this conspiracy. It was stated by Palmer that Sir Thomas Arundel had assured the Tower; that Sir Ralph Vane had two thousand men in readiness to assault the gens-d'armes; that Sir Miles Partridge was to raise London and seize the great seal; and that Sir Michael Stanhop was privy to the plot for the assassination. It is certain that on the scaffold every one of these unfortunate men solemnly called God to witness that Palmer's declarations were false; they asserted that they were guilty of no treason against the King, and had never been parties to any plot for the murder of the Lords of the Council.*

* Carte, vol. iii. p. 264.

As to Crane's evidence, Edward describes it, as for the most part a mere echo of Palmer's; but there is in it one circumstance which seems to show that even by Northumberland and his party it was not believed.  His confession was made on the 26th of October, and he directly accused the Earl of Arundel of being an accomplice in the plot for striking off the heads of the Council; yet this nobleman was suffered to go at large for nearly two weeks.  He was not committed to the Tower till the 8th of November, "because," says Edward, "Crane did more and more confess of him."* And even, after this reiterated accusation, so little credit was attached to the credibility of Crane, that Arundel was never brought to trial.

The only two remaining witnesses whom Edward mentions as having deposed against his uncle, are Hammond, and the Lord Strange; but the points to which they spoke were trifling, and, if true, proved nothing against Somerset.  Hammond said the Duke kept a guard in his chamber, and Strange affirmed that he wished the young King to marry his daughter.  It is for those writers who condemn the Protector, to show by what process of reasoning these offences can be construed into treason or felony.

But enough has been said of that vindication which may be brought forward for Somerset, even out of such imperfect evidence as has too hastily

* Journal.  Burnet, vol. ii.  Appendix, pp. 39, 40.

been described as conclusive against him. I shall now examine the story of his fall and death a little more minutely, and bring to bear upon it some new lights which have arisen out of my recent researches.

It appears that, in the month of February 1550-51, a busy imprudent man, Richard Whalley, a retainer of Somerset's, as we have already seen, and also a correspondent of Cecil's,* had engaged in some intrigues for the restoration of the Duke to the office of Protector. " Some," says Strype, " in the Lower House were consulting among themselves for his restoration to the office of Protector of the King's person, which was taken away from him in his late troubles, but [they] seemed to be prevented by the breaking up of the session. Yet they intended the next session to set about it. In the mean time, the Lords were to be prepared ; and Whalley in particular, the receiver of Yorkshire, endeavoured to persuade divers noblemen to make the Duke Protector next parliament." †

That Somerset himself was a party to these intrigues, has not been shown by any evidence; but their existence at once roused Warwick. The eyes and the emissaries of this subtle politician were everywhere, and Whalley was brought before

* Strype, vol. ii. part i. p. 390. Edward's Journal in Burnet, vol. ii. p. 22. Appendix.

† Supra, vol. i. p. 276.

the Council on the 16th February; upon which occasion, to use the words of the Council Book, "the Earl of Rutland reported certain practices and words used by him (Whalley) very seditious and of great import: whereunto Whalley made denial; but, upon debating of the matter between them face to face, it appeared that Mr. Whalley was culpable, for the which he was committed to the Fleet.* Two days after this, on the 18th February, Sir Francis Leeke was summoned before the Council, and examined as to a conversation alleged to have been held with Whalley, in which they debated (it was said) to which of the two great parties in the state the Earl of Rutland belonged, — whether he was a *Somerset* or a *Warwick;* but Leeke denied that any such conversation had taken place. He admitted that Rutland had informed him of some *foolish prattle* of Whalley's, but the examination brought out nothing against Somerset; and on the 2nd of April 1551, Whalley, upon finding bail, was discharged from the Fleet.*

I have noticed these minute matters, to show with what lynx eyes the conduct of any one connected with the Duke of Somerset, or with his party in the state, was watched by the opposite faction of Northumberland; and to draw the inference, which I think a legitimate one, that as we find at this time no complaint made against him,

* MS. Privy Council Book, 16th Feb. 1550-51.
† MS. Privy Council Book, 2nd April 1551.

and no allegation that he was implicated in these intrigues, we are entitled to conclude that up to this date he was innocent of any grave offence.

It was to be expected, however, that the Duke should be anxious to recover some portion of the power which he had lost; it was natural that Warwick, aware of the activity of his friends, and jealous of his extreme popularity with the lower classes, for this he never lost, should watch him narrowly, exaggerate every fault, and hint that his ambition once more aimed at the Protectorate. In March and April 1551, rumours of a conspiracy and intended rebellion began to be circulated: Sir Ralph Vane, a follower of Somerset, was sent to the Tower for resisting a party of Warwick's retainers;* and seditious bills, exciting the people against the Council, were found scattered in the streets of the metropolis. It was about ten days after this that Palmer, as we have read in Edward's Journal, fixes the date of Somerset's intended rebellion, viz. St. George's day, which is the 23rd April 1551.† We have already seen how suspicious is this man's whole story, taking a general view of the facts stated by him ; but, fortunately, the Privy Council Books enable us to put to the test both the narrative of this witness and the charges of the indictment. The indictment accuses the Duke of a diabolical conspiracy, plotted *on the*

* MS. Privy Council Book, 12th April 1551.
† Nicolas' Chronology, p. 150.

*20th of April,* in the parish of Holborn, for the deposition of the King from his royal dignity, the sei-
zure of the government, and the imprisonment of
the Duke of Northumberland, then Earl of Warwick; and, secondly, of a similar plot hatched, and
to be carried into execution a month later, *on the
20th of May.** Now we know, from the unchal-
lengeable evidence of the Books of the Privy Council, that, on the 19th of April, when this alleged plot
must have been not merely in preparation, but on
the very eve of breaking out, the leader of it sat
as usual in the Privy Council; and that on St.
George's day, the fatal day when, if we are to
believe Palmer, he was to have risen in open rebellion, he was pacifically employed in attending the
feast of the Order, which was held with unusual
magnificence in honour of Henry the Second of
France, recently elected a Knight of the Garter.†
Next day, being the 24th, he again sat as a Privy
Councillor; and, from the 24th April to the 10th
of May, he is found constantly taking his place in
the Council, being present, with a few exceptions,
every day it sits. On the 10th of May, an inquiry took place, before him and the rest of the
Privy Councillors, regarding some seditious letters
which had been sent to one Kelloway, who was committed to the Fleet; and, on the 17th of May, Tracy,

* Howel's State Trials, vol. i. pp. 518, 519.

† He, the Earl of Warwick, and others of the nobility, were
appointed to peruse and amend the Statutes of the Order. Edward's Journal. Burnet, vol. ii. Appendix, p. 25.

a person who had been discovered to have written a
letter to Kelloway, which tended to rebellion, was
committed to the Tower.   Next day, the 18th of
May, being only two days before the indictment
charges the Duke with this conspiracy to raise a
rebellion in the realm, overturn the government,
and seize the Earl of Warwick, in what way do we
find the arch-traitor employed?   Does he, as was
a general practice in those times, when barons
were plotting against the state, does he absent
himself on pretended sickness, or some other affected excuse, from the court?   Is he found increasing his popularity by residing amongst his own
people in the country;  or busy, through his dependants and friends, in collecting arms and making
secret musters?   Nothing of the kind.   On the contrary: for a guilty man, his conduct is the most
marvellous imaginable.   He is discovered placing
himself daily, almost hourly, in the power of his
enemies;  he is seen taking his seat as usual at the
council-table ;* and, most strange to say, this is
the very time seized by the Privy Council to li-
berate those associates who had adhered to him
in his first troubles.   Sir Michael Stanhop, Mr.
Fisher, and Mr. Grey, his confidential servants,
who had been then sent to the Tower, and had
upon bail only procured a conditional liberty, were
now summarily discharged.†   It may perhaps be
said that this conduct only proves Somerset's ex-

* MS. Privy Council Book, 18th May 1551.      † Ibid.

treme anxiety to blind the eyes of the Council to
the plots which he was hatching; and, under a different ruler or minister from Northumberland, the
reply might have some force.   But we have already
met with proofs of the perfection to which the
system of secret information was carried by the
crafty Northumberland; we know that the Duke of
Somerset and his friends were surrounded by his
spies.  Is it credible, had there been the slightest
foundation for the charge in the indictment, or for
the story of Palmer, that the Council and Northumberland, who then ruled them at his will, would have
acted as they did?   And does not their conduct
involve a strong proof of the innocence of the Duke
and of the malice and falsehood of his enemies ?

We have seen that Mr. Richard Whalley,
who is well described by Sir John Hayward as
a " busy-headed man, and desirous to be set on
work," had been imprisoned by the Council for
some intrigues regarding the restoration of the
Duke of Somerset to the office of Protector.*   On
the 26th of June, 1551, we find this same person
addressing the following letter to Secretary Cecil,
in which he gives a minute account of a confidential
conversation which had taken place on the preceding evening (June 25th) between the Earl of Warwick (afterwards the Duke of Northumberland)
and himself on the subject of Somerset.   I shall
first give the letter, which is a remarkable one,
and then draw some inferences from it.

* Supra, p. 16.

## MR. WHALLEY TO CECIL.

*Orig.* St. P. Off. *Domestic.* 26th June 1551.

" Gentle Mr. Cycle. After most hearty commendations. It pleased my Lord of Warwick as yesternight, after he had perused your letters, to discourse with me, and that at great length, the estate and proceedings of my Lord's Grace [*i. e.* Somerset] in sundry things; wherein, Mr. Cycle, it hath seemed unto me that he is a most dear and faithful friend unto my Lord's Grace; for, like as in expressing his mind in the premises, his whole nature, as I well perceived, was not only vehemently troubled, and that with such carefulness and deep consideration of his Grace's proceedings [enterprised] of late; then again, sundry· times overcome (as methought) with the full remembrance thereof, [he] showed most plainly the inward grief of his heart with not a few tears.

" The sum of all was, that my Lord's Grace hath so unadvisedly attempted the enlargement and delivery of the Bishop of Winchester and the Arundells, as also his Grace's late conference, as he taketh it, with my Lord of Arundel, it pleased him, I say, to be so plain with me herein, as he letted not to say the whole Council doth much dislike his late attempts; yea, and partly also, the rest of his proceedings in the Council, wherein his Grace (for lack of good consideration in the order of his proceedings therein) hath brought the whole of the

Council in suspicion that he taketh and aspireth to
have the self and same overdue an authority to the
despatch and direction of the proceedings as his
Grace had, being Protector.

"And further [he] said, Alas! Mr. Whalley, what
meaneth my Lord in this wise to discredit himself,
and why will he not see his own decay herein?
Thinks he to rule and direct the whole Council as
he will, considering how his late governance is
yet misliked? neither is he in that credit and best
opinion with the King's Majesty, as he believeth,
and is by some fondly persuaded. Truly, Mr.
Whalley, like as by discreet order and orderly suf-
fering with the Council, he may both assuredly
have the King his good lord, and also all things
else that he can reasonably desire; so, by the contrary, taking private ways by himself, and attempt-
ing such perilous causes as the said Bishop and the
. . . . * Arundells is, he will so far overthrow
himself as shall pass the power of his friends to
recover.

" These, with a number more of such like effect,
it pleased his Lordship (I say) at large to discourse
of, and with such a careful spirit and love towards
my Lord as meseems ought to be weighed, and
taken as from a most dear friend.

" He declared in the end his good opinion of
you, in such sort as I may well say he is your very
singular good lord, and resolved that he would

* A word illegible.

write at length his opinion unto you in the premises; and, besides, for the better stay unto my
Lord, would prevent his intended journey to the
court, with . . . * speed; minding, as I can judge, to
put in ure your articles for the said Bishop of Winchester.  In the device and most substantial hand-
ling whereof, he did no less many times wonderfully
praise you than . . . . †  For he plainly said, ye
had showed yourself therein such a faithful servant,
and by that, most witty councillor, unto the King's
Majesty and his proceedings, as was scarce the like
within his realm.

" Thus to end, in that ye best know, Mr. Cycle,
that in my wit and will there is too great a difference so to serve his Grace as appertaineth, and as
my heart most desireth ; so, gentle Mr. Cycle, let
your better wisdom duly so consider for the best
preservation of his Grace's estate in these troublesome times ; and never leave him until ye so thoroughly persuade him to some better consideration
of his proceedings, and that he wittily and friendly
concur and continue with my Lord of Warwick,
who, as I perceive, will be very plain with him in
the premises at his coming to the court.   Otherwise, to be plain, meseems peril great will ensue.

" And for that his Lordship is my very good
lord, and hath friendly promised his help in the
furtherance of my suit, I heartily pray you fail
not duly to remember the same : yea, and also,

* A word illegible.        † A word illegible.

when the time shall best serve, to move my Lord Paget thereof in my behalf, who hath most faithfully promised his assistance in the same.

"Thus, never ceasing to trouble you, I rest. At Ware, this morning, Thursday, 26th June 1551.

"Your own assured,

"R. WHALLEY.

"I trust, ye will advertise me by my servant, whom I have appointed to attend you, in case my Lord's Grace's journey shall be stayed upon any respect hereafter, before my return.

" *To the Right Worshipful Mr. Cycle,*
    *with my Lord's Grace.*"

This seems to me a remarkable letter in the story of Somerset's fall, and of Cecil's connection with it. Whalley is no longer busy in his intrigues to procure the restoration of the Duke to the Protectorate. For these he had suffered imprisonment, and been at length released, and when we next meet him, he is the agent and confidant of his great rival Warwick. Secretary Cecil, who was now at court, and attendant upon the Duke of Somerset, had, it seems, written confidentially to Warwick on the subject of Somerset's interference in the affair of the Bishop of Winchester, and had found fault with his conduct. After having perused his letters, Warwick proceeds to discourse on the same point. He professes the

* Edward's Journal.   Burnet, vol. ii. Appendix.

warmest attachment to Somerset: he blames him
for having espoused the cause of Gardiner, the
deprived Bishop, applauds Cecil's " articles "
*against* that prelate, and proposes to put them
in practice immediately. He assures Whalley
that such perilous proceedings as Somerset had
lately been engaged in, occasioned a suspicion in
his mind, and in the rest of the Council, that he
still aspired to the Protectorate. He laments,
as Whalley says, even with tears, that he cannot moderate his ambition, but still will seek to
rule; he asserts that he is far from enjoying such
high credit with the King as many erroneously
believe; he begs him not to hurry on his own
ruin, by taking private courses, but to concur with
the Council, and with himself, the Earl of Warwick, so as to have the King for his good lord,
and all things else that he could reasonably desire.
Warwick concludes, as we see, with pronouncing
the highest panegyric on the wisdom, diligence,
and fidelity of Cecil, for whom he professed the
warmest friendship, and to whom he promised to
write on the subject of the Duke of Somerset.

Whatever sincerity we attach to these professions and proposals from the powerful and crafty
Warwick, we are entitled to draw from them one
inference. They evidently contain the *worst* that
at this moment could be said against Somerset;
and this, we see, amounts to nothing more than
such a general accusation as one powerful leader

or minister was likely to prefer against another. If (as we must believe was the case) the Duke disapproved of the proceedings of Warwick and Cecil in the cause of the Bishop of Winchester, or dissented from their opinion in other matters connected with the government of the state, it was allowable for him not only to declare his opinion, but to endeavour to persuade others to adopt it. Whalley's advice in this conjuncture, — namely, that Cecil would persuade Somerset to forsake his opposition, to concur " wittily and friendly with my Lord of Warwick," and thus to avoid the " great peril" likely to ensue,—shows exactly the relative position of these two rivals ; but it shows also that Warwick, in his complaint against the Duke, did not accuse him of any designs subversive of the government, or of any conspiracy against himself. Up to this date, therefore, the 26th June 1551, Somerset seems to be acquitted of all such intentions by the best of all evidence—that of Warwick himself : and Cecil, by the same evidence, is proved to have sided in this instance with Warwick against the Duke.

It is of importance to examine the conduct of Somerset subsequent to this communication of Whalley to Cecil, and during the months of July, August, and September, which immediately preceded his trial and condemnation. Now, in July, the Duke's proceedings, as far as we can follow them by the light of the Privy Council Books, and

of Edward's Journal, were of the most pacific description; and he appears to have been on perfectly
friendly terms with the King, the Privy Council, and the Earl of Warwick.    The month of
July was almost entirely occupied with the embassy
of the Maréchal St. André to England.    He
brought with him to the King the insignia of the
Order of St. Michael (whom, by the way, with an
excess of puritanical feeling, Edward styles *Mon
Seigneur* Michael) ;* and whether we look to the entertainments given to the French ambassador and
his suite, or to the deliberations on the business of
the state in the Privy Council, we find Somerset
taking his share in both.    Not a whisper is heard
of discontent; no complaints are made against him.
During the succeeding months of August and September, those deliberations took place regarding
the adherence of the Princess Mary to the Romish
faith, and the necessity of restraining her from the
private use of her mass, which so strongly mark
the intolerance of the time, and exhibit the young
monarch under the forbidding aspect of a harsh
and ungenerous persecutor.    Amid these transactions, Somerset, as we know from the records, attended the deliberations of the Privy Council; and,
in common with the Earl of Warwick and the rest
of the councillors, gave his consent to the measures
which were adopted.    Here, it will be allowed,
there is every appearance of amity: and it is well

* Edward's Journal, in Burnet, vol. ii. p. 28-31.

worthy of remark, that so completely had the Duke regained the confidence of the young King and the Privy Council, that in the end of August he was intrusted with the task of putting down a conspiracy; a task which he successfully accomplished, by seizing and executing the leaders. Of the particulars of the plot, or the object with which it was set on foot, we know nothing; but the following entry in Edward's Journal proves the fact.

" 31st August. The Duke of Somerset, taking certain that began a new conspiracy for the destruction of the gentlemen at Okingham, two days past, executed them with death for their offence."*

Up to this date, therefore, namely, the last day in August, we find that Somerset, so far from being himself accused of any plots against the King, the government, or the Earl of Warwick, was employed by the Council as the guardian of the state. The Council were occupied, during the whole month of September and in the commencement of October, by deliberations regarding the coin. They had to dispose also of the complaints made by the French ambassador against the unjust proceedings of the Emperor; and were busy with preparations for the reduction of the northern borders, which, under the too lenient wardenship of the Marquis of Dorset, had fallen into a state of grievous confusion and disorder. Dorset, however, having surrendered his charge, the Earl of Warwick was ap-

* Journal. Burnet, vol. ii. p. 33. Appendix.

pointed to succeed him, with the usual powers of appointing his deputy-wardens. Great as was his authority before, this high office infinitely increased his strength. It placed at his disposal the most warlike portion of the country, and made him almost sole dictator in England. Now, on consulting the Privy Council record, it might at first appear a suspicious circumstance, that during the month of September, the period immediately preceding his arrest, the Duke of Somerset does not once take his seat at the Council; but his absence can be satisfactorily explained. The dreadful disease called the sweating sickness, which we have already noticed, though at this time much abated, does not appear to have completely ceased in England. One of Somerset's household had died of it; and, on the 30th of September, the Council addressed a letter to the Duke, "in which they prayed him, seeing now no danger of sickness from his servant's death is like to ensue, to make no matter of absence thereof, but to repair at his convenient leisure to the court."*

The Duke accordingly did repair to court, and took his place at the Council on the 4th of October, on which day some proceedings occurred which demand notice. Sir Thomas Arundel, as we have already seen, was a friend and supporter of Somerset; and we know, from Whalley's letter to Cecil, that the Earl of Warwick had resented the

* MS. Book of Privy Council, 30th Sept. 1551.

favour shown to him by the Duke.*    On this day,
however, the Council commanded Arundel to be
brought from the Tower; and, after an admonition,
restored him to liberty.†    Is it to be believed that,
had there been at this moment the slightest suspicion entertained of Somerset's treasons, the Earl of
Warwick, who now ruled the Council at his will,
would have liberated Arundel, one of the Duke's
most attached followers?    Yet this was only *three
days* before the meeting between Palmer and
Northumberland, in which, we have seen, the discovery was made of Somerset's alleged conspiracy to
assassinate his enemies and overturn the government.

On this same day, the 4th of October, the King
communicated to the Council his intention of raising Warwick to the dignity of Duke of Northumberland, and of conferring the dukedom of Suffolk upon the Marquis of Dorset.    Paulet, Earl of
Wiltshire, was at the same time to be made Marquis of Winchester; and Sir William Herbert, Earl
of Pembroke.    These promotions accordingly took
place on the 11th; and, on the same occasion, Secretary Cecil, and Mr. Cheek, the King's tutor, received the honour of knighthood.    On the 5th and
6th of October, Somerset,—although he must have
felt that every day increased the power of his enemies,—with what appears to me the fearlessness of

* Supra, p. 21, 22.
† MS. Privy Council Books, 4th October 1551.

an innocent man, took his place at the Privy Council.*  On the 7th, Sir Thomas Palmer accused him of that treasonable conspiracy for which he suffered; but, the matter having been kept secret from him, he with the rest of the nobility attended the Council at Hampton Court on the 11th, on the 12th, and on the 13th.†  On the 14th he began to suspect that depositions had been sworn against him, and challenged Palmer with the fact, who denied it.  He then, as we know, had recourse for advice to one whom his patronage had raised from an inferior condition to a high and influential station — to Secretary, now Sir William Cecil; but here he met with a reception for which he was little prepared.  " The Duke," says the King in his Journal, " sent for the Secretary Cecil to tell him he suspected some ill.  Mr. Cecil answered, that if he were not guilty, he might be of good courage; if he were, he had nothing to say, but to lament him."  This reply, so cold, measured, and unkind, had the worst effect upon the generous and impatient temper of Somerset.  It threw him into a fit of passionate bitterness.  He wrote a letter of defiance to Cecil, whom he now accounted his enemy; whether on any other ground than his keeping aloof from him under his misfortunes, I have no documents which enable me to discover.  Indeed, at this moment, when one or two original letters

* MS. Privy Council Books, 5th and 6th October 1551.
† Ibid. under these dates.

would be invaluable in this investigation, there
occurs the most lamentable *hiatus*.   One fact, however, is certain from Cecil's reply.   It was undoubtedly meant to assure the Duke that he must
rest on his own innocence, and his own exertions,
and look for no help from him.   And this at once
awoke him to the full extent of his danger.   He
felt that a blow was meditated against him; he
knew, perhaps, that in hours of disappointment or
irritation, when he believed that none but friends
were near him, expressions of resentment, or vague
and unformed ideas of revenge, had escaped his
lips, which his enemies might easily wrest to his
destruction.   Under the circumstances in which he
stood, a guilty man would assuredly have fled;
a timid man might have been tempted to do the
same; but Somerset remained firm, and struggled
against the toils which, although still invisible, he
was conscious were daily gathering round him.
He seems to have disdained all idea of escape; and
on the 16th of October, after having again come to
court and taken his seat at the Council, he was,
as we have seen, arrested in the afternoon, and instantly sent to the Tower.   Now, pausing here for
an instant, let me remark, that the result of this
whole examination of Somerset's proceedings, from
February to October, that is, from the first complaints against him to the day of his arrest, as we
have been able to trace them in the authentic Record of the Privy Council Books, is entirely in his

favour; and that there is not only no proof against him, but the strongest presumption of his innocence.

On the same day on which Somerset was arrested, the Privy Council addressed this letter to the justices of peace throughout England.

*Orig. Draft.* St. P. Off. *Domestic.* 16th Oct. 1551.

" AFTER our hearty commendation. You shall understand that we—having knowledge, by God's goodness, of certain heinous and detestable attempts purposed, and almost put in execution, by the Duke of Somerset, with a great confederacy of his adherents, against the state of the realm and governance of the King's Majesty, to the evident peril and damage of his Highness' person, and to the destruction of divers of the nobility, of the only seeking his private singular government,—have for the surety of his Majesty's person, the preservation of the realm, and for the discharge of our duties to God and the world, so secretly and circumspectly travailed therein, that we have quietly committed him by the King's Majesty's commandment to the Tower, with certain of his adherents, as the Lord Grey, and some others. And altho' Sir Ralph Fane, one of the confederates, hereupon fled, yet is he this day with good diligence taken.

" We be most sorry that the said Duke's evil heart and discontented nature hath prevailed in him to be so great a troubler and shame to his country, and to such a peril, as we could none otherwise avoid than thus in doing our duties.

" This matter being of such weight and import-ance as it is of, we thought meet to impart with you, being the justice of peace in those parts, and governor of that portion of the commonwealth committed to your charge, to study and labour by all the means we can possibly to avoid the same; so you, for your parts also, may endeavour yourselves to see good order and quiet observed within the limits of your precinct accordingly.  So fare you well.  From Westminster, the [16th] day of Octo-ber 1551.*

" Your loving friends."

That manufacture of evidence, so commonly re-sorted to in these iron times, is familiar to those who have examined our more ancient criminal records, and has been well described by a late author.

" In state prosecutions," says he, " of all kinds, occurring previously to the Commonwealth, the evi-dence exhibited to the jury consisted almost en-tirely of written depositions and examinations

---

* This draft letter is endorsed, (but evidently by a mistake of the clerk,) 27 Novembris A°. 1551.  The date is fixed by the statement which the letter makes, that on the day it was written Sir Ralph Vane was apprehended; Edward's Jour-nal mentioning that he was apprehended on the 16th of October.

taken before members of the Privy Council, or
commissioners especially appointed for that purpose,
in the absence of the prisoner who was to be incul-
pated by them.   The whole process of manufacturing this kind of evidence may be seen at the
State Paper Office, where a vast number of original depositions are preserved.   In the first place,
the interrogatories to be exhibited to the different
witnesses were prepared by the law officers of
the crown, under the superintendence of the Privy
Council; upon the ' answers' to these, interrogatories were then framed, to be administered to the
party accused.   The statements, if not extracted
by actual torture, [there is no evidence that in
Somerset's trial this horrible engine was used,]
were generally given under the extreme fear of
it, or under a greater or less degree of pres-
sure. * * * The statements thus procured from the
prisoners were perused and examined by the counsel
for the crown previously to the trial; and each deposition being dissected into paragraphs, which
were distinguished by letters on the margin, was
carefully marked with directions to the officer of
the court, to read only certain selected passages.
Thus, in the margins of the depositions examined
by Sir Edward Coke, who was perhaps the most
zealous and laborious Attorney-General who ever
held the office, such notes as these constantly occur in his hand-writing.   ' *Read* A *and* B *only.*'

' *Read not this.*' ' *Cave.*' — (*Beware.* ) ' *Hucus-que.*' — (*Thus far.*) &c. The prisoner, therefore, was not only subjected to the gross injustice of an accusation made behind his back, but, by this skilful pruning of the depositions, was effectually precluded from detecting and pointing out to the jury any inconsistencies in the accusations so made."* This instructive passage, although it describes the state of the criminal law in the time of Elizabeth and James the First, may be taken as still more applicable to its condition under the more despotic reigns of Henry the Eighth and Edward the Sixth; and there is every reason to believe, from all that we know of Northumberland and his agents, that the process of manufacturing evidence, which is above described, now began to be practised against Somerset with great success and activity. We know, in the first place, that no less than thirty-nine persons were apprehended previous to his being brought to trial. Their names appear in the following paper, which is an original, and endorsed with the single word "Prisoners" in a hand-writing which either is Cecil's, or is very similar to it.

* Jardine's Criminal Trials, vol. i. p. 27.

## PRISONERS FOR THE CONSPIRACY OF THE DUKE OF SOMERSET AND HIS ADHERENTS.

*Orig.* HARLEIAN. 249.

1. The Duke of Somerset.
2. The Duchess of Somerset.
3. The Earl of Arundell.
4. The Lord Paget.
5. The Lord Grey.
6. Sir Thomas Arundell.
7. Sir Michael Stanhop.
8. Sir Thomas Holcroft.
9. Sir Thomas Palmer.
10. Sir Miles Partridge.
11. Sir Rauf Vane.

12. Whalley.
13. David Seymour.
14. Hammond.
15. Neudigate.
16. John Seymour.
17. George Vaughan.
18. Crane and his wife.
19. Brande.
20. Banister.
21. Sir Nicholas Poyntz.
22. Tracey.

24. Serjeant Evans.
25. Miles, the Lord Grey's man.
26. Fyscher of the Wood-yard.
27. Fyscher, the Merchant.
28. Brett.
29. Clerk, Vane's son-in-law.

23. Thomas David.

30. Sir Thomas Stradling.
31. St. Albin.
32. Pelham.
33. Jones, Holcroft's man.
34. Sir John Thynne.
35. Herbert, man-of arms.
36. Barteville.

37. Ravyse Clerk.
38. Symonds.
39. Alexander Ste . . *

Endorsed. "*Prisoners.*"

These arrests having been made, the examinations of the various witnesses were taken; but it is unfortunate that, with a few exceptions, none of these examinations are to be found in the State

* The paper here is injured by fire.

Paper Office or in the British Museum. We are thus deprived of the only direct sources of evidence by which we could *positively* have determined the guilt or innocence of Somerset. Yet I have been so far fortunate as to find some original *depositions* and *notes*, which corroborate in the strongest manner the arguments already used, and show, that the design of assassinating the Duke of Northumberland and the Privy Councillors, or of raising a rebellion in the country, imputed to him by Sir Thomas Palmer, was a mere fabrication of his enemies. Such is, I think, a fair inference, from the following paper. It proves that the utmost extent of the Duke's guilt was, the having entertained at one time an idea of *apprehending* the Lords of the Privy Council who were most obnoxious to him. This was talked of by himself, and amongst his friends; but after a little consideration he dismissed it from his thoughts, as either unadvisable or impracticable. We have already seen that Crane was a principal witness against the Duke.

### CRANE'S INFORMATION AGAINST THE DUKE OF SOMERSET AND THE EARL OF ARUNDELL.

*Copy.* ST. P. OFF. *Domestic.*

" CRANE affirmeth that the Duke of Somerset did bid him to tell the Duchess, his wife, that he would no further meddle with the apprehension of

any of the Council ; and commanded that the said
Duchess should bid Stanhop to meddle no more
in talk with the Earl of Arundell.

" Crane deposeth that the Earl of Arundell said
he would have a Parliament so soon as the apprehension was done, to establish things therein ;
lest, peradventure, of one evil might happen a
worse.

" Crane also deposeth that the Duke of Somerset said to him, that he was sorry he had gone so
far with the Earl of Arundell.

" Crane affirmeth that the Duke of Somerset and
the Earl of Arundell had talk of the apprehension
of the Lords of the Council, of whom the Earl of
Pembroke was one ; and the Earl of Arundell said
that the Earl of Pembroke was an honest man, and
would be conformable enough if the others were
taken.

" Crane saith that the Duke and the Earl agreed
that religion should stand as it now doth ; and that
there was privy to the apprehension, the Duke, the
Duchess, and the Earl of Arundell.

" Crane saith that the Duke of Somerset and the
Earl of Arundell had great conference in the garden of Somerset-house, four or five days before the
Duke's going into the west parts, touching the reformation of the estate of the realm.

" Item.—The Earl of Arundell at that time
promised the said Duke to take such part as he

did; and there oft he did desire him by his promise. And their device was for the reformation of the estate, &c. and to apprehend the Duke of Northumberland and the Marquis of Northampton.

" Item.—The Duke of Somerset and the Earl of Arundell agreed that my Lord of Northumberland and the Marquis of Northampton should go to the Tower; and to be used there, as they were when they were there.

" JOHN SEYMOUR proveth the coming of the Earl of Arundell to the Duke of Somerset's house, divers times to Somerset-place; and that he came in a black cloak.

" Crane and Palmer affirm the same.

" The Duke of Somerset told the Duchess, his wife, that the Earl of Arundell would never confess his doings, if they were revealed. Proved by Crane in his examination before Sir Thomas Moyle, &c.

" Item.—The Earl of Arundell refused Mr. Cycell and Crane, and chose Stanhop, as the Duke told Crane, to be the trusty messenger betwixt the Duke and the Earl, &c.

" And after the Duke told Crane how the Earl of Arundell had devised, that, before the apprehension of the Lords, he would have Sir John Yorke to be taken, because he could tell many pretty things concerning the Mint.

" PALMER saith that the Duke desired much to

have assured unto him the Earl of Arundell and others.

" The EARL OF ARUNDELL, upon the question what he and the Duke meant to have done with the Lord Great Master, the Lord Chamberlain, and the Earl of Pembroke; whereunto the Earl answered, that, for his part, he meant no hurt to their bodies, but we would have called them to answer and reform things."

This paper is of much importance, if we consider its character and its contents. It seems to be a note, drawn up probably by some of the crown lawyers, of such evidence against Somerset as could be collected from the depositions not only of Crane, but of Sir Thomas Palmer, of the Earl of Arundel, and of John Seymour. And how utterly trifling is the evidence it contains of the actual guilt of Somerset!—how completely does it support his own assertions made on the trial, that the whole story of a conspiracy to assassinate Northumberland and the members of the Council at a banquet, was a fabrication, and that the measures he had taken in having armed men in his house were solely for his own defence! It would appear that, having talked with the Earl of Arundel of the apprehension of some of the Lords of the Council, he was afterwards sorry that he had gone so far, and resolved to meddle no more with the matter. And

this, making allowance for the probable exaggera-
tions of his enemies, and the misapprehensions
which may have taken place in Edward's mind, accounts for the young King's assertion, that, as to his
determination to kill the Duke of Northumberland
and the Lords, " he only *spoke* of it, and determined after the contrary, and yet he seemed to confess
he went about their death." *

We have seen that the Earl of Arundel, who was
accused by Crane as a main accomplice of the
Duke, was sent to the Tower on the 8th of November.† It appears that, by command of the King,
his confession was taken in the Tower by the Duke
of Northumberland and the Marquis of Northampton. The following paper is this original confession, which I have found in the State Paper Office;
and I may state explicitly, since much vague and
erroneous assertion has been hazarded on this point
by our best English historians, that it is the only
confession or deposition hitherto given in this
question; the only *original* piece of evidence
upon which, in determining the guilt or innocence of the Duke of Somerset, we are entitled
to rest, and to argue with confidence. It is not
dated either in the body of the paper, or, as often
happens, in the endorsement, which is merely
" *Comes Arundeliæ;*" but the confession must have

* Edward's Journal, p. 42.  Burnet's Appendix, vol. ii.
† Ibid. p. 40.

been made between the 8th of November, when
Arundel was sent to the Tower, and the 1st of December, when Somerset was brought to trial.

### CONFESSION OF THE EARL OF ARUNDELL.

*Orig.* ST. P. OFF. *Domestic.*

" AT such time as the Duke of Northumberland
and the Lord Marquis of Northampton were appointed by the King's Majesty's commandment to
hear the confession of the Earl of Arundell in the
Tower ; of whom, when he was brought before
them, and demanded what he had to say, they declared also, how, upon his own suit and request,
they were sent unto him for that purpose.　Who,
after some protestations, with much difficulty, as a
man loath to say any thing that might touch himself, finally confessed these words hereafter following, or the like, to the very same effect.

" ' My Lords, I cannot deny that I have had talk
and communication with the Duke of Somerset, and
he with me, touching both your apprehensions ; and,
to be plain, we determined to have apprehended you,
but, by the passion of God !' quoth he, ' for no harm
to your bodies.'　And when they asked him how he
would have apprehended them, he said, ' In the
Council.'　And when he was demanded how oft the
Duke and he had met together about these matters, he said, ' But once.'

" And after they had showed him (which was
known by the Duke's own confession) that the

Duke and he met sundry times together for that purpose, as well at Sion, as at Somerset-place in London; with that he sighed, lifting up his hands from the board, and said, ' They knew all.'

"And being demanded whether he did at any time send any message to the Duchess of Somerset by Stanhop, the effect whereof was, that she and the Duke should beware whom they trusted; for he had been of late at Barnard's Castle with the Earl of Pembroke, and did perceive by his talk that he had some intelligence of these matters; but, if they would keep their own counsel, he, for his part, would never confess any thing to die for it; he seemed to be much troubled with this demand, and with great oaths began to swear that he never sent no such message to the Duchess by no living creature. And being answered, it might be that he sent the message to the Duke, he sware faintly, ' By the passion of God, no!' But being farther charged by the said Duke and Marquis with the matter, he, perceiving that they had some knowledge of it, finally confessed that he did warn the Duke of the premises by Stanhop, but not the Duchess.

"And afterwards, when Hampton, one of the clerks of the Council, was sent unto him to write all the whole matter, he would in a manner have gone from all again; and, in especial, from the last; saying, he did not will Stanhop to warn the Duke, but only told it to Stanhop. Whereupon the said Duke of Northumberland and the Marquis were

eftsoons sent to him again, in the company of the
Lord Privy Seal and the Earl of Pembroke; at
which time he did, by circumstances, confess the
whole premises, saving the sending of Stanhop to
the Duke; but, nevertheless, he said that he declared it to Stanhop to the Duke, to the intent he
should warn the Duke of it, but in no wise he
would confess again that he sent him.

" NORTHUMBERLAND.    J. BEDFORD.

" WM. NORTHAMPTON.    PENBROKE."

Endorsed.

" *Comes Arundelie.*"


I need hardly point out to the critical reader
how completely this confession of the Earl of Arundel confirms the statements of the former paper,
entitled " Crane's Information ;" and how fully the
story told by this nobleman, and recorded by Northumberland, Somerset's great enemy, supports the
Duke's innocence of any conspiracy to excite a rebellion in the country, and assassinate the Privy
Councillors at a banquet to be given by Lord
Paget. The confession, in short, entitles us to
assert, that the utmost which could be proved
against Somerset was the intention to apprehend
the Duke of Northumberland and some of his associates in the Council. It is stated in another paper,
which gives us Arundel's confession in a more con-
densed shape,* that when this nobleman was asked

---

* This paper is also an original, signed by Northumberland,
Northampton, Bedford, the Lord Privy Seal, Penbroke, and

what he meant to have done with the Lords if he had got them into his power, he answered, " For my part, I meant no hurt to your bodies ; but we would have called you to answer and reform things."

Having examined and taken the confessions of their various witnesses, the next step, as we have seen, according to the mode of conducting a criminal prosecution in these times, was to prepare from the depositions the questions to be put to the prisoner.    From these questions, where they have been preserved, we may form a pretty correct notion, not indeed of his real guilt, but of the extent of the charges made against him ; and in the present case, where, out of five indictments, only one has survived destruction, it is of consequence to ascertain

---

Philip Hoby.    I did not think it necessary to print it in the text, as it was almost word for word a recapitulation of the confession of the Earl of Arundel, there given ; but in the extreme penury of *originals* bearing upon this portion of our history, it may be right to give it in a note.    It is as follows:

*Orig.*   St. P. Off.   *Domestic.*   1551.

" ' Upon suit made by the Earl of Arundell, the Lord Great Master and the Lord Great Chamberlain were willed by the King's Majesty to repair to the Tower to him ; at which time the said Earl, amongst other things, spake these words, or others of like effect.

" ' I cannot deny but that the Duke of Somerset and I have had conference together of the state, and have misliked the order of things.    And being asked what he meant to have done with the said Lord Great Master, the Lord Great Chamberlain, and the Earl of Pembroke, if they had had them in their power, the Earl of Arundel answered,

this.  Now, fortunately for the truth, the questions put to Somerset were found by Sir Henry Ellis amongst the Cotton Charters.  They were and are now in a state of extreme decay, almost of decomposition, from damp ; and this author, anxious to preserve every little plank in that shipwreck of original letters which has been long, and is still going on in this country, has printed them, and arrested their contents before they were lost for ever.  Truth has been said to be the daughter of Time, but in England it would be more just to call her his victim..  Leaving her, however, in his gripe, I must remark that these "questions," although hitherto passed over without comment, are of extreme historical value; they seem to me to establish beyond a doubt this fact,—that Northumberland had abandoned, as utterly hopeless, the charge of assassinating the Lords of the

"'For my part, I meant no hurt to your bodies; but we would have called you to answer and reform things.'  And being asked at the same time whether he had not sent Sir Michael Stanhop in message at any time to the Duchess of Somerset, and for what purpose he had sent the said Stanhop, the said Earl of Arundel answered, that he never sent Stanhop to the Duchess, but to the Duke.  (Said he),. 'I have sent him, willing him to take good heed, for his counsel and secrets were come abroad.    The said Earl of Arundell did also at one other time speak the like words in the presence of the said Lords, and of us, the Lord Privy Seal, the Earl of Pembroke, and Sir Philip Hobbie.

" PENBROKE.        NORTHUMBERLAND.    W. NORTHT.
            " J. BEDFORD.        PHELYP HOBY."
Endorsed.    " *Sir Michael Stanhop.*"

Council, which Dr. Lingard and Mr. Turner consider to be proved against Somerset. The questions are as follows :

### QUESTIONS PUT TO THE DUKE OF SOMERSET.

" 1. Whether did Palmer, the Lord Grey, or both, move you first to keep the field, and to draw northwards?

" 2. What moved you to credit Partridge, when you followed his counsel to remove from Sion, and came to London, contrary to the opinion of some others ?

" 3. To how many did you declare your mind, what time you came to Ely Place to *apprehend the* Duke of Northumberland, then Earl of Warwick ; and who did give you first advice thereunto, and to whom did you repent the not doing of it ?

" 4. Whether did Partridge, or any other, give you advice to promise the people their mass, holy-water, with such other, rather than to remain so unquieted ?

" 5. With how many did you confer concerning the taking of the Isle of Wight, and the fortifying of Poole, or any other place ?

" 6. How many times had you any message or intelligence from Vane, he being in the Tower ; and by whom, and whose means ?

" 7. Whether did you mistrust, after you had spoken secretly with Sir Thomas Arundel, lest he had been purposely set awork to undermine you;

and to whom did you wish that you had not gone
so far with him ?

" 8. What was the uttermost talk that did pass
between you and Sir Thomas Arundel at that
time; and [by] how many noblemen and others
he would be assisted ?

" 9. Whether did you consent that Vane should
labour the Lady Elizabeth's Grace to be offended
with the Duke of Northumberland, then Earl of
Warwick, the Lord Marquis, the Earl of Pembroke, then Master of the Horse, or any others of
the Council; and how and by whom had you intelligence of Vane's proceedings in that behalf?

" 10. How oftentimes have you conferred with
the Earl of Arundel, and he with you, of the misliking of the state and government; and what did
you conclude to be the reformation thereof?

" 11. Whether have you yourself, or any other
for you, at any time conferred with the Lord Paget to the like effect ; and how did you perceive or
know his inclination thereunto ?

" 12. Whether did it proceed first from yourself,
or from the said Earl of Arundel, to have a Parliament immediately upon the attaining of your
purposes; and what matters would you have set
forth at the said Parliament?

" 13. With how many have you conferred for the
setting forth of the proclamation to persuade the
people to mislike the government, and to be offended with the Council; and specially the doings

of the Duke of Northumberland, the Earl of Pembroke, and the Marquis of Northampton ; doing them to understand that they went about to destroy the commonwealth, and also had caused the King to be displeased with the Lady Mary's Grace, the King's sister ?

" 14. What was the effect of the message that Stanhop brought from the Earl of Arundel to you, or to my Lady, concerning of distrust he had conceived of the disclosing of some of the secret points or conferences that had passed between you ?

" 15. What was the effect of the talk that passed between you and Stanhop alone, and between you and Stanhop and my Lady, at your last being at Beddington ; and how often has Stanhop devised with you upon the misliking of the King's Majesty's Council, and specially of the foresaid Lords ; what advice he would give you for the reformation of the same, and whether he would himself offer to take such part as you did; and what other friends he would offer to assist you withal ?"

It has unfortunately happened that the Duke's answers to these questions put to him in the Tower are not to be found; but, judging from the questions themselves, it is remarkable that we have not a single interrogatory as to any purpose of assassinating Northumberland and others of the Privy Council. Does not this nearly amount to proof that the whole story was discovered to be a fabrication, and abandoned as such by his accusers ?

But, looking a little more narrowly into the questions, we can discover, I think, something of the secret history of this tragedy. His enemies were determined to ruin him, to urge him to adopt some measures which might be wrested into treason or felony. For this purpose, Carte informs us that they kept him in a constant state of suspicion and alarm.

" To prepare the way for his destruction," says this author,* " reports were raised of him as a proud and aspiring person, whose ambition had no other bounds than the crown itself; and common rumours were spread abroad that some of his followers had proclaimed him King in several places, to discover how the people stood affected to his elevation. His doors were watched, and notice taken of all that went in or out; his words were observed,— made worse by telling, and aggravated by odious circumstances, to his disadvantage; and no arts of fraud or treachery left unpractised that might bring him into suspicion with the King, and obloquy with the common people. The Duke's friends easily imagined that these practices were a prelude to his and their ruin; but the difficulty was how to guard against adversaries that outdid them in cunning, and were infinitely superior to them in power. It is not unlikely that, in the consultations upon this subject, some hot inconsiderate person, or pretended friend in the pay of his enemy, might propose a

* Carte, History of England, vol. iii. p. 261.

violent attempt against the Duke of Northumberland." This passage seems to me to contain a
true account of the matter, and it is completely
supported by these questions put to the Duke.
They show in a striking manner the state of a man
kept in alarm by the knowledge of plots being carried on for his destruction, and balancing between
the necessity of self-preservation and a desire to
act uprightly: they show, still more, a man worked
on by his friends, rather than working upon them.
Is there a design to take the field and move northwards ?—It is not the Duke who originated it; but
either Palmer, his pretended friend, who afterwards
betrayed him,* and showed himself a mere tool of
Northumberland, or Lord Grey. Does he appear
to have had an intention of leaving Sion-house, his
own residence, and coming to London ?—It was by
the counsel of Sir Miles Partridge.† Is he accused
of alluring the people by a promise of restoring to
them the mass, and advised not to endure any
longer the state of unquietness in which his enemies
kept him ?—This project for gaining popularity
originated, it seems, either with Partridge or some
other ;‡ and so on, through many of the remaining
questions. The most important interrogatory, how-

* " Whether did *Palmer*, the *Lord Grey*, or both, move you
first to keep the field ?"

† " What moved you to credit Partridge when you followed
his counsel to remove from Sion ?"

‡ "Whether did Partridge, or any other, give you advice to
promise the people their mass ?"

ever, is the third ;* and it corroborates in the strongest manner the defence made by the Duke upon his
trial, proving that the utmost extent of his guilt
was a plan to *apprehend*, not to assassinate, Northumberland at Ely-house; formed, as his enemies
suspected, by others, not by himself, and afterwards
abandoned.    It is unfortunate that the Duke's answers to these questions cannot now be found, although we must hope they may yet be discovered.
But, meanwhile, it may be remarked that the remaining charges against him, as they are to be gathered from the questions, are of a minor description, and cannot by any ingenuity be brought under treason or felony.    To have supposed that Sir
Thomas Arundel was employed by his enemies to
undermine him; to have regretted that he had gone
so far with him; to have been aware that Vane endeavoured to prepossess the Lady Elizabeth against
Northumberland and his associates; to have expressed to Arundel or Paget a mislike of the government as managed by this powerful nobleman,
and a desire for some reformation; to have talked
over the best method of persuading the people,
whether by a proclamation or otherwise, to be dissatisfied with Northumberland and the Council; to
have expressed a fear lest the private conferences

* " To how many did you declare your mind, what time you
came to Ely Place to apprehend the Duke of Northumberland,
then Earl of Warwick; and who did give you first advice
thereunto, and to whom did you repent the not doing of it?"

between himself and the Earl of Arundel should have been revealed to his opponents;—all these fears, and regrets, and dislikes, and vague conversations, amount to nothing. Even taking it for granted that Somerset had answered the questions affirmatively, so far from constituting the crimes of treason or felony, they do not imply any higher offence in a minister or statesman than that of being dissatisfied with the state of things; annoyed at his own exclusion from power, and anxious to regain it by the means then commonly in use.

Having thus far examined and presented to the reader the only authentic evidence which now exists against the Duke, it will be unnecessary to go critically through, what I must call, the legal farce of his trial. It took place in Westminster-hall, on the 1st of December; not without great precautions lest the people, by whom he was much beloved, should attempt a rescue. " On the 30th, and last of November," says Stowe, " by commandment from the King's Council, order was taken in London that every householder should see to his family and keep his house, having in a readiness that day a man in harness in every house, but not to go abroad till they should be called, if need were; and further, that, on the night following, there should be kept a good and substantial watch of householders in every ward: which was so done. And on the next morning, being the 1st of December, the Duke of Somerset

was had from the Tower of London by water, and
shot London-bridge at five of the clock in the
morning ; and so went to Westminster, where was
made ready a great scaffold in Westminster-hall ;
and there the said Duke appeared before the Lords
and Peers of the realm ; the Lord William Poulet,
Marquis of Winchester, and Lord High Treasurer
of England, that day sitting under the cloth of
Estate as High Steward of England."*

It was well known that the Duke of Northumberland, the Marquis of Northampton, and
the Earl of Pembroke were the personal enemies
of Somerset ; yet, with that flagrant disregard of
justice which characterizes the law of these times,
they took their place amongst the twenty-seven
Peers who were his judges. The indictments,
being five in number, but of which only one has
been preserved, were then read ; and, the depositions of the witnesses having been produced, the
Duke, after a deliberation of six hours, was acquitted of the treasons, but found guilty of the
felony, and had sentence of death.   And here,
in passing, I must again, for a moment, allude to
Dr. Lingard's account of this trial, and the sentence
which he has pronounced against the Duke.   How
highly all who have studied this historian's works
must respect his learning and acuteness, it is needless to say ; but such rare qualities only make us
the more regret a degree of bias which occasion-

* Stowe, p. 606.

ally infects his mind and prevents the detection of
the truth.    In his remarks on the trial of Somerset,
it seems to me, that he does not write with his
usual caution; and his statement of the evidence
against the Duke is calculated to mislead the reader.

" The indictment," says he, " which had been
found at Guildhall by the grand jury of the City,
accused the Duke of traitorously conspiring with
divers others to depose the King from his royal
estate, and of feloniously inciting several of the
King's subjects to take and imprison the Earl of
Warwick, one of the Privy Councillors.    The witnesses, instead of an examination in open court,
were called, on the day preceding the trial, before
the Lords of the Council and twenty-two Peers and
Noblemen, in whose presence they made oath that
they were not influenced by force or fear, envy or
malice; that they had deposed to nothing which
was not true, and that they had shown to the Duke
of Somerset as much favour as their consciences
would allow.    From their depositions, if they may be
credited, it seems to have been the plan of the conspirators that the Lord Grey should levy forces in
the northern counties,—that Lord Paget should invite Northumberland, Northampton, and Pembroke
to dine with him at his house in the Strand, — that
Somerset's band of one hundred cavalry should
intercept them in the way, or, if they were nume-
rously attended, should assassinate them at table,
—and that the Duke, having raised the City, should

lead his horsemen, 2000 infantry under Crane,* and the populace, to attack the gens-d'armes of the guard. In addition, it appeared that he kept near his chamber, at Greenwich, a watch of twenty armed men to prevent his arrest.

" The Duke, in his defence, contended that the evidence of some of the witnesses ought to be expunged, because they were his men, and bound to him by oaths of fealty; he required, but in vain, that Crane should be confronted with him; he denied that he ever meant to levy men in the north, or to raise the City of London; he asserted that the guard at Greenwich was intended only as a protection from illegal violence; and maintained that the idea of charging the gens-d'armes was too extravagant to enter into the head of any man whose intellect was not deranged. But on that part of the charge which touched him more nearly, the design of assassinating the Lords, he appeared to hesitate. It was indeed true, he said, that he had spoken of it; he had even entertained the notion: but he solemnly declared that, after mature consideration, he had rejected it for ever. The Peers deliberated for some time on their verdict. They acquitted him of treason, but unanimously found him guilty of having conspired to seize and imprison the Earl of Warwick, one of the Privy Councillors; an offence which, by an act of the third of the King, had been made felony without benefit of clergy.

* An evident misprint for Vane.

As soon as the sentence had been pronounced, Somerset fell on his knees, thanked the Lords for their impartial conduct during the trial, asked pardon of Northumberland, Northampton, and Pembroke, whose lives he confessed that he had sought to take, begged them to solicit the King for mercy in his behalf, and recommended his wife and children to the pity of his nephew."*

Such is Dr. Lingard's narrative; and the authorities on which it is founded are stated to be Edward's Journal, the King's letter to Barnaby Fitzpatrick in Fuller's Church History, and Coke's Entries, which contain the indictment. He then sums up his opinion against the Protector in these words : " Those who, in despite of these authorities, persist, like Burnet, in asserting the innocence of the Duke, are compelled to make a number of gratuitous suppositions, not one of which receives any support from contemporary evidence."

Now what is the general impression left upon any reader's mind by this account ?  Burnet represents the Duke of Somerset not as innocent of every charge made against him, for this historian admits that the intention of imprisoning a Peer was proved ;† but he contends that he was guiltless of the

---

* Lingard, vol. vii. pp. 94, 95, 96.

† " All people thought, that being acquitted of treason, and there being no felonious action done by him, *but only an intention of one, and that only of imprisoning a Peer, proved*, that

more aggravated charge of an intention to kill Northumberland and the Lords.    To maintain this,
argues Dr. Lingard, is to make a gratuitous supposition contrary to contemporary evidence.    And
why ?—Because, says he, by *the depositions of the
witnesses, if they are to be credited,* it is proved that
Paget was to invite Northumberland and the Lords
to his house, where Somerset was to assassinate
them.    We have here the depositions of the witnesses
relied on as the grounds of the historian's opinion ;
and any reader would infer, I think, from the words
employed, that the writer had read and weighed
these depositions, and in this way had arrived at
the conclusion that they contain absolute proof
of Somerset's guilt; the only question being, whether they were worthy of credit or not.    But in so
doing he would fall into a material error; and it
is to be regretted that Dr. Lingard's account of
the trial leads him directly into it.    At the time
this author wrote his history, no depositions of any
witnesses had been discovered.    The historian does
not affirm that he had seen any such depositions,
and I think I may state, that no other historian
ever did.    Depositions certainly were taken at the
time, sworn to on the day preceding the trial, and
read at the trial, and of these I have recently discovered two, which the reader has already seen, and

one so nearly joined to the King in blood would never be put
to death on such an occasion."—Burnet's Reformation, vol.
ii. p. 181.

which strongly support the innocence of Somerset;
as to the rest, could we now either see the originals,
or any copy, or had we even an account of their
contents from any author who states that he had
seen them, much light might be elicited on this
obscure subject. But they are lost,—apparently
irrecoverably lost. To speak of them as pieces of
evidence to be credited or discredited,—to quote
facts as if from them, and on these facts to decide
against the Duke,—is unfair to that unfortunate
man, and leads the reader to condemn him upon
very insufficient grounds. Dr. Lingard was probably misled by the inaccurate language employed
by Carte, and more recently by the compiler of
Howell's State Trials, who gives what he denomi-
nates Sir Thomas Palmer's First Examination, and
quotes other evidence under the title of his Second Examination; adding complacently what he
styles Crane's Examination, and Hammond's Examination. These alleged examinations, the historian
has, perhaps, mistaken (and Mr. Sharon Turner has
followed him in the error) for the depositions of
these witnesses; but the State Trials took them
verbatim from Burnet, and Burnet took them from
Edward's Journal, into which, without a word
added more or less, they all resolve. Now Edward nowhere says that he had read or heard
the depositions; and there cannot be a doubt, I
think, that the narrative of Edward was the story
told him by Northumberland as to Palmer's verbal

declaration in the garden, and Crane's and others' confessions. Edward, I must repeat, does not mention that the confessions were made in his presence, or that he had seen any written declarations. To what then does this whole argument amount? If we may believe the story of Somerset's great enemy, told in the manner most favourable to himself, Somerset was guilty. This is clearly no argument at all.

If we attentively consider the trial, it will appear, I think, that the utmost which could be proved against Somerset, and the utmost which he confessed, was an intention, afterwards abandoned, of imprisoning Northumberland, and others of his enemies. " But no," says Dr. Lingard : " he confessed during the trial that he had entertained the notion of assassinating Northumberland ; and, after sentence was pronounced, he again confessed that he had sought to take their lives." In support of these assertions, he quotes Edward's Journal, and Edward's letter to Barnaby Fitzpatrick. Let us look first at the letter of Edward to his friend Barnaby. What does it say?

" After debating the matter from nine of the clock till three, the Lords * * * acquitted him of high treason and condemned him of felony, and which he seemed to have confessed. He hearing the judgment, fell down on his knees, and thanked them for his open trial. After, he asked pardon of the Duke of Northumberland, the Marquis, &c.

*whom he confessed he meant to destroy, altho' be-*
*fore he swore vehemently to the contrary."* *

Now this letter of Edward, when fairly weighed,
instead of supporting, contradicts Dr. Lingard's
statement. The historian says, the Duke confessed
the intention of assassinating Northumberland, both
during the trial and after it. The King says, he
vehemently denied the intention of destroying
Northumberland during the trial, or before sentence had passed, though he seemed to have
confessed the felony,—that is, the plot for the
imprisonment of Northumberland; but he confessed afterwards that he meant to destroy him. Let
us look now to what Edward says in his Journal; and here we find how little dependance
ought to be placed on the evidence of the young
monarch, surrounded as he was by the enemies
of his uncle, and apparently acting under their
influence. In his Journal, again, so far from cor-
roborating, he seems to run counter to his letter.
In the letter it is stated, as we have just seen,
that during the trial he vehemently denied an
intent to kill Northumberland; in the Journal it is
stated that, during the trial, he said he spoke of
killing him and the Lords, and seemed to confess he went about their deaths: but as to what
took place after the trial, the Journal says not
a word of the confession mentioned in the letter,

* Fuller's Church History, vol. ii. p. 341.

about *killing* the Lords, but uses words which seem
to apply to his design of imprisoning them.   It
is very evident, therefore, that either the one or
other of these contradictory pieces of evidence is
erroneous in its statements, and must be rejected :
to found on both, as has been done by Dr. Lingard,
is not allowable.

But I can bring evidence to show that Edward
was misinformed on this point, and it is with this
view that I have reserved for this place an extract
from an original letter of the Marquis of Winchester, who sat as High Steward in this trial,
and who was an enemy of Somerset's ; it seems to
me decisive of the point, that Somerset, neither
during the trial nor after the sentence, made any
confession of an intent to kill Northumberland and
the Lords.   In a letter addressed on the 2nd of
December, the day after the trial, by this nobleman
and the Lords of the Privy Council to the Lord
Admiral Clinton, then in France, we find the following passage :

" Your Lordship shall further understand, that
yesterday the Duke of Somerset was arraigned of ii
[two] several high treasons, and of the procurement
of certain other treasons, which crime is in the case
of a felony as touching the judgment; of which three
several crimes he was before indicted in three
several shires.   At his arraignment, I the Lord
Treasurer, by the King's Majesty, was appointed

High Steward; and we, the Duke of Northumberland and all other Lords of Council, being Barons of
Parliament, with the other Nobles of the realm,
being Lords of Parliament, to the number in all of
26, were as his Peers in the trial; of whom we had
such consideration to eschew rigour and extremity,
declining ourselves to as much equity as might anywise be devised, that altho' the crimes of the treasons were alleged, not only by such as had continual company with him, but also by his own men
nighest to him, as Crane, Neudigate, Hammond,
upon their free confession without compulsion, yet
was he by us his Peers found guilty but of the procurement of certain treasons, which was so mani-
festly and fully proved by many witnesses as in no
reason could be answered or excused.  Amongst
other things of his crimes against the state of the
realm, it was avowed to his face in the presence of
judgment, by the Lord Strange, that he the Duke
had divers times moved the said Lord Strange to
practise with the King's Majesty for the marriage
of his daughter to the King; and, indeed, true it is
the said Lord Strange had so done, and that since
the last treaty for marriage with the French King,
altho' altogether in vain : and yet thereby the said
Duke hath showed himself not only presumptuous,
but also of little consideration of the King's Majesty's honour, and good meaning towards the
wealth of the realm.  For the crimes whereof he is
found guilty ; he is adjudged to be hanged, and so
forfeit as in cases of felony.

" Truly, if we his Peers had but applied ourselves to the justice of the laws in these the Duke's
cases, as we did bend ourselves to show charity and
even so to judge of him as we would that God
shall judge us at the last day of the Lord, he had
been charged and condemned of the other two principal treasons.

" Hereof we thought meet to advertise your
Lordship, to the intent ye may take occasion to declare the same there as you have opportunity."

Let it be remembered that Winchester was
Northumberland's great ally, and Somerset's determined enemy ;* that this letter was written the
day after the trial; and that the object with which
it was written was to furnish the English ambassador with all the facts against Somerset,—with
everything that could justify his condemnation.
Had the accused confessed the intention of assassinating the Lords, would Winchester have omitted
it ?    It seems to me impossible.

Were we not now discussing an affair of life and
death, in which a man was sacrificed for a crime of
which he was guiltless, one might be inclined to
smile at the cant of these noble judges, who plume

---

* Knox, who was then in England, describes Winchester
under the title of Shebna.    " Who was most frank and ready
to destroy Somerset and set up Northumberland ?    Was it
not Shebna ?" Admonition to the Professors of the Truth in
England, p. 53.

themselves upon their lenity. Their argument is
an odd one. The Duke, say they, was arraigned
for two acts of treason, and one of felony. We
found him guilty of the last, and condemned him
to be hanged; but we let him off on the first two,
and so he won't be beheaded. Thus we eschewed
rigour and declined to equity.

We have seen that Cecil was at this time in
high favour with Northumberland; he had been
recently knighted, and, as Secretary of State, must
have possessed great influence. Whether his interference in Somerset's favour could have procured a gentler fate for his former patron, is a
doubtful point: the probability seems to be, that
he saw he was a lost man,—a sheep, as Fuller
says, condemned for the slaughter. To interfere,
might have implicated himself, and could not have
saved the Duke; so he left him to his fate. Yet
this was not done without some trepidation lest
their former intimate friendship and connexion
might be found to cast suspicion upon him. So
at least we may infer from the following letter
of Pickering to Cecil, written from Paris on the
27th of October, a few days before Somerset's trial;
in which he congratulates the Secretary on his
" good fortune in being found undefiled with the
folly of the unfortunate Duke."

### PICKERING TO CECIL.

*Orig.* St. P. Off. *France.* Paris, 27th Oct. 1551.

" Your last letters liked me much; the better
to find therein the form of your good fortune to
be found undefiled with the folly of this unfortunate Duke, whose unlucky and unlooked-for loss
I lament, as charity chargeth; whose disloyal doings I detest, as duty directeth; whose pernicious
purposes proved, I have good right and reason to rejoice, understanding thereby the most happy evition
[evitation] of that dreadful danger wherein our
blessed and most innocent King and commonwealth
was covertly compassed. The King's path, which
you have taken you to travel in, is the right line
that leadeth to that life that is most laudable;
and altho' sometimes a terrible tempest do trouble the traveller in that trade, yet the incompa-
rable comfort of an uncorrupt conscience cannot be so stirred with no storm to scare out of
that way, but holdeth fast by the firm faith that
he hath found in God, to be relieved at length for
his truth's sake. Thus, leaving you with this living Lord, I take my leave: and, if what I may
can stand you in stead, spare not to speak,—for
speed is at hand."        *        *        *

Somerset was a great favourite with the people;
and, whilst his trial was proceeding in Westminster
Hall, an immense crowd waited the result without.

It was then the practice, when a prisoner was found guilty of treason, to have the axe carried before him ; a gloomy ceremonial, which was omitted in the event of his being convicted of felony. When the Duke appeared, it was observed that the axe was removed ; and the people, believing him acquitted, gave such a shout, hurling their caps into the air, that their cry was heard to the Long Acre beyond Charing Cross. A few moments, however, explained the mistake, and their clamours sunk into a melancholy silence.*

I have already pointed out the early prepossessions entertained by Edward against his uncle, and the extraordinary coldness and apathy with which he tells the story of his misfortunes. Hume has justly observed, that care seems to have been taken by Northumberland's emissaries to prepossess the young King against his uncle ; that, lest he should relent, no access was given to the Duke's friends ; and that he was kept from reflection by a constant series of occupations and amusements :† but, had the heart been warm or generous, it could scarcely have been so easily stifled in its young impulses. In the Cotton Collection there is a paper *in the hand-writing* of the young King, dated 18th January, only four days before Somerset's execution. It is entitled by him, " Certain

* Stowe, p. 606.
† Hume, p. 369. Edition of 1832, in one volume. See Cooper's Chronicle, p. 353.

points of weighty matters to be immediately concluded on by my Council;" and of these matters
the third is as follows.

" The matter for the Duke of Somerset and
his confederates to be considered, as appertaineth
to our surety and the quietness of our realm ; *that
by their punishment and execution,* according to
the laws, example may be shown to others."

On the back of this paper a memorandum is
added by Cecil, in his own hand, to this effect.

" These remembrances within written were delivered by the King's Majesty to his Privy Council at Greenwich, in his Majesty's inner Privy
Chamber, the Monday being the 19th of January
1551 [1552], A° 5 of his Majesty's reign.   They were
written with his Majesty's own hand, and received
of his Majesty's own hands by the Marquis of Winchester, being then Lord Treasurer ; being present
these following :

" The L. Treasurer,      L. Admiral,      Mr. Comptroller,
" Lord Great Master,  L. Chamberlain, Mr. Vice-Chamber-
" Duke of Suffolk,       L. Cobham,          lain Gates,
" L. Great Chamberlain,                     The two Secretaries,
" Earl of Pembroke,                             Mr. Sadler,
" L. Privy Seal,                                    Mr. Masone,
                                                          Mr. Bowes."

This minute memorandum seems to have been
drawn up by Cecil, who was himself present, as a
precaution in case any reflections might have been

afterwards made by the King on the subject of his uncle's death. It stamped the originality of the paper, proved that it was delivered to his Council by the young King himself, and proved also, I am sorry to add, that his uncle's execution was fixed at Edward's own request, and without, as far as we can discover, a word being uttered in his favour.

The rest of this melancholy story is soon told. On the 22nd of January the Duke suffered on Tower Hill, at nine o'clock in the morning. He was attended on the scaffold by Dr. Coxe, the young King's tutor; and met his fate with remarkable courage, devotion, and serenity. He addressed the people and asserted his innocence, declaring himself a true man to the King's Majesty and the realm; but observed, at the same time, that as he was condemned by the law, whereunto all were subject, he was content to die to show his obedience. To the last the crowd clung to the hope that Edward would extend mercy to his uncle, and an affecting circumstance occurred to show it. Whilst Somerset was speaking, Sir Anthony Brown was observed gallopping towards the scaffold. The instant the people were aware of his approach, they shouted " A pardon! a pardon!" tossing up their caps and cloaks in the air, and crying, " God save the King! God save the King!" " The good Duke all this while," I use the words of an eye-witness, " stayed, and with his cap in his hand waved the people to come together, saying these words to their words of pardon:

' There is no such thing, good people, there is no such thing; it is the ordinance of God thus for to die, wherewith we must be content; and I pray you now let us pray together for the King's Majesty, to whose Grace I have always been a faithful, true, and most loving subject.'   *   *   At which words the people answered, ' Yea, yea, yea;' and some said, ' It is found now too true.'" †

Fox, the Martyrologist, informs us that he received his account of the behaviour of the Duke of Somerset in his last moments from a nobleman who stood near him on the scaffold.   The last passages in it are minute and pathetic.

" After this," says he, " turning himself again about like a meek lamb, the Duke kneeled down upon his knees; and Dr. Coxe, who was there present to counsel and advise him, delivered a certain scroll into his hand, wherein was contained a brief confession unto God; which being read, he stood up again on his feet without any trouble of mind, as it appeared, and first bade the sheriffs farewell, then the Lieutenant of the Tower and others, taking them all by the hand that were on the scaffold with him.   Then he gave the hangman certain money; which done, he put off his gown, and kneeling down again in the straw untied his shirt-strings; and, after that, the hangman coming unto him turned down his collar round about his neck, and all other things which did let or hinder them. Then lifting up his eyes to heaven, where his only

† Ellis Letters, vol. ii. Second Series, p. 216.

hope remained, and covering his face with his
own handkerchief, he laid himself down along,
showing no manner of token of trouble or fear,
neither did his countenance change, but that before
his eyes were covered there began to appear a red
colour in the midst of his cheeks.

" Thus this most meek and gentle Duke, lying
along and looking for the stroke, because his doublet covered his neck, he was commanded to rise
up and put it off; and then laying himself down
again upon the block, and calling thrice upon the
name of Jesus, saying, ' Lord Jesus, save me!' as
he was the third time repeating the same, even as
the name of Jesus was in uttering, in a moment he
was bereft both of head and life, and slept in the
Lord Jesus."*

So fondly beloved was Somerset by the people,
that many of them crowded round the scaffold, dip-
ped their handkerchiefs in his blood, and preserved
them as relics.

To conclude the subject of this unfortunate
Duke, I trust I have shown that the terms in which
he has been spoken of by Mr. Turner and by Dr.
Lingard,† are unmerited and unjust.   The first author compares him to Cesar Borgia; the second
considers the intention of assassinating Northumberland as proved against him.   To me it appears

* Fox, vol. ii. p. 99.
† Turner, Modern History of England, vol. iii. p. 289.—
Lingard, vol. vii. pp. 95, 96.

that he fell an almost innocent victim to the ambition and craft of Northumberland and his faction : and it is worthy of notice, that Camden observes that he lost his life " for a slight crime, and that, too, contrived by the treachery of his enemies."*

Sir Edward Coke has argued that, even admitting the evidence against him to be true, he was guilty neither of treason nor felony, comparing the charges of the indictment with the clauses of the act on which it is founded ; because there had been no proclamation commanding the Duke and his friends to disperse, and of course no refusal to disperse after such proclamation.   The same argument has been adopted by Burnet and Sir James Macintosh,† and controverted by Collier and Dr. Lingard.‡   I do not pretend to decide upon this legal objection.   It is enough for me to have shown that there is no evidence to convict him of that flagrant crime of which he has been pronounced guilty, in such positive terms by some able historians, — a conspiracy to assassinate Northumberland ; and that the utmost extent of guilt proved by the few original documents which I have discovered was an intention to apprehend this dangerous rival, and wrest from him the power which he found incompatible with his own safety.

* Camden's Britannia, by Gibson, vol. i. p. 98.
† Burnet, Hist. of Refor. vol. ii. p. 180.—Macintosh, Hist. of England, vol. ii. p. 265.
‡ Collier, vol. ii. p. 315.—Lingard, vol. vii. pp. 95, 96.

The greatest stain upon Somerset was his violent
and interested dilapidation of the property of the
church ; one of the greatest stains upon Cecil seems
to me to be his desertion of Somerset.    An accusation has been made by a Romish writer,* who was his
contemporary, that the Secretary not only forsook
him, but betrayed him.    Of this, however, I have
found no direct proof.  It appears, indeed, in Crane's
Information,† that when the Duke of Somerset and
the Earl of Arundel were secretly intriguing for
the apprehension of Northumberland, Somerset had
recommended Cecil or Crane to be the messenger
between them ; upon which, Arundel refused to employ Cecil, and chose Sir Michael Stanhope, who
was afterwards executed as an accomplice of the
Duke.    From this we are entitled to infer that
Somerset, almost to the last, trusted Cecil in his
most secret matters; we know also, from Pickering's letter, already quoted, that Cecil and his
friends thought it great good fortune that, when so
many were brought into suspicion, he should have
escaped undefiled with the folly of the unfortunate
Duke ; we know that he was in habits of intimate
correspondence with Whalley, a principal witness
against Somerset, and that the Duke considered Cecil's conduct so base, that, just when the storm was

* See a rare Tract entitled " An Advertisement written to a
Secretary of my Lord Treasurer's of England by an English
Intelligencer.—British Museum, 698, c. 2.
   † Supra, p. 40.

bursting on him, he wrote him a letter of defiance :
to this we must add, that on the 11th of October, a
few days before Somerset was sent to the Tower,
Cecil is found in the highest favour with Northumberland and his faction, and for his services receiving
the honour of knighthood ; whilst, after the fall and
execution of this unfortunate man, his power, and the
confidence with which he was treated, continued to
increase : all these are suspicious circumstances, but
it is quite possible they might be explained had we
been able to recover more original evidence.  These
facts are undeniable ; that Cecil's earliest, warmest,
and firmest patron was Somerset ; that he left him
in the toils at his hour of utmost need ; and that he
devoted himself with the utmost zeal to the service of his destroyer, the lofty and all-grasping
Northumberland.  We shall soon see that the service was a dangerous one, and conducted him to the
very brink of a precipice.  But it is time to leave
these reflections, and resume our foreign letters.

Having now concluded a disquisition which has
necessarily carried the story forwards to the 22nd
of January, the day of Somerset's execution, the
reader must pardon an anachronism, and permit us
to carry him back a few months, to observe what has
been going on at the court of the Emperor.  To
which end we cannot have a better guide than Sir
Richard Morysine ; who, on the 20th October 1551,
addressed to the Council an interesting letter from
Augsbourg.

At this moment Hungary was the seat of a war between Ferdinand King of the Romans, assisted by his brother Charles the Fifth, and Isabella, the widow of John Zapolski, who had entered into a league with the Turkish Sultan, and had sub- sidised a large Infidel force. One of the most ex- traordinary actors in these scenes was George Mar- tinhausen, who had raised himself from a low origin to be prime-minister to Zapolski, the late King of Hungary. Zapolski, on the death of Louis King of Hungary, in the battle of Mo- hatz, in 1526, had been chosen to fill the throne by one party of the Hungarian nobles, Ferdi- nand by another; and this Prince, having de- feated his rival, Zapolski threw himself into the arms of the Ottoman Porte, and opened Hun- gary to the Infidels, who warmly espoused his quarrel. On the death of Zapolski, Isabella his widow claimed the throne for her son Stephen, whilst Ferdinand prepared to secure it for him- self. Isabella, dreading the power of such a rival, imitated her husband in obtaining the assistance of the Turks; upon which Martinhausen desert- ed her, from disgust, as he alleged, at her selfish and sacrilegious conduct in exposing Christen- dom to the ravages of the Infidels. Those, how- ever, who knew him best, suspected that personal ambition, rather than a zeal for the true faith, regulated his politics; and Ferdinand looked on him with suspicion, though he did not deem it prudent to reject the advances of so powerful an ally. John Baptist Castaldo, whom Morysine mentions in his letter, was sent by the Emperor Charles the Fifth to take the chief command in the Austrian territories in Hungary, and was instructed to co-operate with Martinhausen in the conduct of the war. Petrovitz, whom he also mentions, was a Hungarian Lord, and a relation of Zapolski, the late King. He commanded a portion of the army of Isabella.*

In the following passage of a letter to the Council, dated the 6th of October, Morysine gives us some hints of the motives which at this time swayed the decisions of the Emperor. Rightly to understand his allusions, it must be remembered that the Council of Trent had resumed its sittings on the 1st of May. Pope Paul the Third, having died in the preceding year (1550), had been succeeded by Julius the Third in the papal chair; the beginning of whose pontificate was signalised by a new convocation of this celebrated Council. The bull which he issued for this purpose was far from conciliatory. It was apparent, from the terms he employed, that the holy father proposed to sit in judgment upon the Protestants as culprits, — not to negotiate with them as subjects or children; and even the Emperor deprecated its severe and imperious style.

* De Thou, book ix. p. 423.

\*      \*      \* " Yesterday," says Morysine, " we had all warning that the Emperor within an eight days would go to Inspruck, and so towards Italy. \*      \*      \* The Emperor, by his going to Inspruck, shall be within two days' journey of Trent, and so give stomach to those that be there to do anything, rather than . . . . † once to mean that they ought.

" It is also noised that the King of the Romans will meet with his brother at Inspruck, but few do believe it : that the Turkish Bassa, Beglierbey, with might and main cometh again into Hungary. The King, as they say here, hath a fifty thousand good fighting men. \*      \*      \* The Turks are almost, if men say true, in number . . . . . to Ferdinand his host.    Men think they will pitch a field and . . . . ‡ bloody battle.    If the King have the better, he shall be in rest the next year ; but if, as God forbid, the victory should sway on the other side, all Christendom is shortly like to feel that the Bishop of Ro[me] hath chosen a wrong time to set Christian princes together by the [ears].

" Poor men may mislike things that be amiss, and be sorry that they that may amend them will not ; but, when we have done all that pertaineth to us, we may at the last repose ourselves, and fall asleep in Christ's lap, and assure ourselves, how evil soever things do appear to us, God can and will

† Here the letter has suffered from fire.

‡ Here, and in the former place, the words have been burnt away.

turn the worst of them to his glory, and the commodity and comfort of such as be rightly his.   God
send us a nap with John, while others strive who
may do most harm." *   *   * †

These embarrassments in Hungary, as well as
his constant occupation with the affairs of the General Council, rendered the Emperor unsuspicious of
the intrigues of the Elector Maurice, whom he still
believed his best friend, but who was now secretly
organising against him the most formidable opposition which he had ever encountered.

This extraordinary man had already concluded
a league with the King of Denmark, the Duke of
Mechlenbourg, the Margrave Albert of Brandenbourg, and the son of the Landgrave of Hesse,
against Charles the Fifth ; and with the same object
had, on the 5th of October, entered into a secret
treaty with Henry the Second of France.   Morysine, as we see by the following letter, was not
aware of these transactions, which Maurice had the
address to conceal till the last moment.   The blow
came with stunning force upon the Emperor.

SIR RICHARD MORYSINE TO THE COUNCIL.

*Orig.* St. P. Off. *Germany.  Augsbourg.* 20th Oct. 1551.

" PLEASE your good Lordships, our days of removing are so oft deferred, that tho' every man here
looketh to see the Emperor on horseback upon
Thursday next, yet I must see him gone ere I can

† Orig.   Galba, B. xi. f. 58.

tell whether he will go. It cannot be but he
meaneth to go, and that shortly; he having left
himself almost but such stuff as of necessity must
go in his company, the rest is already at Inspruck.
\* \* \* Yesterday he should have gone, and then
to-day, and now two days hence. For my part, I
wish still new causes to force him to tarry till new-
come money make me able to travel with him.

"Here have been cold rumours that there should
be a battle fought in Transilvania, between Ferdi-
nando's men and the Turks, and that the King
should have the better: but this talk is utterly
ceased, and other news in place; which are, that
the Turks have taken two castles,† that were Petrovitz's, and are about the third; yea, some say
they have taken three, and are about the fourth,
and that they are so many as that Castaldo dareth
not try the matter by a fought field. No, they
now say he would what he can not to come to any
battle, the match being so unequal.

"Yesterday, Duke Maurice's men, that have lien
in company with the others all this while at Xone-
vert, came to town. They say the rest tarry for the
King of Denmark's ambassador, and that they will
be here shortly. More than I have already written
I cannot know, they meaning (as such say that have
been with them) to tell their ambassade first to the
Emperor; and after, as much to others as they con-

† Weisenberg and Dalmatz were two of the castles alluded to.

veniently may. It may be, the matter for the
Bishoprick of Bream, between the King of Denmark and the Duke of Brunswick, be some cause
of the King of Denmark's sending hither.

" Yesterday there came a gentleman of the
Bishop of Rome's chamber hither. He must be
longer here ere all his errand can be known.
They say, that may talk with him, he talketh very
stoutly, even as though the Bishop were like to do
what he meaneth against France. The Bishop, he
saith, maketh in Rome 8000 footmen, and 2000
more in Bologna. The Spaniards that be at
Sienna, which are counted a 1500, go to Parma
by the Emperor's appointment; and those 2000,
that be gathered up at Bologna, go by the Bishop's
appointment to Vienna, in three places. The Emperor also maketh 1500 horsemen more hereabouts
at this present.

" Cardinal Vesali is by this almost in France;
one being sent after him with some new instructions, even when this his chamberlain came from
his *Holowness*.* Here is a talk that the Bishop
is in hand with the Venetians to borrow money of
them, upon one or two of his towns, Imola, Faenza,
Ravenna, or Cervia; which, a forty years since, the
Venetians were in possession of. It is thought the
French King doth make them a far better offer;
that is, to help them to all these, and more, without

---

* Hollowness.—Morysine, who is a wit, writes ' Hollowness'
for ' Holiness.'

disbursing of so great sums of money as the Bishop would have for one of them.   Thus there are ways daily and hourly sought out to make the Venetians declare themselves friends either to the one side or the other.   If the Turk bar them of such corn as they of necessity must have out of his country, men guess they must go, and will, where he appointeth them.

"These of Trent, that would men should take this their conspiracy against God and his word for a Council General, be doing, and have made answer to the French King's protestation.   The copy is either not yet come hither, or only come to the Bishop's nuncio this last night.   I trust, by the next, to get it.   The Imperials say, the Turk's navy is gone towards Constantinople, and will winter at home.   Few do think the news true, for that the time serveth ill now to seek new havens.     *     *     *
Here was news risen that the young Scottish Queen should be dead; but since there is come a post out of Flanders, to tell the Emperor that his sister, the French Queen, is like to die.   He hath in all haste sent a gentleman of his chamber, called Workern, to visit and comfort her.

"The Prior of Capua is now thought to be parted in earnest from the French King's service, for that he hath written letters which do declare just causes of his going away; alleging this as one, that the Constable of France hath sought many ways to have him killed.   Some think Mirandola

will be in great hazard if the French King do not
levy the siege the sooner.*    They have, as we
say here, great want of all things but of corn.
Their wine is almost spent, their flesh eaten, their
salt and oil consumed.    Yea, th' Imperials say they
were driven of late to send out their horses, for
that they have neither meat to feed them with, nor
salt to powder them in.    Of late, they sent out
two soldiers of theirs appareled like market-men;
they had their panniers and capons, such as called
and cried when they forced them so to do: which
noise when Alessandro Vitelli's men heard, they
thought there was cheer at hand for them; but
while they thus fondly sought capon's flesh, they
lost their own flesh.    A 25 of Alessandro's best soldiers slain in this bickering; the rest, content to
avoid their hurt, by seeing their fellows' harm,
would trouble the market-men no longer.

" I send your Lordships an Italian letter, which
telleth wonders of great companies of wolves that
have been, and yet are, about Pistoja and Florence.    If he that wrote it writeth truly, these
wolves, no doubt thereof, are as apt a figure to set
out the cruelty of this time as can be devised.    For,
besides that in cattle they kill as many as come in
their way, they wax familiar and come into men's
houses, and devour young children, even in their

* Mirandola was at this time held by the French, and besieged by the Emperor's forces.—De Thou, book vii. sub anno
1551.

cradles. The like company of wolves was seen in Italy in the year 1525, when the French King was taken at Pavia.

" I have heard it oft, that Francisco Sforza, the Duke of Milan,† was fain to promise by proclamation four crowns to every one that did bring to him a wolf; and found the charges to be such, as he came after to revoke his proclamation, with promise to give a ducat for a piece. He was weary of this price also, and came at the last to a testoon; and then they brought him no more wolves, nor he gave them no more money.

" And being now come to the end of this letter, we have constant word brought us that the Duke of Saxony hath warning to depart to-morrow with his band of Spaniards towards Inspruck; and that the Emperor himself, to-morrow, will also set forward on his journey. * * * From Augusta, 20th October 1551.

" RICHARD MORYSINE."

We must now turn our eyes once more to the court of France, which we shall find enlivened by a royal christening, and connected with it an English embassy extraordinary. Catherine of Medicis had brought the King a son in 1551, who afterwards ascended the throne by the title of Henry the

---

† Francis Sforza, Duke of Milan, born 25th July 1401, an illegitimate son of James Sforza, surnamed the Great, and Lucia Trezana. He died in 1466.

Third. Soon after his birth, Henry the Second, who, as we have seen, was at this moment desirous of maintaining the most friendly relations with England, requested its young monarch to stand godfather to the child: he consented; and, early in November, sent the Lord Clinton into France to act as his representative at the christening.

The King sent in Clinton's suite a young gentleman named Barnaby Fitzpatrick, who had been educated along with Edward, and to whom he appears to have been much attached. Fuller terms him the King's *proxy for correction;* a quaint phrase, by which we are to gather that, when Edward broke Priscian's head, Sir John Cheeke, his worshipful tutor, broke Barnaby's: yet he adds, when such execution was done, as Fitzpatrick was beaten for the Prince, the Prince was beaten in Fitzpatrick.* Barnaby commenced life under the fairest auspices: the young King drew up, with his own hand, instructions for his conduct when abroad; and some letters from Edward to Fitzpatrick, with others from the young favorite to his master, have been published by Fuller and Walpole. Cecil, also, corresponded with Barnaby, and watched over his education; whilst the French Monarch received him graciously, and took him into his household. The death of Edward, however, overcast all these fair prospects. — Clinton was an able naval commander and statesman, and in both capacities

* Fuller, vol. ii. p. 342.

had already been employed in services of high moment. Having been ill before setting out, he was seized on his arrival with a relapse, which rendered it impossible for him to fulfil one of the objects for which he had been sent,—to deliver his Majesty's token to the Princess Elizabeth, being a fair diamond in a ring.

These remarks will enable the reader to enter into the spirit of the following letter from Sir Wm. Pickering to the Council: at the time it was written, Somerset, it will be seen by the account given of the conspiracy, was still alive, and a prisoner in the Tower. This slight anachronism must be pardoned; as it was necessary, in discussing the question of the Protector's guilt, to throw all the letters directly illustrative of the subject into one series.

### SIR. W. PICKERING TO THE COUNCIL.

*Orig.* St. P. Off. *France.* 27th Oct. 1551.

" Please it your Lordships to be advertised that your letters of the date of the last of Sept. came to my hands the 12th of Oct. inclosed in a letter of the Constable's; and the 24th of this inst. Francisco arrived at Melun with your Lordships' letters of the 16th of the same; so that I had spoken with the Constable not past three days before, concerning the effect of your first letters. * * * Upon the receipt of your Lordships' last letters of the date of the 16th, delivered me at Melun by Francisco, I repaired with all convenient speed towards

the court, the King being then newly arrived at
Chantilly, good forty English miles from Melun;
and the same night I came to Paris, from whence
I sent my man in post with my letters unto the
Constable, for the knowing of the King's pleasure
for my repair to his presence.

" Upon Friday, my man returned again with
his answer, that the King had so appointed his
hunting and pastime abroad, that, as he thought,
it would be Sunday before I might have him
at any convenient leisure. Nevertheless, the Constable willed me to repair to a fair town called
St. Lies, distant from Chantilly two leagues;
where he said I should find good lodging, and
be well intreated. According to his appointment
I came thither the same day, and found neither of both. Upon Saturday, early in the morning, I sent my man to him again to show him
that I was already there, abiding the King's Majesty's will and pleasure. He sent me word that
the King was that morning ready to go à l'assem-
blée, (as he was, indeed, by my man's report,) and
therefore prayed me that I would come to him on
Sunday to dinner; which I did, and was accompanied with the Cardinal of Lorrain, and marvellously
feasted. Then was I brought to the King's presence;
where, after the King's Majesty's right hearty commendations, I declared how the King my master
did congratulate his Majesty on the birth of the
young Prince, his son, and that he prayed God to

send him many such fruits of ripe and hoary years,
accepting most thankfully his good brother's request in choosing him his Christian *compère*, whereunto I said his Highness was no less ready than his
Majesty desirous to require him to the same; and
for this intent I told him that my Lord Admiral
prepared his journey towards these parts with as
much speed as he might conveniently to supply the
King's Majesty's room as his deputy in that behalf.

" From this I came to the contents of your
Lordships' last letters, and told him that the King
my master would communicate with his Majesty,
not only all his prosperous success as occasion served, but those hard adventures also that chanced
unto him much contrary unto his Grace's expectation; for so, I said, required the strait amity betwixt their Majesties. Wherefore I told him that I
was commanded to open unto him a perilous conspiracy lately purposed in England, very dangerous
to the King's Majestie: howbeit God, that ever preserved the same in other perils, had not likewise
forsaken him in this jeopardy, of all other most
dangerous; for, by his most merciful favour, the
thing was revealed in time, and the chief attempt-
ers already, by his Highness' commandment, committed to prison. And thus I entered, according to
your Lordships' commandment, how the Duke of
Somerset, seeking his private sole governance, purposed, and almost put in execution, certain heinous
and detestable attempts, with the confederacy of his

adherents, against the state and governance of the
King's Highness and of his realm, to the evident
peril and danger of his Majesty's person, and to the
destruction of divers the nobility of his realm; for
avoiding of which enormities he is now committed
by the King's Majesty's commandment, with certain
of his adherents, as the Lord Grey and others, to
the Tower of London; and Mr. Vane, one of the
same confederates, was apprehended with great diligence, as he thought to have escaped away, and is
now forthcoming among the rest.

"The King, seeming amused* of this matter,
paused a great while; and at length answered, that
he was right sorry to understand of any such mis-
demeanor amongst his good brother's subjects; and
specially that he, which ought by all good right to
have been the most earnest defender of his Prince,
and the chiefest upholder of his country, should by
any means pretend the hurt of the one, or the
overthrow of the other; and marvelled much that
neither God's laws, nor man's laws, nor yet the law
of nature, could move the stony heart of the Duke,
not from doing, but from thinking, any such pernicious thing against the Prince and commonweal,
wherein he hath much overpassed both the limits of
reason and nature.    Nevertheless, he said, that, on
the other part, he most heartily rejoiced to perceive
how, by the singular provision of Almighty God and
your Lordships' good and diligent circumspection,

* In a muse, a reverie.

his good brother and son was so well preserved, and
his realm in so good time delivered from such imminent danger.    By means whereof he trusted that
this scourge, though it were grievous for a time,
should be for the best, and none other thing than
a good admonition to the King's Highness and to
your Lordships hereafter to look more warily to
yourselves, and to the good governance of the
realm ; and called God to witness that, if any thing
had happened to the King's Highness otherwise
than well, (that God forbid at any time !) the same
should have been unto him no less grief than if it
had chanced to any of his own natural children.

"Sir, quoth I, his Highness hath that for so fully
persuaded, that I dare boldly assure your Majesty
that he standeth in the like terms of sincere affection and brotherly love towards you, and wisheth to
you the same good luck he desireth to himself.    In
conclusion he wished, for the more surety of the
King's Majesty's person, that, like as the chief at-
tempter was forthcoming in a sure place, even so
might the rest of his adherents with no less diligence be weeded out and brought to light.    Thus,
after his rejoicing that the mischievous purpose of
the King's Majesty's enemies was espied out in good
season, he commanded me to do his most affectuous recommendations to his good brother and son,
and so entered into other purposes.

"He told me of a picture of the King his good

brother's, that Mons. Gerniacque* brought with him
out of England, and said that it was very excellent;
and yet that the natural, as he was persuaded,
much exceeded the artificial. Here he asked me
what news I had of the Emperor, which he never
faileth at every mine access to his presence.   Sir,
quoth I, I have none other but that I hear he pass-
eth towards Trent, and so determineth his journey
into Italy.—Nay, quoth he, that is not so; for he
intendeth to repair shortly into his Low Countries.—
Sir, quoth I, it may well be; for I received these uncertain news but of a courier of the King my master's, that came long since out of the quarters
where he now remaineth.—Well, quoth he, let him
come when he will; he is prepared for, and shall
be received.   Thus, after other communication of
small importance, his Majesty licensed me to depart.

" After this, taking my leave on the Constable,
I demanded of him if he had any news that he
would participate with the King my master, and
with the Lords of his Council.   Monsieur l'Ambassadeur, quoth he, as for news, we have no great store
at this present, but that our men have given an
overthrow to the Spaniards about Asta in Piedmont, and slain of them to the number of two hundred at least.

" Here he entered once again, as he had done be-

* Jarnac.

fore, into communication of the Duke ; and said, if
the King my master had need of men or arms to
suppress or punish the wickedness of his evil-willers
within his realm, that there is good store in France,
which he assured me should be ready at his Majesty's beck and commandment.

" I gave him thanks, on the King's Majesty's
part and your Lordships', of his gentle offer in his
master's behalf, and that herein he showed himself
no less than he was well known and holden for in
England ; howbeit, I told him that your Lordships'
vigilant and discreet governance was ever such that
we should have no need of foreign aid for the administration of justice in our realm for punishment of
offenders according to their demerits.

" Well, quoth he, let my Lords of the Council beware that the Emperor be not a part in those matters ; for, saith he, he searcheth very often to sow
the mischievous seeds of discord in divers places,
and the commodity serveth him right well in England, by the means of some that are nearer of kin-
dred unto the King than the Duke. Here I pressed
him, as much as reason would, to declare more
plainly what his meaning was therein ; requiring him,
if he had intelligence of any of these matters, to
show himself as he was taken and esteemed of my
master ; and, if it pleased him to utter the same to
me, I would serve him as his secretary in English,
and [his] instrument, to advertise the King's Majesty
of his mind and opinion therein. Other thing I could

not get at his hands of any precise knowledge, otherwise than that he mistrusted the Emperor's *tromperie* in every business. And therefore would he, he said, that we, his master's dear friends, should be well ware of him, his friends, and all his kins-folks in England. Here, after my leave-taking of him, he returned to the King, and committed me to Mons. Maury and Mons. Lansacque; commanding them to show me his esquiery, his armoury, and all other commodities and pleasures about Chantilly.

" Since my last letters to your Lordships these be our occurrents. Pedro Strozzi arrived here by post, and will shortly depart hence again. The Cardinal, that I wrote to your Lordships of, cometh not yet hitherward, as I can hear. There is one Ludovici depesched from hence to Malta for the revocation of [the] Prior de Capua, but it is thought that he will not return hither again. The Turk's galleys were lately dispersed into divers coasts; some to Previzi, Figaro, and some to Valona. Divers of them perished by reason of a great tem-pest, insomuch that the common judgment here is that they shall not be able by this great disorder-ing to do any thing of importance this next year.

" This day the King removeth from Chantilly to Equoan, whereas he intendeth to keep the feast of All Saints; and within two days after he cometh to Paris, and from thence within two other days to Fontainbleau, where he will attend my Lord Admi-ral's arrival for this baptism.

" Thus, having none other occurrents to write at this present, but that I feel your Lordships' present sorrow my most just grief, I beseech the Lord to comfort you, and bring all things to your Lordships' good desired end and purpose.

" At Paris, the 27th of October.

" Your Lordships' most humble to command,

" W. PYKERYNGE."

Whilst the miserable tragedy of Somerset's trial and death was acting in England, the preparations for that great contest between the Emperor and the Protestant Princes led by the Elector Maurice, began to develope themselves more openly than before. In the following letter from Chamberlayne, who was at this time resident ambassador in the Netherlands, we have the first intimation of that famous league or coalition which Maurice the Elector had secretly organised against his former friend and patron the Emperor.

CHAMBERLAYNE TO THE COUNCIL.

*Orig.* ST. P. OFF. *Flanders.* Nov. 16th, 1551.

" PLEASETH your most honourable Lordships to be advertised. Since the time that I did last write of my proceedings here with the Queen about the molestations done unto the merchants, I have had no matter of moment to certify until now, that I have secretly learned that these folks have discovered somewhat of a *confederacy* between Duke

Maurice, Duke Albert of Brandenburg, and divers others,* pretending for to seek the Landsgrave's liberty by force ; and some will say that Maurice hath levied his siege beside Magdeburgh, having been within the town and banquetted with them, and [they] are thought to be all in *one confederacy ;* wherewithal it is said that the Emperor is very perplexed, and doth travail with the Switzers all that he may for to induce them to his side, but, as it is thought, all in vain.    Mons. D'Aremberg and one Barlement, of this Council, are depesched in post

* When the Elector Maurice was secretly forming this confederacy of the Protestant Princes of Europe against the despotic designs of the Emperor, he sent an envoy to England, soliciting Edward the Sixth to join the league. (Carte, vol. iii. p. 258.) The following paper contains Edward's reply, declining to become a party; and, as it is drawn up in the handwriting of Cecil, I give it, (although hurriedly composed, and in some places false in its latinity,) as containing the best account of the King's answer to this important message. The Protestant Princes had not authorised their envoy to enter into a treaty, his mission being only to sound Edward's inclination; and it is not improbable that the request he made at the same time, for an advance of four hundred thousand dollars, rather cooled the zeal of the English Council. The paper furnishes us also with another proof of the confidence reposed in Cecil by the young King and Northumberland at this moment.

*Orig.* 19 Nov. Anno 5 Edwardi VI. 1551. *Germany.* St. P. Off.

" Responsio R. Maj. ad Oratorem Ducis Mauritii Electoris, Joannis March. Brand. et Ducis Megalopolensis, missum ad R. Maj^m.

" Regia Majestas optimè affecta est, quod causam hance promovendi Evangelii libertatem susceptum est, quicquid

towards Gueldres and Friseland,—men think, for
that the said Maurice and the other had gotten
the same into their confederacy, for the better
agreeing of their purpose.   Whatsoever there is,
it is some great matter that is in hand, wherewith
these people are perplexed, and do not make much
talk thereof.

" It is told me that there hath been a battle
foughten in Hungary, the particulars of which I
cannot yet learn.

" The French galleys at Marseilles, as it is said,
have taken eight rich ships coming out of Spain
towards Genoa, with the King and Queen of Bohe-
mia's treasure and stuff.   The saying goeth here,

bonâ cum ratione excogitari possit, ad tuendum liberam confes-
sionem Evangelii, Romanique Pontificis tyrannidem propellen-
dam, non solùm e suis finibus, verùm etiam à reliquâ Christianâ
R. P. *

" Verùm quoniam Maj. sua intelligit, oratorem hunc legatum
esse tantùm à tribus Principibus, sciatque certò magnum esse
numerum Principum in Germaniâ, qui antehâc protestationes
ediderunt adversùs cæcam illam et inmanem tyrannidem R.
Ecclesiæ, et adhuc, ut spes est, causam tam piam non deserue-
runt, consultum esse duxit — ut priusquam fœdus aliquod inea-
tur, clarè, perspicuè, et certè intelligi possit qui reliqui Princi-
pes, sive Reges, sive Duces, sive Marchiones, sive Comites,
sive Civitates et Respub. expectandi atque accessendi sint ad
hanc communitatem, societatemque fœderis tam pii, tamque
magni momenti et ponderis, ut, quò causa sit gravior, eò majore
prudentiâ sit prosequendum; nam qui prudentiam serpentis
simplicitati columbinæ miscuerit, is neque ex prudentiâ malig-
nitatem, neque ex simplicitate stultitiam, sentiet.   Multoque
consilio salus inest, ut ait ille."

* Republica.

that the Frenchmen have made courses into the land of Liege, by reason whereof the Bishop hath called the states of the country together; which have granted to contribute towards the wars, and take the Emperor's part against the French King. Marry, I have no great belief that the bruit should be true.  \* \* \* \*

"THOMAS CHAMBERLAYNE."

THE COUNCIL TO THE LORD ADMIRAL, BEING IN FRANCE FOR TO CHRISTEN THE FRENCH KING'S SON.

*Orig. Draft.*  ST. P. OFF.  2nd Dec. 1551.

" AFTER our hearty commendations to your good Lordship : the same shall understand that Francisco the courier arrived here with your letters upon Monday in the forenoon ; and, being empesched with other great businesses, we could not return the messenger before this time.

" Touching the letters of Mr. Pickering, we commend his wisdom and diligence.  And for that your Lordship moves us to know our opinions whether it were best for yourself to go with the King's Majesty's token to the Lady Elizabeth who is at Blois, distant from Fontainbleau the space of sixty miles, we think, if your Lordship's estate for your sickness might commodiously suffer you so to do, the same were very necessary, considering what she is now to the King's Majesty our master; and, what honour soever your Lordship shall do to her Grace,

the same shall redound to his Majesty's good contentation.    Marry, if your sickness shall so increase
and grow upon your Lordship that you cannot
without your great trouble take the journey upon
you, then we think it convenient that your excuse
be so made as it may evidently appear the same to
be the cause of your not going ; adding thereto
also, if your Lordship shall think meet, the respect
ye have to forbear the coming to her Grace, and the
rest of the King's Majesty's the French King's
children, with the ague being upon you ; and upon
that excuse, ye may, we think, send the King's
Majesty's token by Mr. Pickering.    * * * *

"This day the French ambassador is here, who,
upon Monday at night late, advertised us of certain
letters sent to him from the French King his master,
signifying to him that upon the first day of December, which was the next day, that is to say, yesterday, the christening should be of the French King's
son, and the treaty ratified by the said King that
present day, whereof he did advertise us to the intent the like might be here for the ratification of
the King's Majesty's part; but, upon knowledge that
he had himself of the affairs the next day, he offered the putting off that day until this day, for the
which purpose he is now come hither; and, after dinner, himself first hath made collation of the treaty,
with the very treaty sealed by the commissioners
and ambassadors of the French King; finding the
same to agree, received it of the King's Majesty in

the presence of all of us his Majesty's Council, with a number of others of the nobles of the realm.

" Furthermore, the King's Majesty sendeth presently by this bearer a chain of gold of the value of three hundred crowns and upwards, which his Highness' pleasure is your Lordship shall cause to be delivered unto Monsieur L'Aubespine the French King's Secretary,* as in present from his Majesty, with also his Highness' thanks for the said Mons. L'Aubespine's goodwill and diligence always used towards the affairs of this realm." * * *

Although Clinton was unable to visit the fair Princess who had been espoused to his young master, he so far recovered strength as to deliver his credentials in person to her father the King. Sir Wm. Pickering, in a letter to the Council, dated at Melun, on the 8th December, informs them that the Lord Admiral "had been well welcomed and right honorably received, and much better had been if the quality of his fervent disease had not let their purpose therein. Uppon Sunday at night," he continues, " his Lordship was sumptuously feasted with the King, where it pleased his Grace also to place me at his own board, and the rest of the gentlemen at

* Claude de l'Aubespine, Lord of Châteauneuf, successively Secretary of State to Francis the First, Henry the Second, Francis the Second, and Charles the Ninth. He was much trusted by Catherine of Medicis. On the day in which the news of the battle of St. Denis reached the court, she came to his bedside, he being too weak to rise, and consulted with him. He died next day.

a side table.   Mr. Granado hath taken his leave, and hath in reward three chains, one of the King, the Queen, and Dolphin, in value by estimation viii$^c$ (800) crownes.   The King's Ma$^{tie}$ shall have sent him from hence 6 cortalls, 3 Spanishe horses, one turke, a barbery, one courser, and two little mules.   Thus, after my most humble recommendations, &c." *

On the 15th December, Clinton addressed the following letter from St. Denis to the Council.

### THE LORD ADMIRAL LORD CLINTON TO THE COUNCIL.

*Orig.* St. P. Off, *France.* 15th Dec. 1551.

" AFTER my most humble commendations unto your good Lordship.   It may please you to be advertised that, upon Monday was se'enight, I departed from the court of France, and in Paris I have reposed myself these six days, in hope to have recovered some health to have been able to have presented the King's Majesty's token, and done his Highness' most hearty commendation to Madame Elizabeth, being at Blois, according to the King's Majesty's commandment.   But I find so little amendment that I shall scant be able to maintain my journey into England, being most heartily sorry that my fortune is so evil that I am not able to do my duty in that commission committed to me.   I

* Orig.   St. P. Off.   France.   11th Dec. 1551.

have delivered Sir Wm. Pickering, according to your Lordships' pleasure (signified unto me in your last letter), the King's Majesty's token, and declared unto him his Highness' most hearty commendations and message; and also required him to declare my infirmity, and let of doing my duty, according to my commission from the King's Highness; and incontinently he will depart towards Blois to accomplish the same. I have been, ever since my coming hither, at the French King's charge for my table only, and most favourably and courteously used, with offer of all pleasure and commodity that might be had within this town by the French King's special commandment, for the King's Majesty's his good brother's sake. And Mons. de Geye and Mons. de Lensec hath still accompanied me. And, as touching the gift which the French King sent me, [it] is in value three thousand four hundred crowns, all in gilt plate, saving two small cups of gold which maketh up the just sum aforesaid.

" I have no news to advertise your Lordships worthy the writing, other than that the Legate which came from Rome lyeth here in Paris, tarrying a larger commission to come from the Bishop of Rome, to treat of the peace between the French King and the said Bishop. This day I have taken my journey towards Calais, being evil able to travel, having a double quartan; trusting your Lordships will consider what small service I am able to do, being in this case, touching the commission I

have for the view and taking order at Calice and
Guysnes, so that my hope is your Lordships will
discharge me thereof, and appoint some other more
apt and able man for that purpose.    Beseeching
your good Lordships that your pleasure therein may
be signified unto me by the bearer.    And thus, beseeching Almighty God to send your Lordships
long life, with much honour, I humbly take my
leave of the same.

    " From St. Denis, the 15th of Dec. 1551.

" E. CLYNTON."

    The letters addressed by the Duke of North-
umberland to Sir William Cecil from the time
of the second fall of the Duke of Somerset, to the
death of Edward the Sixth, on July 6th, 1553, demonstrate that Northumberland entirely managed
the government, and that Cecil, as Secretary of
State, enjoyed under him a large share of power
and favour.    Although numerous, these letters do
not possess any great interest, but relate chiefly to
the distribution of offices and the common routine
of state business.    The two which follow may serve
as a specimen of the correspondence.    It is evident
from them, that in all principal affairs the Duke's
will was supreme, and that the Secretary, like
most of his colleagues in the Council, enjoyed office
at the price of being entirely subservient to Northumberland; who, although the most courteous of
correspondents when permitted to direct all accord-

ing to his own will, was impetuous and violent in the extreme if opposed. So completely did Cecil feel this, that, in a remarkable entry in his private diary, he describes himself as having no will of his own under Edward, and as only recovering the rights of a free agent by the death of the young King,—" *Libertatem adeptus sum morte Regis, et ex misero aulico factus liber et mei juris.*" *

### NORTHUMBERLAND TO CECIL.

*Orig.* St. P. Off. *Domestic.* 8th January 1551-2.

" After my hearty commendations. These be even so to require you to have in remembrance the letters to be sent unto the Lord Conyers for his repair unto the parliament; and also the other letters to be sent unto Sir Ingram Clifford for to repair unto Carlisle, and there to remain for the time for the supplying of the place of the Captainship of the town of Carlisle, and Deputy-warden of the West Marches, in the absence of the Lord Conyers, and till such time as the King's Majesty's pleasure shall be to him farther known in that behalf.

" And forasmuch also as the Lord Deputy of Calais hath wilfully proceeded in the matter between him and my brother, contrary to my Lords of the Council's late letters, and to the renewing of

---

* Private Journal. Lansdowne, 118. Of this Journal, which is exceeding brief, Dr. Nares has given a fac-simile.—Life of Burleigh, vol. i. p. 60.

more unquietness between them and their reti-
nues, which is to be eschewed and removed, lest
farther displeasure might rise and grow between
them; methinketh now my Lords have good
cause, upon this new matter of unquietness which
he hath made, notwithstanding their letters written
in the King's Majesty's name, and also his device
for demanding the rearages of the rents during the
time of the wars past, without first making my
Lords of the Council privy thereunto; — their
Lordships hath now, in mine opinion, just cause to
look upon such indiscreet dealing, rather than
to suffer the man's wilfulness to be occasion of
greater inconvenience; which I pray you to set
forth as shall seem good to your wisdom. And so I
bid you most heartily well to fare. From Ely
Place, the 8th of January 1551.

<blockquote>
" Your assured loving friend,

" NORTHUMBERLAND."
</blockquote>

## THE DUKE OF NORTHUMBERLAND TO SECRE-
## TARY CECIL.

*Orig.* St. P. Off. *Domestic.* 28th Jan. 1551-2.

" THE ambassador of France mindeth to be here
this afternoon, for that he had no leisure, as he
saith, the other day to accomplish such things as he
had to declare to the Lords; wherefore either the
Lords must mind to come immediately after dinner
from the Star Chamber hither, or else he must
have word respiting his coming till to-morrow,

which, if the affairs in the Star Chamber after dinner requireth any time, I think it best to be so.
Wherefore I would you move this to the rest of the
Lords that do sit to-day there.   And so send me
word if they will have him deferred till to-morrow,
and thereupon I will send one purposely to stay
him for this time.

" His secretary also showed me that —— Paris,
who brought the present, desireth his depesche;
and therefore it were well done that you came
hither to put these things in order, ( . . . . . )*
and the rather to defer th' ambassador's coming
till to-morrow : wherefore send me word forthwith.

" Your assured friend,

" NORTHUMBERLAND."

Endorsed.—"28*th Jan.* 1551.
   " *The Duke of Northumberland to*
      *Sir W. Cecil.*"

In a letter written at this time by Pickering to
Cecil, Barnaby the King's favourite, whom he had
sent to improve himself in the court of France,
again makes his appearance.   His allowances from
England seem to have been scanty; and his " entertainment" by Henry the Second, who, out of
compliment to Edward, had taken him into his service, was apparently still more parsimonious.   Cecil had meanwhile given him all he could afford,
—" wise letters of good counsel."

* Here the letter is torn.

SIR WILLIAM PICKERING TO SIR WILLIAM CECIL.

*Orig.*  St. P. Off.  12th February 1551-2.

" Sir.—For your good news of the beginning of
the parliament, and of the good expectation all
men have in the proceedings of the same, I would
requite you with th' occurrents of this court, if I
were not more than certain that ye should fully understand them by my Lords of the Council. Therefore, leaving the same as rather superfluous than
needful, I assure you that I look with great desire to hear that a good conclusion were annexed
unto the first parts of your syllogism, which I trust
shall be so perfect, that it shall lack neither in
form nor in metal, or else my patience will be soon
spent. I am right sorry that the courier used you
so evil in the delivery of your books. His promise
to me was much otherwise. I wish him therefore
the worst I can—a rope for reward.

" Mr. Barnabie standeth [in] great need of a good
solicitor to procure the augmenting of his entertainment here, and specially as the season now
serveth, to the end he may compare fellowlike in
these wars with his equals ; otherwise it should be
a reproach to the place he cometh from, and a dis-
couraging, peradventure, to his forwardness, that
meriteth in my judgment any preferment. Wherefore, knowing you his very good friend by the diligent care you have in oft advising him, as your
wise letters of good counsel to him do well witness,

I beseech you likewise to assay what may be done for the setting forth of his person, as reason requireth, in this time. Three hundred pounds will stand him in small stead, tho' his horses be sent him out of England. The dearth of all things, and specially belonging to war, are such, that a great deal maketh a small muster in these quarters.

" Thus far entered in making you a solicitor, I most heartily require you to have this bearer, my servant Morgan's long suit, recommended. His greatest business is Mr. Barnaby's matters, which I would he should well despatch before his return, and then it may please you to hasten him hither again.

" Thus, after my hearty recommendations, I wish you health. At Paris, the 12th of February, at four of the clock, afternoon.

" Yours to command,

" W. PYKERYNGE."

*" To the Right Honourable Sir W. Cecill, &c."*

The execution of the Duke of Somerset was not long afterwards followed by the disgrace of Lord Paget. We have seen him sent to the Tower as an accomplice in the alleged plot for the assassination of Northumberland, which, as some of the witnesses are said to have affirmed, was to be perpetrated at his house; yet it is worthy of observation, that, when Paget's turn came to be punished, the charge against him was not a design or attempt to

assassinate Northumberland, or any of the Council,
but malversation in his office as Chancellor of the
Duchy of Lancaster. He was tried in the court
of Star Chamber, confessed his guilt, paid a
heavy fine, and was degraded from the order of the
Garter.* " None of the Duke of Somerset's friends
or followers," says Carte,† " had stuck to him in all
his troubles with so much fidelity as the Lord
Paget,"— a most erroneous panegyric. We have
seen that Paget betrayed him in his first fall;
and there is strong reason to believe that he had
some hand in involving him in his final troubles,
which ended in his death.‡

### NORTHUMBERLAND TO THE LORD CHAM-BERLAIN.

*Orig.* St. P. Off. *Domestic.* 30th May 1552.

" THIS shall be to advertise your Lordship that
I have received your letters, together with the several submissions of the Lord Paget, and also the
late Master of the Rolls; finding a great variety
and difference between the first and second submission of the said Lord Paget : and like as your
Lordship, and others my Lords, have in my opinion
done right honourably in the refusal of his first submission, which indeed was farsed [stuffed] with sub-
tilty and dissimulation, only to abuse the King's

* Stowe, p. 608.          † Carte, vol. iii. p. 264.
‡ Strype's Memor. vol. ii. part i. p. 537.

Majesty's clemency and your Lordships' goodnesses,
as by his latter submission it doth and may right
well appear; so for my part I do think it very requisite that the submissions of Beaumont, both the
first and second, should be better set forth in articles by some of the King's learned counsel, more
especially declaring and setting forth the nature of
his several offences, in such manner and form as
the said Lord Paget's latter submission is.   And as
touching the setting at liberty of the Countess of
Sussex and Harlypoole's wife, methinketh by your
Lordship's better advice that matter would be
somewhat better tried and searched; the rather
for that she is charged to have spoken and said
that one of King Edward's sons should be yet living.   And as touching Brett and Fisher, I am of
your Lordship's opinion, that for their offences
they have been sufficiently punished.   Marry, by
the Duke's own confession to me, he declared Brett
to be of a very evil nature.   He sought all the
ways he could to irritate the said Duke against me;
whereby it should seem he cared not to have had
a ruffling world: nevertheless, I trust this punishment will be a warning to him for [ever].   And
thus, with my right hearty commendations to your
good Lordship, I commit the same to the tuition
of the Almighty.   From Otford in Kent, this 30th
of May 1552.

"Your Lordship's own assuredly,

"NORTHUMBERLAND."

"*To my very good Lord my Lord Chamberlain, this.*"

The friendship between Cecil and the lofty and magnificent Northumberland, whose train in his progress was too great to admit of its burdening any private house, is strongly marked in the two following letters. The Duke's promise to visit Richard Cecil, the Secretary's father, were it only to drink a cup of wine with him at the door, and Sir William Cecil's anxiety to attend him in person, are worthy of notice as marking devotedness and intimacy.

### NORTHUMBERLAND TO CECIL.

*Orig.* St. P. Off. *Domestic.* 30th May 1552.

" I HAVE received your two sundry letters, the one by my Lord of Huntington, the other by a post ; marvelling that in neither of them it appeareth that you have received mine of the 28th of this present, wherein was inclosed a letter which I then received from my brother. And as touching the several submissions of the Lord Paget and the late Master of the Rolls, it seemeth to me that the learned counsel have more seriously proceeded by special articles to the Lord Paget than to Beaumont, as I have partly written to my Lord Chamberlain ; and I am of opinion that it is requisite that Beaumont's submission should be particular and special as the other is.

" And for your gentle and most friendly request to have me to your father's in my way northwards, I do even so semblably render my hearty thanks

unto you, assuring you I will not omit to see him
as I go by him, though I do but drink a cup of
wine with him at the door ; for I will not trouble
no friend's house of mine otherwise in this journey,
my train is so great, and will be, whether I will or
not. And for your own being there, like as I think
myself much beholden to you that would take so
much pains, and to me a singular pleasure to
have so much of your company; so could I rejoice,
for your own health, that you might have such a
*cantell* of recreation. And even so, with my hearty
commendations and like thanks for your overpaid
friendship always towards me, I leave the rest of
this conclusion until our next meeting; praying you
I may be commended to Mr. Secretary Petre.

" At Otford, this last of May,

" Your assured loving friend,

" NORTHUMBERLAND."

Endorsed.—" *Ultimo Maii* 1552.

" *To my very loving friend,*

" *Sir Wm. Cycyll, &c.*"


NORTHUMBERLAND TO CECIL.

*Orig.* ST. P. OFF. *Domestic.* May 31, 1552.

" AFTER my most hearty commendations.
Herewith I do return again, as well the letter written from my Lords to the Lord Conyers, which in
my mind cannot be amended ; and also the letter
which I have written to the Greemes, being liked by
my said Lords. Other I have not at this present ;

but trusting to see you at the court upon Saturday noon-time of the day, or on Monday before dinner, God willing.

" My Lord Marquis hath been with me, I thank him ; and some good fellows with him : we have been merry.   To-morrow he departeth from me by five of the clock in the morning towards my Lord Cobham's, who, as I understand from them this day, is in no little peril of life.   Thus I leave, wishing to you the good that your own gentle heart can desire.

" At Otford, this last of May, at ten in the night.
" Your assured faithful friend,
" NORTHUMBERLAND."

Endorsed.—" *Ultimo Maii*, 1552.
" *To my very loving friend,*
*Sir Wm. Cecil.*"

We have already become acquainted with Whalley under various lights,—as an intimate correspondent of Cecil, a tool of Northumberland, a busy adviser of Somerset, and lastly, a witness against him : he is now stript of his office, (which may have been the reward of his taking part against the Duke,) for divers notable misdemeanors.

### NORTHUMBERLAND TO THE LORD CHAMBERLAIN.

*Orig.*  ST. P. OFF.  *Domestic.*  1st June 1552.

" AFTER my most hearty commendations to your good Lordship, with the like to you Mr. Vice-

Chamberlain.  And whereas it hath pleased the King's Majesty to be so gracious Lord unto this bearer, John Fisher, one of his Grace's pensioners, to give the reversion of the receivership of Yorkshire, which Whalley had, who for divers notable evil demeanors, as well in his office as else, is thought unworthy any longer to occupy the same ; beseeching you both, and all the rest of my Lords, that this his Majesty's honest servant may enjoy the gift which his Highness hath appointed unto him ; for whom I dare be bound in all the land I have, he shall honestly and truly serve in it.

"And where it hath pleased God to call out of this life the wife of my son Ambrose, and hath left no child alive, her next heir now is the son of one Harwood, whose father was my servant, and slain at Musselburgh Field, and held his lands of me. Now, by the death of my said son's wife, he is ward to the King's Majesty for such lands as he shall have after my son Ambrose's life, which he holdeth by curtesy of England, because he had a child by her.

"It may therefore please you, at this my request, to move his Majesty only if I may have of his Highness the preferment of the child ; which child, before the death of this woman, was my ward : and thus I cease not to molest you both in all my pursuits, which I know not how to recompense but with my faithful goodwill and friendship, as knoweth God, who grant you the desires of both your own gentle hearts.

"From Otforde, the 1st of June 1552.

"Your Lordship's,

"and your assured faithful friend,

"NORTHUMBERLAND."

"To my very good Lord, my Lord
Chamberlain; and my very loving
friend, Mr. Vice-Chamberlain."

The following letter is curious, as containing a minute account by Northumberland of the symptoms of that awful scourge called the sweating sickness. It is strange, that not a word of sorrow escapes the lips of the father who saw his little daughter hurried in a few hours from the midst of the joyousness of childhood into the grasp of this fell disease; and yet it would be hard to blame him, for the deepest is often the stillest grief. At this moment, indeed, Dudley's mind had much to engross it, for he was about to set out on his splendid progress;* and Clinton, the Lord Admiral, as we see from his letter which follows, proposed to meet his Grace and Sir Wm. Cecil between Burne, Cecil's native village, and Richard Cecil's house. It must have gratified old Richard Cecil to see the boy who had left his father's roof with no such bright prospects, return to it Secretary of State, and friend and confidant of the first man in the

* Supra, p. 111.

state. But had he known the cares and dangers of the office, he would have hesitated to change his own cloth of frieze for his son's cloth of gold.

NORTHUMBERLAND TO THE LORD CHAMBER
LAIN AND SIR. WM. CECIL.

*Orig.* ST. P. OFF. *Domestic.* June 2, 1552.

" AFTER my most hearty commendations. — Whereas I perceive by your letter of this instant, that, except the death of my daughter might seem dangerous and infectious, the King's Majesty's pleasure is that neither I should absent myself nor stay my son; whereupon I have thought good to signify unto you what moveth me to suspect infection in the disease whereof my daughter died. First, the night before she died, she was as merry as any child could be, and sickened about three in the morning, and was in a sweat, and within a while after she had a desire to the stool ; and the indiscreet woman that attended upon her let her rise, and after that, she fell to swooning, and then, with such things as they ministered to her, brought her again to remembrance, and so she seemed for a time to be meetly well revived, and so continued till it was noon, and still in a great sweating; and about twelve of the clock she began to alter again, and so in continual pangs and fits till six of the clock, at what time she left this life. And this morning she was looked upon, and between the shoulders it was very black, and also upon the one side of her cheek ; which thing, with the suddenty, and also [that] she could brook nothing that was ministered to her from the beginning, moveth me to think that either it must be the sweat or worse, for she had the measles a month or five weeks before, and very well recovered, but a certain hoarseness and a cough remained with her still.　This [is] as much as I am able to express, and even thus it was: wherefore I think it not my duty to presume to make my repair to his Majesty's presence till further be seen what may ensue of it ; neither my son, nor none that is in my house, except his Majesty, shall command the contrary, or that your Lordships' wisdom shall think it without peril, being no more nor no less than before is declared ; requiring your Lordships' farther answer hereupon, and accordingly I will [endeavour] myself.

"　Thus I commit your good Lordships to the tuition of the Almighty.

"　From Oteforde in Kent, this 2d of June.

"　Your own most assured,

"　NORTHUMBERLAND."

THE LORD CLYNTON TO SIR WM. CECIL.

*Orig.*　St. P. Off.　*Domestic.*　15th June 1552.

"AFTER my hearty commendations unto you, These shall be to desire you that you will send me word by the bringer hereof, as near as you can, what time my Lord of Northumberland's Grace will be at your father's ; and whether he mindeth to dine there, and about what time, and what way he will come to my house.

" Burne, in my opinion, is his best way, and therefore am minded to meet his Grace between that and your father's house ; whereof because I would be loath to be disappointed, I most heartily desire you to advertise me what you think therein.

" I trust you will accompany his Grace hither to my house. Thus you shall do me great pleasure, which I will not fail to requite. From Sempringham, the 19th of June 1552.

" Your loving friend,

" E. CLYNTON.

" I pray you let my Lord's Grace be guided thro' Boron, [Burne,] which is his Grace's next way, and so shall I be sure to meet his Grace ; or else I may be disappointed, which I would be very sorry to be. If his Grace dine in any place by the way, I pray you send me word of it."

It is pleasant once more to meet with so agreeable a lady as the Duchess of Suffolk, and to find Sir William Cecil in her company, cased, not as usual in his Secretary's robes, but in a hunting-jacket, meditating the death of a buck. Latimer, it appears, had been desirous of having a venison pasty at the feast of his wife's churching; but " wild things," as the Duchess says, " be not ready at commandment," and he was forced to go without it.

### THE DUCHESS OF SUFFOLK TO CECIL.

*Orig.* Sᴛ. P. Oғғ. *Domestic.* June 1552.

" Bʏ the late coming of this buck to you, you shall perceive that wild things be not ready at commandment; for truly I have caused my keeper, yea, and went forth with him myself on Saturday at night after I came home, (which was a marvel for me,) but so desirous was I to have had one for Mr. Latimer to have sent after him to his wife's churching; but there is no remedy but she must be churched without it. For I have, ever since you wrote for yours, besides both my keepers, had . . . . . . * about it, and yet could not prevail afore this morning; and now I pray God it be any thing worth.

" But, as touching your hunting here, I would be sorry you should leave it undone on any such respects as you spoke of, for I am not so uncharitable but I can well suffer them to come and hunt in your company; yea, and gladly would wish, not for any great need, I thank God, that I have of them, but for goodwill, that they would so neighbourly use me to hunt with my licence, tho' they leave not hunting whilst they left not one deer in my park; for their honest behaviour, being my neighbours and the worshipful of the shire, should be more pleasant to me than any sport that

---

\* Some words here are not to be made out. Indeed, both the spelling and writing of the Duchess are very bad.

any wild beast in all the world could make me. Yea, and were it not more for the pleasures of such, than for my own commodity, profit, or pleasure, I would not leave one such beast about me as might make any neighbour I have fall out with me : and that were now soon adone, for, I assure you, I have not to my knowledge two bucks more in my park. But that must not discharge you from hunting; for, if it please not you to take the pains to kill them, I am sure I get them not, unless I kill them out of hand : wherefore I would desire you to take the pains, and take your part of them ; and also you may have as good sport at the red-deer, and I pray you take it, for I am very glad when any of my friends may have their pastime here, and nothing grieves me but when I cannot make the pastime with them ; and therefore at your pleasure come, and bring with you whom you will, and you shall be welcome, and they also for your sake. And so, with my hearty commendations to yourself, your wife, your father and your mother, I bid you all farewell in the Lord. From Grimsthorp, this present Wednesday, at six o'clock in the morning ; and, like a sluggard, in my bed.

> " Your assured to my power,
>> " K. SUFFOLK.

" Master Bertie is at London, to conclude if he can with the heirs; for I would gladly discharge the trust wherein my Lord did leave me, before I did, for any man's pleasure, any thing else."

" *To my very friend, Mr. Secretary Cecil.*"

Sir Richard Morysine, in his embassy to the Emperor in 1550,* and during his residence at the imperial court, in 1551 and 1552, was accompanied by one who, although then in the inferior situation of his secretary, has become better known to the world of letters than the ambassador. This was the noted, amiable, facetious, and learned ROGER ASCHAM, the Latin tutor of Elizabeth, the friend of Cecil, Saddler, Cheek, Smith, and, we might almost say, of every able statesman or honest scholar in England. His "Report and Discourse upon the affairs of Germany," which has been frequently printed, is perhaps one of the most graphic, spirited, and amusing dissertations on that country, ever given to the world. Unlike the common laborious state papers of this time, (or indeed, we might add, of every other time,) it is neither dry nor tedious ; but, with much valuable information, is relieved by anecdote, sparkles with kind and gentle wit, and abounds in such minute portraits of the eminent men of that age as are nowhere else to be found. Ascham was in truth no common man. I know not where we shall find a better description of what a good history ought to be, than in this brief sentence. "When you and I" (he is writing to his old schoolfellow John Astely) "read Livy together, if you do remember, after some reasoning we concluded both what was in our opinion to be looked for at his hand that would well and advi-

---

* See supra, vol. i. p. 342.

sedly write a history. The first point was, to write nothing false. Next, to be bold to say any truth, whereby is avoided two great faults, flattery and hatred; for which two points Cæsar is read to his great praise, and Jovius the Italian to his just reproach. Then, to mark diligently the causes, counsels, acts, and issues in all great attempts: and in causes, what is just or unjust; in counsels, what is proposed wisely or rashly; in acts, what is done courageously or faintly; and of every issue, to note some general lesson of wisdom or wariness for like matters in time to come, wherein Polybius in Greek, and Philip Comines in French, have done the duties of wise and worthy writers. Diligence also must be used in keeping truly the order of time, and of describing livelily both the site of places and nature of persons, not only for the outward shape of the body, but also for the inward disposition of the mind, as Thucydides doth in many places very trimly, and Homer everywhere, and that always most excellently." *

Ascham, who, as will be seen by some passages of the letters now published, was a zealous Protestant, could scarcely expect to rise in the reign of Mary, although many of his more accommodating brethren contrived to get over this obstacle; but it is strange that, when his pupil Elizabeth came to the throne, we should not find him again emerging into notice; and it is certain that he died poor,

* Ascham's English Works, by Bennett, p. 5.

leaving little to his orphans and widow but a high reputation and an empty purse. It may be feared that, with all his classical and statesman-like attainments, there is too much truth in the assertion of Camden,* that he was much addicted to dice and cock-fighting,—two strange pursuits for the most learned scholar of his age. It may be suspected also, from his naïf éloge upon the Rhenish wine,† and the gusto with which he describes the fat capons of Bruges, that honest Roger was a sincere admirer of old wine, as well as of old books and old coins. One of his most delightful works, "The Schoolmaster," took its origin from a dinner at Lord Burleigh's, (then Sir William Cecil,) given when the Queen was at Windsor, in 1563. The party consisted of ten, most of them men of eminence: Sir William Petre, Sir John Mason, Dr. Wotton, Sir Richard Sackville, Sir Walter Mildmay, Mr. Haddon, Mr. Astley, Mr. Hampton, Mr. Nicasius, and Roger Ascham. At dinner, Cecil observed that strange news had come from Eton; that several scholars, in consequence of the extreme severity of the masters who had over-whipped them, had run away from school. Upon this, Petre, a severe old fellow, called them presumptuous little dogs, and pleaded warmly for the use of the rod. Dr. Wotton in a gentle voice supported Cecil, who had blamed the masters, and disapproved of such seve-

---

* Annals of Elizabeth.   Kennett, vol. ii. p. 416.
† English Works of Ascham, by Bennet, p. 372.

rity in education.   Haddon sternly seconded Petre's
views, and asserted that the best schoolmaster then
in England was the "greatest beater."   Sir John
Mason bantered both sides, but adhered to neither.
(This was exactly the plan the same gentleman
adopted in more serious questions.)   At last, Roger Ascham deemed it his time to say something;
and, to the praise of his good heart, taking the boys'
part, remarked, in answer to Haddon, that if the
smartest scholars were those who had smarted most
under the birch, he ascribed it rather to the supe-
riority of the mental, than the flea-ing of the material, parts of these young gentlemen.   With this
view Cecil and Sackville were mightily pleased;
and Sackville having afterwards found Ascham in
the Queen's private apartment, where her Majesty
had been reading with him an oration of Demos-
thenes, entreated him to write something on the
subject; observing that, although he had said nothing at dinner, he had *felt* the subject deeply,
having had all love of learning fairly *birched* out of
him at fourteen,—a course he was determined to
avoid in the education of his little grandson Robert.   From this conversation arose " The Schoolmaster" of Ascham.

One of the most amusing letters of Ascham's is
a kind of daily journal, written on the road, but
addressed from Augsbourg to Mr. Raven and
others of his dear college friends and cronies, de-

tailing all the wonders he had met with in his
travels, and introducing personal descriptions of
the Emperor, his son Philip, Ferdinand, King of
the Romans, the Electors, John Frederick and
Maurice, with many other noted persons.   A consi-
derable portion of this letter has been printed by
Mr. Bennett in his edition of Ascham's English
works,* but a large part has been omitted; and
what is given appears to have been taken from a
mutilated and imperfect copy made by Dr. Birch †
from a manuscript of Mr. Baker's.   An original
draft, in a handwriting which I suspect is that of
Ascham himself, is in the Lansdowne, 98. No. 10;
and from this the reader will be pleased to see
some interesting passages not hitherto printed.   On
arriving at Brussels, he had an opportunity of seeing Eleanor, the French Queen Dowager, widow of
Francis the First, and sister to Charles the Fifth;
and is minute in his observations.

ORIG.   Lansdowne, 98. 10.

  " 5th. Oct.—WE tarried," says he, " at Brussels
all Sunday: I went to the mass, more to see than for
devotion, will some of you think.   The Regent was
with the Emperor at August [Augsbourg]; but the
French Queen, the Emperor's sister, was there: she
came to  mass clad very solemnly all in white cam-
bric, a robe gathered in plaits wrought very fair  as
need be with needle white work, as white as a dove.

---

  * London, 4to.1761.        † Brit. Mus. Ayscough, 4164.

A train of ladies followed her, as black and evil as
she was white.  Her mass was sung in pricksong by
Frenchmen very cunningly, and a gentleman played at the organs excellently.  A French Whipit
Sir John bestirred himself so at the altar as I
wished Patrick by to have learned some of his
knacks. * *  The Queen sat in a closet above;
her ladies kneeled all abroad in the chapel among
us.  The Regent of Flanders had left at Bruxelles
a sort of fair lusty young ladies: they came not
out, but were kept in mew for fear of gosshawks
of Spain and France; yet they came to [view] and
stood above in windows, as well content to show
themselves as we to see them.

   " They had on French gowns of black velvet,
guarded down right from the collar with broad
guards, one with another, some of cloth of gold,
some of cloth of silver, great chains arr—— [ar-
ranged] with precious jewels.  On their heads they
had glistering cauls of goldsmith work, and black
velvet caps above, [with] frills of great agletts of
gold, with white feathers round about the compass
of their caps.  They seemed boys rather than ladies,
excellent to have played in tragedies.  There was
not one well-favoured among them, save one young
lady, fair and well-favoured.  The Queen went
from mass to dinner; I followed her; and because
we were gentlemen of England, I and another was
admitted to come into her chamber where she sat
at dinner.  She is served with no women, as great

states are there in England; but altogether with men, having their caps on their heads whilst they come into the chamber where she sits, and there one takes off all their caps. I stood very near the table and saw all.

" Men, as I said, served ; only two women stood by the fire-side not far from the table, for the chamber was little, and talked very loud and lewdly with whom they would, as methought.

" This Queen's service, compared with my Lady Elizabeth's my mistress, is not so princelike nor honourably handled. Her first course was apples, pears, plums, grapes, nuts ; and with this meat she began. Then she had bacon and chickens almost covered with sale onions, that all the chamber smelled of it. She had a roast caponet, and a pasty of wild-boar ; and I, thus marking all the behaviour, was content to lose the second course, lest I should have lost mine own dinner at home.

" After dinner, Mr. Berwick's brother, which dwells with Mr. Chamberlayne, came to me, and gently led me to see the city ; for this ye must consider, in every town I come in, as leisure will serve, I went in to see all abbeys, friaries, churches, libraries, stationers for books, goldsmiths for old coins. I marked the manners, order, and raiment of each age : I marked the site, the building, the strength, the walls, the ditches, gates, ports, and havens of every town, and what opportunities either by water or land each town stood by.

" These matters cannot be well packed up in a
small leaf of paper; but, if I were with you at a Pro-
blem† fire, I could make you partakers of a great
deal of my journey. If I had had one Mr. Helande
or Ed. Raven with me, to have used freely the
company of his legs, eyes, ears, and tongue in this
journey, I had seen and known both more than I
do, or more than most part of men do that have
journeyed this way. Our young gentlemen care
not for this knowledge. * * *

" At this town's [Tongres] end we met the
Queen of Hungary ˙posting from Augusta into
Flanders, having a thirty in her company, for she
had outridden and wearied all the rest, passing that
journey in thirteen days, that a man can scarce do
in seventeen. She is a *virago:* she is never so
well as when she is flinging on horseback, and hunting all the night long.

" This Tongres is notable in Cæsar's Commenta-
ries; the old walls of the old town be yet apparent
in the fields.

" 8th Oct.—From Tongres to Maestricht, called
Trajectum, nine miles. A fair city standing on the
river Mosa, as good as Trent. In the midst of this
stand mills betwixt two boats that never lack water.
I marvel that Tongres hath not the like; and here,
at a goldsmith's shop, I saw the first old coin after
I came out of England. The goldsmith told me
that a great sort were found at Tongres, which we
past from the day before.

† So in the original.

" 10th Oct.—As we rode out of Maestricht, there stood in a shop fair white bread to be sold, the loaves being bigger than ever I saw two loaves at Cambridge. My lady sent her footman to buy a stiver's worth, which is twopence. At the first word, the maid proffered him thirty-two for his stiver; and he, having as many as either his conscience could require, or his lap could hold, would ask no more.

" This day we rode to Vulick, called in Latin Fuliacum of J. C. [Julius Cæsar] the founder. The country, by the way, may compare with Cambridge-shire for corn.

" This know, there is no country here to be compared for all things with England. Beef is little, lean, tough, and dear. Mutton likewise; a rare thing to see a hundred sheep in a flock. Capons be lean and little. Pigeons naught; partridge, black, ill, and tough; corn everywhere, and most wheat. Here is never no dearth, except corn fail. The people generally be much like the old Persians that Xenophon describes, content to live with bread, roots, and water; for this matter, ye shall see round about the walls of every city, half a mile compass from the walls, gardens full of herbs and roots, whereby the cities most part do live. No herb is stolen, such justice is exercised. These countries be rich by labour and continuance of men, not by goodness of soil.

" If only London would use, about the void places

of the city, these gardens full of herbs, and if it were but to serve the strangers that would live with these herbs, beside a multitude whom need, covetousness, or temperance would in few years bring to the same, all England should have victuals better cheap.

" I think also there is more wine indeed drunk in England, where none grows, than even there from whence it cometh. It is pity that London hath not one goodman to begin this husbandry and temperance.

" At Bruges in Flanders we had as fat and good great mutton, and fatter, better, and greater capons than ever I saw in Kent; but nowhere else. But now let us come to Onlick, a town of the Duke of Cleves, standing in Guelderland, burned of late years by the Emperor, having goodly deep ditches and strong walls, with a great marsh of the one side the town : yet the Duke of Cleves is building it anew again, enlarging the town three hundred feet round about from the old walls ; making so broad and deep a ditch, so strong and thick a wall, with so many scouring bulwarks point to point, every one answering other, with vaults under the ground to serve infinite loopholes for great pieces, scouring and sweeping within two foot of the earth the whole country about; having within, to back the wall, such a broad rampart of earth as nothing can burst down, that to my judgment neither the strength of Calais or Antwerp doth pass it. At the

east side of the town is building a castle so fair and
large as the Emperor might dwell in; so strong [as]
to repulse the Great Turk.

" I told myself, about this little town, five and
thirty brick-kilns. The Duke, hereby, will be so
strong as be once able again to bide the Emperor
basse [*sic*] ; but the Emperor is a wise prince, which
can suffer men to beat themselves with their own
purses.

" 11th Oct.—From this town to [Colen] is eighteen miles. We left Aquisgrave, where the Emperor
is crowned, on the right hand. This day's journey
was much through woods, jeopardsome for thieves
called *snaphanses,* in complete harness. There is
one vale so good for corn as no piece of Cam-
bridgeshire is like.

" When we came nigh Colen, being a fair day,
there fell such a mist, because Rhenus fluvius was
so nigh, that we lost the view both of the country
and also of the city. Coleyne is not so well build-
ed, by my judgment, as the towns in Brabant and
Flanders, nor as here Surnia et Rhetia. We, entering the town, had thought every man had been a
butcher, for almost in every shop there hung an ox
and half a dozen sheep. The manner is, at this
time to kill their store for the whole year, and, at
killing of his ox, he makes a feast to his kinsfolks
both of the country and city.

" Arnold Brickman, Mr. Spering's kinsman,
showed me much gentleness; and I made him again

good cheer at my Lord's table, and by him I wrote into England. * * * Ye will not believe how constantly every one doth talk here of Reynold of Mount Aborie, one of the sons of Hamon, which is said to have wrought at this church more for a penny than other seven could; and so, for envy, was slain sleeping, and cast into the Rhine, and found and buried there as a good man, and now here taken as a saint, and for his death, they say, the work could never go forward. Some of you have read the story. Ye may believe it as much as you list, for I only tell you what men here generally say and do talk. The Three Kings be not so rich, I believe, as was the Lady of Walsingham.

"If I could have tarried in Coleyn, I would have sought out them, and written now to you what certain old monuments of writing they have at Coleyn for the bringing thither of these three kings.

"St. Ursula there, with the 11,000 virgins, be more to be marvelled at. A nun showed us the church and relics; there is in the church no stalls, but five-and-thirty double stone graves, one upon another, made like troughs, and covered over with stone. In an inner chapel stood St. Ursula, formed down to the middle all of silver, not massy, but hollow, standing within a hollow tabernacle. In the wall about her, in the same order and height, stood ladies and noblemen, (the King's son of Brabant, which should have been her husband, stood next her,) to the number of fourscore or more,

K 2

made even after the same sort, of silver, or sawle [sic], which have many of them great wounds. There be heads clothed in velvet and satin, set in lockers orderly, with so many bones, couched* [sic] likewise in order, that books stand not fairer in a study, as I ween two carts would scarcely carry them. There be also many heads of children, new-born, or else ripped out of their mothers' womb, for they were not all maids, but many of them noble-men's wives."            (20th Jan. 1550-51.)

The Council in their instructions, sent about this time to Sir Richard Morysine, the English ambas-sador at the Emperor's court, had directed him, in the account which he should give of his interview, to recount not only all that the Emperor said, but to mark minutely his gestures, behaviour, and ge-neral manner, so that they might understand, from the exhibition he made of his " passions of joy and grief," the exact temper in which he received their communication.    These instructions will be found in the British Museum, Galba, B. xii. fol. 233. Lord Hardwicke† has printed Morysine's reply to the English Council, in which he informs them of the manner in which he had fulfilled their com-mission.    It is long, and in many places uninter-esting ; but the following passage, in which he de-scribes his hospitable reception by D'Arras, the

---

* Couched—perhaps " lying."
† State Papers, vol. i. p. 32.

prime minister, and proceeds to recount with characteristic minuteness his interview with the Emperor, is worth inserting.   Granvelle was Bishop of
Arras.

" The Bishop said he would let me alone till I
had changed my apparel: while my men brought
me such things as I did mind to wear, his servants
did fetch me a brush, water for mine hands;
and, after this, they cast a couple of napkins upon
the table, and brought in a pasty of red-deer, and
said there was a couple of partridges at the fire,
and would shortly be ready.   I told them that I
had dined at Spires; and yet the Bishop, now
knowing that my men had done with me, came
again, and willed me to taste of the venison, that I
might taste of his wine.   I saw a dish of olives, and
so did eat one of them; and brought him good-
luck in a cup of wine, which he would needs I should
taste: the kindness was very great, in comparison
of any that ever I received in this court; and I
thought my good-lucks came together, for Bernardine was gone that morning toward England,
as he told divers, and I was thus certain of the
Bishop at afternoon; which both were such news to
me, and so welcome, that I wist not whether I was
gladder that Bernardine was gone from this court,
or for this my rare entertainment with D'Arras.

" But I must on in order with my matter.   I,
for that I had more list to talk than to eat, would
no venison; and therefore the pasty was carried to

my men, and they much made of.  He and I fell to
talking again ;  he groping to know mine errand,
and I keeping it for th' Emperor.  He asked me
whether the ports were shut up in England, as he
had word from Flanders, or no.  I said, I neither
knew of any cause why they should be kept, or
heard of any keeping of them more than that he
had said.

"And while we thus talked, his chamberlain
came from the court, and told him that the Emperor did now look for me.  D'Arras, seeing my
horse without a foot-cloth, did offer me his mule,
but I gave him thanks; and, saving your Honours, in
buskins and spurs, and other short apparel, made
my horse serve me well enough ;  and going, I said,
I knew well mine errand would not be long hid
from him.  He brought me forth of his house, and
tarried abroad till I was on horseback; then also
courteously, with his cap in hand, taking leave of
me.  And thus, being come to the court, I found
Adrian of the Chamber waiting for me, who was so
ready to bring me in to the Emperor, that I was
fain to intreat him to give me leave to breathe me
a little, for that I had run apace up a long pair
of stairs.

"Upon this short pause I followed Adrian,* and

* This Adrian was a Groom of his Chamber, and a special favourite with Charles.  Pedro Mexia, speaking of Charles' habits, observes, "After dinner he gave audience, and sometimes, retiring himself into some secret place, he passed his time

found the Emperor at a bare table, without a car-
pet or any thing else upon it, saving his cloak, his
brush, his spectacles, and his picktooth.    At my
coming in I offered to stand at the side of his Majesty which was next to the door, but, it being on
his left hand, he willed me to go almost round
about the table, that I might stand on his right
side, perhaps for that he heareth better on th' one
side than on the other; but, as I took it, he did it
to h[onour] the King my master.    Here, after the
delivery of the King's Highness' letters, [which]
his Majesty received very gently, putting his hand
to his bonnet and uncovering the upper part of his
head, I did efforce myself with as good countenance as I could, and with as good words as my
wit would serve me to devise in the riding of
almost twenty English miles, to show the glad-
[ness] of the King my master, both that for his
Majesty in so long and painful a journey either
had his health continually, or was, by being some-
time sore accrased, soon brought to perfecter
health.    I did say besides much more, there could
be few that did more rejoice at his Majesty's so
honourable and fortunate approaching towards the
Low Countries than did the King my master, which

in drawing the plot of some fortress, or other edifice ; but most
commonly he used to jest with a Polonian dwarf which he had,
or with one Adrian, a Groom of his Chamber."—Pedro Mexia's
Imperial History, p. 636.    Translated by W. T. and published
with a Continuation, by Edward Grimstone.

did repute all his Majesty's good successes to be as
his own.   *   *   *   *   *   *

"He did not suffer me to go on, but, on the
least pause that I could make, he did utter unto
me in gentle words that he took the King his good
brother's letters in very thankful part; *   * saying as well as he could, (for he was newly rid of
his gout and fever, and therefore his nether lip was
in two places broken out, and he forced to keep a
green leaf within his mouth at his tongue's end,—a
remedy, as I took it, against such his dryness as
in his talk did increase upon him,)—saying, therefore, as well as he could, he neither had nor
could forget the King's Majesty's father's love at
sundry times showed unto him, nor deceive that
trust which at his death he put him in, recommending unto his trust the King his son.   He
had not forgot the amity that so many years had
lasted between the realm of England and the house
of Burgundy; he trusted the King his brother had
in these his young years found friendship, and no
. . . . *, at his hands; and that he had seen a desire
in him perpetually to preserve this ancient amity,
using this sentence, 'that old amities, which had
been long tried and found good, are to be made of;'
and this he spake a little louder than he did the
rest, as tho' he would indeed have me [think] that
he did earnestly mean that he said: and yet hath
he a face unwont to disclose any hid affection of

* Here the original has been injured by fire.

his heart, as any face that ever I met with in all
my life ; for where all white colours (which, in
changing themselves, are wont in others to bring a
man certain word how his errand is liked or misliked,) have no place in his countenance, his eyes
only do betray as much as can be picked out of him.
He maketh me oft think of Solomon's saying, ' Heaven is high; the earth is deep ; a King's heart is un-
searchable.'    There is in him almost nothing that
speaks beside his tongue ; and that at this time, by
reason of his leaf and soreness of his lip, and his
accustomed softness in speaking, did but so-so utter
things to be well understand, without great care to
be given to his words: and yet he did so use his
eyes, so move his head, and order his countenance,
as I might well perceive his great desire was that I
should think all a good deal better meant than he
could speak it."

Morysine proceeds to detail the message which
he brought from Edward the Sixth, which was an
offer to combine with the Emperor against the
Turk, the common enemy of Christendom, whose
" successes in Hungary began to threaten the peace
of Europe, and to alarm all good Christian princes."
Charles, as the ambassador describes it, listened
kindly but coldly, saying nothing; "thinking," to use
the words of the letter, " in very deed, as I might
perceive, to have heard somewhat of joining forces
against another enemy of his, to whom he beareth

as little good-will as to the Turk ; and here," (adds the ambassador,) "he having so good an occasion to have said somewhat of the French King, whether it was for that he spake with some pain, or whether he would that I should speak first against him, did not so much as once name him." \* \* \* Charles soon after putting his hand as he could to his cap, the ambassador took his leave for that time.

The Emperor afterwards sent a message, through his prime minister, to the English ambassador, and seemed anxious to hear whether he brought no other commission from his master. Morysine answered, none as ambassador ; neither was it possible for him to say a word beyond his instructions : but, if D'Arras pleased, he would talk with him on the state of matters in Europe, not as an ambassador, but " privately, as a poor friend might speak with an Emperor's great councillor." He then argued that the Turk could do no hurt to Christendom, if Christian princes did not back him ; "and here," says he in his letter, " D'Arras said enough against the French King, and said he would show me a pretty way of writing news ; and going to a coffer of his, he brought out a couple of blanks† sent by D'Arramont from Con-

† This mode of sending blanks signed by particular persons, to be filled up with such facts or communications as were most likely to mislead and render abortive the measures of a rival power, was much practised in the crafty diplomacy of the times. We find it used by Mary of Guise during her regency in Scotland.

stantinople to the French King, wherein might be
written such news as might serve the French
King's purpose, and be taken for news come from
the Turk's court, because D'Arramont had subscribed both the blanks with his hand and name.
I saw both the blanks ; but whether they were
D'Arramont's, or like to be his, I know not."†

In the following extract from a letter of Morysine's we have a glance at the state of the Papal
Court in Oct. 1552.

*Orig.* GALBA, B. XI. f. 129. 26th Oct. 1552. *Spira.*

\* \* " Of late, the Bishop, meaning, as men
guess, to enjoy his papacy and live like a Pope,
hath wound himself out of all business, leaving the
charge of his whole doings to five Cardinals, with
power absolute to do what they shall think good ;
only requiring them that, as occurrents happen, he
may hear of them.

" Il Cardinal di Monte is appointed to oversee the
Bishop's revenues, and to take order for things of his
Holiness' Chamber. Cardinal Pigghin [Pigghini]
is appointed to matters of judgment, for to appoint
consistories and such like. Cardinal Cicada hath
in charge to look to the Bishop's lands and castles,
such as are not appointed to legates already.
Cardinal Mignanelli, or rather Mangiagnelli, is

† The letter is dated Spire, 7th Oct. 1552. It is in Galba,
B. XI. fol. 117, and in several places has been injured by fire.

made superintendent, to see that religion amend in
no place where he hath to do.*  But Cardinal
Dandino is he that hath to do in matters of state—
in things between the Bishop and Princes of Christendom; and it is thought Dandino will do his best
to deserve such pensions as the French King giveth
unto him, and fail of that he seeketh if he get not
some more.  *  *  It is like the Bishop meaneth
to make his excuse by these five Cardinals, in case
any thing be done that the Emperor may mislike.  He that wrote the news from Rome saith,
that his Holiness is not in so extreme love with
Cardinal di Monte as he was."  *  *  *  †

The late Dr. M'Crie, in his Life of Knox, mentions two conflicting statements as to the manner
in which this celebrated reformer procured his liberty from imprisonment on board the French galleys: one, that the galley on board which he was
confined was taken by the English; the other, that
he was delivered from his long servitude by orders
of the French King.†  This last account we have
already shown to be the true one.

The moment he procured his freedom Knox passed
over to England, where he was favourably received
by Cranmer and the English Council, and sent to
officiate as a preacher at Berwick.  This was in

* *Mignanelli.*—Morysine puns on Mignanelli and Mangiagnelli (lamb-eater).  The Cardinal was probably a *gourmand*.
  † Life of Knox, vol. i. p. 75.

1549.   In April 1550, he publicly disputed against the Mass, at Newcastle, before the Council and congregation ; amongst whom were the Bishop of Durham, the learned and amiable Tunstal, and his doctors.*   In the month of Dec. 1551, he was made one of King Edward's chaplains ; and, in Oct. 1552, was employed in revising the Articles of Religion previous to their ratification by Parliament.†   It appears, by the Book of the Privy Council, that on the 27th of this same month he received forty pounds as the King's Majesty's reward.‡   Beza has informed us that the reformer refused a bishoprick ; and Knox himself, in a manuscript letter which has been quoted by Dr. M'Crie, alludes to the high promotions which had been offered him by Edward the Sixth.§   Neither the date of this offer, however, nor the bishoprick which he was invited to fill, have yet been discovered.

The following letter from Northumberland to Cecil fixes both.   The proffered see appears to have been the bishoprick of Rochester, and the offer was made and declined by Knox in the same month in which he had been consulted upon the Articles of Religion, and had received a reward, or, as Dr. M'Crie thinks, a pension from the King.   The expected services of this stern partisan of Protestant-

---

* Life of Knox, vol. i. p. 85.

† MS. Privy Council Book.   Oct. 2nd, 1552.

‡ Ibid. Oct. 27th, 1552.

§ Bezæ Icones.—M'Crie, vol. i. pp. 100, 101.

ism,—the hope expressed by Northumberland that he would operate as a *whetstone* to the gentler Cranmer, and as a hammer against the furious Anabaptists,—are not the least characteristic parts of this letter.

## NORTHUMBERLAND TO CECIL.

*Orig.* St. P. Off. *Domestic.* 28th Oct. 1552.

" I would to God it might please the King's Majesty to appoint Mr. Knocks to the office of Rochester bishoprick; which, for three purposes, should do very well.   The first, he would not only be a whetstone, to quicken and sharp the Bishop of Canterbury, whereof he hath need; but also he would be a great confounder of the Anabaptists lately sprung up in Ként.

" Secondly, he should not continue the ministration in the North, contrary to this set forth here. Thirdly, the family of the Scots, now inhabiting in Newcastle chiefly for his fellowship, would not continue there, wherein many resorts unto them out of Scotland, which is not requisite.

" Herein I pray you desire my Lord Chamberlain and Mr. Vice-chamberlain to help towards this good act, both for God's service and the King's.

" And then for the North, if his Majesty make the Dean of Durham Bishop of that see, and appoint him one thousand marks more to that which he hath in his deanery,—and the same houses which he now hath, as well in the city as in the country, will serve him right honourably,—so may his Majesty receive both the castle, which hath a princely site, and the other stately houses which the Bishop had in the country, to his Highness; and the Chancellor's living to be converted to the deanery, and an honest man to be placed in it; the Vice-chancellor to be turned into the Chancellor; and the Suffragan, who is placed without the King's Majesty's authority, and also hath a great living, not worthy of it, may be removed, being neither preacher, learned, nor honest man: and the same living, with a little more to the value of it—a hundred marks, will serve to the erection of a Bishop within Newcastle.   The said Suffragan is so pernicious a man, and of so evil qualities, that the country abhors him.   He is most meet to be removed from that office and from those parts.

" Thus may his Majesty place godly ministers in these offices as is aforesaid, and receive to his crown 2000$^{li}$ a year of the best lands within the north parts of his realm.   Yea, I doubt not it will be iiii$^m$ marks a year of as good revenue as any is within the realm; and all places better and more godly furnished than ever it was from the beginning to this day. * *

" Scribbled in my bed, as ill at ease as I have been much in all my life.

" Your assured friend,   NORTHUMBERLAND."

Endorsed in Cecil's own hand.

" *Duke of Northumberland to*
  *Sir W. Cecyll.   28th Oct.* 1552."

In the following extract from a letter of Morysine, written to the English Council from Spires,
we have a graphic picture of an interview, in the
camp before Metz, between the Emperor and the
Margrave Albert.   Charles was remarkable for his
graceful horsemanship.   He rode, says Mexia,
when fully armed, with so much majesty, and
managed his horse so gallantly, that no more
accomplished knight could be found.*

Ascham, in his Discourse on the State of Germany, has given us, from personal observation, a
minute portrait of Albert Margrave of Brandenbourg.   This leader, one of the most powerful
and able, but least respectable of the Protestant
Princes, had refused to subscribe the pacification at
Passaw; actuated apparently by a jealousy of the
Elector Maurice's increasing power, and by a turbulent imperious disposition which took delight in war
and confusion.   Soon afterwards, however, he was
reconciled to the Emperor; and having routed and
taken prisoner the Duke D'Aumale in the battle of
St. Nicholas, he joined the army with which Charles,
in the month of November 1552, laid siege to Metz.
"Marqhes Albert," says Ascham, "is now at this
day (June 1553) about thirty-one years old; of a
good stature, neither very high nor very low; thick
without grossness, rather well-boned for strength
than overloaded with flesh; his face fair, beautiful,

* Imperial History, p. 635.

broad, stern, and manly; somewhat resembling my
Marquis of Northampton when he was of the same
years : his eyes great and rolling, making his countenance cheerful when he talketh, and yet, when he
giveth ear to others, he keepeth both a sad look
without sign of suspicion, and also a well-set eye
without token of malice; and this behaviour I
marked well in him when I dined in his company at
the siege of Metz, in the Count John of Nassau's
tent.   His voice is great, and his words not many,
more ready to hear others than to talk himself."†

SIR RICHARD MORYSINE TO THE COUNCIL.

*Orig.* Galba. B. xi. f. 132.    *Spires.*   30th Nov. 1552.

\* \* " Men think the Emperor also meant to increase this opinion in us, [that Metz was about to
surrender or be taken,] who, the 20th of November,
came riding fair in harness upon a great courser of
Naples into the camp, and found many occasions
to talk to divers, to thank whom he knew had
done any thing well, and to encourage others, fill-
ing men with hope as he went: and when he
came where Marquis Albert and Marquis Marignian were, they both lighted from their horses ;
whereupon the Emperor, looking with a very loving countenance upon Marquis Albert, did put out
his hand to him, and shook him twice or thrice
at once, as the Almains are wont to do.   The
Marquis had his eyes still fast upon the Emperor's

† Ascham's English Works, by Bennet, pp. 25, 26.

countenance, as one that meant to see whether there were any looks that would betray thoughts commanded to keep in. When he saw all was well, or at the least could not see but all seemed well, he, standing and not kneeling, spake a few words to the Emperor, which the Emperor did seem to take in very good part; and giving him words for words, a good many for a few, he took him by the hand again. The Emperor dined that day with the Duke of Alva; and lieth where the Duke lieth, in an abbey hard by Metz. \* \* \*

" The Palsgrave, my Lords, hath so feasted me and others that came at my desire, as he must think me an ungrateful man if I make not as much suit as I can to purchase him thanks from the King's Majesty. \* \* He showeth a singular affection to the King's Majesty, a constant memory of the great goodness showed to him and to his family by the King's Majesty's most noble father.

" His wife beareth the title of a Queen, and yet by no intreaty would he suffer her to wash with me.† When we went a hunting, he would needs I should leave my horse and go in waggon with him; setting me in his lady's place, and sending her amongst her women. He came within a mile of Spires, because I did not come to him; and lay there three days ere I could go to him. \* \* \*

" He said at his table, his hemet,‡ that is his shirt, was never so nigh his skin as the King's Majesty's

---

† So in the original. This passage is obscure.
‡ Probably for " hemd," which is the German word?

father was, and should be while he had any breath
in him, nigh his heart. His Queen would fain have
me to send or bring my wife thither.  \*  \*  \*
Men think, within eight or nine days this matter of
Metz will grow to some conclusion."

The conclusion to which this memorable enterprise grew is well known. The Duke of Guise,
to whom the defence of Metz had been entrusted,
having with him the flower of the French nobility, baffled every effort of the Emperor; and compelled him, after experiencing severe loss, to raise
the siege.† The first great cannonade was opened
four days after the date of Morysine's letter on
the 24th Nov. De Thou gives a most spirited account of the siege.‡

Northumberland's kind intentions for Knox's
preferment to a bishoprick appear to have been of
short duration; for we see, from the next letter,
that the Duke and the reformer had met, and,
after a stormy interview, had separated with little
regret on either side. Knox had too much acuteness not to detect the ambition and selfishness of
this domineering statesman, and too much sincerity
not to tell him of his faults to his face. In the
reformer's "Admonition to the Professors of the
Truth in England," he shows an intimate knowledge of the characters of Northumberland and
Paulet, Marquis of Winchester: the first, as he
says, "ruling the roast by stout courage and proud-

† January 1552-3.        ‡ Book xi.

ness of stomach;" the other, under the name of Shebna the Treasurer, acting like " a crafty fox, showing a fair countenance to the King, but under it concealing the most malicious treason." *

The most interesting portion of this letter, how-ever, is that in which Northumberland alludes to his own religious faith; which, he assures us, had continued firm to the Protestant creed for twenty years : little more than a year elapsed, when this unhappy man was executed, professing himself a Roman Catholic.

NORTHUMBERLAND TO CECIL.

*Orig.*  St. P. Off.  7th Dec. 1552.

" MASTER KNOX's being here to speak with me, saying that he was so willed by you, I do return him again, because I love not to have to do with men which be neither grateful nor pleasable.  I as-sure you I mind to have no more to do with him but to wish him well, neither also with the Dean of Durham, because, under the colour of a false con-science, he can prettily malign and judge of others against good charity upon a froward judgment. And this manner you might see in his letter, that he cannot tell whether I be a dissembler in religion or not : but I have for twenty years stand [stood] to one kind of religion, in the same which I do now profess; and have, I thank the Lord, past no small dangers for it.

" I do send you herewith the letter which I do

* Admonition to the Professors of the Truth in England, p. 53.

mind to send to the Constable of France by Vellan-
dry, because the Constable sent me one by him,
which the King's Majesty did see; praying you to
know his Highness' pleasure in it, and to send me
word by this bearer. I have also thought good to
put you in remembrance eftsoons of the matter
revealed by the Dean of Durham, for that it seemeth not good to me it should lie in *hogarmogar*,† for
the matter is perhaps of more importance than it
is taken for. If it be proveable, it is without all
doubt meet for his Majesty to know the truth of it,
with all the circumstances and adherents, *nisi fortè
veniant Romani.* *  *  *

" I remember well your considerations concerning
what might be judged by evil people of me, as
though it might be imagined that I should be the
procurer of the matter against the parties for displeasure, or for that I would be alone, or for to
have some of his inheritance. As touching that
first, it is known to the King's Majesty and some
others of the Council who is the revealer of the matter; and, while it is now fresh in memory, I think it
meet the matter were so handled as the revealer,
while he is here, should be eftsoons asked and
caused to declare under his handwriting by what
means he came to the knowledge of this matter,
and how long he did know it before he did utter it

† *i. e.* in a secret state.—The matter revealed by the
Dean of Durham was, a conspiracy against the government,
of which Bishop Tonstal was alleged to be cognizant without
revealing it.

unto me, and by whom the matter was first broken unto him.

" And this done, with the advice and consent of some others of my Lords of the Privy Council, it shall the better and more livelier appear to their wisdoms what is farther to be done in it, chiefly for the King's Majesty's surety. * * * And, for my own part, if I should have past more upon the speech of the people than upon the service of my master, or gone about to seek favour of them without respect to his Highness' surety, I needed not to have had so much obloquy of some kind of men ; but the living God, that knoweth the hearts of all men, shall be my judge at the last day with what zeal, faith, and truth I serve my master.   And though my poor father,† who, after his master was gone, suffered death for doing his master's commandments, who was the wisest prince of the world living in those days, and yet could not his commandment be my father's charge after he was departed this life ; so, for my part, with all earnestness and duty I will serve without fear, seeking nothing but the true glory of God and his Highness' surety : so shall I most please God and have my conscience upright, and then not fear what man doth to me. *    *

" From Chelsey, this 7th of Dec. 1552.

" Your assured friend,

" NORTHUMBERLAND."

* Edmund Dudley, executed August 15th, 1510.

The Duke of Northumberland, in repeated letters, exhibits the utmost anxiety for the appointment of a bishop .to the vacant see of Durham ; Tonstal having been deprived on account of his alleged privity to a conspiracy against the government. * Northumberland's plan was carried into effect in the Parliament which sat in the following month of March. It was, as we have seen, † to dissolve the old bishoprick, and erecting two sees, one at Durham, the other at Newcastle, to endow them moderately,—Durham with two thousand, and Newcastle with one thousand, marks a year. The temporalities of the dissolved bishoprick, which was a county palatine, were to be vested in the King; and on these the ambitious Duke had an eye for himself. Nor was he unsuccessful. They were granted to him, but the King's death interrupted and ultimately put an end to the scheme.

These circumstances must teach us to receive with caution Northumberland's remarks on the godless state of the country. The zeal of the Duke for the recovery of the straying sheep was of an interested kind. It is strange to find this rigid supporter of the Reformation abusing the Protestant bishops and pastors as " new, obstinate doctors, without humanity or honest conditions, and so sotted with their wives and children as ut-

* Supra, p. 149. Hayward in Kennet, vol. ii. p. 323.

† Supra, p. 143.

‡ Hayward in Kennet, vol. ii. p. 323.

terly to neglect their calling." But we must not attach much credit to this tirade. The key to it is to be found in the conclusion of the letter. Their possessions were too great, and Northumberland longed to reduce them to a reasonable size by helping himself to a large portion of the county palatine.

### NORTHUMBERLAND TO CECIL.

*Orig.* St. P. Off. *Domestic.* 2nd Jan. 1552-3.

" Forasmuch as this old year past was not happy for old Durham to receive a new bishop, I would wish, if so it might please the King's Majesty and my Lords so to consider it, that that country should no longer be deferred from a pastor, where there is already so many straying sheep. And if so great a matter as this is, both for God's cause, the quiet of the country, and the King's Majesty's honour, shall be so little regarded, notwithstanding the continual calling upon it which I have from time to time done, I would that some other that seemeth to make the matter so light had mine office there, and I discharged thereof; and then they shall perhaps know better what it means to have the rule and government where God shall be neglected and forgotten. And what order was lately taken with the Dean of Durham I neither yet did hear nor have been made privy to it; and where he is, and how he is employed by the order of my Lords, whether he be gone home, or whether he remain here, I know not; but wheresoever he be, I have been much deceived by him, for he is undoubtedly not only a greedy, covetous man, but also a malicious, and an open evil speaker; and thereof there is enough now can make report: therefore, for the love of God, let not the See be so long destitute of some grave and good man; yea, rather a stout honest man that knoweth his duty to God and to his Sovereign Lord, than one of these new obstinate doctors without humanity or honest conditions. These men, for the most part, that the King's Majesty hath of late preferred, be so sotted of their wives and children that they forget both their poor neighbours and all other things which to their calling appertaineth; and so will they do so long as his Majesty shall suffer them to have so great possessions to maintain their idle lives. Beseeching God that it may be amended.

" From Chelsey, the 2nd January 1552.

" Your loving friend,

" NORTHUMBERLAND."

" *To my very loving friend,*
*Sir. Wm. Cecil, Knight,*
*deliver this.*"

Northumberland, one of the most crafty, domineering, and grasping of men, and whose ambition aimed latterly at nothing less than kingly power, assumes, in the following letter to Cecil, the garb of a recluse, wearied with the world, studious of rest, and longing for his departure from a scene in

which he had witnessed so much vanity.  The epistle
is an accomplished piece of hypocrisy, but it was
addressed to one who could see through it all.   It
is worthy of note also, that this letter is written at
the time when the young King began to fall into that
declining state of health from which he never afterwards recovered.   This illness, probably, had sug-
gested to Northumberland his great design against
the crown; and his absence from the Council may
have been connected with the organising his plot
for the alteration of the succession.

### NORTHUMBERLAND TO CECIL.

*Orig.*  St. P. Off.  *Domestic.*  3rd Jan. 1552-3.

" FORASMUCH as it seemeth to me, yesterday, by
your friendly persuasions for my coming to the
court, that the same, with some others my friends,
either did not thoroughly understand mine estate, or
might judge in me some great negligence for being
so long absent, I have thought good with these further to declare unto you, that whosoever do think
that for any respect I do now withdraw or absent
myself from the King's affairs, saving for lack of sufficient health, he judgeth me wrong.  Albeit, I must
needs think that if all things were considered in me,
as I am able to declare by myself, and easy enough
to be judged of others, mine absence might be the
better borne ;  but this moveth me to remember the
Italian proverb, which, though it become me not
to say of myself, yet the saying is true, that of a

faithful servant shall become a perpetual ass.  So, though I were able to bear the burden, I trust my Lords do not mind so to use me once, if my body were as healthful as any man's.  I assure you, both for the King's honour and my poor estimation, it is high time for me to seek a way to live of that which God and his Highness hath sent me ; and to keep the multitude of cravers from his court, that hangeth now daily at my gate for money, so long have I passed forth this matter in silence and credit, that shame almost compelleth me to hide me.  What comfort think you may I have, that seeth myself in this case after my long travail and troublesome life, and towards the end of my days ?  And yet, so long as health would give me leave, I did as seldom fail mine attendance as any others did ; yea, and with such health as, when others went to their sups and pastimes after their travail, I went to bed with a careful heart and a weary body ; and yet abroad no man scarcely had any good opinion of me.  And now, by extreme sickness and otherwise constrained to seek some health and quietness, I am not without a new evil imagination of men.  What should I wish any longer this life, that seeth such frailty in it ?  Surely, but for a few children which God hath sent me, which also helpeth to pluck me on my knees, I have no great cause to desire to tarry much longer here.  And thus, to satisfy you and others whom I take for my friends, I have entered into the bottom of my care, which I cannot do without sorrow : but if God would be so merciful to mankind as to take from them their wicked imaginations, and leave them with a simple judgment, men should here live angels' lives; which may not be, for the fall of Adam our forefather procured this continual plague, that the one should be affliction to the other while we be in this circle, out of which God grant us all his grace to depart in his mercy. And so I leave, wishing the good unto you that your own self can desire.

    " At Chelsey, the 3rd of January 1552.

            " Your assured loving friend,

                    " NORTHUMBERLAND."

" *To my very loving friend,*
   *Sir Wm. Cycill, Knight.*"
Endorsed by Cecil himself.
" *D. of Northumberland to W. Cecill,*
   3 *Jan.* 1552."

We have already seen how earnestly Northumberland exerted himself for the promotion of Knox to the bishoprick of Rochester, when the advancement of this great enemy of the Romish Church suited the state purposes of the ambitious Duke : we have seen also that the reformer proved, probably too honest, certainly too stubborn, to lend himself to the designs of a selfish and crafty statesman ; for which reason he was sent back to Cecil as a man neither " grateful nor pleasable."*

It appears however that Knox was a favourite of

* See supra, p. 148.

the young King, or perhaps we should rather say of
Cheek, Cecil, Bedford, and others of the puritan
party,—from whom Edward imbibed many of his
opinions and predilections.   It is known at least,
that on the 2nd October 1552, he was consulted in
the revision of the Articles of Religion previous
to their ratification by Parliament; and that, on the
27th of the same month, he received forty pounds
as a reward from the King, under the title of his
Majesty's Preacher in the North.*

On his return to Newcastle, the reformer's custom
of alluding in the pulpit to affairs of state brought
him into new trouble.  Northumberland took offence because he lamented the fall of Somerset;
and the Roman Catholic party in the Council
caught fire at an assertion which he made, that all
who were enemies to the Protestant faith were secret traitors to the crown and commonwealth.†

For this attack he was brought before the Privy
Council, but the King's good opinion and the interest
of the puritan party again bore him out unhurt; and,
having been heard in his defence, he was absolved
from all blame,‡ and permitted to return to the scene
of his labours.   It was a return, however, to strife
and persecution.  Lord Wharton, the most powerful man in these quarters, was his enemy; the
Mayor of Newcastle brought forward new accu-

* MS. Privy Council Book, 27th Oct. 1552; and under the
date 2nd Oct. 1552.

† M'Crie's Life of Knox, vol. i. pp. 92, 93.        ‡ Id. p. 95.

sations; and, as Northumberland writes, " uttered against him his malicious stomach." Their united opposition seems to have embittered his life, and drew from him a letter to this nobleman, which, from the manner in which he alludes to its contents, must have been desponding and melancholy, a tone very different from that in which he generally expressed himself: it is much to be regretted that this letter of Knox, which was sent enclosed by Northumberland to Cecil, is not to be found. It sounds strange to our ears to hear the rigid and indomitable reformer, whose voice made princes and nobles tremble, described, almost in a style approaching to contempt, as " a poor soul" to whom it would be charity in Cecil to minister a few words of comfort in his perplexed and broken-hearted state.

### NORTHUMBERLAND TO CECIL.

*Orig.* St. P. Off. *Domestic.* 9th Jan. 1552-3.

" After my right hearty commendations.—Herewith I do return unto you as well Mr. Morison's letters as also the Lord Wharton's, and do also send with the same such letters as I have received from the said Lord Wharton of the 2nd and 3rd of this instant, with also one letter from poor Knoxe, by the which you may perceive what perplexity the poor soul remaineth in at this present; the which, in my poor opinion, should not do amiss to be remembered to the rest of my Lords, that some order might be taken by their wisdoms for his recomfort. And as I would not wish his abode should be of great continuance in those parts, but to come and to go as shall please the King's Majesty and my Lords to appoint him, so do I think it very expedient that his Highness' pleasure should be known, as well to the Lord Wharton as to those of Newcastle, that his Highness hath the poor man and his doings in gracious favour; otherwise some hindrance in the matters of religion may rise and grow amongst the people, being inclined of nature to great inconstancy and mutations. And the rather do I think this meet to be done, for that it seemeth to me that the Lord Wharton himself is not altogether without suspicion how the said Knoxe's doings hath been here taken : wherefore I pray you that something may be done whereby the King's Majesty's pleasure to my Lords may be indelayedly certified to the said Lord Wharton, of the King's Majesty's good contentation towards the poor man and his proceedings, with commandment that no man shall be so hardy to vex him or trouble him for setting forth the King's Majesty's most godly proceedings, or [what he] hereafter by his Majesty's commandment shall do ; for that his Majesty mindeth to employ the man and his talent from time to time in those parts, and elsewhere, as shall seem good to his Highness for the edifying of his people in the fear of God. And that something might be written to the Mayor for his greedy accusation of the poor man, wherein he

hath, in my poor opinion, uttered his malicious
stomach towards the King's proceedings if he might
see a time to serve his purpose; as knoweth God,
to whose infinite goodness let us pray that all
things may prosper, to his glory, and to the honour
and surety of the King's Majesty.

" From Chelsey, this 9th of January 1552.

" Your assured loving friend,

" NORTHUMBERLAND."

" *To my very loving friend,*
  *Sir. Wm. Cecil, Knight,*
  *deliver this.*"

The following letter from Northumberland to
the Lord Chamberlain, written in contemplation of
the meeting of the last Parliament of Edward the
Sixth, is full of interest. The preparation of the
speech by Cecil, the manuscript notes " scribbled "
on it by Northumberland, the insight we obtain
into the different political views of these remarkable men, the previous consultations on the choice
of a speaker, and the query as to the continuation
of a service which one would have supposed to
have been long since abolished—the Mass of the
Holy Ghost, are all points of importance.

## NORTHUMBERLAND TO THE LORD CHAM-
BERLAIN.

*Orig.* St. P. Off. *Domestic.* 14th Jan. 1552-3.

" AFTER my most hearty commendations to your
Lordship. I do return to the same herewith

the arguments and collections of Mr. Secretary
Cecil, left with me by your Lordship at your late
being at Chelsey; which, as I did then partly declare my opinion in some points, seeming to me
your Lordship not to mistake the same, hath made
me the bolder to scribble a part of my simple
mind upon the margin; which, by your wisdoms,*
when you shall have seen and perused, and not
like the same, there is no harm but to strike it out
with a pen, for the text remaineth, so as Mr.
Secretary can easily find out his own.

" The cause why I have scribbled the book so
much is, that I am of opinion that we need not
to be so ceremonious as to imagine the objects †
of every froward person, but rather to burden
their minds and hearts with the King's Majesty's extreme debts and necessity, grown and
risen by such occasions and means as cannot be
denied by no man; and that we need not to seem
to make account to the Commons of his Majesty's
liberality and bountifulness in augmenting or advancing of his nobles, or of his benevolence showed
to any his good servants, lest you might thereby
make them wanton, and give them occasion to
take hold of your own arguments; but as it shall
become no subject to argue the matter so far, so, if

---

* Although the letter is addressed to the Lord Chamberlain
only, the notes of Dudley were meant for the consideration
both of this nobleman and Cecil.

† Objects—*i. e.* objections.

any should be so far out of reason, the matter will always answer itself with honour and reason, to their confuting and shame : praying your Lordship, and also Mr. Secretary, to bear with me in this my folly, the rather for that I know your minds was that I should declare my opinion, (tho' I know small need there is of the same,) otherwise you would not have left the instrument with me.

"And further, touching my Lady Elizabeth's Grace's communication with Mr. Chancellor concerning Durham Place, this bearer can declare the same unto you. It hath not been much from that I did therein conjecture : nevertheless, her Grace seemeth by the report of the said Master Chancellor to be fully satisfied, but not without conceiving some displeasure before against me, for that I would make labour or means to have the house without first knowing her mind; wherein I must appeal to the King's Majesty's most gracious goodness, and to your Lordship's friendly remembrance, whether ever I made means or suit for to have it. And herein I trust his Highness will defend me unto her Grace, who indeed I would not offend willingly, knowing her [relation,] as I do, to his Highness. Her Grace hath presently sent to cause the house to be delivered, wherein I rest to know his Majesty's further pleasure. Her Grace also hath sent me word by Master Chancellor, that she is determined about Candlemas to come to see the King's Majesty, and is desirous that she might borrow St.

James' to lie in for the time, because she cannot have her things so soon ready at the Strand House ; but I am sure her Grace would have done no less, though she had kept Durham House still.    And thus I commit your Lordship to the tuition of the Almighty.    From Chelsey, the 14th of January 1552.    " Your Lordship's assured loving friend,

" NORTHUMBERLAND.

" Postscripta.—In my poor opinion, it is time the King's Majesty's pleasure were known for the Speaker of the House, to the intent he might have secret warning thereof, as always it hath been used, because he may the better prepare himself towards his preposition; otherwise he shall not be able to do it to the contentation of the hearers.    It would also be considered who shall that day preach before the King, and what service shall be said in the stead of the old service, which was wont to be of the invocation of the Holy Ghost ; or whether his Majesty will have the communion for all his Lords and Prelates to communicate together at the said service in his Màjesty's presence, or not.    And also, that his Majesty's pleasure were known concerning the bringing in by writ some heirs-apparent into the parliament-house, whereby they may the better be able to serve his Majesty and the realm hereafter.

" *To my very good Lord my Lord*
    *Chamberlain, deliver these.*"
Endorsed in Cecil's hand.
    " 14*th Jan.* 1552.
    " *Duke of Northumberland to my Lord Chamberlain.*"

The Duke of Northumberland was not contented with the possession of the greatest power which perhaps was ever enjoyed by any English subject. He aimed yet higher; tottered on the highest step of the ladder, lost his balance in grasping at the crown, and brought upon himself swift and utter ruin. Yet his plan, as far as human foresight could reach, seemed artfully and strongly laid. It is well known. The young King, whose constitution had never been robust, fell into a declining state of health in January 1552-3;[*] and Northumberland, aware that the most prominent feature in Edward's character was an apprehension, it might almost be called a horror, for the re-establishment of the Roman Catholic faith in England, conceived the project of inducing him to settle the crown upon the Lady Jane Grey, descended by her mother's side from the youngest sister of Henry the Eighth, and thus setting aside Mary, who was the true heir. During the month of May 1553, the young King seemed convalescent; and Northumberland selected this as a proper time to lay his plans, and consolidate his power by a marriage between the Lady Jane and his fourth son, Lord Guilford Dudley. At the same time, his daughter, Catherine Dudley, was married to Lord Hastings, eldest son of the Earl of Huntingdon; and Lord Herbert, the Earl of Pembroke's eldest son, and a nobleman entirely de-

* Hayward in Kennet, vol. ii. p. 323.

voted to the Duke, was united to the Lady Catherine Grey. These alliances strengthened his hands, and he knew that the Council were most of them his creatures. The readiness with which Edward lent himself to a project so unjust and nefarious is extraordinary. He agreed to disinherit Mary, to set aside Elizabeth, to pass over Mary Queen of Scots, the lineal descendant of the *eldest* sister of Henry the Eighth; and, contrary to the will of that monarch, and to the act of parliament which had declared the next heirs to be the Ladies Mary and Elizabeth, he by his own sole prerogative settled the crown on Jane Grey, Henry's great grand-daughter.

The scene in which this memorable piece of injustice was carried into execution must have been an extraordinary one; and there is fortunately preserved an account of it by the Lord Chief Justice Montague, who was himself a principal actor. It appears that, on the 11th June 1553, this Judge received a letter from the Council at Greenwich, requiring him to attend next day at court, and to bring with him Sir John Baker, Mr. Justice Bromley, and Gosnold and Griffin, the Attorney and Solicitor General.*

* It is worthy of notice that this letter, which may be considered as the first step towards setting aside Mary's title, was signed not only by Secretary Petre, and Sir John Cheek, who, on the 2nd of June, had been sworn as a third Secretary of State, but also by Cecil.—MS. Privy Council Book, 2nd June 1553: and Narrative of Sir Edward Montague; Fuller, Church History, vol. ii. p. 369.

Montague accordingly came to court, and was brought to the King's presence, with whom he found the Marquis of Winchester, Lord Treasurer, the Marquis of Northampton, Sir John Gates, and others of the Council. Edward declared that his long sickness had caused him to think seriously of the state of his realm; that he was resolved the crown should not go to the Lady Mary, who might alter the religion; and that therefore he had called him to receive the royal commands regarding the drawing up a deed, by which he meant to alter the order of succession. The King then showed him some written articles, which had been prepared with this design, and ordered him to draw out a deed of settlement according to their tenor. To this Montague replied, that such a proceeding would be illegal, and directly against the Act of Succession, which was an act of parliament. The King, however, was peremptory; and the old Judge, receiving the articles, required an interval to consult the statutes and deliberate.

Next day, the 12th of June, Secretary Petre sent for Montague to Ely Place, Northumberland's palace, and informed him that the affair required speedy despatch; upon which the Chief Justice hastened to court, and coming before the Council, and probably speaking the more boldly because the Duke was absent, declared that, after having considered the King's wishes, the opinion of himself and his colleagues who were with him

remained unaltered.   To make such a destination
of the crown as had been proposed, would, he affirmed, be not only treason in them, but treason in all
their Lordships.   Upon this, Northumberland, to
whom this opinion had been communicated, burst
into the Council-room, pale and trembling with
anger; and, amongst other outrageous talk, called
the Chief Justice traitor, and swore that he would
fight in his shirt with any man in that quarrel.

Next day, the 14th June, Montague received
an order from the Council to repair instantly to
court, with the same official persons who at first
accompanied him.   On passing through the rooms,
" all the Lords looked upon them with earnest
countenance, as though they had not known
them;" by which Montague and his brethren began to fear that things would go hard with them.
Nor were they deceived.   On being introduced to
the royal presence, Edward, " with sharp words
and angry countenance," demanded why they refused to obey his order ; commanded them on their
allegiance to make quick despatch; and declared
he would afterwards have it ratified by Parliament.
Some Lords, who stood behind the Chief Justice,
said, if they refused to draw the deed, they were traitors.   And Montague, as he himself says, being a
*weak old man and without comfort,* professed at last
his willingness to consent upon two conditions ; the
first, that the King would give him his commission
under the great seal, enjoining him to draw the

instrument; the second, that a general pardon for having drawn it, should be made out at the same time.   To this Edward agreed: Mary was declared illegitimate, and the crown settled upon the Lady Jane Grey.

Montague's own words upon this point are remarkable: "And so," says he, "the doers and makers of the said book (or settlement), with sorrowful hearts and with weeping eyes, in great fear and dread, devised the said book, according to such articles as were signed with the King's proper hand, above, beneath, and on every side." *

This will having been thus drawn, Northumberland insisted that it should be signed by all the Council, as well as by the Judges; a request which, after more or less hesitation, was at length obeyed by all except Sir James Hales.   Some idle controversy and recrimination has arisen between Catholic and Protestant writers on this point of Edward's change of the succession; and the Councillors who signed the will having been partly Protestants and partly Catholics, historians, as they belong to the one or to the other persuasion, have attempted to excuse their friends and to blacken their opponents.   Nothing can be more absurd; because nothing can be more certain than that the

---

* Fuller, vol. ii. p. 372.—The Articles have been printed by Strype, from a MS. described as belonging to D. Wm. Petyt. Edward has headed them, "My devise directing the Succession."   See Life of Cranmer, vol. ii. p. 912.

conduct of the whole Council, with one fine exception in the case of Hales, was selfish, timid, and time-serving.

I have already observed that Cecil's desertion of Somerset, and his devotedness to Northumberland, brought him to the brink of a precipice. The moment of trial was now come, and it is curious to trace him under it:* yet let us do it with every allowance. The times were dreadful—and in the vocabulary of statesmen to lose your place, and to lose your head, were then almost convertible terms.

On his first suspicion of the desperate game which Northumberland was playing, Cecil appears to have adopted an expedient not uncommon in those days with councillors who wished to get rid of a dangerous question. He became very sick, and absented himself from court. This at least is Strype's conjecture,* and there is every reason to believe it correct.

Many of his friends, however, thought him really ill; and amongst these Lord Audley, who loved and studied the healing art, undertook his cure, as appears by the following humorous recipe and epistle.

LORD AUDLEY TO CECIL.

*Orig.* St. P. Off. *Domestic.* 9th May 1553.

" Good Mr. Cecil.—Be of good comfort, and pluck up a lusty merry heart, and thus shall you

---

* Strype's Memorials, vol. ii. p. ii. p. 109.

overcome all diseases : and because it pleased my good Lord Admiral lately to praise my physic, I have written to you such medicines as I wrote unto him, which I have in my book of my wife's hand, proved upon herself and me both ; and, if I can get any thing that may do you any good, you may be well assured it shall be a joy to me to get it for you.

### " A good medicine for Weakness or Consumption.

" Take a sow-pig of nine days old, and flea him and quarter him, and put him in a stillatory with a handful of spearmint, a handful of red fennel, a handful of liverwort, half a handful of red nepe,* a handful of celery, nine dates clean picked and pared, a handful of great raisins, and pick out the stones, and a quarter of an ounce of mace, and two sticks of good cinnamon bruised in a mortar ; and distil it together, with a fair fire ; and put it in a glass and set it in the sun nine days ; and drink nine spoonfuls of it at once when you list.

### " A Compost.

" Item.—Take a porpin, otherwise called an English hedgehog, and quarter him in pieces, and put the said beast in a still with these ingredients : item, a quart of red wine, a pint of rose-water, a quart of sugar, cinnamon and great raisins, one date, twelve nepe.

" If there be any manner of disease that you be

* Turnip.

aggrieved with, I pray you send me some knowledge, and I doubt not but to send you a proved remedy.

" Written in haste at Greenwich, the 9th day of May.

" By your true hearty friend,<br>" JOHN OF AUDLEY."

Cecil's disease, however, was deeper fixed than to be cured by soup formed from the distillation of a sow-pig boiled with cinnamon and raisins, or a compost of a porpin or hedgehog stewed in red wine and rose-water. It was Northumberland's plot that troubled his digestion.

As the month of June approached, his quick eye had detected more decided symptoms of the Duke's daring scheme, and we learn from an authentic paper that he viewed it with the utmost alarm. He probably knew, what afterwards was so strikingly shown, the hatred with which the people regarded the Duke, and their strong attachment to legitimacy. There was then in Cecil's service, and treated by him with much confidence, one Mr. Roger Alford; and Strype has published in his Annals* a letter from this person to Lord Burleigh, which gives us some interesting particulars of that great statesman's conduct at this trying crisis. It is strange that these should have been so little noticed by the writers of his life, although well worthy of attention. In walking in Greenwich Park, the court being then at Greenwich, Cecil, it appears, told Alford in con-

* Vol. iv. p. 349.

fidence, that he had secret information of a device of King Edward's regarding the succession. He had heard of it, he said, not as a councillor, but covertly from a friend. The object of the device was to set aside Mary, and to make Lady Jane Queen. When the project was riper, he considered it likely, he said, that he would be called to give his opinion; but he emphatically declared that, whatever became of him, he *never would be a partaker in that device.* The plot was then confined to a few members of the government; and Cecil, having resolved at all hazards to resist being brought in as an accomplice, absented himself from the Council.* This was a dangerous step: Northumberland was violent, and we have Alford's testimony to the fact, that Cecil dreaded assassination; he went about armed, contrary to his usual practice; he resorted to London, often under cover of night; he had his money, plate, and evidences conveyed out of his house; he meditated flying from the country, but, when Gosnold and Hales refused to sign the will, he plucked up new courage and remained. The power of Northumberland, however, and the importunity of the young King, having at last prevailed over all opposition, Cecil was called upon last of all to give his consent. Here, as the passage is important, I must use Alford's own words.

* This absence of Cecil from the Council was from the 22nd of April till the 2nd of June 1553. This was the time Lord Audley prescribed his hedgehog soup.

" Afterwards, the matter thus proceeding, and the Judges' opinions prevailing so far, who, together with Mr. Gosnold, and all others required thereunto, had subscribed, saving yourself, you told me that being called for before the King, upon his commandment that you should subscribe his instrument, you answered it, that allowing it as a councillor you could not, for causes you showed him. Whereupon, as I remember also, he said, he willed you to subscribe as a witness that it was his pleasure to have it so to pass, which you have no reason to deny ; and so as the last man you subscribed."

This account of Cecil's opposition to Northumberland's iniquitous scheme, of his being the last who was induced to affix his name to the will, and of his signing *as a witness* to the King's signature, not as consenting to the deed, has been adopted by all the writers of his life ; and Alford, as we see, states that he received it from Cecil's own lips. I must frankly confess, however, I give no credit to the story. It is contradicted by evidence under his own hand. If it was true that *to the last* he was utterly against the scheme, and determined at all hazards to have no hand in it, how does it happen that, at the first, that letter which Chief Justice Montague received upon the 11th of June, requesting his presence at the noted interview in which the scheme for the disinheriting of Mary was first broached, was signed by Cecil as well as by the other Secretaries, Sir William Petre and Sir John Cheek ? But there is much stronger proof against Alford's story than this. Not only is the King's will signed by Cecil, without there being the slightest symptom that his name (which occurs not last, but in the middle of all the other signatures,) was there placed as a witness; but it appears that, after the framing of the will, the King, or the Duke, to make assurance doubly sure, had directed a new instrument to be drawn out, by which certain members of the Council engaged " upon their oath and honour to adhere to *and carry into effect* all the articles contained in the King's settlement." Now this second deed is signed by four-and-twenty councillors, and amongst these occurs the name of William Cecil. The story, therefore, of his determined opposition to Northumberland, and of his signing, not as a principal but as a witness,—a tale so oft repeated without due examination,—seems to me to have been manufactured to meet the exigency. Alford's letter, it must be observed, was written in 1573, twenty years after the events it describes; it was drawn up at Cecil's own request, and was evidently composed with the most favourable feelings towards his old master, who was then Lord Treasurer and Prime Minister of Elizabeth. It states some part of the truth, but not the whole truth. The distress and alarm of Cecil when he first heard of the scheme of Northumberland to set aside Mary, and his resolution to resist it, " whatever became of him," are emphatically dwelt on, and are certainly true; but

he has suppressed the fact that these honest reso-
lutions faded away, and that the feelings of the
courtier proved in the end too strong for the determination of the patriot. Northumberland, however, had no doubt detected his unwillingness ; and,
on the 2nd of June, Sir John Cheek was sworn in
as a third Secretary of State. It is difficult not
to connect this extraordinary step with Cecil's absence from the Council, and indisposition to the
plot against Mary. It appears to me that Northumberland meant to show him that, unless he
went all lengths with him, he must cease to be Secretary. And the argument was not lost upon him.
During the interval between the 2nd and the 11th
of June, there was, I have little doubt, a painful
conflict in his mind. It was during these eight
days that Northumberland matured his design ; and
on the 11th, as the reader will recollect, the letter
was written to Montague, which may be regarded as
the first public step against Mary. This letter, we
know from Montague's account, was signed by Cecil ; and that signature demonstrates, I think, that
he had determined to retain his place, whatever sacrifice it might cost him. And as we shall soon see,
it did cost him dear ; for he was driven by it to
falsehood, to evasions, and to little subterfuges,
from which every upright mind would have recoiled. But this discussion upon Cecil's behaviour in
perhaps the most trying crisis of his life has carried
me too far. 1 must resume the series of our letters.

Whilst these dangerous intrigues were being carried on at home, the continental relations of the country were not neglected.

Dr. Wotton and Sir Thomas Challoner had been sent on a mission to the French King in the beginning of April 1553. On April 15th, 1553, they addressed a letter to Cecil, dated at Monstrieul, which has been printed by Haynes.* It mentions the sudden muster of the Imperial army under the Prince of Piedmont, their investing Therouenne, and the consternation of Mons. de Loches commandant of that place; who, being absent from his charge, had, in an attempt to re-enter the town, suffered a defeat by the Burgundians. The French King, they say, was at St. Germain, expecting the Queen's *accouchement*, and had sent for all his children. Sir William Pickering, the English ambassador at the French court, was afterwards joined in the commission with Wotton and Challoner. The following letter gives an account of their negotiations. †

* MS. Privy Council Book, 1st April 1553. — Haynes, p. 148.

† In the Ambassades de Noailles, vol. ii. p. 9, there is a letter from the Constable Montmorency to Noailles, giving an account of the conferences of the English ambassadors with the French ministers. The English names are sadly mangled. Challoner is Monsieur *Charanger*, and Maistre Woton is in a note explained to be "Nicolas Malherbe, Doyen des Eglises de Cantorbery et d'York." Wotton was born at Bockton *Malherbe*, in Lincolnshire. Hence, probably, the ludicrous mistake as to his name.

About the same time, Edward the Sixth, or rather the Duke of Northumberland, who had the whole management of affairs, despatched an embassy not only to the court of France, but to the Emperor ;* the object of both being the same, to promote a reconciliation between these two rival princes, and to restore peace to Christendom through the mediation of England.   The Emperor had not as yet given an audience to the ambassadors, and the preliminary demands of the French monarch were so extravagant, that there seemed little prospect of the negotiation being attended with success.   In a letter of Secretary Petre to Secretary Cecil, dated Greenwich, 15th May 1553, he remarks,   " Our ambassadors with the Emperor have not yet spoken with him, but only with the Regent, of whom they have yet no answer.   In France they had access long ago ; many fair words and certain *small* requests : the realms of Naples, Sicily, Arragon, and Navarre ; the duchy of Milan, the county of Ast [Aosta], the sovereignty of the Low Countries.   Things go slowly forward ; whether it be the Emperor's weakness, or the expectation of some other mean, or that they will not hear of peace, I know not." †

The reader will remark the allusion in the latter part of the following letter to the news which had reached France, of Edward " being a little *sick and*

* MS. Books of Privy Council, 27th March 1553.
† Haynes, p. 150.

*accrased,*" a feeble phrase to express that mortal malady which had seized the young King ; but Wotton and his colleagues were either themselves ignorant of its fatal nature, or wished to disguise it from the French King and his ministers.    This, however, would have been a vain attempt, for, on the 13th of this same month, Noailles had written to the Constable Montmorency that there was but little hope of his recovery.*    We know that at this moment the Duke of Northumberland was engaged in organising the plot by which he raised Lady Jane Grey, wife of his fourth son, Guilford Dudley, to the throne, on the decease of Edward, which took place little more than six weeks after.

## WOTTON, PICKERING, AND CHALLONER, TO THE COUNCIL.

*Orig.*  St. P. Off.  *France.*  May 16th, 1553.

" After our most due commendations.   It may like your good Lordships to be advertised that, upon our first access to the French King, we sent a special messenger with our letters of the 1st of this instant unto your Lordships, containing at large the substance of our conferences with the said King and Constable.   Since which time we have not received any letters either from your Lordships or from my Lord of Norwich and his colleagues in Flanders ; which giveth us half a doubt that perchance, by means of the Emperor's sickness, or

* Negociations de Noailles, vol. ii. p. 25.

otherwise, they have not had such speedy audience
as we, or else perchance have had such answer as
is cause of more delay in the signification thereof
unto us.

" In the mean time, according to the advertisement of our former letters, yesterday arrived at
Paris a Cardinal Legate from the Bishop of Rome,
called Capo di Ferro ;* who heretofore, what time I
the Dean of Canterbury was here ambassador resident, came hither in like office of Legate ; who now,
at his entry into Paris, was solemnly received with
the accustomed processions, and, for more special
honour, the Bishop of Cahors there met and
received him ; from whence he cometh as to-morrow to this town of Poissy, his lodging being
already prepared, and shall have his audience at
the court.

" Now, forasmuch as even lately the news have
been spread in this court (albeit we think it not
most certain) that they of Sienna and the Imperials
are at an appointment of peace, so as the 10th day
now past of this instant, as these men affirm, the
writing of the said appointment should be capitu-
lated, and thereby accorded that the armies, as well
French as Imperial, withdrawing from Sienna, the
said city and territory thereof should remain clearly
discharged, and restored to the ancient liberty, of
which appointment and restitution the Bishop of

* Jeronimo Capi-Ferri, Cardinal of St. George. — Noailles,
vol. ii. p. 45.

Rome is said to be the only mediator; therefore
it is thought by some discoursers here, that the
said Bishop pretendeth by means of his Legates,
sent presently, the one to the Emperor and the
other to the French, to bear a great stroke in the
composition of the rest of their quarrels and differences, so as a peace by his means may follow:
which thing we shall endeavour ourselves, as much
as we may, to attain knowledge of, and advertise
your Lordships from time to time with diligence
how this Legate shall demean himself, and how he
shall be used here.

" And albeit we had thought, for a day or twain
longer, to have deferred the writing hereof until the
said Legate's access unto the French court; by
which time also it might be that we should have received some packet from your Lordships, which we
much desire; yet upon occasion of a message this
day brought unto me, Sir Wm. Pickering, by
Mons. De Manny from the Constable, we thought
good to despatch unto your Lordships this present
letter out of hand, to give the same to understand
that, according to the said Manny's message, Mons.
the Secretary De L'Aubespine is already in order
to repair into England, intending this night to set
forwards by easy posts, of purpose (quoth the said
Mons. De Manny) to visit, from the King my master,
the King his good son and brother, who, as the
King my master hath been advertised, hath been a
little sick and accrased. And therewith the said

Manny asked me whether I had not lately heard
thereof; whereunto I answered, that since his Highness' late accrasement, taken of a cold, I heard
nothing of any other sickness that his Majesty
should newly sustain; trusting it was not so. Well,
quoth he, in case you purpose to write any thing by
Mons. L'Aubespine into England, I am come to
give you notice of his departure, and so he took his
leave, not declaring otherwise the cause of the said
L'Aubespine's going. The occasion, therefore, of
his repair into England we know not, otherwise
than in this sort; and yet we think it may be some
further matter than an errand of visitation. And
whether these men, besides the answer they have
made to us, mean to declare the same to the King's
Majesty more particularly by some man of their
own of special credit, (such as De L'Aubespine is,)
and perchance therewithal to make overture of some
further matter, we know not. * * *

  " The French Queen yesterday, after a long
and perilous travail, was brought a-bed of a daughter; and the voice goeth, that, within these four
days, the King removeth from St. Germain's to
Paris, and from thence into Picardy, nearer the
places subject to the Imperials' danger. Pietro
Strozzi is returned out of Italy, and from the Duke
of Ferrara hath brought (as is said) this answer:
that in case the French King do send an army into
Italy, competent for any great enterprise, the Duke
will show himself, on his part, both his good cousin,

ally, and special confederate ; otherwise [he] would
be loath to discover himself altogether French without notable purpose.    Capt. Riffenberg is said to
have newly entered covenant with the French King
to make up his band to the number of six thousand
lansknechts, accounting those which he hath already
in regiment. * * *

    " Your Lordships' at commandment,
       " N. Wotton.    W. Pykerynge.
               " Thos. Challoner."

We have just mentioned the embassy to the
Emperor, the object of which was a desire upon
the part of Edward and his ministers to mediate
a peace between this potentate and France.    The
following is the letter from the ambassadors,—the
Bishop of Norwich, Sir Philip Hoby, and Sir R.
Morysine.

## THE BISHOP OF NORWICH, SIR P. HOBY, AND SIR R. MORYSINE, TO THE COUNCIL.

*Orig.* St. P. Off. *Germany.* 9th June 1553.

" Pleaseth your Lordships, yesterday in the
afternoon, about five of the clock, Messieurs De
Baldemont and Gerard, two of the Emperor's
Council, set us from our lodging unto the court,
where first we had access unto the Queen ; by
whom, after a short excuse made of the long delay
of our answer, it was told us that like as the King
our master, in travailing of this sort to pacify the

present wars, had not only showed himself a very sincere friend unto the Emperor, but also a well-willer of the tranquillity of all Christendom according to the office of a good king, so the Emperor, for his part, did not only yield unto his good brother his most hearty thanks, but also assured us that, whensoever those reasonable conditions were offered that might appear to tend unto a perfect and an unfeigned peace, it should well be known that the Emperor doth presently no less covet the quiet of all Christendom than as a good Christian prince should, and as he hath ever coveted and travailed for it.

" And since the cause of these wars is unknown unto the Emperor, being begun by the French King of that sort that all the world knoweth, it is therefore reason the offers also begin there; or else let them that have begun show what grounds they have to begin it, that it may be seen by indifferent men in whom the fault is; and then, look what may with the Emperor's honour in reason be required, and it shall be seen whether he meaneth not indeed as she now had said unto us.

" Wherewith she left that matter, and told us that we should immediately speak with the Emperor himself, and should at his hands perceive whether this were true or not. Whereupon she caused us to be led down to the Emperor's chamber, from whence, after a little pause, we were brought into his privy chamber, and there found

him set on a chair with his feet on a stool, looking
very pale, weak, lean, and feeble ; howbeit nothing
so ill as we before believed of him, for his eye was
lively enough, and his speech sensible : but what we
should judge of him we cannot tell, for he hath
escaped so many perils of sickness, that tho' his
colour and his flesh be gone, yet he may endure a
while.    Marry, to judge him by our sight, we must
say that he appeareth unto us rather a man of short
time than of continuance.*

   " Thus, when we were come to his presence and
made due reverence, we made the King's Majesty's commendations to him, and in few words
touched the King's Majesty's affection towards his
Majesty, and then the cause wherefore we were
sent.    Whereunto briefly he answered us of this
sort : that he was sorry of our long delay here,
but his sickness had been the cause, wherefore he
prayed us to bear withal ; and for our message he
did specially thank the King our master, his good
brother, both for the good affection that he always
findeth in him, and also for his zeal unto the concord and peace of all Christendom, giving him the
title of a good and virtuous king ; showing himself
much pleased that the King's Majesty did so ear-

---

* Sir Philip Hoby, in a letter to Secretary Cecil, dated at Brussels, 20th June, and printed in Haynes, p. 151, gives much the
same account of the Emperor's extreme weakness ; adding, that
his credit and estimation in Germany, Italy, and other places,
decayed as rapidly as his body.

nestly follow this good purpose, so friendly by him taken in hand ; assuring us that, upon offer of reasonable conditions, (his honour being saved,) we should well see how much he tendered peace. And so, he praying us to make his most hearty commendations again unto the King his good brother, we took our leave at him, wishing to his Majesty strength and long health. And, either this day or to-morrow, we look to hear of the Legate's † access unto him.    *    *    *

"THOMAS NORWICENS.

"PHELYP HOBY.

"RICH. MORYSINE."

"Bruxelles, 9th June 1553."

On the 6th of July, Edward, who had been sinking for some months under a pulmonary complaint, expired at Greenwich. His death was probably hastened by the prescriptions of a female empiric, to whose care he was committed after the physicians had pronounced the case hopeless.‡   Next day, the 7th, Cecil wrote in his Diary that singular and inexplicable sentence to which I have already alluded in the first volume : "*7th Julii libertatem adeptus sum morte Regis, ex misero aulico factus liber et mei juris.*" That Cecil, under the latter part of the reign of Edward, should have found himself an unhappy courtier who had no will of his own, I can well believe.   It is demonstrated by many authentic

† The Papal Legate Dandino, sent to meditate a peace between the two monarchs.

‡ Carte, v. iii. p. 278.   Giffet, p. 3.

papers; but the death of the young King, so far from giving him freedom, and permitting him to follow his own inclinations, which, according to his own assertion, were all on the side of Mary, chained him more hopelessly to the will of the proud Duke, and compelled him to support the cause of the Lady Jane. What meaning then can we attach to the words " *factus liber et mei juris*" ?

But, leaving this riddle to be solved by future antiquaries, I proceed to observe that Northumberland and his faction, the moment the young King breathed his last, shut the gates of the palace, doubled the guards, intercepted all communication with the country, and resolved to conceal his death for a fortnight, till they had obtained possession of the persons of Mary and Elizabeth, and secured themselves against all opposition. * Previous to the King's death, a request had been sent in Edward's name for the repair of the Lady Mary to the court, and she was on the point of falling into the snare ; she had advanced on her journey as far as Hoddesdon, near London, when a secret message was brought her that Edward was dead, and that if she advanced she was lost. Dr. Lingard ascribes this important piece of service to the Earl of Arundel ; Mr. Jardine, in his Criminal Trials, to Sir Nicholas Throckmorton.† Unfortu-

* Roger Alford's letter to Cecil. Strype's Annals, vol. iv. p. 349. Noailles, vol. ii. p. 70.

† Lingard, vol. vii. p. 151. Jardine, Crim. Trials, vol. i. pp. 43, 44.

nately, both authors have omitted to state their authority; but, be this as it may, Mary instantly mounted on horseback, and rode at speed to Kenninghall in Norfolk, where she deemed herself in safety.*   This occurred on the 7th July ; and, early in the morning of the same day, Lord Clinton, by Northumberland's order, seized the Tower, in which were the royal treasures, with the munitions of war.   He was accompanied by the Lord Treasurer Winchester and the Earl of Shrewsbury.   They turned out the Constable, Sir James Crofts; fortified it more strongly, by bringing in additional ordnance;   and prepared it for the reception of the Lady Jane as Queen.   On the same day, the Lord Mayor and some of the leading aldermen and citizens were sent for to the Council, informed of the King's death and will, commanded to keep the event secret, and dismissed, after having taken the oaths to the new sovereign.

The whole Council, with others of the principal nobility, were now in the Tower, strictly watched by Northumberland, who dreaded intrigue, aware that he had heads as crafty as his own to deal with.   On the 9th, a letter was brought from Mary, which she wrote to the Council in the character of Queen, expressing her astonishment that they had not proclaimed her, and requiring them instantly to repair this omission.   To this an answer was returned, reminding her of her alleged

* Holinshed, vol. iii. p. 1065.

illegitimate birth, declaring that the Lady Jane was their Queen, to whom their allegiance was due, and recommending her to submit to her lawful sovereign. It is important to observe that this letter was signed by Cecil, as well as by the rest of the Council.* All this took place whilst the Lady Jane was totally ignorant of the high destiny intended for her; but, on the 9th, Northumberland, with the Duke of Suffolk, the Earl of Pembroke, and others of the nobility, repaired to Sion House, where she and her husband, Lord Guilford Dudley, had resided since their marriage. She was struck with an unusual deference and respect in their manner; and soon after, her mother, the Duchess of Suffolk, having entered the apartment, Northumberland explained to her the will of the late King, saluted her as Queen, and, falling on his knees with the rest of the nobility, declared that they would defend her title with their blood.†

She was much overcome, burst into tears, and accepted their homage with unaffected sorrow and humility. On the 10th she was proclaimed, publicly assumed the government, and made her royal entry into the Tower, where she was received with all the honours due to a Queen of England.‡

So far Northumberland's project had been crowned with complete success; and judging from the

* Holinshed, vol. iii. p. 1067.

† Lingard, vol. 7, pp. 153, 154.   Carte, vol. iii. p. 281.

‡ Stowe, p. 610.

precautions which he had adopted, and the power
which he seemed to possess, the cause of Mary
appeared desperate. But the leader in this great
change was hated by the people. They dreaded his ambition; they called to mind the ruin
which he had brought on their favourite Somerset,
they accused him of making the young King a mere
tool to execute his own plans; and hinted that
Edward had been poisoned. It was noticed that
when Jane took her progress to the Tower, the
crowd gazed upon her in silence, offering no
congratulations; and we know from Bishop Godwin,* that this circumstance gave encouragement
to some of Queen Mary's friends in the Council,
who secretly favoured her cause, though compelled for the time to dissemble. It is from this
moment that I believe Cecil, who was now keenly
observing every turn, commenced his double play,
of which I shall speak immediately.

In the mean time, nothing could be more extraordinary than the rapidity with which the short
and lamentable episode of the Lady Jane hurried to
its conclusion. Scarcely had the Council despatched their answer to Mary's summons, when the appal-
ling news arrived that she had been joined by the
Earls of Bath and Sussex; to this it was soon added,
that she had been proclaimed Queen in some places
amid universal acclamations; that Sir Edward
Hastings, brother of Lord Huntingdon, had joined

* Kennett, vol. ii. p. 329.

her with four thousand foot; and that her forces increased every hour. It was necessary for Northumberland to act on the instant, but he was distracted with difficulties. If he left the Tower, he dreaded the intrigues of the Council and the disaffection of the capital; if he remained, whom could he trust to command the army? At last, he determined to proceed against Mary in person; and, having spent the 11th and 12th in collecting his force, he left the city, and trusted to surprise his antagonist before she was able to cope with his troops.* In this, however, he was miserably disappointed. The Queen, encouraged by the enthusiasm of the people, acted with uncommon decision and vigour; she had on the 16th July left Kenninghall, and ridden without drawing bridle to Framlingham, where, in a few days, she saw herself at the head of thirty thousand men.† Northumberland soon heard of this; it was added, that he had been proclaimed a traitor, and a price set upon his head: he dreaded that his communication with the capital would be cut off; and, losing courage, fell back from Bury upon Cambridge.

From this moment all was lost. The Council, who were still conducting the government of the Lady Jane in the Tower, becoming assured of the real state of affairs, deemed it prudent to discover that she whom they had so recently

* Speed, p. 1108.
† Holinshed, vol iii. p. 1067.

branded as an illegitimate usurper was their only
lawful sovereign.    This wheel was executed on the
19th of July, and, on the 20th, Mary was proclaimed
at St. Paul's Cross amid extravagant demonstra-
tions of popular joy.    After which Arundel and
Paget hurried with the good news to Framlingham.
On the 20th also, the Duke of Northumberland,
who had attempted when too late to make his peace
by proclaiming Mary, was arrested for high treason; and that same day the Lady Jane saw herself despoiled of the ensigns of royalty by her own
father, who joined the stronger party.    She was permitted to depart to Sion House, whilst Northumberland and his associates were lodged in the Tower.

The diligence of Strype and other collectors has
preserved some of the public instruments and letters which illustrate the transactions of these nine
eventful days; but they contain little secret history, and I have found no private letters to guide
me.    In truth, it would be almost vain to expect them, as the rapid whirl of events and the
peril of the time made the actors in them too busy
and too timid to write.

There is, however, among the Lansdowne manuscripts one valuable paper which enables us to resume our examination of the conduct of one of the
greatest men who figured in these extraordinary
scenes.    I mean Cecil.    It is a defence of himself
which he presented to Mary.    The paper is in his own
hand-writing; and, as the only printed copy which I

know is a very inaccurate one,* I give it here from
the original in the British Museum.    It is entitled

## " A BRIEF NOTE OF MY SUBMISSION AND OF MY DOINGS."

*Orig.* LANSDOWN. 102. F. 2.

" 1. First, my submission with all lowliness that
any heart can conceive.

" 2. My misliking of the matter when I heard it
secretly ; whereupon I made conveyance away of
my lands, part of my goods, my leases, and my
raiment.

" 3. I also determined to suffer, for saving my conscience ; whereof the witnesses, Sir Anthony Cooke,
Nicholas Bacon, Esq. Laurence Eresby of Louthe,
(ii.) two of my suite, Roger Alford and William
Cayewood.

" 4. Of my purpose to stand against the matter,
be also witnesses Mr. Petre and Mr. Cheke.

" 5. I did refuse to subscribe the book, when
none of the Council did refuse : in what peril, I
refer it to be considered by them who know
the Duke.

" 6. I refused to make a proclamation, and
turned the labour to Mr. Throckmorton, whose

---

* It is difficult to understand why Strype should not have
printed the original, but contented himself with an abstract in
his notes on Hayward, Kennett, vol. ii. p. 352.    We owe its
first appearance to Mr. Howard, in his Life of Lady Jane Grey,
pp. 310, 313, but owing to the inaccurate transcription and
typography, the blunders entirely deform the sense.

conscience I saw was troubled therewith, misliking the matter.

" 7. I eschewed the writing of the Queen's Highness bastard, and therefore the Duke wrote the letter himself which was sent abroad in the realm.

" 8. I eschewed to be at the drawing of the proclamation for the publishing of the usurper's title, being specially appointed thereto.

" 9. I avoided the answer of the Queen's Highness' letter.

" 10. I avoided also the writing of all the public letters to the realm.

" 11. I wrote no letter to the L. (Lord) Lawarr, as I was commanded.

" 12. I dissembled the taking of my horse, and the rising of Lincolnshire and Northamptonshire, and avowed the pardonable lie where it was suspected to my danger.

" 13. I practised with the L. Treasurer to win the L. Privy Seal, that I might by the L. Russel's means cause Windsor Castle to serve the Queen ; and they two to levy the west parts for the Queen's service. I have the L. Treasurer's letter to L. (Lord) St. John for to keep me safe if I could not prevail in the enterprise of Windsor Castle, and my name was feigned to be Hardinge.

" 14. I did open myself to the Earl of Arundel, whom I found thereto disposed ; and likewise I did the like to the L. (Lord) Darcy, who heard me with good contentation, whereof I did immediately tell Mr. Petre for both our comfort.

" 15. I did also determine to flee from them if the consultation had not taken effect, as Mr. Petre can tell, who meant the like.

" 16. I purposed to have stolen down to the Queen's Highness, as Mr. Gosnold can tell, who offered to lead me thither, as I knew not the way.

" 17. I had my horses ready at Lambeth for the purpose.

" 18. I procured a letter from the Lords that the Queen's tenants of Wymbledon should not go with Sir Thomas Caverden; and yet I never gave one man warning so much as to be in a readiness, and yet they sent to me for the purpose, and I willed them to be quiet. I might, as Steward there, make for the Queen's service an hundred men to serve.

" 19. When I sent into Lincolnshire for my horses, I sent but for five horses and eight of my servants; and charged that none of my tenants should be stirred.

" 20. I caused my horses, being indeed but four, to be taken up in Northamptonshire; and the next day following I countermanded them again by my letters, remaining in the country, and notoriously there known.

" 21. When this conspiracy was first opened to me, I did fully set me to flee the realm; and was dissuaded by Mr. Cheke, who willed me for my satisfaction to read a dialogue of Plato, where Socrates, being in prison, was offered to escape and flee, and yet he would not.   I read the dialogue, whose reasons indeed did stay me.

" Finally, I beseech her Highness that in her grace I may feel some difference from others that have more plainly offended, and yet be partakers of her Highness' bountifulness and grace: and if difference may be made, I do differ from them who I served, and also from them that had liberty after their enforcement to depart, by means whereof they did, both like noble men and true subjects, show their duties to their Sovereign Lady.   The like whereof was my devotion to have done, if I might have had the like liberty ; as knoweth God, the searcher of all hearts, whose indignation I call upon me if it be not true :

" Justus adjutorius meus Dominus, qui salvos facit rectos cord (corde) :

" God save the Queen in all felicity !

" W. CECILL." *

It is singular that so important a paper as this should have been so little consulted by the writers of Cecil's Life, whose besetting fault it is to indulge in vague and unlimited encomium.   Yet the facts which it contains are not only interesting as

---

* Endorsed by Cecil himself,—" No. xxxx.  1553.  *Ante et p$^t$ mortem Ed.* 6$^a$ ;" and in another old hand on the back, " His apology for himself as to his actings in Queen Jane's business."

illustrating his character, but are in truth all we know of the secret history of the revolution which unseated Jane and placed Mary on the throne. I request the reader to observe how completely this paper corroborates the view already given of the absurdity of the story that Cecil only signed Edward's will as a witness: for what says he himself of this?—" I refused to subscribe the book (i. e. the will) when none of the Council did refuse; in what peril, I refer it to be considered by them who know the Duke." Is it to be believed that he would have here omitted to add, that he signed it only as a witness, and not as consenting to the deed? Yet had Cecil the disingenuity to invent for the credulous ear of Alford this excuse, which he did not dare to plead to the Queen, and to consent in future years that the story, which he deemed, perhaps, a " pardonable departure from the truth," should be retailed by his dependants.    Such little beings are our greatest men!

Equally ungenerous and selfish was his conduct when Northumberland commanded him as secretary to draw the proclamation in favour of Jane. What says he here?

" I refused to make a proclamation, and turned the labour to Mr. Throckmorton, whose conscience I saw was troubled therewith, misliking the matter."

Thus was poor Sir Nicholas saddled by Cecil with an act of treason from which his conscience recoiled; and the Secretary, whose eye was looking forward to coming events, found the means by this cunning suggestion to place one man at least between himself and the scaffold. Under the reign of Elizabeth, Throckmorton and Cecil were keen political opponents. Was not this enough to account for their enmity ?

It is evident from the paper, that, the moment Northumberland left the Tower to take command of the army, Cecil and the Council began to plot against him. It had been first resolved by the Duke that he should remain in the capital, and that Suffolk should command the army against Mary; but the Lady Jane, earnestly and with tears, implored the Council that her father should not be separated from her;* and they, who by this time had secret information of Queen Mary's success, were eager to get rid of Northumberland, whose presence awed them into subjection. The account given by Holinshed of Northumberland's consent to lead the army, and of his speech to the nobles before leaving the Tower, is interesting, and has some fine touches which seem to stamp its authenticity. † After alluding to the arguments used by the Lords to prevail upon him to take the expedition on himself, he thus gives the Duke's answer :

" ' Well then, since ye think it good, I and mine

* Stowe, p. 610.

† On the margin it is said to be copied from the report of an eye-witness. Holinshed, vol. iii. p. 1068.

will go, not doubting of your fidelity to the Queen's Majesty, which now I leave in your custody.' So that night he sent for both lords, knights, and others that should go with him, and caused all things to be prepared accordingly. Then went the Council in to the Lady Jane, and told her of their conclusion, who humbly thanked the Duke for reserving her father at home, and beseeched him to use his diligence; whereunto he answered, that he would do what in him lay. The morrow following, great preparation was made; the Duke, early in the morning, called for his own harness and saw it made ready at Durham Place, where he appointed all his retinue to meet. The same day carts were laden with ammunition, and artillery and field pieces were set forward.

"The same forenoon the Duke moved eftsoons the Council to send their powers after him, as it was before determined, to meet with him at Newmarket; and they promised they would. He said further to some of them, 'My Lords, I, and these other noble personages, with the whole army that now go forth, as well for the behalf of you and yours, as for the establishing of the Queen's Highness, shall not only adventure our bodies and lives amongst the bloody strokes and cruel assaults of our adversaries in the open fields; but also we do leave the conservation of ourselves, children, and families at home here with you, as altogether' committed to your truth and fidelities: whom, if we

thought ye would through malice, conspiracy, or
dissension, leave us your friends in the briers and
betray us, we could as well sundry ways foresee and
provide for our own safeguard, as any of you, by
betraying us, can do for yours.   But now upon the
only trust and faithfulness of your honours, whereof
we think ourselves most assured, we do hazard our
lives; which trust and promise if ye shall violate,
hoping thereby of life and promotion, yet shall
not God count you innocent of our bloods, neither
acquit you of the sacred and holy oath of allegiance made freely by you to this virtuous lady the
Queen's Highness, who by your and our enticement
is rather of force placed therein than by her own
seeking and request.   Consider also, that God's
cause, which is the preferment of his word, and
fear of Papists' entrance, hath been (as ye have
here before always known) laid the original ground,
whereupon ye, even at the first motion, granted
your good-wills and consents thereunto, as by your
handwritings appeareth; and think not the contrary, but if ye mean deceit, though not forthwith,
yet hereafter God will revenge the same.   I can
say no more, but in this troublesome time wish you
to use constant hearts, abandoning all malice,
envy, and private affections.'   And therewithal the
first course for the Lords came up; wherefore the
Duke shut up his talk with these words: 'I have
not spoken to you in this sort upon any mistrust I
have of your truths, of which always I have hitherto

conceived a trusty confidence, but I have put you in remembrance thereof, what chance of variance soever might grow among you in mine absence; and this I pray you, wish me not worse good-speed in this journey than ye would have to yourselves.'

"'My Lord,' said one of them, 'if ye mistrust any of us in this matter, your Grace is far deceived, for which of us can wash his hands clean thereof? And, if we should shrink from you as from one that were culpable, which of us can excuse himself to be guilt-less? Therefore, herein, your doubt is too far cast.' 'I pray God it be (quoth the Duke); let us go to dinner.' And so they sat down. After dinner, the Duke went in to the Queen, where his commission was by that time sealed for his lieutenantship of the army; and then took his leave of her, and so did certain other Lords also. Then, as the Duke came through the Council Chamber, he took his leave of the Earl of Arundel, who prayed God to be with his Grace; saying, he was sorry it was not his chance to go with him and bear him company, in whose presence he could find in his heart to spend his blood even at his feet.

Then the Earl of Arundel took Thomas Lovel, the Duke's boy, by the hand, and said, 'Farewell, gentle Thomas, with all my heart.'

" Then the Duke, with the Lord Marquis of Northampton, the Lord Grey, and divers others, took their barge and went to Durham Place, and to Whitehall, where that night they mustered their men ; and next day, in the morning, the Duke departed with the number of six hundred men or thereabouts ; and, as they rode through Shoreditch, said the Duke to the Lord Grey, ' The people press to see us, but not one saith God speed us.' " *

It is worth remarking, that Northumberland seems to have been ruined by his own excess of caution. In order that he might do nothing upon his own warrant, he insisted on having his route and marches prescribed by the Queen and Council ; whilst the Lords, in their turn, as craftily assigned to him short journeys, "not without the politic forecast," says Holinshed, " of some in favour of the Lady Mary; for, the longer the Duke lingered in his voyage, the Lady Mary the more increased in puissance, the hearts of the people being mightily bent unto her."†

Having thus artfully procured the absence of Northumberland, and presented to him such orders as they knew must ruin him if executed—having at the same time sworn to him and to the Queen inviolable fidelity, the Council proceeded busily in their intrigues against both ; and of these intrigues, Cecil, as he himself informs us, was the principal author.

" I practised," says he, " with the Lord Treasurer to win the Lord Privy Seal, that I might by the Lord Russel's means cause Windsor Castle to serve the Queen ; and they two to levy the west

* Holinshed, vol. iii. pp. 1068, 1069.      † Ibid. p. 1069.

parts for the Queen's service. I have the Lord
Treasurer's letter to the Lord St. John for to keep
me safe if I could not prevail in the enterprise of
Windsor Castle, and my name was feigned to be
Hardinge."

"I did open myself," he continues, "to the
Earl of Arundel, whom I found thereto disposed;
and likewise I did the like to the Lord Darcy, who
heard me with good contentation, whereof I did immediately tell Mr. Petre for both our comfort."

These practices of Cecil when in the Tower, and
the success with which he secretly laboured with
the Lord Treasurer and others, to assist Queen
Mary, are still more distinctly described in Roger
Alford's letter.   Of this, part has been already
quoted, but the following concluding narrative is
well worthy of attention.

"After this," says this confidential servant, "you
showed me in the Tower that you had a conference
with the last Lord Treasurer,* and withal showed
me out of your bosom a letter of credit of his to
my Lord Marquis of Winchester that now is, his
son, to credit you, and to follow your devices and
directions.   And, for the better execution of this
your determination, I kept in a store certain blank
passports, before in my custody, where the Council's hand was already set, for that the despatches
then were quick, to escape more surer.

"I remember further, at that time, of a wrote

* Alford is describing in 1573 what took place in 1553.

postscript in a letter of the Council's to the Duke, whereby was signified to him the revolt of Bethal and others with the navy to the late Queen, that your horsemen, which should have gone to the aid, were empesched by John Villiers, because you meant not to give any aid at all to their so much misliked enterprise. At that time you remembered also to me that the late Earl of Bedford was broken withal, as a misliker of that device, and Sir Wm. Petre also. * * * * After this, the Lords not long after agreed to go to Baynard's Castle to the Lord of Pembroke, upon pretence before in Council to give audience to the French King and Emperor's ambassadors, that had been long delayed audience ; and that the Tower was not fit to him to enter into at that season. At which time my Lord of Arundel, upon some overture of frank speech to be had in Council in respect of that present state, said secretly to his friend, (as I take it yourself or Sir Wm. Petre,) *that he liked not the air.* And thereupon it was deferred to Baynard's Castle ; from which place the Lords went and proclaimed Queen Mary. And yourself was despatched after my Lord Arundel and my Lord Paget to her Grace, being at Ipswich ; where, being sent by you a little before, my Lady Bacon told me that the Queen thought very well of her brother Cecil, and said you were a very honest man.

" Marry, there was a letter of late written from the Council to the Duke, intercepted, whereby it

appeared you had armed horsemen against her; but
that they were impesched by Northamptonshire
men, which had done you much hurt. Whereupon,
being privy to the matter before, I laughed, and
told her the matter.

" At your coming to Newhall, you exhibited your
Submission to her Majesty, wherein you repeated
your whole actions in that case, which I wrote.
Upon the delivery whereof, you kissed her hand at
Sir Wm. Petre's house at Ingerstone, before any
other of the Council men. And I am to remember
you further, that Mr. Cheeke answered Queen
Mary's letter, sent by Hungate to the Council; for
that you shifted as you could all dealing in those
matters, and said, if Hungate had taken a good
time to deliver his letter, you thought the Council
would have taken her offer. This, all for this
present.

　　" From Hitchin, the 4th of Oct. Anno 1573.
　　　　" Your Lordship's ever to command,
　　　　　　　　　" Roger Alford.

" You have the copy of your Submission, wherein
your whole dealing therein is remembered. If not,
I think if Mr. Fothergill, who had the keeping of
the Council chest at that time, were spoken to,
he would find it among the Council matters at
that time." *

This paper of Cecil's, entitled " his Submis-

* Strype, Annals, vol. iv. p. 349. The " Submission," is
the paper printed above p. 192.

sion,"* which is an original in his own handwriting, and the letter of Alford's, his old servant, who we see was with him in the Tower at the time, enable us to fill up a portion of English history hitherto left a blank by all our best writers, and to add some important facts to the life of Lord Burleigh. We see that when shut up with the Council in the Tower, he was prime agent in the re-action in favour of Mary. We can trace the doublings by which he deceived Northumberland, seduced the Council from the allegiance which he and they had sworn to Queen Jane, and, whilst he appeared to fulfil his oaths to this amiable person, really broke them, and acted against her. Thus, if an order must be given in favour of Jane, it was followed by a counter intrigue which rendered it abortive; and care appears to have been taken to preserve evidence of the fact. If obliged to send for his horsemen to assist the army against Mary, he managed that they should be attacked and " empesched" on their journey, meaning not to give any aid to their misliked enterprise. This circumstance of the detention of Cecil's horsemen had been mentioned by the Council in a letter written from the Tower to Northumberland. The letter was intercepted by Mary; and she accused the Secretary to Alford of having armed soldiers against her. But Alford, we see, laughed, and explained the stratagem to the Queen. We have already seen the caution with which he shifted the

* Printed above, p. 192.

writing of Jane's proclamation upon Throckmorton: we find from Alford, that when Queen Mary's letter from Kenninghall was to be answered, a similar devolution of the dangerous duty took place upon his unfortunate brother-in-law, Sir John Cheeke; and we know from himself, that he not only had the address to decline drawing the paper which branded Mary with illegitimacy, but that his refusal had the effect of making Northumberland write the letter himself. This very letter, in Northumberland's handwriting, with many interlineations and erasures, is now in the British Museum.* Upon the whole, there is presented in these papers of Cecil and his servant, a picture of successful craft, disingenuity, and, I must add, falsehood,† which has, perhaps, never been equalled in the history of statesmen.

We have learnt from Holinshed the fervency

---

* Lansdowne, 3, f. 24. Northumberland's draft was afterwards copied by a clerk, signed by Queen Jane, and sent to the Marquis of Northampton. It also is amongst the Lansdowne, 1236, f. 24, and has been printed by Ellis, Archaeologia, vol. xviii. p. 269. He conjectures that it was the composition rather of the Dudleys than the Lady Jane; not aware of the extraordinary circumstances under which it was written by the Duke himself. Both these remarkable papers were afterwards carefully preserved by Cecil. On the back of the first, there is written by him, "12th July 1553, first copy of a letter to be written from the Lady Jane, when she came from the Tower."

Written by the Duke of Northumberland, on the back of the second, the emphatic words "Jana non Regina!"

† See p. 193. "I avowed the pardonable lie." Cecil's own words.

with which the Earl of Arundel, on the departure
of Northumberland to the army, declared the devotedness of the Council, and implored a blessing
upon his Grace.   We know from Alford the quaint
observation by which he conveyed to his brethren
his opinion that "the air of the Tower" was un-
favourable to free discussion; hinting the impos-
sibility of carrying any counter-revolution into
effect till they were out of its disagreeable pre-
cincts.   To accomplish this formed the difficulty;
but Suffolk, who had the charge of keeping
them within that fortress, appears to have been a
very weak man.   It was pretended to him that the
Council must have a conference with the French
Ambassadors, regarding the foreign auxiliaries who
were to join Northumberland.*   He consented that
for this purpose they should leave the Tower.   They
did so; sent for the Lord Mayor, and instantly
proclaimed Mary.

It remains only to conclude the drama by the
following graphic account of the arrest of the
once lofty and all-powerful Duke.   It is from
Stowe; and Arundel is still a principal figure in
the picture.   The chronicler, after describing the
letters which the Council on the 20th of July addressed to the Duke, commanding him on pain of
treason to lay down his arms, thus proceeds:

"The rumour of these letters was no sooner

---

* Rosso.  I successi d'Inghelterra dopo la morte de Odoardo
Sesto, pp. 15, 16.  Ferrara, 1560.

abroad, but every man departed; and shortly after
the Duke was arrested in the King's College by
one Master Slegge, Serjeant-at-arms.   At the last,
letters were brought from the Council at London,
that all men should go each his way; whereupon
the Duke said to those that kept him, 'Ye do me
wrong to withdraw my liberty.   See ye not the
Council's letters, without exception, that all men
should go whither they would ?'   At which words,
they that kept him, and the other noblemen, set
them at liberty.   And so continued they for that
night, insomuch that the Earl of Warwick was
ready in the morning to have rode away; but then
came the Earl of Arundel from the Queen to the
Duke into his chamber, who went out to meet
him, and as soon as he saw the Earl of Arundel he
fell on his knees, and desired him to be good to
him : ' For the love of God, consider,' saith he, ' I
have done nothing but by the consents of you and
all the whole Council.'   'My Lord,' quoth the
Earl of Arundel, 'I am sent hither by the Queen's
Majesty, and in her name I do arrest you.'   'And I
obey it, my Lord,' quoth he.   ' I beseech you, my
Lord of Arundel,' quoth the Duke, ' use mercy towards me, knowing the case as it is.'   'My Lord,'
quoth the Earl, 'ye should have sought for mercy
sooner ; I must do according to my commandment.'
And therewith he committed the charge of him and
of other to the guard and gentlemen that stood by."*

* Stowe, p. 612.

Such was the conduct of this noble Earl, who but a few days before had assured Northumberland, in the name of the whole Council, not only of their inviolable resolution to keep their oaths to Queen Jane, but of his own particular anxiety to shed his blood at his Grace's feet.

It is instructive to turn from this revolting scene, as we find it in authentic letters, to the rosy hues of indiscriminate panegyric with which Mr. Lodge has invested two such questionable politicians as Arundel and Winchester. But many of the "characters" of this writer, when tested by contemporary evidence, will be found to be little else than elegant aberrations from the truth. Nor is Mr. Lodge their only advocate; Mr. Turner has observed,* " that there is no occasion to charge, and no evidence to prove, any perfidy or treachery upon the part of the Council ;"— an extraordinary opinion, contradicted almost by every step they took, by their own letters, by Cecil's submission, by the narrative of Stow and Holinshed, and by their express declaration to Mary, that all along they had remained her true subjects.

* History of England, part ii. 4to. p. 226.

# INTRODUCTION TO PERIOD THIRD.

## 1553—1558.

CONTEMPORARY PRINCES.

| England. | France. | Germany. | Spain. | Scotland. | Popes. |
|---|---|---|---|---|---|
| Mary. | Henry II. | Charles V. | Charles V. | Mary. | Julius III. |
|  |  | Ferdinand. | Philip II. |  | Marcellus II. |
|  |  |  |  |  | Paul IV. |

THE brief and inglorious reign of the Princess who on the death of Edward succeeded to the throne, and the state of England and of the Continental powers at this period, do not demand any lengthened introduction to this concluding division of our letters. I have already said that I believe Mary to have been an amiable woman before she succeeded to the throne; I am equally ready to allow that her history as a Queen affords a memorable instance how feeble a barrier is the best natural disposition against the dreadful influence of fanaticism. The truth seems to be, that the principle of toleration, whether we look to Catholics or to Protestants, was utterly unknown. In this respect Gardiner and Knox, Pole and Calvin, Mary and Elizabeth, stand pretty much upon the same ground.

Of Mary's reign the leading events are easily recognised. The restoration of the Roman Catholic faith, the cruel persecution of the Protestants, the marriage with Spain, the rebellion of Wyatt, the war with France, and the temporary subserviency of England to the political views and the grasping ambition of the Emperor, — these are the great and gloomy features in the picture at home.

Looking to the Continent, we find that, in the commencement of the year 1554, Charles the Fifth, in conformity with engagements which he had contracted at the pacification of Passau, summoned a diet to assemble at Augsbourg. Its principal object was to take into consideration the religious differences which divided the empire, and to restore, if possible, something like tranquillity and peace to both parties. It did not commence its sittings, however, till the year 1555.

In the mean time, the condition of Europe gave but faint hopes that the two great powers which domineered over its destinies were anxious for rest; the war between Charles and Henry the Second continuing with even greater exasperation than before. It had been expected that Cardinal Pole, who, on his road from Italy to England, had visited both these monarchs, might have prevailed upon them to agree to some terms of accommodation; and so universal was this feeling amongst the people of France, that his progress was attended by crowds, who hailed him as the messenger of peace, and scattered flowers in his path.

But these anticipations were completely fallacious; and never was there a more cruel campaign than that in which the French King, having divided his whole military force into three great armies, attacked the Emperor in Flanders, upon the points of Artois, Avesne, and Ardennes. These three armies were commanded respectively by Charles de Bourbon, Prince de la Roche sur Yon, the Constable Montmorency, and the Duke de Nevers. Henry the Second, having joined the united armies of the Constable and De Nevers immediately after they had stormed Marienbourg, made himself master of the towns of Bouvines and Dinant, put the inhabitants to the sword, ravaged Hainault, burnt Mariemont—the beautiful palace of the Queen Regent, and sat down before the strong castle of Renty. The place was the key to Artois, and, if lost, must have rendered the conquest of this fine district almost inevitable. The Emperor in person advanced to its relief; and a battle took place under the walls of this castle, in which the military skill and conduct of the Duke of Guise, and the impetuous bravery of Tavannes, were conspicuous. The victory was claimed by the French, and they certainly remained masters of the field; but Charles retreated in good order, took up so strong a position that the enemy did not venture to attack him, and Renty was not taken.

On the side of Italy, Henry experienced a severe reverse in the defeat of his favourite general Pietro

Strozzi, at Marciano, by Medechino, Marquis of
Marignano; a disaster which ultimately brought
with it the loss of Sienna, after a siege of ten
months.

The most important event of the succeeding year
(1555) was the Diet of Augsbourg, in which, after
long debate, a complete liberty of conscience was
granted to those States and Princes in the empire
who had embraced the Protestant opinions. All
their legitimate rights and privileges were confirmed to them; their ministers were permitted to
enjoy their ecclesiastical livings, and those who in
any way attempted to attack them on the ground
of religion were declared enemies of the public
peace. At the same time it was declared that
such privileges belonged to Lutherans alone, no
other sect of the Reformers being permitted to
enjoy them; whilst Ferdinand, the King of the
Romans, inserted into the agreement a clause,
named the Ecclesiastical *Reservat,* by which every
Romish incumbent who should afterwards become
a Lutheran was deprived of his benefice.

In Italy, Brissac made himself master of Casal
in Monferrat, with the surrounding country; but
Porto Hercole having been attacked by Vitelli on
the land side, and blockaded by Doria, was compelled to surrender; the French troops in the
garrison being allowed to retire with their arms,
whilst the Italians became prisoners of war. During the following year (1556), the eyes of Europe
were fixed on an extraordinary spectacle: Charles

the Fifth, wearied with the cares of government, and broken in constitution and in spirits by the discomfiture of those vast schemes of ambition which had occupied his life, resigned his dominions into the hands of his son Philip the Second, and, stipulating only for the payment of a moderate annuity, buried himself in the seclusion of a convent, where he died in 1558.

The Emperor at the same time invested Octavio Farnese with the duchies of Parma and Piacenza, and concluded a truce for five years with France ; but the engagements into which Henry the Second had entered with Pope Paul the Fourth stood in the way of a permanent peace : the pontiff saw himself attacked by the Spaniards, he appealed to France for protection, and, after a brief interval, war soon burst out with as much fury as before.  In the campaigns which followed in Artois and in Italy, the arms of France were unfortunate.  The Duke of Guise failed in his attack upon the kingdom of Naples, and, after having attempted in vain to bring the Duke of Alva to a battle, appeared ready to give up the enterprise in despair.  In Artois, the reverse was still more complete.  Philip having assembled a formidable army in the Low Countries, commanded by the noted Emanuel Philip, Duke of Savoy, was joined by a fine body of ten thousand English, sent over by Mary; who, contrary to the wishes of her subjects, had declared war against France.  With this force, which amounted to near sixty thousand men, the Duke of Savoy invested St. Quentin. Montmorency advanced to its relief with an inferior force, and after having thrown some troops into the town, imprudently exposed himself to an attack by the Spanish cavalry in the rear and on both his flanks. The defeat was rapid, sanguinary, and so decisive, that there seemed little to prevent the united armies from an instant advance upon Paris. " Is my son at Paris ?" were, it is said, the first words which Charles the Fifth addressed to the messenger who brought to his monastic solitude the news of this great victory.

Henry the Second was, however, consoled for this severe reverse by the success of the Duke of Guise, who, having invested Calais,—a town strongly fortified, and which for more than two hundred years had been in possession of the English crown, — made himself master of it in the brief space of fifteen days. The accounts of this disaster were received in England with a burst of sorrow and indignation ; but none of her subjects felt the blow so poignantly as the Queen. During her last illness she declared that, if her body were opened, the word " Calais" would be found written on her heart.

She died on the 17th of November 1558, on which day Elizabeth succeeded to the throne, and Sir William Cecil, whose early career we have traced in these letters, was chosen her principal minister.

## PERIOD THE THIRD.

### 1553—1558.

CHARLES THE FIFTH had never forgiven the Elector Maurice the mortification and defeat which he
had met with at his hands ; and it was with the secret but joyful connivance of the Emperor that the
fierce and impetuous Albert of Brandenbourg refused to become a party to the pacification at
Passau, and turned his arms against the Protestant
Princes. The Imperial Chamber denounced against
Albert the ban of the Empire, and committed the
execution of the sentence to the intrepid Elector of
Saxony. This led to the celebrated battle of
Suershausen, fought on the 9th of July, only three
days after the death of Edward the Sixth. In this
engagement Maurice completely defeated Albert ;
but himself received a mortal wound, of which he
died two days after.

The following letter gives us some particulars of
the battle, and touches on its consequences. It is
addressed to the English Council by Christopher
Mundt, one of their foreign agents or correspondents, for whose imperfect English allowance must
be made. De Thou has given us a graphic picture

of the same fierce and heady fight. " The armies,"
says he,* " were now come almost in sight of
each other; Albert having traversed all Saxony by
long marches, and crossed the Weser, pitched his
camp in the diocese of Hildesheim, near the castle
of Peine, in the duchy of Lunenbourg, on a hollow
spot of ground surrounded on all sides by woods,
into which the passage lay through a rocky valley
forming a very narrow pass. Maurice held the
upper open field over against him. Treaties for an
accommodation had been all along carried on by
the intercession of the Princes; and on the very
day of the fight, which was the 9th of July, copies
of articles were interchanged between them. And
now it was near one o'clock in the afternoon; at
which time Albert's soldiers, having dined, and
drunk a large quantity of wine, were more disposed
for quarrelling than peace. Albert himself rising, as he was wont, half-intoxicated after dinner,
and being of a most turbulent temper at the best,
when some trifling article could not be agreed
upon, instead of a copy of the conditions, insolently
sent back to Maurice a flag, the usual token of a
challenge; and, advancing haughtily with his men,
provoked him to battle. Maurice, incensed at the
other's insolent carriage, instantly let loose his
troops, who were already prepared; and the minds
of both armies were so irritated, that, before they

---

* I have slightly altered Wilson's translation, vol. i. pp.
555, 556.

had put themselves in order, they rushed upon one another as to a mutual butchery. The wing where Maurice took his station, began to give way; and when this great leader exerted himself to rally his men, and galloped up and down, addressing the soldiers by their names, he was struck to the ground by a small ball which entered his right side near the bowels, and was immediately carried back by his men into the camp.

" The victory, however, because he was stronger in horse, after a long dispute, fell to his side, but turned out a very bloody one; Henry of Bruns-wick's two sons, · Charles Victor and Philip Fre-derick Duke of Lunenbourg, and the Counts Barbu and Bickling, were slain. Some say that Albert himself was taken prisoner in the flight; but that, either not being known, or immediately paying down his ransom, he got off, and escaped safe to Hanover.*    Sixty-four foot and sixteen horse colours were taken from him, and presented to Maurice,—a small comfort to a dying man ! * *

" Before he died," adds this historian, " Maurice sent letters to the Bishop of Wurtzbourg, informing him of his success, and admonishing him to beset all the ways, to intercept Albert in his flight." It is of this letter, which exhibited all the energy of this great man, although written when he knew his

---

* It was first suspected that Albert was slain, as we learn from a letter of Henry the Second to his Ambassador Noailles, dated 19th July 1553. Ambassadés de Noailles, vol. ii. p. 77.

wound to be mortal, that Mundt sent a Latin translation to the Council. "Afterwards," says De Thou, "when he felt certain symptoms of approaching death, being a man of high and invincible spirit, he settled his military and domestic affairs with great tranquillity of mind, and declared himself perfectly willing to leave the world; adding that he found himself, to his exceeding joy, supported by his faith in the Son of God, and did not feel any fond desire of this life, in which he had been engaged in a continual hurry of business, had experienced so much of the fickleness of human minds, and met with such ill returns to his merits. * * * At length, on the 11th day of July, about nine o'clock in the morning, he expired in his tent, in the thirty-third year of his age." The historian adds a curious passage upon the portents which are said to have preceded his death. "Many prodigies," says he, "are related to have portended his death: dogs were seized with a rabid fierceness, which incited them to fight till they killed one another; rumblings were heard in the air, and noises of men and horses during a tempestuous night in the same field where the battle was fought; howlings were heard in towns, and in the castle of Perlin the head fell from Maurice's statue without any force offered; the Elector himself appeared in a dream to a man of great worth, surrounded with flames; and bloody drops were seen upon the leaves of plants, not only in those parts, but also at Strasbourg, in the beginning of June."

The message which Mundt mentions as having been sent by the Emperor to the Margrave Albert and the Duke of Brunswick, commanding them to lay down their arms, furnishes us with another trait of the crafty policy of Charles the Fifth. As long as the Margrave Albert was engaged in war with Maurice, the Emperor seems to have felt no disposition to restore peace to Germany; his object being to weaken his enemy, the Elector, who had not only already checked his progress to almost universal dominion in Europe, but at the very time of his death was secretly plotting how he might distress him in the Netherlands.*   But, on the death of this formidable man, Charles was seized with a fit of pacification; the truth being, that he was afraid the Margrave Albert might become as troublesome and imperious as Maurice.   The message of defiance sent by Albert to the Duke of Brunswick is not mentioned by De Thou.

CHRISTOPHER MUNDT TO THE COUNCIL.

*Orig.*   ST. P. OFF.   *Germany.*   15th August 1553.

" PLEASETH your Lordships to understand, that, because of diversities and uncertainties spread ever from the battle had between Duke Maurice and the Marquis, I can write nothing assuredly; sup-

* De Thou, Book xii. sub anno 1553.

posing that your Lordships were better informed of all these doings from the Low Countries than we here.　At this present I do send a translation of a letter sent from Duke Maurice, of all these doings, to the Bishop of Wartzberg.*　After the death of Duke Maurice, his body is carried to a town in Misnia, called Dresen, where it is buried by his brother Augustus; †　the which likewise of the Electorship, as Mauricius was, is now returning even now out of Denmark, where he went with his wife, the King of Denmark's daughter, when his brother began this business.

" Mauritius hath left but a daughter, now ten years of age.　Augustus hath as yet but a daughter; he had a son, the which is dead.

" All men are in good hope that between Joannes Fredericus‡ and Augustus better love and amity shall follow than before.　Then, Augustus is given to peace and quiet, and hath all times lovingly and friendly entreated Joannes Fredericus' children; so it is reported that Mauritius hath required and admonished his brother in his testament, to keep love and amity with Joannes Fredericus and his children.

" Joannes Fredericus is now at Gota, having all

---

* See Spondanus Epitome Baronii, vol. ii. p. 546.

† His funeral oration was spoken by the celebrated Camerarius at Leipsic, on the 19th of July.　De Thou, book xii. sub anno 1553.

‡ The old Elector of Saxony, who had been deposed, and afterwards restored, by Charles the Fifth.

his councillors about him. In the assembly had at Eydelberg, it was determined and concluded, and money disbursed to the chief captain, called Hatsleyn, that an army should have be gathered with all celerity; the which should have be send into Saxony, for to command peace to both Duke Maurice and the Marquis in all the Electors' names; and the which part would not have observed the peace, the same should have been suppressed with the aid of the other: but before this army might be made ready, the field was fought in Saxony.*

" The Marquis gathereth again men about Bremen; and, as it is reported, he hath a great army together, and hath sent word to the Duke of Brunswick, (even he called, in a writing sent to the same Duke, the chief captain and defender of the untrue and false priests,) that he do make him ready, then he will shortly offer him a just battle, then that is past be but a skirmishing. The Duke hath about eighteen enseigns of footmen and two thousand horsemen, the which he doth divide in high places to keep them. His two sons, so likewise one bastard son of his, be slain in the field. His third son Julius, hearing the death of his brethren, is shortly after departed.

" The Emperor hath sent to the Marquis and to the Duke of Brunswick, commanding them peace,

* De Thou, book xii. sub anno 1553, gives an account of the conferences at Heidelberg (March 1552-3), but does not mention this resolution.

and that they shall send all their men of war to him. So the Emperor hath sent likewise to the city of Nuremberg, and to the Bishop, exhorting them to peace; the which would be glad to be in peace if they might.

" The King of Romans hath sent aid to the city of Nuremberg; then he is joined with them, the which be enemies to the Marquis, and he and Duke Maurice both had [proclaimed] war against the Marquis openly in writing; the which have burned and destroyed the Marquis' country, so that, besides two or three castles, he had nothing else besides. The King of Romans' son, Maximilian, is in continual sickness and [grief]? At the Diet, indict at Augusta : nothing is here spoken. And thus, &c.

"CHRISTOFF MUNDT."

"Argentyn, 15 Augusti 1553."


Once more turning our eyes to England, we find, that on the 18th of August 1553, the Duke of Northumberland was brought to his trial in Westminster Hall. The Duke of Norfolk sat as High Steward ; and some of those pliant nobles, who had been the assistants and advisers of Dudley in his late practices, were now seen among his judges. His guilt was so clear that he attempted no denial of the facts ; but, making great reverence to the judges, requested the opinion of the court upon two points. First, " Whether a man doing any act by authority of the Prince and Council, and by warrant of the Great Seal of England, and doing nothing without

the same, may be charged with treason for any
thing he might do by warrant thereof." Secondly,
"Whether any such persons as were equally culpable in that crime, and those by whose letters and
commandment he was directed in all his doings, might
be his judges, or pass upon his trial as his peers."

In this pertinent question Northumberland evidently, I think, alluded to the commands of Edward
the Sixth, and the warrant under the Great Seal of
England affixed to his will. Yet it is strange that
all our historians* misunderstand the question, and
suppose with the judges, (who seem purposely to
have evaded Northumberland's meaning,) that his
allusion was to the great seal of Queen Jane. A
reference to the copy of the will itself, taken out of
the original under the Great Seal, will show that
the Duke rested his defence on his having carried
into effect King Edward's "*true mind* and intent"
declared by his will, evidenced by his sign-manual,
and corroborated by *his* Great Seal.† Taking it
in this light, the query was somewhat difficult to be
answered. The only reply to it was, that the King
himself could not alter the law as fixed by Parlia-

* See Carte, vol. iii. p. 287. Hume, p. 374. Edition in one vol.
London, 1832. Lingard, vol. vii. p. 127. Fourth edition, 1838.
Mackintosh, vol. ii. p. 290.

† Copy of the will, entitled "Edward's counterfeit will."
Harleian 35, f. 364. Thus attested. "This is a true Copy
of Edward the Sixth's Will, taken out of the original under the
Great Seal, which Robert Cotton delivered to the King's Majesty, 17th April 1611, to be cancelled."

ment; that Edward's own act was illegal. But the judges, as I have said, purposely mistook and evaded Northumberland's meaning. They answered that the Great Seal which he laid for his warrant was not the seal of the lawful Queen of the realm, but of an usurper, and therefore could be no warrant to him; and, as to his second question, it was replied, that if any were as deeply to be touched in that case as himself, yet so long as no attainder were of record against them, they were, nevertheless, persons able in law to pass on any trial, and not to be challenged therefore, but at the Prince's pleasure. The Duke, upon this, continues Holinshed, saw that to stand upon uttering any *reasonable* matter, as might seem, would little prevail; he therefore confessed the indictment, (as did his companions, Gates and Palmer,) and moved the Duke of Norfolk to be a mean unto the Queen for mercy." *

When sentence was passed, he stood up and said, " I beseech you, my Lords, to be humble suitors unto the Queen's Majesty, and to grant me four requests. First, that I may have that death which noblemen have had in times past, and not the other; secondly, that her Majesty may be gracious to my children,† which may hereafter do good service, considering they went by my commandment

---

* Holinshed, vol. iv. p. 4.

† It is well known that Robert Dudley, the fifth son of this unfortunate Duke, became afterwards the famous Earl of Leicester, the favourite of Elizabeth.

who am their father, and not of their own free
wills; thirdly, that I may have appointed to me
some learned man for the instruction and quieting
of my conscience; and fourthly, that she will send
two of the Council to commune with me, to whom
I will declare such matters as be expedient for her
and the commonwealth; and thus I beseech you all
to pray for me." *

It is much to be regretted that no notes of the
secret communications which Northumberland desired to make before his execution, are to be found
in the State Paper Office; or, as far as I have yet
searched, in the British Museum.    Dr. Lingard
informs us,† that it is stated by Parsons, in his
" Warn Word," (a rare volume, which I have not
been able to procure,) that Gardiner and another
member of the  Council, whose name is not given,
visited Northumberland in the Tower, when the
Duke pleaded hard for his life; and Gardiner, it is
said, not only interceded for him with the Queen,
but had in a manner obtained her consent, when
Northumberland's enemies wrote to the Emperor,
who by letter persuaded Mary that his pardon was
incompatible with her safety.    This story must, I
think, be erroneous; as there was no time between
Northumberland's trial and execution to communicate with the Emperor. ‡    Before the Duke's trial,

* Holinshed, vol. iv. p. 4.        † Vol. vii. pp. 127, 128.

‡ Northumberland was  tried on the 18th of August, and
executed on the 22nd of the same month.

however, Charles the Fifth had given advice to
Mary to punish with rigour the leaders of the conspiracy, and to be lenient to the rest.  There can
be little doubt that from the first the Queen had
determined to take Northumberland's head.  I am
the more disposed to question Dr. Lingard's, or
rather Parsons' account, as the only instance I
have found of anything like a vindictive feeling
in Mary relates to Northumberland.  In her secret
interview with Commendone, who was eager to
leave London and carry her message to the Pope,
she insisted that he should remain two days, that
he might witness the execution of the Duke.*

There is a manuscript in the Harleian,† which
gives us some interesting particulars of this miserable man and his companions.  It informs us
that, on the 21st day of August 1553, before forty
of the citizens of London, the Duke of Northumberland, my Lord Marquis of Northampton, Sir
Andrew Dudley, Sir Henry Gates, and Sir Thomas
Palmer, came into the chapel, where they first
knelt down each upon his knees and heard mass,
every one of them saying the *Confiteor.*  " Mass
being finished," it continues, " the Duke rose up and
looked back upon the Lord Marquis, and came
unto him, asking them all forgiveness, one after the
other upon their knee, one to another ; and the

---

* Graziani, Vie de Commendon, traduite par Flechier, p. 53.

† Harleian, 284 ; fol. 128. d.   I have since found that Stow's
account, p. 614, coincides almost verbatim with this manuscript.

one did heartily forgive the other.  And then they came all together before the altar, every one of them kneeling, and confessing to the Bishop that they were the same men in the faith according as they had confessed to him before, and that they all would die in the Catholic faith.  When they had all received the sacrament, and all was done, they turned to the people every one of them, the Duke saying, ' Truly, good people, I profess here before you all that I have received the sacrament according to the true Catholic faith ; and the plague that is upon this realm, and upon us now, is, that we have erred from the faith these sixteen years, and this I protest unto you all from the bottom of my heart.'   And the Lord Marquis likewise did affirm the same with weeping tears ; and also Sir Andrew Dudley, Sir Henry Gates, and Sir Thomas Palmer."  It must have been on the evening of this day that Dudley wrote that piteous letter to the Earl of Arundel, which has been so frequently printed.*  He addresses this nobleman as his especial refuge,  declaring how woful was the news which he had received that evening from the Lieutenant of the Tower, that he must prepare to-morrow for his deadly stroke.  "Alas! my good Lord," he exclaims, " is my crime so heinous as no redemption but my blood can wash away the spots thereof?  An old proverb there is, and that most

* By Howard, in his Life of Lady Jane Grey, pp. 322, 323 ; Tierney, in his History of Arundel, p. 333 ; and by Lodge, in his Life of Dudley, Duke of Northumberland.

true, ' That a living dog is better than a dead lion.'
Oh, that it would please her good Grace to give me
life ! yea, the life of a dog, if I might but live and
kiss her feet, and spend both life and all in her honourable service !" This affecting appeal, however,
led to no extension of mercy, and the law was
allowed to take its course.

There are so many versions of the last words of
the Duke of Northumberland,\* that it is not easy
to discover the exact truth regarding his deport-
ment upon the scaffold. The number of these
copies seems to indicate an uncommon importance attached by both parties to his behaviour at
the last. Fox says † that he had promise of pardon, even if his head was upon the block, if he
would *recant* and hear mass; and Burnet, in his
History of the Reformation,‡ affirms, that " certain
it is that he said he had been always a Catholic
in his heart." The reader will observe from the
following confession, which is in the latter portion
of it a different production from the speech, as
reported by Stow,§ that Dudley says nothing in the
least degree similar to the words imputed to him
by Burnet, but rather the contrary. " On the
22nd of August," I quote from Stow, " Sir John
Gage, Lieutenant of the Tower, delivered to the

---

\* There is, besides the " Confession" printed in the text, one
in the Cotton Collection, Titus, B. II. f. 162 ; another in the
Royal MSS. British Museum, 12 A. 26, in Latin ; another
later abstract in the Harleian, 2194.      † Fox, vol. iii. p. 13.
‡ Vol ii. p. 243.      § Stow's Annals, p. 615.

Sheriffs of London by indenture these prisoners following. First, Sir John Gates was brought forth, and set at the garden-gate; then the Duke of Northumberland was likewise brought forth, and Sir Thomas Palmer after him.

"When the Duke and Sir John Gates met, 'Sir John,' saith the Duke, 'God have mercy upon us! for this day shall end both our lives; and I pray you forgive me whatsoever I have offended, and I forgive you with all my heart, although you and your counsel was a great occasion hereof.' 'Well, my Lord,' quoth Sir John Gates, 'I forgive you as I would be forgiven; and yet you and your authority was the original cause of all together; but the Lord pardon you, and I pray you forgive me.' So, either making obeisance to other, the Duke proceeded; and when he came upon the scaffold, he, putting off his gown of grain-coloured damask, leant upon the east rail, and spoke to the people—"*

I do not give Stow's edition of the speech of Northumberland, as the following confession is probably a more authentic document.

THE OPEN CONFESSION OF JOHN DUKE OF NORTHUMBERLAND, WHO SUFFERED AT TOWER HILL, 22nd of AUGUST 1553.

*Orig.* HARLEIAN, 284; fol. 127.

"GOOD people. Hither I am come this day to die, as ye know. Indeed, I confess to you all that I

* Stow, p. 614.

have been an evil liver, and have done wickedly all
the days of my life; and, of all, most against the
Queen's Highness, [of] whom I here openly ask forgiveness (and bowed his knees) : but not I alone the
original doer thereof, I assure you, for there were
some other which procured the same; but I will
not name them, for I will hurt now no man. And
the chiefest occasion hath been through false and
seditious preachers, that I have erred from the Catholic faith and true doctrine of Christ. The
doctrine, I mean, which hath continued thro' all
Christendom since Christ. For, good people, there
is, and hath been ever since Christ, one Catholic
church; which church hath continued from him to
his disciples in one unity and concord, and so
hath alway continued from time to time until this
day, and yet doth throughout all Christendom,
only us excepted; for we are quite gone out of that
church. For, whereas all holy fathers, and all
other saints throughout all Christendom, since
Christ and his disciples, have ever agreed in one
unity, faith, and doctrine; we alone dissent from
their opinions, and follow our own private interpre-
tation of Scriptures. Do you think, good people,
that we, being one parcel in comparison, be wiser
than all the world besides, ever since Christ? No,
I assure you, you are far deceived. I do not say
so for any great learning that I have, for, God
knoweth, I have very little, or none; but for the
experience which I have had.

" For I pray you, see, since the death of King Henry the Eighth, into what misery we have been brought; what open rebellion, what sedition, what great division hath been throughout the whole realm; for God hath delivered [us] up to [our] own sensualities, and every day [we] wax worse and worse. Look also in Germany, since they severed from the faith; unto what miserable state they have been brought, and how their realm is decayed. And herewith I have [braved] these preachers for their doctrine, and they were not able to answer any part thereof, no more than a little boy. They opened the books, and could not [reply to] them again. More than that, good people, you have in your Creed, *Credo Ecclesiam Catholicam,* which church is the same church which hath continued ever from Christ, throughout all the apostles', saints', and doctors' times, and yet doth, as I have said before. Of which church I do openly profess myself to be one, and do steadfastly believe therein; I speak unfeignedly from the bottom of my heart. This good man, the Bishop of Worcester, shall be my witness (and the Bishop said, ' Yea'). And I beseech you all bear me witness that I die therein. And I do think, if I had had this belief sooner, I never had come to this pass: wherefore I exhort you all, good people, take you all example of me, and forsake this new doctrine betimes. Defer it not long, lest God plague you as he hath me, which now suffer this vile death most worthily.

" I have no more to say, good people; but all those which I have offended I ask forgiveness, and they which have offended me I forgive them, as I would God forgive me. And I trust the Queen's Highness hath forgiven me : where as I was with force and arms against her in the field, I might have been rent in pieces without law, her Grace hath give me time and respect to have judgment.

" And after he had desired all the people to pray for him, he humbled himself to God, and covered his own eyes with a cloth, and he suffered execution meekly."

In looking into Sepulveda's Annals of Charles the Fifth, we find, in the speech there ascribed to Northumberland, that general similarity with the above " Confession," which proves, I think, that both contain a pretty fair report of the real behaviour of Dudley on the scaffold.* I may notice, by the way, that there is an interesting letter of Sepulveda's, addressed to Cardinal Pole,† which shows that the Spanish historian sent the Cardinal the manuscript of the twenty-ninth book of his History, embracing the account of England under Mary; requesting him to add to it and correct it. It is not

---

* Sepulveda De Rebus Gestis Caroli V.   Sepulvedæ Opera, vol. ii. p. 483.

† Sepulvedæ  Opera;  Madrid, 1780, 4 vols. 4to.  Vol. 3, Lib. vi. Epistola xiv.—I owe the knowledge of this curious letter to my friend Mr. Holmes, of the British Museum.

unlikely, therefore, that Dudley's speech was the interpolation of Pole, who arrived in England in the month of November of the succeeding year, and enjoyed the best opportunities of procuring accurate information. In the same letter to Pole, Sepulveda informs us, that, amongst other materials for the English portion of his history, he had access to the letters of Philip the Second, written to his sister Joanna. But if his Highness' epistles to his sister were not somewhat more minute and communicative than those to his wife, Queen Mary, which I have met with in the State Paper Office, the Spanish author would not be much the richer by the acquisition. As to the assertion of Fox, that Dudley was induced to profess himself a Roman Catholic by a promise of pardon, I have nowhere found any good authority to support it.

Having thus seen the miserable fall of the once lofty Northumberland, we must turn our eyes for a moment to the Courts of Brussels, France, and Rome.

The embassy sent to the Netherlands a short time before the death of Edward has been already mentioned. The joy of the Queen Regent, sister to the Emperor Charles the Fifth, on the accession of Mary to the English throne, and the sumptuous dinner which she gave to Sir Thomas Cheyne the ambassador, and his colleagues, on the occasion, are vividly painted in the following letter.

CHEYNE, misnamed Cheyney, by Lloyd in his Worthies,* was a knight of ancient family, and an early favourite of Henry the Eighth and Wolsey, with whom he had served on the continent. Lloyd's reverence for royalty, and his courtly style of writing, are amusingly marked in the sentence where he speaks of Cheyne's excellence as a juster. " Not long after," says he, " he encountered the King himself at Greenwich, where he had the great honour of a strong and valiant knight, and a greater of having been *overthrown* by his Majesty."* Cheyne also served with the Earl of Hertford against the Scots, and was not long after made Warden of the Cinque Ports. He was a man much after Mary's heart, a zealous Romanist, and an advocate for absolutism in government.

THE BISHOP OF NORWICH, SIR P. HOBY, SIR R. MORYSINE, AND SIR THOMAS CHEYNE, TO THE QUEEN.

*Orig.* ST. P. OFF. *Germany.* 25th August 1553.

" PLEASE it your Highness: albeit we did not think to write any letters unto your Grace before our return, yet not having our despatch, which we looked for daily, and thinking our abode long, we could not but send to your Grace these few lines to declare the cause of this delay, which hath

* Lloyd's Worthies, p. 466.

been, as we think, for that the Regent might have time, by feasting of us, to show how dearly the Emperor's Majesty and her Grace loveth your Highness.

" Yesterday, being St. Bartholomew's day, her Grace prayed us to dine with her, where we had such a dinner as we have seen few the like in all our lives; with such her Grace's carving and entertainment to me, Sir Thomas Cheyne, as the greater could not be devised. The dinner lasted very long, and the place was such as strangers might freely behold all the manner thereof.

" The French Queen was first placed; the Regent the next; I Sir Thomas Cheyne by her; next, I the Bishop of Norwich; after, I Sir Philip Hoby; and last, I Sir Richard Morysine; being all placed of one side of the table. And tho', while the dinner lasted, the cheer was as great as could be wished, yet the Regent devised how after dinner her latter entertainment might overcome and far exceed the former. The table being taken away, her Grace called for chairs, and giving the first to the French Queen, I Sir Thomas Cheyne had the second, and was set by her; the third her Highness sat in herself, and I the Bishop of Norwich hard by her; next sat the Duchess of Lorraine, and I Sir Philip Hoby placed by her; last sat I Sir R. Morysine, whom Monsieur Molambees, one of the Order, and Grand Master of her Household, did accompany. This sitting and devising lasted

above an hour.    The effect of our talks your Grace
shall know at our coming home.    *    *    *

"TH. CHEYNE.
"THOMAS NORWICEN.
"PHELYP HOBY.
"RICH. MORYSINE."

On the same day on which this dispatch was
written, Charles the Fifth addressed a letter to
Mary, which is preserved amongst the Royal Letters in the State Paper Office; † but as it contains little more than expressions of compliment
and congratulation, I do not print it.

The news of Mary's accession to the throne was
received with extreme joy by Pope Julius the Third;
and in a consistory held at Rome on the 5th of
August, it was resolved to select Cardinal Pole as
the Legate to be sent to England.‡    Pole, whose
health was feeble, had at this moment retired to
the Convent of Maguzano, on the banks of the Lago
di Garda, and, well aware of the disordered state
in which he would find his native country, he resolved not to precipitate his departure.    In the
mean time, Cardinal Dandino, the Papal Legate in
Flanders, despatched Francis Commendone (afterwards the well-known Cardinal of that name)
with instructions to pass secretly into England.
He did so; and arriving in London in the middle of

† Royal Letters, I, B 26.
‡ Raynaldi, Continuatio Annal. Baronii, vol. xxi. p. 83.

August, found everything in great confusion. "The heretics," says Graziani, in his Life of Commendone, " were still proud of the authority they had exercised under the former reign, and decidedly hostile to the re-establishment of the Roman Catholic faith. Mary had the name of a Queen, but she was not mistress in her kingdom. *" Commendone found great difficulty in getting access to the Queen. At length he met a gentleman of family, a near relative of the Duke of Norfolk : his name was Lee, and the Papal envoy had formerly known him at Rome. Lee was in the confidence of the Queen, and by his means Commendone had a secret interview with Mary. She assured him of her inviolable attachment to the Romish Church, and of her resolution to restore its worship ; but implored him to conceal himself, and to act with the utmost caution. She was already, she said, in treaty with the Emperor, who had offered her his son in marriage. Northumberland was about to stand his trial, and every day she hoped to become more secure, but still much was unsettled.

After some days Mary again sent secretly for this envoy. She informed him that she had concluded her league with Charles the Fifth, and had resolved on her marriage with Philip. She intrusted him with letters to the Pope ; assured him again of her resolution to reconcile her kingdom to

* Vie de Commendon, par Graziani, Traduite par Flechier, p. 49.   Noailles, vol. ii. p. 245.

the Holy See, and entreated the presence of Pole in England.*

Commendone, having only waited to be present at the execution of Northumberland, set out for Italy. He travelled night and day, and although he made a diversion from the direct route to visit Pole at his convent, arrived in Rome on the ninth day after quitting London. It may be easily believed that the letters which he brought were highly acceptable to the Pope. Julius, according to Graziani's account, was much overcome, burst into tears, and thanked God that his Pontificate should be marked by the restoration of so beautiful a country as England to the obedience of the church.†

The Papal Envoy had left London, as we have seen, on the 23rd of August, and the succeeding months of September and October were busily occupied by Mary and her councillors. She had to celebrate her coronation, to summon and meet her parliament, to restore the ancient religion, to decide upon renouncing or retaining the title of Supreme Head of the Church,—a knotty point, upon which Pole and Gardiner took different sides ;—and to complete the negotiations for her marriage. It was necessary, also, to adopt some definite line of action regarding those eminent persons who, by their late conduct, had brought

* Vie de Commendon, p. 53.
† Vie de Commendon, pp. 53, 54, 56.

themselves within the pains of treason.  Northumberland, indeed, the arch-rebel, had been executed; but his accomplices, of whom it is not
easy to say whether they were most the victims of
his power or the sharers of his guilt, remained.  Of
these, the greatest, Winchester, Arundel, Paget,
Pembroke, Petre, Cecil, and others, had already
secured their pardon, in what manner we have just
seen.  Two of the immediate retainers of the Duke
had been executed with their master : these were
Gates and Palmer ; the last, that person whom we
have formerly met with as the principal cause of
the ruin of the Duke of Somerset.  Here, for the
present, Mary's severity ended.  Jane, indeed, and
her husband, Lord Guilford Dudley, were kept
prisoners in the Tower, but this was a necessary
precaution ; her father and mother, the Duke and
Duchess of Suffolk, were pardoned, and set at
liberty.

The coronation took place on the 1st of October ; the Queen having come to the Tower in the
midst of a splendid procession the day before.
The whole ceremony was unusually magnificent.
Mary's head-dress seems to have made a deep impression on our chroniclers.  It was a caul of cloth
of tinsel enclosed by a massy circlet of gold, " so
heavy with jewels, " says Stow, " that the Queen
was fain to bear it up with her hand."  She sat in
a litter, or chariot, drawn by six horses; and following her, in another chariot, covered with cloth

of silver, were seen the Lady Elizabeth and the Lady Anne of Cleves, both (says Perhn, who was an eye-witness,) " in silver habits, according to the French fashion." * While on the subject of dress, I must for a moment express my doubts of the singular state-ment of Griffet, that the new sectaries who governed England during the minority of Edward the Sixth, not contented with depriving the Church of all the pomp of her ceremonies and splendour of her wor-ship, forbad the women to wear colours, or to use embroidery. A slight glance at the portraits of the time—and, fortunately, we have Holbein for the great painter of the period—will convince us that the opinion is a chimera of Griffet's and No-ailles', and that the privilege of dressing themselves *à la Française*, with gold-lace, embroidery, and long sleeves, the indefeasible rights of the toilet, as it was never taken from the ladies by Ed-ward or his councillors, could not be restored by Mary.† But this error of Griffet's has misled a higher authority. " As the time of her coronation approached," says Dr. Lingard, " the Queen intro-duced within the palace an innovation highly gra-tifying to the younger branches of the female no-bility, though it foreboded little good to the reform-ed preachers. Under Edward, their fanaticism had

* Descrip: des Royaumes D'Angleterre et D'Ecosse. Re-printed, London, 1775. Nichols.

† New Lights on the History of England, from the French of Griffet, p. 12. Lingard, vol. vii.

given to the court a sombre and funereal appearance.   That they might exclude from it the pomps
of the devil, they had strictly forbidden all richness
of apparel, and every fashionable amusement.   But
Mary, who recollected with pleasure the splendid
gaieties of her father's reign, appeared publicly in
jewels and coloured silks; the ladies, emancipated
from restraint, copied her example; and the courtiers, encouraged by the approbation of their sovereign, presumed to dress with a splendour that
became their rank."*   This is playfully ironical,
and it is quite allowable, for

" Without black velvet breeches—what is man?"

but, I suspect, the whole is founded on an erroneous assumption.   Edward's own Journal proves
that, instead of sombre and funereal, his court was
uncommonly gay and splendid; and as to dress, if
Dr. Lingard will but examine the portraits of that
young prince and his lords and ladies, he will find
no want of jewels, ermined bodices, coloured silks,
and other pardonable little vanities.

Mary met her first parliament on the 5th of October.   Burnet, in his account of its proceedings,
introduces to us one Beal, Clerk of the Council in
the reign of Elizabeth, and a violent leader of the
puritans in those times, who has asserted, that every
kind of bribery, influence, and intimidation was
employed by the court to control the elections

* History of England, vol. vii. p. 125.

and procure the return of Roman Catholic members :* but I agree with Collier that the character of the man renders his evidence suspicious ;† and I have found no letters to show that the court were now more active in the elections than was then the practice of the time.

In this parliament the Queen retained the title of Supreme Head of the Church ; whilst the House passed an act, by which it was declared that she was born in lawful wedlock.   Mary herself saw the inconsistency of this, and it had been clearly explained to her by Pole, that her first step must be to renounce a title which had been wrested from the Pope and usurped by her father.   The validity of her mother's marriage, as he justly observed, rested on the fact, that the Pope was supreme head of Christ's church on earth ; and it was impossible for her to be head of the church and a lawful Queen.   Pole, in a paper of instructions preserved in the Cotton Collection, ‡ declares that he knew the Queen's own wish was to renounce the title ; but his advice was opposed by Gardiner and the rest of her council, and the Queen submitted to their dictation.   Nothing, however, could be more inconsistent than the conduct of the council; for whilst with one breath they advised the Queen to retain her own supremacy, with

* Burnet, vol. ii. p. 252.
† Collier's Ecclesiastical History, vol. ii. p. 348.
‡ Titus, B. ii. f. 114.

another, they brought in an act which tacitly acknowledged the supremacy of the Pope.

A bill was next introduced, which in three lines destroyed the whole superstructure of Protestantism, and replaced it by that form of divine service which had been used in the last year of King Henry the Eighth. " In one single act," says Strype, " they cut off and repealed at a clap no less than nine Acts of Parliament made under King Edward, all relating to the Reformation." *

The impression made upon the great body of the people by this sudden depression of the doctrines and mode of worship which had been so strenuously maintained under the former reign, was at first favourable to this change. This is stated in a curious pamphlet of the time, which Strype believes to have been written by Coverdale. " The common sort," says he, " argued thus. If this (the Protestant faith) were God's words—if this people were God's children, surely God would then bless and prosper them. But now, instead of that, there is no doctrine so much hated, no people so much persecuted as they be—therefore it cannot be of God. This is of God which our Queen and old bishops have professed. For how hath God prospered and kept them! What a notable victory hath God given to her ! " †

But if the people, erroneously assuming success as the test of truth, were reconciled, if not pleased,

* Strype, vol. iii. part i. p. 83.     † Ibid. p. 86.

to return to the faith of their fathers, they had also
the national prejudices of their fathers, and hated
the idea of that Spanish match, which was now
the subject of common talk.   A union between
Mary and Philip, had, indeed, been projected even
before Edward's death; for on the 23rd of June,
when the Prince was despaired of, Cardinal Dandino, the Papal Legate at Brussels, wrote to Ca-
pisuca, Cardinal St. George, the Legate at Paris,
that the Emperor was resolved on the match.*

But the Emperor was always averse to hurry forward any important measure : he had a suspicion
that Pole was against the marriage ; that he
was interested to promote a union between Courtenay, the young Earl of Devonshire, and Mary;
and he perhaps dreaded that the Cardinal might
precipitate the changes in religion before the Spanish match, which he regarded as a matter of para-
mount importance, was settled.   It has been supposed by some writers that Mary had thoughts herself of marrying Pole and, as he was only a Cardinal Deacon, the event was possible ; but he was
fifty-three years of age, a formidable objection.
Be this as it may, Charles flew into a violent passion when Pole came into Flanders on his way to
England, and sent peremptory orders for him to
remain at Delinghen or Liege.   " Unless," says the
Cardinal, writing to the Pope, " he had wished
" pigliar *in mano il Bastone* e cacciarmi, non mi po-

* Carte, vol. iii. pp. 287, 288.

teva far maggior violentia con parole." *    When a
cardinal comes to think that he had barely escaped
being "cudgelled by the Pope," the affair must have
been serious.

The best account we have of Pole, is that of his
friend Beccatelli, translated by Pye, and illustrated
by some good notes.    It forms a necessary accom-
paniment and antidote to Philipps' Life of Pole,
which is not to be quoted without examination.
Wotton, we see, was evidently misinformed as to
Charles' great partiality.    It is stated in a note
to a letter of Mons. de Noailles, that, when at
last admitted by the Emperor to an audience at
Brussels, "ce Prince lui dit avec dureté qu'il se seroit
dispensé de la peine qu'il avoit prise de revenir." †
Pole took all this with great meekness and submission, and remained " enveloppé sous les ailes de
cette grande aigle," till the imperial bird, having
feathered his nest by the marriage of his eaglet
Philip to Mary, allowed the old Cardinal to take
his flight over to England.

In the two following letters of Wotton, the first
to Sir William Petre, the second addressed to the
Queen, we have some important intelligence from
France and the court of the Emperor ; in return for
which the Dean manifests a strong desire to be made
acquainted with the proceedings at home under the
new reign.    These he rightly terms "no small mat-

---

* Quirini, vol. iv. lett. li.    † Noailles, vol. iii. p. 187.

ters;" and we see they were no less than the marriage
with Spain, and the restoration of the Roman Catholic faith in England.   It is mortifying, but not un-
instructive, to mark the speedy accommodation of
the minds of many of the most zealous Protestants
under Edward to the religious views of the new
sovereign.   What was Romish blindness in this
pliant Dean's estimation on the 6th of April 1547,
has now become a matter of such moment and
necessity, that he prays God to prosper it, and his
heart longs to hear of it, " quemadmodum cervus
desiderat fontes aquarum."

## DR. WOTTON TO SIR W. PETRE.

*Orig.*  St. P. Off.  *France.*  26th Oct. 1553.

" Sir.—The bearer shall deliver you those few
books I wrote you of; at the least, if they be
come home, for I never heard word of them since
I sent them away.  And if I had been of late at
Paris, as I have not, for the plague that reigneth
there, peradventure I might have found out some
other book that might have pleased you; but that
shall be for another time, and, God will, when Paris
is clear of the plague.  If you have not my Lord
of Winchester's book called Marcus Anthonius Con-
stantinus, I will send it you.

" I have no special news to write you of, but that,
' quemadmodum desiderat cervus fontes aquarum,
ita desiderat anima mea' to hear somewhat of your

proceedings at home, which God prosper, for they be no small matters that you have in hand.

" Here was on Sunday last at the court, in the presence of the King, a Jew solemnly christened, who was named Catherinus, for that the Queen was his only godmother, without any godfather. The Jew's father being a physician, and learned in the Jews' Talmud, is christened likewise, but not now; who, with his wife, was present at their son's christening. The father, being now called Ludovicus Carettus, hath made a little book in Hebrew, turned into Latin, which you shall receive herewith. I sent to Paris for more of them; but the printer is dead of late, and the books cannot be sold till the executors be agreed of the inventory and other things. It seemeth he will prove a valiant champion for us, against his own nation, if he may live. But the sport was, that when the Cardinal de Lorraine, who did minister himself the baptism, should have given him his ' *candidam vestem*,' it would not be found at the least in half an hour; and some good fellows were there who said he was no Jew at all, and that his name was Jehan de Lion. Now, whether it be so or not, I know not; but if they had made an Anabaptist of him, I would say he were a false Jew. And thus I beseech Jesu long to preserve you in health and prosperity, &c.

" N. Wotton."

DR. WOTTON TO THE QUEEN.

*Orig.*  St. P. Off.  *France.*  27th Oct. 1553.

" La Ferte, Melun.

" PLEASETH your Highness to be advertised that here hath been of late at this court an Italian called the Abbot of St. Salu, belonging to the Cardinal Pole, and sent from him to the French King, who hath declared here to divers of his acquaintance that the Pope hath made the said Cardinal Legate *de latere* to the Emperor and to this King, and having done with them, to your Highness.

" His errand to the Emperor and to the French King, as this Abbot saith, is to see whether he can do any more good with these two princes, for the reconciliation of them, than the other two Legates did. And like as it is well known that the Emperor hath the Cardinal Poole in very good estimation, which appeared well at the last vacation of the papacy, where the Imperial Cardinals laboured all they could to have him made Pope; so the French King, and such as are great about him, have an honest opinion of him also, but yet not without a little suspicion of him for the favour which they saw th' Imperials bare unto him at that time.  Nevertheless, it is thought that, if any of the Cardinals shall be able to do any good in this matter, this man is most like to do it, being esteemed among many to be of an honest mind and virtuous life.

" And albeit that this Abbot speaketh of his master's going into England, yet, as far as I can learn, it is after this sort, that when the Cardinal hath done with these two princes, then he will tarry to see whether he shall be admitted and received into England; and, by this said Abbot's saying, the said Cardinal is by this time well forward on his journey, so that the Abbot thinketh he will be within these few days with the Emperor.

" And now, for because that if he come hither, (as it is reckoned assuredly he will do,) it will much be marked and noted of the world how I behave myself unto him, I therefore humbly beseech your Highness it may please you to let me know your pleasure therein, whether I shall resort to him; and, in case I do, after what sort I shall use myself unto him; and, knowing your Highness' pleasure therein, I will endeavour myself to follow the same in all points the best I can.

" Here are presently no great news.    The saying is, that the Prince of Salerne, Petro Strozzi, and in a manner all the Italians of this court, prepare themselves to go into Italy; for what purpose I know not as yet.    But it may seem not unlikely that, seeing that Don Ferrant maketh a good number of men, and that the Genoese are entered a league with the Duke of Florence, (though somewhat late,) and that the Prince Doria hath his galleys ready, (as it is said,) therefore these French Italians go into Italy to attempt somewhat there, whereby the other may be stayed from going into Corsica for the recovery of it, as the French be well fortified there; who, being suffered to continue there quietly this winter, will so fortify the places they have or the spring of the year come on, that it shall not be easy for their enemies to recover them. The Great Master of Rhodes or Malta is dead, in whose place is chosen a Frenchman; for, as I understand,* the Spaniards and French, who are the greatest nations in number amongst them, have agreed that they will choose ever, by course, one time a Spaniard and next a French, so that neither Italian nor any of other nation shall be able to be Master amongst them.

" I am advertised from Lyons, that the French ambassador at Venice hath made shift there for his master for fours ——† and ten thousand crowns, and the French King . . . [has taken] up at Lyons, at the last fair, four hundred thousand francs for fourteen in the hundred, and did owe there before that a million and a half of gold. The fort which was spoken of should have been made by [beside] Hesdin goeth not forward, for because (as these men say) that the time of the year serveth not for it.

" These Italian ambassadors have sure advertisements that the Sophy's ambassador was with the

---

* Wotton's information was correct. Claude de la Sangle was chosen Grand Master.

† A word here is unintelligible.

Turk at Constantinople, and spake with him the 20th of August; but that notwithstanding, the 28th of that month, the Turk with the four Bassa's embarked himself with his youngest son, and took his journey towards Aleppo, to be ready there against the spring of the year, to march then against the said Sophy.   They have also news that two ambassadors from the King of the Romans arrived at Constantinople the 25th of August, and spake with the Turk ere he departed, but they know not how they sped.*

" They have news also that the Turk's armata, that was in Corsica, † hath been seen in the sea drawing homewards towards Levant, whereof hath been much doubted here whether they would back again this time, or winter on this side; but, if they be gone indeed, it shall be time for the Genoeses to

---

* The ambassadors, as we learn from Isthuanffus, book xix. c. i. p. 229, were Bishop Anthony Verantius, and Francis Zauis, Admiral of the fleet of the Danube.   The information given by the Italian ambassadors to Wotton was erroneous.   Solyman, the Turkish Emperor, had left Constantinople previous to the arrival of Ferdinand's ambassadors; having committed the government of his capital to Ibrahim the Eunuch.   Soon after, the ambassadors took their journey through Bithynia, and had an audience of the Turkish Emperor, who, elated by his late triumph over the King of Persia, rejected their proposals for peace with haughty contempt.

† This Turkish fleet had been joined by some French ships of Marseilles; and their united armament had made themselves masters of Corsica, which belonged to the Genoese.—Sleidan, book xxv. sub anno 1553.

bestir themselves, if they intend to do any good in Corsica.

" And thus I beseech, &c.

" Written at La Ferte, Melun, 27th Oct. 1553.

" N. WOTTON."

In our next letter our old acquaintance Sir John Mason presents us with a sketch of the intended matrimonial policy of the Emperor, and, as is usual with him, touches rapidly on the state of Europe.

### SIR JOHN MASON TO THE COUNCIL.

*Orig.* ST. P. OFF.  *Flanders.*  28th Nov. 1553.

" MY humble duty remembered to your good Lordships, the same may please to be advertised that it is now resolved that the Count of Eggemmond,* Mons. Lallayng, who is elder brother to Mons. de Hochstracht, Mons. de Courrieres,† and Negri, Chancellor of the Order, shall come ambassadors into England. The matter hath been long in debating, and the Prince of [Orange,] Mons. de Burce, and Mons. Hochstracht, were in the election,

---

* The well known Lamoral Count Egmont, born in 1522, of an ancient and noble Dutch family. In 1544, he served in the army of Charles the Fifth, in his great African expedition. The most brilliant part of his career was posterior to the date of this letter, when, in 1557, his bravery and military conduct were the chief cause of the great victory gained by the Spaniards and the English over the French at St. Quintin; nor was his conduct less conspicuous at the battle of Gravelines, in 1558.

† John de Montmorency, Lord of Courieres.

but in the end such be determined upon as I have before written; and yet both these that tarry, and the Duke of Savoy, do merely say that those shall be the avant-couriers, and they will follow in the battle.    The Prince of Aurenge's wife is newly brought a-bed, and Mons. de Hochstracht hath the principal charge of all the finances of these Low Countries, which be the occasion of their stay.

" The said ambassadors mind to come very honourably accompanied with many gentlemen, and with the number, as I am informed, of not much under two hundred horses.    They depart from hence within seven or eight days after the date hereof; and, when they shall be in the way, they intend to make good speed.*

"Mons. de Boyssa, Master of the Horses, cometh also into England, and so doth Mons. de Beteres; whether at this time or not I am not certain, but long behind them they will not be.    Their errand is not to join in commission with the other, but to pass the seas into Spain, and to conduct the Prince into these parts.

" I am advertised by divers ways, that our young men at Antwerp use their talk very wildly, as well in the declaration of their misliking of our proceed-

---

* They did not, however, arrive in England until some weeks after the Parliament was dissolved.    It was in this Parliament that the Commons carried the address which gave great offence to the Queen, entreating her not to marry a foreigner.

ings in matters of religion, as of the other great matter also, which in this court is taken as a thing utterly concluded.   They have had a late bickering with the Spaniards, which hath so tickled them as they let not in all places to declare their discontentation with the whole nation.   Your Lordships, in mine opinion, shall do well to despatch their governors unto them with some speed, at whose hands they might receive some such threatening lesson from the Queen's Highness and your Lordships as they might learn hereafter how to temper their tongues.*

" Here is spread in this court very gladsome news of a great quantity of gold arrived at Sevilla in Spain.   The sum is named five millions.   I pray God it be half so much.   Whatsoever it be, it maketh us merry in the mean season whilst the certainty thereof is a-learning.

" The sending of a power by the Duke of Florence to the recovery of Corsica causeth the French King to make his account as if he had declared against him ; and therefore hath he in despite sent his mortal enemy Pietro Strozzi to be his lieutenant in Italy, whilst Mons. de Termes shall remain in Corsica.

* The disgust at the Spanish match was still deeper in England than among these young gentlemen, whom the prudent Mason describes as talking so wildly at Antwerp.

Anonymous attacks upon Philip, representing him as haughty, cold, tyrannical, and bigoted, were published in the City, and even dropped in the Queen's chamber.—Carte, vol. iii. p. 297.

" The said French King hath sent to Argel, to
hire the navy thereof to the number of twenty galleys. I trow, if the devil were to be treated with,
he would entertain him. Oh Lord! put him into a
better and more Christian mind, by whose means
the enemies of Christ's faith learn all the secrets of
our manner of making of war at the expenses of
Christian men.

" The Sophy hath met, as the tidings come here,
with a fleet of the Turks laden with spice. Out of
Hungary we have uncertain news of a great overthrow given lately to the Turks by Christian men.
God send the said Turk ill luck against the Persians; for, if he return with the victory, the matters
of Hungary will soon be revenged. Other news
there be not here for the present; the matters of
England so occupying the talk of every man, as all
other news be put to silence. *   *   *

" JOHN MASON."

It has been asserted by most of our historians,
that Mary was attached to Courtenay, whom she
had created Earl of Devonshire, and that she
meant to marry him. It is certain that she showed
him great favour, and the people were eager for the
match. Gardiner, at first, espoused his interests;
and the Queen chose Lady Exeter his mother as her
bedfellow and confidant. From all these circumstances, the report of such a union became general;
and Noailles, the French ambassador, intrigued

busily to bring about the match. But I have met with no direct proof that Mary herself ever seriously thought of Courtenay. If she did, it was an evanescent preference ; and her wishes soon centred in Philip, who was then the greatest marriage in Europe. There is a passage quoted by Strype,* from an unpublished manuscript of Sir Thomas Smith, which insinuates that the Queen had fallen in love with the Prince's picture. " I heard not many years ago," says Smith, " of *a certain lady*, who having the picture sent unto her of one whom she never saw, who should be her husband, was so enamoured thereon, and so ravished, that she languished for love, and was in a manner out of her wits for his long tarrying and absence.—But I ween hot love was soon cold, and not long after repented."

There can be little doubt of Strype being right in his conjecture, that Smith here alludes to Mary. The passage occurs in a discourse whether Queen Elizabeth should marry a stranger or an Englishman. We know from Noailles, that, as early as October 1553, the Prince of Spain sent Don Inigo de Mendoza † with a private message to Mary ; and it is by no means improbable that such a love-envoy should bring with him a miniature of his young master. If we may believe Titian's pencil, Philip was a handsome man ; and the following minute description of his features and figure, by one

---

* Strype, Memor. vol. iii. part 1, p. 196.

† Ambassades de Noailles, vol. ii. pp. 223, 226.

who drew from the life, may excuse Mary's impatience. It occurs in a rare tract or letter, written by John Elder, *the Redshank* or Highlander, who, in 1542, addressed to Henry the Eighth a wild proposal for uniting Scotland with England.* Elder was then in London amongst the spectators of Philip's entry into the city ; and thus wrote to his friend the Bishop of Caithness. " Touching his (Philip's) height," says he, " I can well compare him to John Hume, my Lord of Jedward's kinsman. Of visage he is well-favoured, with a broad forehead and grey eyes, streight-nosed and manly countenance. From the forehead to the point of his chin, his face groweth small ; his pace is princely, and gait so straight and upright as he loseth no inch of height ; with a yellow head and a yellow beard. And, thus to conclude, he is so well-proportioned of body, arm, leg, and every other limb to the same, as nature cannot work a more perfect pattern. And," as I have learned, " of the age of twenty-eight years. Whose Majesty I judge to be of a stout stomach, pregnant-witted, and of most gentle nature." †

Towards the end of the session of her first parliament, the match with Spain was generally can-

* Printed in the Bannatyne Miscellany, vol. i. p. 1, from a MS. in the Royal MSS. Brit. Mus. 18 A. 38, transcribed by the Secretary, Mr. Laing.

† The letter is dated "From the City of London, this new-year's day and the first of the kalends of January."—Ames, Typographical Antiquities, vol. i. p. 563.

vassed, and gave rise to an animated discussion in
the House of Commons, in which the feeling was
loud and unanimous against it.  They sent their
Speaker with an address praying the Queen not to
marry a stranger ; but Mary, in this instance, seems
to have sacrificed the wishes of her people to her
ambition.  She was determined to have the Prince
of Spain ; and whatever little preferences she may
have shown to Courtenay were probably rather
blinds to quiet the discontent of her subjects,
and afford her time to finish her negociations, than
any real intentions in his favour.  As for the idle
and romantic tales of Vertot regarding Courtenay's
love for Elizabeth, and Mary's jealousy and revenge, they have been successfully refuted by Griffet.*  It is to be regretted that they should remain
embalmed in the history of Hume, who was probably
misled by Vertot ; but it is still more extraordinary
that the French author should have contradicted
the letters of Noailles, which he himself published.

The following letter from Dean Wotton, the
English ambassador at the court of France, contains an interesting account of the conversations
which he held with Henry the Second, and his
prime minister the Constable Montmorency, on the
subject of the Queen's marriage with Philip of
Spain.  Taking into view the war which then

---

* Griffet, translated under the title of " New Lights thrown
upon the History of Mary," p. 57.  Hume, 8vo. edition, in one
vol. p. 375.

raged between France and Spain, and the extreme
jealousy with which Charles and Henry regarded
each other, we are not to be surprised that the
French monarch's countenance was sad, his words
few, and his dislike of the match "marvellously
great," to use Wotton's expressions.   Indeed, notwithstanding his reiterated assurances of amity and
love for "his good sister," it is well known, to all
who have looked into Noailles' letters, that Henry
had taken every possible method to defeat Mary's
wishes and disappoint the Emperor's ambition;
that his ambassador at the English court had even
endeavoured to attain this object by holding secret
intercourse with the disaffected, and exciting civil
disturbances in England.

In his panegyric on his royal mistress, Wotton
declares that, "even when in fear of her life, Mary
had never been induced to assent to anything contrary to her conscience or to her honour."   He had
forgotten that the Queen's constancy had failed
on one memorable occasion, when she wrote letters with her own hand to her father, (which, says
Camden, I myself have seen,) "wherein she not
only for ever renounced the Pope's authority in
England, but also acknowledged her father to be
supreme head of the Church of England under
Christ, and her mother's marriage to have been
incestuous and unlawful."

It must be remembered, however, that when this

was done the Queen trembled under her father's tyranny, and was no doubt fearful for her life.*

It is impossible not to be struck with the clear sagacious views of Montmorency, and the soldier-like bluntness and vigour with which they are expressed. No English statesman could have more ably pointed out the evils to be dreaded from the Spanish match.

### DOCTOR WOTTON TO THE COUNCIL.

*Orig.* St. P. Off. *France.* 23rd Dec. 1553.

" It may please your Lordships to understand, that, the 13th of this present, I received yours of the 7th of the same; and, sending to the court for audience, I was appointed to have it the 17th of this month; and that day, going thither, I dined with the Constable.† And after dinner he showed me that the King had taken a great cold, and came not out of his chamber all that day, though it was Sunday, so that he stood in doubt whether I might then speak with him; but he would go up to him and show him of my coming, and, in case he were in state to be spoken withal, I should not fail to speak with him : and so going up, and at the last returning again, showed me that the King was so hoarse that men could not perceive what he said, and that therefore he desired me to be content to take the pains to come again the next day, when he

---

* Camden in Kennett, vol. ii. p. 367.
† The Constable Montmorency.

trusted to be somewhat better. And, so doing, I
had audience of him; and found, indeed, that he had
taken a great cold, as did very well appear by his
speech.

" After I had delivered him the Queen's Highness' letter, and declared unto him the effect
of mine instructions as well as I could, the King
answered me : That, at the Queen's Highness' coming to the crown, she sent Mr. Sentleger hither to
declare unto him that she intended to live in peace
and amity with him, and the like I myself had
divers times declared unto him, and that the Queen
herself had often said as much to his ambassador
in England; whereat he said he rejoiced not a little,
and for his part promised likewise to do the same
with her Highness; the which thing, quoth the
King, I have observed and kept, as you do know
how I have caused your merchants to be heard
favourably in all their suits, and others besides.
And now, quoth the King, if the Queen my good sister shall marry with him that is my chief enemy,*
and even during this war-time,—although I know it
is not my part to appoint her where, nor with
whom, nor when she shall marry,—yet it must needs
be a grief unto me to consider what advantage mine
enemies will think to have thereby upon me. And
yet, whatsoever they think thereof, I have hitherto
defended my country from mine enemies, and with
God's grace so will I do hereafter. And where you

* Philip the Second.

say that the Queen my good sister intendeth and promiseth now again to continue still in peace and amity with me, whether she marry or marry not, and what second husband soever she have,* I am very glad to understand her good mind therein.

" But yet Mons. l'Ambassadeur, quoth the King, it is to be considered that a husband may do much with his wife; and it shall be very hard for any wife to refuse her husband any thing that he shall earnestly require of her; and you, that have been abroad in the world, do well know how subtle and crafty Spaniards are; so that, of what mind soever the Queen my good sister be of now, it is to be doubted how she shall be able to continue in it. Nevertheless, seeing she doth now make this promise unto me again, both for the good opinion I have of her, and that I think she would not make such a man as you are tell me such a tale as you have here told me, unless she did intend to keep her promise, I will trust to it; and, for my part, she shall be assured to find me ready to continue the peace and amity which hath been betwixt us, and to show her any pleasure that shall be in me to do besides.

" Whereupon I said unto the King, that indeed I took it to be true that a man might obtain much of his wife; but, like as that was true, so I took it

---

* An expression, used by Mary in allusion to her first marriage being to her kingdom. See Ambassades de Noailles, vol. ii. p. 325. " Elle avoit epousé son royaulme et non poinet les hommes."

again that a wife of wit and discretion might do as
much with her husband.  And therefore, the Queen
my mistress having determined and promised to enter into no war with him for any husband's sake she
might have, being endowed of God with so much
wisdom as she is, I doubted not should be well able
to obtain so reasonable a thing of her husband as
to forbear to constrain her in such a matter, so
much against her promise and the wealth of her
country.

" And Sire, quoth I, the Queen my mistress and
her Council, I doubt not, have very well considered
this to be true, that a husband may do very much
with his wife, and that if the marriage should ensue betwixt her Highness and the Prince of Spain,
and the wars continue betwixt you and the Emperor, it is not unlikely but that the Prince would
much wish that her Highness would take part with
the Emperor, and would move her thereto by
the best means he could; and how loath a wife
would be to say nay to her husband : all these
things, quoth I, I doubt not have been weighed and considered; and seeing they have been
weighed and considered, and yet nevertheless the
Queen doth eftsoons make you this earnest promise again, it may well appear, Sire, that her
Highness and her Council will well consider and
provide also how her Highness shall be well able
to avoid and shift off any such request that by
the said Prince might be made unto her; for, if

she doubted any whit thereof, what needed her to renew now this promise unto you again, and that so earnestly as I have here declared it unto you? And this, Sire, quoth I, I shall be bold to say unto you, that you never were acquainted with Prince or Princess of a more constancy than you shall find in the Queen my mistress; whereof she hath given great experiment divers times already, who neither by fair means, nor yet for danger of her life, could ever be induced to assent to any thing either contrary to her conscience or to her honour.

"Wherefore, Sire, I am certainly persuaded that you shall find her stedfast and constant in this her promise now so earnestly renewed unto you. And in case this marriage with the Prince of Spain should take effect, I do hope that her Highness shall rather thereby be the better able to treat some good agreement betwixt you and the Emperor, than that therefore she should enter into war with you.—Well, quoth the King, then shall there no fault be found on my part, but I will likewise continue the good peace and amity which I have with the Queen my good sister; and so I pray you to advertise her. I declared also unto him some of the acts passed by the Parliament, but he seemed to have known them before: and when I spake of the repealing of the sentence of divorce, Why should it not? quoth the King, for no doubt it was done against all reason. And when I showed him how the Queen's Highness had not only forgiven those that conspired with the Duke of Northumberland their offences, but also the fines which were therefore assessed upon them, It is done, quoth the King, like a noble Princess, and a merciful, for the which she ought much to be commended.

" But, what words soever the King used to me, his countenance was very sad ; yea, and his words but few, and not pronounced with such assuredness and alacrity as he used to do, but sometimes staying in his tale and repeating his words again, as though his mind were somewhat troubled. Whereby, and by the communication which I had with the Constable of these self matters, it seemeth unto me that they mislike it marvellously, and do much fear the breach of amity betwixt us.

" Talking with the Constable, who did set a better face upon the matter than the King did, and used me at both these two days as familiarly as he did at any time, amongst other things he said unto me, As for you, being not of that vocation, it is no marvel though you perceive not so well how much a man that of himself hath any wit, or will be advised by good counsel, may obtain of his wife. We that are married may better perceive by what occasions, and means, and times, we may win them.

" Sir, quoth I, I do not think otherwise therein, indeed ; but yet the Queen my mistress would not now renew this earnest promise if she would be won to the contrary.—I believe, in good faith, quoth the Constable, that she doth now mean and intend as she doth promise; but if she marry the Prince, he, being her husband, will by such means induce and persuade her that that thing which she now reckoneth to be good for the realm of England, (that is to say, this amity with us, which is indeed very commodious and necessary for both the realms,) she will then peradventure think not to be so.

" Although, quoth I, I allow that wives will be much persuaded by their husbands, yet I take that to have more place in private persons than in this case which we are in; for, like as the Queen is wise of herself, so is she content to have wise counsel about her, so that neither she herself, nor yet her Council, can so lightly by words be deceived as to be made believe that thing to be ill for the realm which is good indeed.

" Why, quoth the Constable, when the Prince hath married the Queen, he shall be King himself, and then what councillors will or dare counsel against his King's pleasure and will?—The right, quoth I, of the crown of England is grounded on the Queen's Highness, whosoever shall be her husband. And grave councillors, quoth I, will not fear to declare their minds, according to their duty and conscience.—No [one] will, quoth the Constable; I report me to you how they have done it in the late King's time. And, when he is King, who shall be councillors but such as shall please him?

" As for these things, quoth I, that a husband may do much with his wife, yea, and as you say, a

King with his subjects; and that, the war continuing betwixt you and the Emperor, it is very likely the Prince, having married the Queen my mistress, will travail to induce her to take part with the Emperor; these things, quoth I, are such as no doubt have been well considered and foreseen by the Queen's Highness and the Council already ; and therefore, seeing they have foreseen it, and yet nevertheless her Highness doth promise so earnestly for no second husband's sake to enter into war with France, it seemeth to me it cannot be otherwise but that she intendeth so to provide for that matter aforehand as she shall ever be able to keep her promise.

" What provision, quoth the Constable, can be made for such a matter but a few lines written, which Spaniards use to keep as long as they make for their purpose? —If it lay, quoth I, only in their power to do it, peradventure they would; but such a great matter as this is cannot be brought about but by the consent of the whole realm, and they know that the breach of the amity were not good for them, and so will not consent to it.—You may say so, quoth the Constable, and I pray God it prove so ; but it is much to be doubted that what good mind soever the Queen be of now, that she shall have much ado to continue long in it.   And for because, quoth the Constable, that I have used to talk ever frankly with you, I cannot but say unto you as I think, that I do much lament your state of England.

" Why so, sir ? quoth I.—Why so ? quoth the Constable.  You are a man that hath travelled abroad, and you know in what state all countries are where Spaniards bear any rule.  Sicily, Naples, Lombardy, Sienna when they had it, and all other places where they have had any authority, do you not know how they are oppressed by the Spaniards? in what a bondage and misery they live ?  Even so must you look to be in England : for at the beginning, as they do everywhere, they will speak fair and genteely unto you, till the time they have made themselves somewhat strong in the realm, and won to them some great men of the realm ; and then will they begin to get your ships into their hands, and likewise those few forts which you have, yea, and will build new in places meet for their purpose ; and so a little and a little usurp still more and more, till they have all at their commandment.—As for other countries, quoth I, where Spaniards bear authority, I intend not much to speak of, nor what authority they should bear in England if this marriage take effect I know not, for that the Queen's Highness hath communicated nothing thereof unto me ; but, if I shall speak to you as I think, surely I believe that the Queen and the Prince will appoint no rulers or ministers in England but Englishmen, who know best how to rule and order the people of England. — No! quoth the Constable : why not as well as in Naples and other places ?—Whatsoever they do, quoth I, in Naples, I am sure that

Spaniards bear no rule in Flanders, and yet is there
a great deal more cause why they should do it there
than in England; unless, quoth I, you think we
shall be less able to provide for our realm than
Flemings are for their country.

" An it were not, quoth the Constable, for
that the Emperor feareth that Flanders would
rather give themselves up to the King,* than they
would be oppressed by the Spaniards, no doubt
Spaniards should have as great authority there as
in other places.—I know not, quoth I, whether
that be the cause or not; but, if Spaniards fear
such an inconvenient, this may they likewise fear,
that if they should go about to take any such
authority upon us in England, that the people
would show that they were not contented with it;†

---

* The King of France.

† This was Wotton's best reply, for the Spanish match was
wonderfully unpopular in England; but this hatred of the people proved but a feeble obstacle in these days of high prerogative and aristocratic subserviency. Mary's first parliament,
as we have seen, showed a strong aversion to the marriage,
and the House of Commons presented an address against it.
On being made aware of this, the Queen declared " that she
would prove a match for all the cunning of the Chancellor
(Gardiner); and, sending the same night for the Imperial ambassador, bade him follow her into her private oratory, where,
on her knees at the foot of the altar, and before the sacrament,
she first recited the hymn ' Veni, Creator Spiritus,' and then
called God to witness that she pledged her faith to Philip
Prince of Spain, and while she lived would never take any
other man for her husband."—Lingard, vol. vii. p. 144. This
was on the 30th of October.—Griffet, p. 47.

so that even for that consideration they will look for no such authority there, no more than they do in Flanders. But, whatsoever I said therein, the Constable still persisted that we should feel his words to be true within a while.

" The Constable showed me also, that the King had news, that the Emperor had already caused to be published in Rome that this marriage was thoroughly concluded and agreed upon, and that the capitulations and conditions of them were sent hither from Rome, which the Constable caused to be sent for, and read unto me by the Secretary Bourdin. But, for because the chamber was full of people giving both good ear and eye to us, he read not so loud that I could perceive all that he read ; but part of it is this:

" That the Prince of Spain hath declared that he will not go thro' with the marriage with the Lady Mary Infant of Portugal, under pretext of the long days of payment of the money which the Prince should have with her. That the matrimony is concluded betwixt the Prince and the Queen of England. That the Prince, by the month of February next, shall pass over into England with seven or eight thousand Spaniards, there to solemnize and accomplish that matrimony. That, if God send a son of this matrimony, that he shall have all the Low Country with England. That, if there be two sons, the first shall be King, and the second shall have the Low Countries, for because the Low

Countries cannot well endure to be under a stranger.    There was also somewhat of daughters, but I
perceived it not well.

" That for because that by this means Spain
shall forego the Low Country, therefore the
Queen's Highness shall resign her right she pretendeth to France to the Emperor and his posterity, for a recompense of the Low Country.

" That the Emperor shall send an army into
Guienne to recover it; and the Queen shall send
thither likewise, at her charges, a number of her
men to assist the Spaniards;    *     *     *     *
that whatsoever should be so taken (if I understood it well) should be put to the keeping of
Englishmen, till it might appear that the Low
Countries should be dissevered from Spain, and
then all that to be restored to the Spaniards.
These were the principal points which I carried
away of that matter. *

" The Constable had a long talk with me at this
time, and all the while used a gentle countenance
unto me, which was well marked, and letters written abroad of it that self day; for already was
all the court full of the news of the marriage betwixt the Queen's Highness and the Prince, and
the matter taken to be fully agreed and concluded

* The reader may compare Wotton's recollection of the
terms of the treaty with the deed itself, by turning to Rymer,
vol. xv. pp. 387, 388; or to Carte, vol. iii. p. 301.

upon, for the French ambassador † had sent hither a man of his, but a few days before.    *   *   *

"And where your Lordships would know what the talk here is of this marriage, the truth is, that at the court, amongst in a manner all sorts of men, there is none other thing so much talked of as that is; for the marriage in this court is taken for concluded and determined. And therefore, whensoever they meet with any of my men, or any other Englishman, straight they are in hand with him of that matter; and commonly all do use this talk, that they are very sorry, and lament much that we shall now become subjects to Spain; and then begin to describe the intolerable pride and the unsatiable covetousness of Spaniards, whom, they say, if we did know as they do, we would never suffer to bear any rule over us. And when they have talked their pleasure herein, for because that is not the very place where it grieveth them, sometimes they burst further out and say, that now it appeareth we will no peace with them; for, if we did, the Queen our mistress would not marry with their enemies. Finally, they take it to be a great punishment that God hath sent upon us.

"One of the chief ambassadors here, talking with certain other of that matter, said, Will you see the works of God? England and Scotland,

† Monsieur De Noailles, whose letters have been printed, and present a full account of the French intrigues against the marriage.

which have thus long been two realms, ruled by
themselves, and able to compare with any other
realms, are now even about one time, for because
they shall not laugh at each other, brought under
strangers;—the Englishmen under Spaniards, and
the Scots under Frenchmen. Thus men speak of
it as their fancies serveth them. And, out of
doubt, they take it here all to be the worst news
that almost could chance unto them; and now they
begin to perceive what a loss they had of King
Edward the Sixth, on whose soul God have mercy.

" I understand that it is taken here at the court,
that the Emperor would not that the Cardinal
Poole should go into England, fearing lest he would
go about to let* this marriage of the Queen and the
Prince of Spain. I understand also, that Cardinal
Poole had put these men in a good hope that the
said marriage should take none effect; having certified the French King, by the Abbot whom he
sent hither, that, as for the Queen's Highness, he
was as well assured of her mind concerning that
marriage as he was of her mind concerning matters of religion, and that that marriage should take
no place : whose words these men trusted much
unto.†

" The Pope hath been sore sick, so as it was

---

* To hinder.

† If this be true, we cannot wonder at the Emperor's harsh-
ness to Pole, and the long detention of the Cardinal before he
was permitted to come into England.

thought he could not escape; but now the saying is, he amendeth.

" The Great Turk, going towards Aleppo, sent for his eldest son to come to him ; who, trusting to be well received of his father, was most cruelly murdered in his father's presence, and by his commandment.    Men that have seen the said son, say that, of all Ottomans' posterity, there was never none so like to attempt great enterprises, and to achieve them to his honour, as he was.    The cause hereof is taken to be the favour and love which the Turk beareth to the children he hath by another woman—not mother to him that is slain.    But his other sons are nothing of that towardness and activity that this man was of. *

" The Scots here say, that the governor of Scotland at the last is content, and doth submit himself to meddle no further in the government of the realm of Scotland, after that the young Queen† shall be twelve years old, than she shall appoint him to do.    And, indeed, he sent so lightly, and without advisement, the young Queen and his two sons hither, that he must needs now dance as these men list to pipe; whereas, if he had kept them at home, it is very likely his own son should have married the Queen, and have been King himself.

* The reader will probably remember the interesting historical episode, in Robertson's Charles the Fifth, upon this domestic tragedy.    The name of the unfortunate Prince was Mustafa.

† Mary Queen of Scots.

" The French army by sea, going into Corsica, was taken with a great storm; and eight or nine of the galleys, wherein were the Captain Polin, the Great Prior of France, brother to the Duke of Guise, and the Duke of Sunie, fugitive of Naples, were driven back to Marseilles and that coast, and could not tell whether Petro Strozzi and the rest were saved or not. And I cannot perceive that the King hath as yet received certain news that they are saved; for altho' their chance were to escape the danger of the tempest, yet are their enemies stronger on the sea there about Corsica, than these galleys which are missed are. The loss of Petro Strozzi and the said galleys were like to be of such importance to the French King, that the loss of Corsica were most likely to ensue of it.

The French King seeketh all means to get money; and it is commonly talked that he taketh every man's plate to coin money of it, which he will restore again when he hath money enough.

\*       \*       \*       \*

" Written at Melun, the 23rd December 1553.

" N. WOTTON."

A few days after the despatch of this letter, in which the French monarch and his ministers so clearly pointed out the probable consequences of the Spanish match, the Emperor's ambassadors left Calais, and on the 2nd of January they arrived in London.\* They were instructed to make a formal offer of the hand of the Prince of Spain. This they did soon after in a public audience; and Mary, observing that it did not become a woman to treat personally of her own marriage, referred them to her Council. To the high dignitaries who composed it Charles had not been sparing of golden promises, and it was confidently anticipated that all would be easily arranged. But the antipathy of the English gentry and of the great body of the nation to this alliance increased every hour. It was believed, and not without good ground for the anticipation, that England would sink into a province of Spain; their country, it was said, would be trampled on, its liberties invaded, its commerce ruined, its very name forgotten.

I have met with some criminal examinations in the State Paper Office which demonstrate the intensity of this feeling. It appears that, on the 23rd January 1553-4, William Cotman, a smith, who lived in the county of Kent, was committed. He declared that " William Ishley, Gent. eldest son to Sir William Ishley, Knt. came this morning to his shop, two hours before day, to shoe his horse, where he tarried the making of a shoe, and there used these words: ' that the Spaniards were coming into the realm with harness and hand-guns, and would make us Englishmen worse than enemies, and viler; for

* Griffet, p. 72.

this realm should be brought to such bondage by them as it was never afore, but should be utterly conquered.' And, at his taking of his horse, he said with a loud voice, that all the street might hear it, it being scarce day, ' Smith, if thou beest a good fellow, stir and encourage all the neighbours to rise against these strangers, for they should have lawful warning and help enough,' * * *

" ' Why,' quoth the smith, ' these be marvellous words, for we shall be hanged if we stir.' ' No,' quoth Ishley ; ' ye shall have help enough ; for the people are already up in Devonshire and Cornwall, Hampshire and other counties.' "†

Such were the bitter feelings of a large body of the gentry and the people against this Spanish marriage ; and so busily did Mary's enemies work upon them, that, within a few days after this declaration, a rebellion broke out, which had its ramifications through some of the principal counties in the kingdom.

The history of this formidable conspiracy, known by the name of Wyatt's plot, its complete failure, and the additional strength and security which it conferred on the Queen's government, are subjects familiar to our readers. Sir Thomas Wyatt undertook to manage the rising in Kent; Sir Peter Carew, in the west of England ; and the Duke of

† *Orig.* St. P. Off. " The saying of William Cotman, in the county of Kent, smith, this present Tuesday, 23rd January 1553."

Suffolk, the father of the Lady Jane, who owed his life to Mary's clemency, in the midland counties. Noailles, the French ambassador, who had been instructed by his master to foster the discontent and encourage the enemies of the Queen, was deeply involved in the plot; [*] and there seems strong reason to believe (although it is still a contested point), that the Lady Elizabeth was at least acquainted with the designs of the conspirators, if she did not actually encourage them. In a letter from Renard, the French ambassador, to Charles the Fifth, he informs the Emperor that, in a conversation with Mary, she had told him " that Lord Russell's son, who was a prisoner in his father's house, had already declared that during the rebellion he had received letters from Wyatt directed to the Lady Elizabeth, which he conveyed to her." [†] But more of this presently.

Two causes seem to have led to the ill success of the plot: the precipitancy of Carew, who forced Wyatt to discover himself before his measures were complete; and the remarkable courage and decision of the Queen. On the advance of the rebels to London, the Duke of Norfolk, with the Queen's guards and five hundred men belonging to the trained bands of the city, hurried off against them; but, on coming in sight of the enemy, Brett, the

---

[*] Noailles, vol. iii. pp. 36, 37.

[†] Griffet, p. 90.

captain of the trained bands, with his whole force,
went over to Wyatt, the Duke retired, and the bold
rebel, at the head of fifteen thousand men, advanced
to Deptford.   It was at this crisis that Mary's own
vigour and courage were the means of saving herself and her throne.   The whole city was in dis-
may ; her ministers, awakening her at two in the
morning, implored her to fly, and had provided a
boat to convey her by water from the capital.*
Amid the confusion, men ran about armed, or with
such weapons as they could hastily seize ; and
not only the mayor and aldermen wore their steel
coats, but the serjeants-at-law, and other barristers
in Westminster Hall, pleaded in harness.†   In the
midst of all Mary was calm ; she consulted the
Spanish ambassador, and he wisely counselled her
to remain on the spot.   She instantly resolved to
do so ; commanded her nobles and a few of her
women to accompany her to Guildhall ; and, on
arriving there, addressed to the magistrates, and the
people who had crowded round her, a speech which
had a powerful effect.   Fox, an author strongly
prejudiced against the Queen, has preserved it, " as
near out of her own mouth," says he, " as it could
be penned." It has every mark of an extempore
harangue ; and I am induced to give some sentences from it, were it merely to show how little
ground there is to animadvert, as has been done by

* Griffet, p. 82.
† Jardine's Criminal Trials, vol. i. p. 52.   Stow, p. 619.

some popular writers, upon her narrow capacity and extreme ignorance. *

" ' I am come,' said she, ' in mine own person, to tell you what you already see and know, how traitorously and rebelliously a number of Kentish men have assembled against us and you. Their pretence was for a marriage determined for us, to the which, and to all the articles whereof, you have been made privy: but since we have caused certain of our Privy Council to go against them, the marriage seemed to be but a Spanish cloak to cover their pretended purpose against our religion; so that they arrogantly demanded to have the governance of our person, the keeping of the Tower, and the placing of our councillors.

" ' Now, loving subjects, what I am ye right well know;—I am your Queen, to whom, at my coronation, when I was wedded to the realm and the laws of the same, you pronounced your allegiance and obedience. And that I am the right and true inheritor of the crown, I take all Christendom to witness. My father possessed the same regal estate, and to him ye always showed yourselves most faithful and loving subjects; and, therefore, I doubt not that ye will so show yourselves likewise to me, and not suffer a vile traitor to have the order and governance of our person, and to occupy our estate.' * * * She concluded her address with

* Hallam, Const. Hist. vol. i. p. 144.—Hume, 8vo. edition, pp. 374, 389.

these words, ' Good subjects, pluck up your hearts, and like true men stand fast against these rebels, both our enemies and yours; and fear them not, for, I assure you, I fear them nothing at all.'"*

The effect of this speech was highly favourable to the Queen. Twenty-five thousand men immediately enlisted for her defence. Wyatt's force, by desertion, sunk from fifteen to two thousand; and, although to the last he acted with extraordinary courage, his troops were defeated, and himself seized and lodged in the Tower. Meanwhile, Sir Peter Carew, after a feeble attempt in Devonshire, had escaped to the Continent; and the Duke of Suffolk, having been equally unsuccessful, was made prisoner, with his son Lord Thomas Grey, and sent to join Wyatt in the Tower.

Of the persons implicated in this rebellion, and the state of public feeling at the time, there is much valuable information to be gleaned from the manuscript letters of Simon Renard, the Emperor's ambassador at the court of London, to his master Charles the Fifth. Of these I shall speak immediately; but I must first give two letters of Wotton's.

It appears that, whilst such was the stirring and dangerous course of events in England, this ambassador, either unconscious of the impending crisis, or afraid to discuss the subject, despatched the following quaint epistle to Sir William Petre, now

* Fox, p. 1290.

Chancellor of the Order of the Garter, in which he makes his first appearance as a herald. Will Somers, to whose apophthegm he alludes, was a favourite fool of Henry the Eighth.*

WOTTON TO SIR WILLIAM PETRE.

*Orig.* St. P. Off. *France.* 26th Jan. 1553-4.

"Sir.—I thank you much for the promotion whereto you have promoted me by your last letter, but I am sorry you forgot to send me my title and name whereby I should be called,—whether it be Yellow Cross, or Green Mantle, or Obscurentius, or such other; for that would have set me well forth *pardy*, and have made me welcome here, at the least amongst my fellows the Heralds.

"And seeing you have made me a Herald, though you have poured no bowl of wine on my head, I intend to show you some part of my cunning; and therefore I send you herewith a certain declaration, whereby may appear (as I take it) certain degrees of consanguinity and affinity wherein the Queen's Highness and the Prince of Spain are knit together. But I remember very well, that I have

* Will makes his appearance in a little illumination upon the Psalter of this monarch, which is preserved among the Royal Manuscripts in the British Museum. An engraving from this exquisite miniature is prefixed to the first volume of Sir Henry Ellis's Letters. In it the King is represented sitting at a table playing on a small harp. His jester stands beside him, his hands clasped before his breast, and one huge ear cocked up, as if drinking in the royal melody.

oftentimes heard my fellow Will Somer (God keep him warm, wheresoever he be!) say, that he would abide by no saying of his; and, forasmuch as it is ever good to learn of a wise man, I intend therefore, in this matter, to learn a lesson of him. And, therefore, I do protest unto you, that as well in this case as in any other concerning pedigrees, whatsoever I say or write, or shall say or write, I intend not to abide by it, but shall refer myself for the truth of it to them that do: *quam protestationem volo semper et ubique pro repetita haberi, exnunc prout extunc, et extunc prout exnunc.* Under this protestation it shall not greatly force to whom you show it. And altho' I intend not to affirm either these, nor any other, to be true; yet would I be loath to declare or speak any such thing, but that I had read it before in some book or pedigree.

\*　　\*　　\*　　\*　　\*

"And where you would have me move yet more doubts; I am sure you do well remember the old saying, '*Qui nihil scit, de nullo dubitat:*' seeing then I know nothing at all of your treaties and doings of this matter, how were it possible for me to consider any such doubt of them? Nor those few doubts whereof I wrote to you before, could I now have thought on unless, by my Lord's letter from home, I had learnt that there had been some communication of this marriage; and that, by these men's report here, I understood that the Emperor did offer the Queen the Low Country.

" And where I understand that our preachers' rooms at Canterbury shall now be void, I trust, my masters, you courtiers will not take the gift of them from me, to whom it belongeth, and entitle the Queen to it by a thing called the King's prerogative, who is *cousin-german* to the præmunire; for no man living knoweth neither the one nor the other, but even as it pleaseth you to be, so must it be a prerogative, or a præmunire.

" For because I shall be sure never to hear no news from you, my masters, out of England, I intend, therefore, to send you some news from hence. We say here, that the Emperor requireth a good number of hostages of the Queen, for the safeguard of the Prince while he shall be in England; which fable, whether it be true or not, I cannot tell; but, as I hear, it giveth them here occasion of much mad talk, sounding not most to the honesty of poor England. And thus I beseech Jesu long to preserve you in health and prosperity! Written at Paris, the 26th of January 1553.

" Yours assuredly, N. WOTTON.

" Postscripta.—Since perceiving how I am fallen into this sickness upon so little occasion, to my knowledge, I am half in despair to be able to do the Queen's Highness any service here, for this cause; and also for that, because of this marriage, I think it will be very hard to avoid the war betwixt us and France, the war continuing between the Emperor and France, I have the less desire to continue here; therefore, if you see any good occasion of my revocation, I pray you omit it not; and by the next I pray you to signify to me whether you see any hope of my revocation, or not; and, in case you do, about what time."

We have seen that Sir Peter Carew, after his failure in Devonshire, fled to France, where he engaged in intrigues with the French King against Mary's government. The moment Wotton ascertained the fact of his being in Paris, he requested an interview with Henry. We have an account of it in the following letter to the Queen.

### DR. WOTTON TO THE QUEEN.

*Orig.* St. P. Off. *France.* 12th Feb. 1553-4.

" PLEASETH your Highness to understand that, knowing Sir Peter Carew to be here, and hearing it bruited abroad that there was a great *My-lord* (for so they call him here) come hither to require succour and aid against your Highness, I thought it meet for me to speak with the King and with Monsieur le Connetable of it, and to feel their minds what they intended to do therein; and so required audience, which I should have had sooner than I had, but for that a servant of mine was sick, and his face began so to break out that I feared it had been the measles, and therefore durst I not go to the court till I was by the physician certified that it was no contagious thing.

" And so had I audience the 10th of this present,

and spake first with Monsieur le Connetable, to whom having declared the cause of my coming, he made me answer that there was no such man come, nor the King nor he knew of none; and that I should be assured the King intended to keep the peace and amity with your Highness, as he had ever said he would do.

" This was the effect of his answer concerning that matter.   And then he entered in talk of these news of the commotion in England, and showed me what he heard, and asked me what I had heard. Whereas, indeed, I had very little to answer him, having received no news at all thereof; and yet by conjecture, reasoning with him thereof, I showed him, that if your Highness were in any danger, or found the matter hard to pacify, I doubted not but your Highness would have sent to the King your good brother knowledge of it ere this; but, seeing you did not so, it might thereby well appear that you would not trouble him with that matter till you had reformed it by such means as you should think best; and told him that, seeing your Highness had had so good leisure to prepare for that matter, I doubted not but that you should very shortly, with little business, bring it to a good end.

" So, after a good long communication of this matter, he brought me to a chamber next to the King's chamber ; and, he going before to the King, within a little while after I went to the King too. And having first given the King thanks for certain

gentle messages and offers which he sent me in my
sickness time, I said unto him, that I had heard
that in Kent there was a commotion of the people, murmuring for certain causes wherewith they
were not contented; and the like I said I had
heard of some other parts of England: nevertheless, for that because, by all that was spoken of it,
it seemed to me that the matter was such as your
Highness might ever, when it should please you,
either with a few words pacify, or, if you were
otherwise minded, you might right well by might
and power chastise the beginners and offenders
thereof, therefore I said, that if I had heard none
other news, I would not at this time have troubled the King therewith.   But because there was
another bruit noised since that time throughout all Paris, that there was *un grand Milord* come
out of England unto him to require succour and
aid to maintain their rebellion against your Highness, I said I thought I ought not to dissemble
that matter, nor could do no less than to require to
speak with him of it.

"I said, his Majesty knew what promises your
Highness had ever made him, and likewise what
promises he had ever made your Highness again.
And seeing, therefore, that you were friends, and
intended to continue that friendship and amity, I
said I trusted assuredly he would never give ear
to such a sort of men, and much less give them
succour nor aid.

" The King made very strange at my tale, and said that he knew of no great Lord come out of England. Marry, he said, it was true that the Cardinal Farnese would have borne him in hand that the Earl of Devonshire was seen here by a man of his, who said he knew him very well ; but that there was no such thing indeed. 'And, nevertheless,' quoth the King, 'you have done well to speak to me of it, seeing you heard such a tale. And, as I have ever said unto you, I will keep peace and amity with the Queen my good sister, your mistress ; nor I do not help nor succour no rebels against her. And you know yourself,' quoth the King, ' that not only I am content to entertain the peace and amity which we have together, but that for my part I could have been content to have made it straiter and surer ; but, seeing she thinketh this to be sufficient, I am content with it too, and therefore you shall not need to mistrust that I will do any thing contrary to the amity betwixt us.'

" 'Sir,' quoth I, ' I did never mistrust it ; but yet is it true that there is come hither a gentleman of the west country, named Sir Peter Carew, whereupon by likelihood this bruit rose.' ' I have not seen him,' quoth the ' King, nor know him not. Marry, I remember I have heard speak in times past of one of that name, that was Master of the Horses in England.' ' Yea, Sir,' quoth I, ' there was one such indeed, but this is not he.' ' Whatsoever he be,' quoth the King, ' I assure you I have not seen him, nor know him not.' 'Sir,' quoth I, 'assuredly he is fled out of his country, and should have been taken, as some other were, if he had tarried; and therefore, Sir, if he or any other (for it is not unlikely that others shall be constrained to flee likewise or it be long) come to your Highness for any such purpose, altho', Sir, you were not in such amity as you are with the Queen my mistress, yet, in my simple mind, it were neither for your Highness' profit, nor for your honour, to meddle with a matter desperate and without recovery, for surely their matter is none other. If these men that make this commotion had suddenly marched forward, they might peradventure have found the Queen my mistress, doubting no such matter, unprovided for it, and therefore might perchance have put her to somewhat the more trouble; but it is now a fortnight ago since they began, or more, and in this space it is not to be doubted but that her Highness hath so provided for all things, that she shall easily have her mind of them, and, specially, seeing that you hear not of any one of the great Lords that taketh part against her. The King said, that whosoever should come to him for any like matter, he would not comfort nor aid them against your Highness.

"'Is it then,' quoth I, 'your pleasure that I so advertise the Queen my mistress?' 'Yea, marry, I pray you,' quoth the King, 'for I will not fail so to do.' This is the effect of the answer I have had of the King at this time. † *    *    *    *

" The said Sir Peter Carew departed hence the 9th of this present in post, as I hear, to go to Roan, as some say, to tarry there a while to see how things shall pass in England.

" Having written thus far, I hear say that the King had yesterday news from Boulogne, that my Lord Cobham should have skirmished against them that are up in Kent, and that he hath lost about five hundred of his men. And that, after that, my Lord of Norfolk went against them with a great company, who forsook him; and, besides that, slew five hundred Spaniards who were come in their company.‡    *    *    *    *

" I understand that the Duke of Florence hath determined to make war against the Sienneses, and hath an army ready for that purpose. § *    *    *

" It is certain, also, that the King of Portugal's son is dead; and that the Princess his wife, the Emperor's daughter, within twenty days after was delivered of a son, which much recomforted all that country, being, as reason was, right sad for their Prince's death. The Duke Octavio Farnese and the Conte de Pitigliano return home into their country, and the Conte de Mirandola followeth shortly after.

† Here follows a part in cipher.
‡ Here occur more sentences in cipher.
§ More in cipher.

" And thus I beseech Jesu long to preserve your Highness in health, honour, and much felicity. Written at Paris, the 12th of February 1553.

" N. Wotton."

The conspiracy of Wyatt, and the difficulty of tracing the rebellion in all its ramifications, sealed the fate of Lady Jane Grey and her husband. Her father, the Duke of Suffolk, had been treated with much generosity by Mary, and, after having received his life at her hands, had a second time risen in arms against her. He was now executed; but it was a piteous measure, not to be justified under the plea of necessity, to bring the youthful Jane and her husband, Lord Guilford Dudley, to the scaffold. Mary, it is said by some writers, wished to pardon them, and there is reason to believe it; but the Emperor inculcated severity, and her own councillors, — those very men who had placed Jane upon the throne,—now urged the expediency of her execution. Their conduct is strongly animadverted on by Bishop Ponet, who knew much of the intrigues of these times. " They," says he, " that were sworn chief of the Council with the Lady Jane, and caused the Queen Mary to be proclaimed a bastard through all England and Ireland, and that were the sorest forcers of men, yea, under the threatened pain of treason, to swear and subscribe unto their doings, * * * afterwards became counsellors, I will not say procurers, of the innocent Lady Jane's death; and at this present are in the highest authority in the Queen's house, and the chiefest officers and doers in the commonwealth." " Perhaps," adds Strype, in quoting this passage, " the Marquis of Winchester, the Earl of Arundel, and the Earl of Pembroke were intended by this writer as some of the chief of these notable temporizers."* Yet, strongly as we may stigmatize such conduct, we must equally blame Mary for her weakness in giving way to their cruel policy.

Their youthful and innocent victim suffered within the Tower on the 12th of February, her husband having been beheaded a short time before on Tower Hill. The particulars have been often told, and I need not repeat the sad story, but refer my readers to the pathetic narrative of Sir Harris Nicolas.† By an unhappy oversight, when the Lady Jane was preparing to walk to the scaffold, which had been erected on the green over against the White Tower, the cart containing the headless body of her husband was driven under the window of her prison, so near that her eyes met the horrid spectacle.‡ Yet, though pale and shook, she retained her tranquillity. " She came forth," says Stow, " the Lieutenant leading her, with countenance nothing dismayed, neither her eyes anything moistened with tears, with a book in her hand,

* Ponet, quoted by Strype, vol. iii. part i. p. 141.
† Life of Lady Jane Grey, prefixed to her Works.
‡ Holinshed, p. iv. p. 22.

wherein she prayed until she came to the scaffold.
Whereon when she was mounted, this noble young
lady, as she was endowed with singular gifts both
of learning and knowledge, so was she as patient
and mild as any lamb at her execution."*

There is something deeply affecting in the whole
history of Jane. Her royal birth was her bane, and,
even in the gay and happy season of girlhood, this
fatal greatness clouded all her sunshine. Her parents were strict and severe. The speech she made
to Roger Ascham at Broadgate, when he found her
reading Plato at a time when her young friends
were hunting in the park, gives us a dismal glimpse
of the misery of her young years. Though the passage must be familiar to some of my readers, yet,
as nowadays the " Schoolmaster" of Ascham is but
little read, I may give it. " Before I went into
Germany," says he, " I came to Broadgate in Lei-
cestershire, to take my leave of that noble Lady,
Jane Grey, to whom I was exceeding much beholden. I found her in her chamber reading
Phædon Platonis in Greek, and that with as much
delight as some gentlemen would read a merry tale
in Boccacio.

" After saluting and duty done, with some other
talk, I asked her why she would lose such pastime
in the park  Smiling she answered me, ' I wis all
their sport in the park is but a shadow to that
pleasure that I find in Plato. Alas! good folk,

* Stow, p. 622.

they never felt what true pleasure meant.'  'And
how came you, Madam,' said I, 'to this deep
knowledge of pleasure, and what did chiefly allure
you unto it; seeing not many women, and but very
few men, have attained thereunto?'

" 'I will tell you,' quoth she, 'and tell you a
truth which, perchance, ye will marvel at.  One of
the greatest benefits that ever God gave me is,
that he sent me so sharp and severe parents, and so
gentle a schoolmaster.    For when I am in presence
either of father or mother, whether I speak, keep
silence, sit, stand, or go; eat, drink, be merry, or
sad; be sewing, playing, dancing, or doing anything
else, I must do it, as it were, in such weight, measure, or number, even so perfectly as God made the
world; or else I am so sharply taunted, so cruelly
threatened, yea, presently sometimes with pinches,
nips, and bobs, and other ways, which I will not
name, for the honour I bear them, so without
measure misordered, that I think myself in hell,
till time come that I must go to Mr. Aylmer, who
teacheth me so gently, so pleasantly, with such fair
allurements to learning, that I think all the time
nothing whilst I am with him.    And when I am
called from him I fall a weeping, because whatever
I do else but learning is full of grief, trouble, fear,
and whole misliking unto me.    And thus my book
hath been so much my pleasure,    *    *    that, in
respect of it, all other pleasures in very deed be
but trifles and troubles unto me." †

† Ascham's Schoolmaster, pp. 222, 223.

How wretched must have been the years passed
under so harsh a system, and how pleasant is it to
turn from the austerity of the parents to the amiable
Aylmer, and the quiet love of literature which he so
gently fostered.    Nor were these earliest sorrows
the worst; when torn from her studies and constrained to be Queen, the nine days she wore the
crown were embittered by domestic misery and dissension.    Her husband quarrelled with her because
she conscientiously refused to make him King; his
mother, the Duchess of Northumberland, behaved
with such extraordinary violence, and evinced such
hostility, that she was apprehensive of her life; and
there can be little doubt of the perfect sincerity of
her speech to the Duke her father, when he an-
nounced to her that she was no longer Queen:
" This news pleases me better than that which told
that I was to have the throne." *

It appears to be Mr. Turner's opinion, that Jane
suffered her ambition to be dazzled by the splendour of the prize offered her, and that she really
believed in Mary's superior right when she accepted
the crown; so, at least, I gather from some of his
remarks.    " She had descended," he says, " from
her social probity to take a royalty which was
another's inheritance : and although importunity
had extorted her acquiescence, yet her first reluctance gave testimony even to herself that she had
not erred in ignorance of what was right; and

* Lettere de Principi, vol. iii. p. 138.

no one but herself could know how much the temp-
tation of the offered splendour had operated, beyond the solicitation, to seduce her to what she
ought to have continued to refuse."* This is hardly
just, I think : nor do I see any reason for disbe-
lieving her own simple account in her last words on
the scaffold, that, in receiving the crown, she submitted to the superior judgment of those " who
should seem to have further understanding of things
than I, who knew little of the law, and much less
of the titles to the crown." This, be it observed,
is completely corroborated by her own account of
the solemn words she used when she accepted
the throne. " I turned to God and humbly pe-
titioned and supplicated him, that, if what had been
given to me *were rightfully and lawfully mine,* he
would grant me so much grace and spirit that I
might govern these kingdoms to his glory and
service."† And it also corresponds with the expressions she uses in her last pathetic and beautiful letter to her father. " And yet, tho' I
must needs acknowledge that being constrained,
and, as you well know, continually assailed, in
taking the crown upon me, I seemed to consent, and therein grievously offended the Queen
and her laws ; and yet do I assuredly trust that
this my offence towards God is so much the less,

* Turner's History of Edward the Sixth, Mary and Elizabeth, p. 229, first edition.

† Jane's Letter to Mary. Lettere de Principi. vol. iii.
p. 375.

in that, being in so royal an estate as I was, my
inforced honour never mixed with my innocent
heart."* Having this letter before me, I cannot
subscribe to the opinion of Dr. Lingard, that Jane's
" contempt of the splendour of royalty, and her re-
luctant submission to the commands of her parents," are to be considered as the fictions of historians.†

The Lady Jane, if we judge from the portrait in
Lodge, engraved from an original in the collection
of the Earl of Stamford, had sweet though rather
diminutive features; but her figure was finely
formed, and there is a simplicity in her dress
which becomes it well. It is so plain, that Griffet
might at first sight have quoted it as supporting his supposed puritanical costume of Edward's
time; but, on a nearer look, the richly flowered
tucker, the string of pearls round the neck,
the flowers in her bosom, and the little jewel
clasping the tight spencer, confute his notions,
and show that Plato permitted his pupil some little leisure for the toilet. Challoner,‡ in his " De-
ploratio," speaks of her as surpassingly beautiful :

> —— " Formosa fuit : divina movebat
> Sæpe viros facies."

And Granger quotes an anonymous epigram, which,
in two lines, has much matter :

* Biogr. Britt. article ' Jane Grey,' p. 2420.
† History of England, vol. vii. p. 113, fourth edition.
‡ Strype's Eccles. Mem. vol. iii. p. 190, Appendix.

> " Quicquid dulce animum compleverat, utile quicquid;
>    Ars cerebrum, pietas pectus, et ora sales."

> " Her mind all sweets, all virtues did comprise;
>    Fair, holy, kind, accomplished, witty, wise."

SIMON RENARD, who held the office of Lieutenant
or Bailli of Daumont, in Franche Compté, was sent
by the Emperor as his ambassador to the English
court some little time before the death of Edward
the Sixth.*   His original letters from England to
Charles the Fifth are preserved in the public
archives at Brussels; but a transcript of them, in
three volumes, is to be found in the public library
at Besançon, from the study of which Griffet composed his interesting little work on the reign of
Mary.†   The first portion of Renard's correspondence, to my great regret, I have not seen; but
access has been politely given me ‡ to the later
letters which he addressed to the Emperor, transcribed, by order of the late Record Commission,
from the originals at Brussels, and some of these,
which have never been printed, are well worthy of
attention.   They are written at the same time,

---

* Carte, History of England, vol. iii. p. 288.

† Eclaircissemens sur l'Histoire de Marie Reine d'Angleterre.   These valuable letters are referred to by Dr. Lingard, in the fourth edition of his History, now in the course
of publication.

‡ By the Right Honourable Lord John Russell, under whose
custody, as Secretary of State, they now are.

often on the same day, as Noailles' despatches; and are valuable, not only as enabling us to correct the highly coloured and overcharged pictures of this ambassador, who was strongly prejudiced against Mary, but from the new lights which they occasionally throw on this portion of our history. The two following letters, alluding to what took place immediately subsequent to Wyatt's rebellion, when the plot had failed, and the Tower was crowded with prisoners, are interesting. It had been discovered that the French and Venetian ambassadors were both deeply implicated with Wyatt; and we accordingly find Sebastian Cabot, the celebrated navigator, who, although a Venetian by blood, was born, and had been nearly all his life in the service of England, accusing the Venetian ambassador of secret practices against the government. Clinton, too, the Lord Admiral, arraigns him of having furnished the rebels with arms.

Renard, from his letters, was evidently jealous both of Bishop Gardiner the Chancellor, and of Cardinal Pole. Nor is it difficult to discover the reason. The Emperor and his ambassador had their hearts intent upon one great object — the marriage of Mary and Philip. Gardiner insisted that, Mary's first thoughts should be given to the state of religion and the restoration of the ancient faith; but he deprecated the immediate renunciation of the title of Supreme Head of the Church : whilst Pole loudly asserted that, till the kingdom was reconciled to Rome, and this usurped supremacy restored, nothing was rightly done, and nothing could be expected to prosper. Charles believed that, between them, the people would be stimulated to a third explosion, and the marriage prevented. It was for this reason that the Emperor detained the Cardinal so long on his road to England, and that Renard received instructions to watch the Chancellor.*

Renard's second letter is, however, the most interesting, from the information it communicates upon Wyatt's plot, and the connection of Courtenay and Elizabeth with this rebellion. The picture of Elizabeth uncovering her litter, and, although pale and reduced by sickness, proudly and severely eyeing the crowds who flocked to gaze on her, is finely drawn. Whether she did or did not encourage the plot, is still a disputed point in English history, upon which some new and important information is to be gleaned from this Spanish correspondence. But it is time to listen to the ambassador. A few lines of the French letters being of minor importance have been omitted in the translation.

* See an interesting letter of M. De Selves, the French ambassador at Venice, to the Constable Montmorency, in Ribier Memoires D'Estat, vol. ii. p. 457, dated as early as September 12, 1553. De Selves had been ambassador in England in the time of Edward. He knew Mary well, and had then formed the opinion that she would never marry a subject.

### SIMON RENARD TO THE EMPEROR.

20th February 1553-4.

" SIRE.—The whole Council of the Queen of
England have resolved to summon parliament for
the fifteenth day after Easter, that the articles of
the marriage of the Queen to his Highness may be
ratified and approved; for this purpose, letters and
summons are already in preparation, to be sent
with all despatch to the different counties and districts, as it is the custom always to give six weeks'
notice before the assembling of any parliament.

" The Chancellor still obstinately insists that
they shall debate the subject of the Queen's right
to be supreme head of the Church, which some
members of the Council oppose; nor am I without
suspicion that the Chancellor is advised to this by

---

### SIMON RENARD TO CHARLES THE FIFTH.

*Trans. from Orig. at Brussels, in cipher.* 20th February 1553-4.

" SIRE.—Tout le Conseil de la Royne d'Angleterre s'est
resolu que l'on doit assembler le parlement pour le xv^e
jour apres Pasques, pour faire approuver et auctorizer les articles de mariage de la dicte dame avec son Altesse par icelluy;
et se depeschent les lettres en toute diligence pour les envoier
au pays et contrees, pour ce que, quant il est question d'assembler le parlement, l'on a toujours fait la publication six se-
maines devant. Le Chancelier insiste toujours que l'on propose l'article du titre de Supreme Chief de l'Eglise, ce que
aucuns du Conseil ne trouvent bon; et ne suis hors de suspicion que le dit Chancelier se face par l'advis du Cardinal

Cardinal Pole, that he may accumulate difficulty upon difficulty. A point, the truth of which I hope to fathom, and to discover if he is to be trusted or not.

" The Cardinal has not written to the Queen, nor sent any reply to two letters which she addressed to him,— one received on his journey, the other at Brussels; by which she required his advice how she should, without scruple of conscience, provide for the vacant sees, and whether he had authority to pronounce the requisite confirmation. This shows that he entertains some resentment against the Queen, because she had sent him no notice regarding the marriage; and, accordingly, one of the principal servants about him, a theologian, named William Peto, has addressed a letter to Mary, which she received three days ago, giving her advice not to marry, but to embrace celibacy; interspersing in his letters several texts of the Old and

---

Polo, pour mettre difficulté sur difficulté, ce que j'espere enfoncer plus veritablement, et assentir s'il a malvais ou bon humeur.

" Le Cardinal n'a escript à la Royne ny respondu à deux ses lettres qu'elle luy a envoyé, l'une qu'il a receu de chemin, l'autre à Bruxelles, par lesquelles elle desiroit savoir comme elle pourvoieroit aux eveschez vacans sans scrupule de conscience, et s'il a mandement pour donner les confirmations requises; que demonstre qu'il ait quelque sentment contre la dite dame de ce qu'elle ne luy a fait communication de mariage, à cě conforme que l'un des principaux qu'il a avec lui, qui se nomme Wiliem Peto, theologien, luy a escript puis trois jours, luy donnant conseil de non se marier, et de vivre en celibat, meslant en ses

New Testaments, and repeating ten or twelve times that she would fall into the power and become the slave of her husband,—nay, that at her advanced age she cannot hope to bear children without the peril of her life ; a speech which has been often enough repeated.  He concludes by an offer to come to visit her, and tell her something more.

" The Venetian ambassador has had an audience of the Queen and the Council to offer his apology regarding the arms which the rebels took from the Venetian ship, to which I alluded in my last letters. He insisted that they only carried off ten swords, ten partisans, and five or six arquebuses ; that they took away no guns, and entered the ship by force.  To this the Admiral replied, that he was well assured to the contrary.  And, the day before, Cabot had accused the said ambassador, before some of the Council, of secret practices carried on by him and his secretary, by which the evil intentions

---

lettres plusieurs allegations du Vieux et Nouveau Testament, repetant x ou xii fois qu'elle tombera en la puissance et servitude du mari, qu'elle n'aura enfans sinon soubz danger de sa vie pour l'age dont elle est, qu'est ung sermon recordé, offrant de venir vers la dite dame pour lui dire de surplus.

"L'ambassadeur de Venise a eu audience devers la dite dame et le Conseil pour s'excuser des armes que les rebelles prindent en la nave Venetienne, dont j'ai fait mention par mes dernieres lettres ; disant qu'il ne prindrent sinon dix espees, dix partisannes, et cinq ou six harquebouses, et qu'ilz ne emmenerent l'artillerie, et qu'ilz entrarent par force : à quoy a respondu l'Admiral que l'on sçavoit le contraire, et le jour precedent CABOTO avoit accusé le dit ambassadeur deverz aucuns du

which he has against the Queen and his Highness were evidently proved, there being a strong suspicion that the conspiracies were entered into in his house ; especially with Courtenay, who did not venture to go so openly to the house of the French ambassador.

" It is certainly known that a courier passed over by Dover, who brought money to assist Wyatt. Condemnations of several noblemen occur from day to day, but the executions do not follow.

" I have received a letter by this bearer from his Highness, in which he informs me that he has sent the necessary powers to your Majesty. Nevertheless, I shall pretend that I have received letters from him.

" And thus, Sire, I pray the Creator to grant you the accomplishment of your exalted and noble wishes. From London, the 20th Feb. 1553.

" *From the original in cipher.*          " SIMON RENARD."
      " *To the Emperor.*"

---

Conseil de propos tenuz par luy et son secretaire, tesmoignans la malvaise volunté qu'il a à la Royne et son Altesse, estant suspecte que en sa maison les conjures soient esté faictes, signamment avec Cortenay, qui n'osoit aller au logis de l'ambassadeur de France si ouvertement.

" L'on a sceu pour verité qu'il y a passé ung courier à Douvres qui portoit argent pour le secours de Wyat. L'on condempne de jour à autre plusieurs gentilshommes, mais les executions ne s'ensuyvent.

" J'ay receu lettre de son Altesse par ce porteur, par lesquelles il m'advertit qu'il a envoyé les pouvoirs à vostre Maj$^{te}$, et pourtant je feray semblant avoir receu lettres de luy.

### SIMON RENARD TO THE EMPEROR.

#### 24th February 1553-4.

" SIRE.—Wyatt has plainly confessed in his deposition that the Sieur Osell, when he passed through this kingdom into Scotland with the French ambassador, now resident there, spoke to one named Crofts, at present a prisoner, to persuade him to hinder the marriage of his Highness and the Queen, to raise Elizabeth to the crown, to marry her to Courtenay, and put the Queen to death : that he had before this spoken to Mr. Rogers, also a prisoner; and to Peter Carew, by one named South, and Pickering, to become accomplices, having promised money, assistance, and men on the part of the King of France. And that,

---

" A tant, Sire, je prie le Createur donner à vostre Maj^te l'accomplisement de ses treshaultz et tres nobles desirs. De Londres, le xx de Febrier 1553.

" SIMON RENARD."

" *D'après l'original en chiffre.*

    "*A l'Empereur.*"

### SIMON RENARD TO THE EMPEROR.

*Transcript from Orig.*   *Brussels.*   24th Feb. 1553-4.

" SIRE.—Wyat a plainement confessé par sa deposition comme le Sieur D'Osel passant par ce royaume pour aller en Ecosse, avec l'ambassadeur de France, qui est resident par deça, parlarent à un nommé Croff, à present prisonier, pour empescher le mariage de son Altesse avec la Royne, haulser à la couronne Elisabeth, et la marier à la Cortenay, et fair mourir la Royne, et ja auparavant parlé à M. Rogers, aussi prisonier, et à Pierre

to enable them more easily to carry on the chief enterprise, this monarch was to make a simultaneous attack on the side of Scotland, Guyenne, and Calais, at the moment that they on their sides conducted the principal enterprise. With this object, the French had sent several officers into Scotland, and intended to despatch the Visdame with artillery, ammunition, money, and soldiers, to begin the war, in conjunction with the Scots, in that quarter; whilst the Marshal St. André is to make the attack on the side of Guyenne. * * * And now as the principals in the conspiracy are prisoners, and the design on this side has failed, there is great doubt whether the King of France will pursue his enterprise on the side of Scotland and Guyenne. * * *

---

Caro, par ung nommée South, et Pequeryn, interposer, aians de la part de Roy de France promis argent, ayde, et secours de gens ; et que, pour plus aisement conduire à chief ceste practique, le dit Roy feroit emprisne du coustel † d'Ecosse et de coustel du Guyenne et Calaix en ung mesme temps, et pendant qu'ilz executeroient de leurs coustels la principale practique ; et à cest effect les François avoient fait passer plusieurs capitaines en Ecosse, et deliberoient envoier le Vidame avec artillerie, munition, argent, et gens de guerre, pour, avec les Ecossois, guerroier de ce coustel-là ; et de coustel de Guyenne le Marechal de St. André devoit commencer. * * * Et comme les principaulx de la conspiration sont prisoniers, et que le desseing de ce coustel cesse, l'on doubte si le dit Roy poursuivra son emprinse du coustel d'Ecosse et de Guyenne.

---

† *Coustel* for *côté* (side).

"Thus the practices of the French are discovered; to prevent which, the Queen had despatched
the Earl of Derby to enlist soldiers, and to take
four counties under his government. The Earl of
Westmoreland, and some others, have also a command; and, besides them, every member of the
Council has one hundred foot-men and fifty horse
under their command, as their ordinary guard.
The Admiral in haste is arming all the ships that
he can get afloat; they are fortifying and provi-
sioning the sea-ports, and orders have been sent to
their governors, directing them to favour the ships
of your Majesty, as well Flemish as Spanish. * * *

"The parliament is fixed to be held at Oxford on
the 7th of April next; a proceeding which gives
umbrage to the Londoners, who foresee that, if the
Queen leaves the city, it will soon be impoverished

---

"Ainsi la practique des François est decouverte: pour laquelle prevenir la dite dame a depesché le Compte Darby pour
asseurer gens de guerre, et gouverner quatre contiees du royaulme comme lieutenant, le Comte de Westmorlant a aussi
charge et plusieurs autres, et à l'entour d'elle tous ceux du
Conseil ont chacun cent hommes depied, et cinquante chevaux
soubdoyez d'elle, pour la garde ordinaire. L'Admiral en toute
diligence arme les plus de navieres que l'on peult, l'on munit
les portz de mer de ce qu'est necessaire, et a l'on escript à tous
les gouverneurs d'iceulx de favoriser les navieres de vostre
Majesté tant de Flandres que d'Espaigne. * * *
"Le parlement est assigné à Opfort [Oxford] pour le vii[e]
jour d'Avril prochain, dont ceulx de Londres ne sont contens,
prevoians, si la dite dame esloigne la ville, en peu de temps elle
sera appovrie; et mesmes pour ce que la dite dame delibere

\* \* \*   To-day the Duke of Suffolk is to be executed; \* \* and all possible expedition is made in the trials of the criminals, who are very numerous, as the enclosed list shows,—there being more than twenty whose names are not given in it.

" The Queen has granted a general pardon to a multitude of people in Kent, after having caused about five-score of the most guilty to be executed. Numerous are the petitions presented to her Majesty to have the pains of death exchanged for perpetual imprisonment, but to this she will not listen.

" As to the divisions in the Council, I understand that Paget makes head against the Chancellor, the

---

aller en York, et resider celle part, pour estre le peuple catholique, et avoir port de mer prochain, et sont apretz les bourgeois de Londres pour supplier la dite Royne de ne sortir de la ville, et luy promettre toute asseurance, et consentir à tel mariage qu'elle voudra.

" Ce jourduy l'on execute le Duc de Suffocq, qui ne s'est jamais voulu reconnoistre quant à la religion ; aiant fait admonestement au peuple pour non se revolter contre la Royne, à laquelle il demandoit mercy. Et fait l'on tout ce qui est possible pour achever le procez des criminels, qui sont en si grand nombre que la enclose demonstre, et plus de vingt d'avantage qui ne sont nommez.

" La Royne a fait pardon general à la multitude de peuple de Caempt [Kent], apres avoir fait executer environc ou v$^{xx}$ des plus culpables. Chacun poursuit devers la dite dame pour convertir les paynes de mort en prison perpetuelle, à quoy elle ne veult condescendre ny prester l'oreille.

" Sur la partialité de Conseil j'entens que Paget fait teste au

Grand Chamberlain, and the Comptroller ; nor am I without apprehension that, from animosity against the Chancellor, he may conduct himself contrary to the expectations which the Queen entertains of his fidelity.    It is now more than six days since he has been absent from the Council, excusing himself on the plea of indisposition, and retiring to his house about twenty miles distant.    Suspicions have risen against him, because Croft and Wyatt have repeatedly insisted on having an interview with him in secret, which is not permitted.

" The Lady Elizabeth arrived here yesterday, clad completely in white, surrounded by a great assemblage of the servants of the Queen, besides her own people.    She caused her litter to be uncovered, that she might show herself to the people. Her countenance was pale; her look proud, lofty, and superbly disdainful ; an expression which she assum-

---

Chancelier, Grand Chamberlan, et Contrerolleur, et me doubte que par depit du dit Chancellier il face chose contre à l'espoir que la dite dame a eu ; et y a plus de six jours qu'il n'a esté au Conseil, s'excusant qu'il soit indisposé, et est allé en sa maison distante de ce lieu vingt miles ; et y a suspicion contre luy de ce que Croff et Wyat demandent continuellement de parler à luy en appart, ce que l'on ne veut permettre.

"La dame Elisabet arriva hier habillé tout de blanc, avec grande compagnie de gens de la dite dame et des siens, et fait decouvrir la litiere pour se monstrer au peuple, aiant visage pale, fier, haultain et superbe, pour desguyser le regret qu'elle a.    La dite dame ne la voulut veoir, et la fait loger en ung quartier de sa maison duquel elle ne peult sortir, ny ses servi-

ed to disguise the mortification she felt. Mary declined seeing her, and caused her to be accommodated in a quarter of her palace from which neither she nor her servants could go out without passing through the guards. Of her suite, only two gentlemen, six ladies, and four servants are permitted to wait on her; the rest of her train being lodged in the city of London.

"The Queen is advised to send her to the Tower, since she is accused by Wyatt, named in the letters of the French ambassador, suspected by her own councillors, and it is certain that the enterprise was undertaken in her favour. And assuredly, Sire, if, now that the occasion offers, they do not punish her and Courtenay, the Queen will never be secure; for I have many misgivings that, if, when she sets out for the parliament, they leave Elizabeth in the Tower, some treasonable means

---

teurs, synon qu'ilz passent parmy la garde, et luy a laissé seulement deux gentilzhommes, six femmes, et quatre serviteurs, et la reste de son train est logé en la ville de Londres.

"L'on luy conseille de la faire mettre en la Tour, puisque elle est accusé par Wyatt, nommée par les lettres de l'ambassadeur de France, suspitionnée par ses propres conseilliers, et qu'il est certain l'entreprinse estoit en sa faveur. Et certes, Sire, si, pendant que l'occasion s'adonne, elle ne la punyt et Cortenay, elle ne sera jamais asseurée; car je doubte, que la laisant en la Tour quant elle partira pour le parlement, que par trahison l'on ne la delivre ou Cortenay, ou tous deux, que seroit erreur pire que le premier.

"L'ambassadeur de France fait grande instance pour recou-

will be found to deliver either Courtenay or her, or both, so that the last error will be worse than the first.

" Since the publication of the act which I sent your Majesty for the expulsion of strangers, the people have been in much better spirits here ; and its effect in purging the kingdom will be most useful and seasonable : but your Majesty ought to take care that such as retire into your dominions should be arrested, as amongst them many French heretics will be found.

" Spinola has gone with Fitzwater into Flanders, rather as a spy than for any other business ; nor should I have known of this unless a cousin of his had told me some days since.  *    *    *

---

vrer l'original de ses lettres, et Paget donnoit l'avis qu'il se fait ; mais le Chancellier a conseillé le contraire, pour non perdre le temoignage des practiques ; et ja en avois parlé à la dite dame pour retirer le dit original, ce qu'elle a fait, et ne s'en dessaissira.

" Puis la publication de l'edit pour faire sortir les etrangiers, que j'ay envoyé à vostre Majesté, le peuple a esté fort remis en ce lieu, et sera tres apropos et utile, par lequel le royaulme se repurgera ; mais il sera expedient vostre Majesté fasse prendre garde que ceulx qui se retireront es pays de vostre Majesté soient arrestez, pource que parmy eulx l'on trouvera plusieurs François heretiques.

" Spinola est allé avec Fealtre en Flandres, plustot pour espier que pour aultre occasion ; et ne le sçavois jusques à ce que ung syen cousin m'en a adverty puis deux jours. Je fais toute l'instance possible pour faire retirer le Chevalier Bernard, mais la Royne n'a tant de credit envers aucuns de Conseil que le

" And thus, Sire, I pray the Creator to grant you the entire accomplishment of your noble and exalted desires. 24th Feb. 1553-4.

" *To the Emperor.*"          " SIMON RENARD."

I may give the following short letter of Secretary Bourne to the Council, as it alludes to the examinations regarding Elizabeth's supposed accession to Wyatt's plot.

## MR. SECRETARY BOURNE AND OTHERS TO THE COUNCIL.

*Orig.* ST. P. OFF. *Domestic.* 25th Feb. 1553-4.

" OUR duties remembered to your good Lordships. We have this morning travailed with Sir Thomas Wyot touching the Lady Elizabeth; and her servant, Sir William Saintloo. And your Lordships shall understand that Wyot affirmeth his former sayings; and says further, that Sir James Croft knoweth more, if he be sent for and exa-

---

portent† . . . . il est certain qu'il traffique ordinairement avec les François par le moiens de l'ambassadeur de Venize.

" A tant, Sire, je prie le Createur qu'il donne l'entier accomplisement à vostre Majesté de ses treshaultz et tres nobles desirs.          " De vostre Majesté,

          " Tres humble et tres obeissant

                    " Subject et serviteur,

" A l'Empereur."               " SIMON RENARD."

---

† A word occurs here which cannot be made out.

mined.   Whereupon Crofts has been called before
us ; and, examined, confesseth with Wyot, charging
Saintloo with the semblable matter, and further as
we shall declare unto your said Lordships.   Wherefore, under your correction, we think necessary and
beseech you to send for Mr. Sayntlo, and to examine him, or cause him to be sent hither by us
to be examined.

"Crofts is plain and will tell all.   And thus our
Lord preserve her Highness, the realm, and your
Lordships all!  From the Tower, this Sunday.

            "Your own to command,
                    "Jo. Bourne.    Rich. Southwell.
                    "Thos. Pope.    John Hyggins.

"My Lords.   In anywise search for the Lady
Fitzwilliam's second son.   It is a great and marvellous importing, but not hasty or now dreadful,
thanks be to God !"

Addressed.   " To the Right Honourable the
    Lord Chancellor and Mr. Secretary Petre."

The instructions of Charles the Fifth to Count
D'Egmont, dated the 18th February 1553-4, at Brussels, are preserved amongst the archives in that
city.   The following letter informs us how the
ambassador proceeded to fulfil them.

## SIMON RENARD TO THE EMPEROR.

### 8th March 1553-4.

SIRE.—On the arrival of the Sieur D'Egmont here, which took place on the 2nd of the present month, the Queen of England sent to him the Sieur Mason, who has been appointed ambassador in the place and absence of the Bishop of Norwich, the Earl Guerret * and the Sieurs Perrot and Howard, who met him near this city, and accompanied him to my house, where he is accommodated for the few days he will remain here ; and the same day, having seen, read, and re-read his instructions, we were of opinion that I the Lieutenant D'Amont should go to the Queen and her Council to inform them of his arrival, and of the occasion of his voyage, so that by their advice he might proceed to the execution of his charge and commission.

---

## SIMON RENARD TO THE EMPEROR.

*Transcript from Orig. Brussels.* 8 Mars 1553-4.

" SIRE.—A l'arrivee de Sieur D'Egmont en ce lieu de Londres, que fut le second du mois present, la Royne d'Angleterre envoya audevant de luy le Sieur Masson qu'a esté sorrogué ambassadeur au lieu et absence du Sieur de Norwitz, le Conte Guerret, et les Sieurs Parret et Haward, qu'ilz le recontrerent pres de ce lieu et accompagnarent jusques en mon logis, où il s'est acomodé pour le peu de jours qu'il avoit à demeurer par deça ; et le mesme jour ayant veu, leu, et releu son instruction,

---

* Perhaps for ' Warwick.'

" Five or six days ago, I had already held a consultation with the Chancellor, Petre, Paget, and the
Comptroller, on the affairs of this realm, and of the
Queen, on the question whether they ought to proceed further in the negociations about the marriage ;
more especially on the point whether his Highness, coming here, would be secure ; and what
things they desired should be done on the part
of your Majesty; all being debated in the presence and by the command of the Queen, with open
and express declaration, that if the condition of the
kingdom did not permit it, or if they saw that his
Highness and the Queen were likely to fall into any
danger, then they ought to consider it never could be
the will of your Majesty that an alliance should go
forward out of which distress might arise ; especially such troubles as would expose to hazard those

nous fumes d'avis que je le lieutenant Damont iroit devers la dite
dame et son Conseil pour l'advertir de son arrivee, et occasion
de son voyage, pour, par leurs advis, proceder à l'exploit et execution de sa charge et commission.

" Et ja, cinq ou six jours auparavant, le dit lieutenant avoit
assenty du Chancellier, Peter, Paget, et Controlleur l'estat des
affaires du royaulme, et la dite dame, et s'il leur sembloit que
l'on deust passer oultre au negoces de mariage, et expressement
si son Alteze venant par deça seroit asseuré, comme, et ce qu'ilz
desireroient fut fait de la part de vostre Majesté, le tout en
presence et par commandement de la dite dame, avec ouverte
et expresse declaration que si les affaires du royaulme ne le
comportoient, ou s'ilz veoient que les personnes de son Altese
et de la dite dame deussent tumber en danger, qu'ilz deussent
penser la volunté de vostre Majesté n'avoir esté que de l'alli-

from whose fall the whole Christian republic, the
kingdom, and provinces on both sides, and their
subjects and vassals, would be affected with the most
deplorable changes and calamities.

" In the same audience it was stated that it
became them gravely to weigh this matter, and
to adopt in it a firm and constant resolution
either to delay further proceedings, or to abandon
them in the state in which they were, or to carry
them forward; that your Majesty had been always
accustomed to proceed in your causes with sincerity,
and on plain and justifiable grounds, as you wished
to do for the future; especially with the Queen and
the kingdom of England, on account of the ancient
friendship and the ties of relationship and neigh-
bourhood so often remembered and renewed, requesting them with all confidence to reply to me :
and pointing out to them that the Sieur D'Egmont

---

ance, inconvenient deust sortir, principalement tel que seroit
celluy, si les personnes tumboient en hazaid, dont la republique
Chrestienne, les royaulmes et pays des deux coustelz, subjectz et vassaulx, recevroient à jamais troubles, prejudice, et
alteration regretable ; qu'il convenoit meurement peser cette
matiere, et y prendre resolution ferme et constante, ou delayer,
ou de la laisser imparfaite, ou de l'advancer; et que vostre
Majesté avoit toujours accoustume proceder en toutes les
actions sincerement, cleiement, et justifiement, comme elle
vouloist faire à l'advenir, signamment avec la dite dame et
royaulme d'Angleterre, pour les occasions de parantaige et
ancienne amitié et voisinance souvent reprinses et memorez ;
les piiant en toute confidence m'en respondre ; leur specializant

had brought along with him the ratification of the treaty, that he had power to complete it upon the part of his Highness, that he was in possession of the necessary briefs of dispensation on account of the consanguinity, that he had powers after this for the completion of the alliance by betrothment and words *de præsenti*, to pass into Spain and conduct his Highness into this kingdom for the consummation of the marriage, and finally to conclude upon all the circumstances which were in dependence.

"Having heard this, the Queen and the Council answered in nearly the same terms in which they had already replied to me upon the negociation above mentioned: that they could see no reason or danger which should cause any delay in prosecuting a marriage so salutary and honourable; that, thanks to God, the heretics and the

---

que le dit S<sup>r</sup> D'Egmont avoit apporté les ratifications du traité, avoit povoir de son Altese pour de sa part le ratifier, avoit les brefz de la dispense necessaire pour la consanguinité, avoit pouvoir pour asseurer l'alliance par fianceaille, et promesse de present, pour ce fait passer en Espaigne, et conduire son Altese en ce royaulme pour la consommation du mariage, et finalement conclure sur toutes circonstances en deppendans.

" Quoy entendant, la dite dame et les ditz du Conseil dirent ce que ja auparavant ilz avoient respondu au dit lieutenant sur la negociation cy dessus touchée ; qu'ils ne veoient moyen ou danger pourquoy l'on deust retarder ou differer de passer oultre en la dite matiere de mariage tant salutaire et honorable ; que, grace à Dieux, les hereticques et rebelles estoient reserrez, la

rebels were in prison, the conspiracy detected
and their guilt proved, and that in a short time
its actors would meet with an exemplary punishment; that for the future the Queen would take
such good order in her affairs as to give her the
strong hand and full command over her subjects;
that they had not the slightest doubt about his
Highness passing into this country in perfect safety,
provided he took precautions against the force
which the French prepared at sea to intercept and
give him battle, of which they told us they were
well advertised; that the Sieur D'Egmont was most
welcome, and that they had despatched the Earl of
Pembroke and the Admiral to salute him on the
part of the Queen; and that, as soon as it pleased
him to have audience, they were ready to hear him
and to communicate upon the rest." * * * *

It would be tedious to give the dry deliberations
on the articles of the marriage; but the passage in

---

conjoure decouverte et preuvée, et dont l'on feroit chastoy ex-
emplaire et en brief temps; que, pour l'advenir, la dite dame
donneroit si bon ordre à ses affaires que la main forte luy de-
meurera, et en toute auctorité pourra commander à ses subjectz; qu'ilz ne doubtent aucunement que son Altese puisse
passer seurement en ce royaulme, pourveu qu'il se donne garde
de l'armee des François qu'ilz preparent en mer, comme ilz di-
soient, estre advertys, pour le rencontrer et combattre : que le
dit Sʳ D'Egmont estoit le bien venu, et avoient envoyé devers
luy les Conte de Pembroch et Admiral pour le saluer de la part
de la dite dame; que, quant il lui plaira avoir audience, ilz
seroient pretz pour l'ouyr, et communicquer sur ce que reste.
* * * *

which Mary replies to Renard's remarks on the guilt of Courtenay and Elizabeth is well worth inserting.

" To this the Queen, after the usual words of courtesy, replied that she and her Council were labouring as much as possible to discover the truth as to the practices of Courtenay and Elizabeth; that it was certain Courtenay was convicted by many of the other prisoners of knowing, consenting, and assisting in the plot; that he was in possession of a cipher cut upon a guitar, by means of which he corresponded with Peter Carew; that the enterprise was in his favour; that he had intrigued with the French King; that he had been ready to fly into France if Wyatt had not prevented him; that Carew forwarded the marriage of him and Elizabeth; and that he [Courtenay] found himself most gravely implicated and guilty. Yet as the law of

---

" A ce la dite dame, apres les remerciations ordinaires, repondit qu'elle et son Conseil traveillent et diligentement tout le possible pour tirer la verité des practiques de Cortenay et de la dite Elisabeth; qu'il estoit certain le dit Cortenay estoit convaincu par plusieurs autres prisonniers qu'il estoit participant, saichant, et consentant de la dit conjure, qu'il avoit une ziffre avec Pierre Caro taillé sur une guitaire, que l'emprinse estoit en sa faveur, qu'il tenoit practique avec le Roy de France, qu'il avoit esté pret pour aller en France, mais que Wyat l'avoit diverty et que Caro * brassoit le mariage de luy et de la dite Elisabeth, et qu'il se trouvoit grandement chargé et culpable; mais que comme la loy establye par le Parlement d'Angleterre

---

* i. e. Carew.

England does not affix a capital penalty to those who have simply consented to treason, if there be no proof of an overt act, but only condemns them to perpetual imprisonment and the confiscation of their property, the Council was exerting itself to find proof of some overt act, so as to bring him in for the punishment which he deserves. And lastly she added, that for this end no exertions of hers should be wanting, since he had shown so little regard either to her crown or to her life.

"As for Elizabeth, she observed that her examination by the Chancellor, Arundel, Petre, and Paget would take place that day, and that they would be guided by her answers in what was best to be done; that they had already found by the confession of the son of the Lord Privy Seal, who was arrested in his father's house, that this young man had received letters from Wyatt during the time of his rebellion, which were addressed to Elizabeth,

---

ne perscryvoit peyne de mort contre ceulx qui ont consentu en trahison s'il n'y a heu demonstration du fait, ains seulement ordonne qu'ilz seront condamnez à prison perpetuelle et confiscation de tous leurs biens, le Conseil estoit apres pour entendre ce que l'on pourroit descouvrir des actes qu'il pourroit avoir fait, pour parvenir à la peyne qu'il merite ; qu'elle y tiendra la main, puisque il n'a eu respect à sa vie et couronne.

" Que, quant à la dite Elisabeth, elle seroist interroguée le mesme jour par le Chancelier, Arondel, Petre, et Paget, pour, selon les responses, advizer ce que l'on en fera ; et que l'on trouvoist par la confession du filz de Privesel, qu'est arresté en la maison de son pere, qu'il a receu lettres de Wyat pendant la rebellion addressans à la dite Elizabeth, et qu'il luy a fait

and had delivered these letters to her ; and, in short, that her conduct had been such as they had always found it and judged of it.   With regard to the other prisoners, they will be condemned and executed before our departure from this place.   She added, that she would never cease to demand the enforcement of the laws, which would be a terror to others who were disposed to malign her : it was her hope, she said, to set out soon for Windsor for the holidays, and then to proceed to Oxford to hold her parliament ; but, before the parliament, she would take care to make strict order and provision for the safety of the Tower.   Regarding the City, she had already communicated with the Lord Mayor.

\*        \*        \*        \*        \*

" As to the marriage, besides all the promises she had already made to the Lieutenant Damont, her Majesty observed, that every thing should be done to ensure it ; that all precautions should be taken for

---

delivrer ; et qu'elle est telle qu'elle l'a toujours trouvée et jugée. Et que, quant aux autres prisonniers, ils seront condemnez et executez avant que partir de ce lieu, et ne cessera de solliciter l'exploict de justice pour terrer autres qui auroient volunté de maligner ; qu'elle espere de partir de brief, pour aller à Windsor faire ses festes, et dois la à Opford pour tenir le parlement ; que avant son parlement elle laissera bon ordre et provision pour la garde de la Tour de Londres.   Et pour la ville, qu'elle a deja communiqué avec le Maire.   \*    \*    \*    \*

" Que, quant au mariage, encore qu'elle ayt ja promis devant le Sacrement au Lieutenant Damont, elle fera tout ce que sera requis pour l'asseurance d'icelluy ; qu'elle fera tout le possible

\*        \*        \*        \*        \*

the security of his Highness' person ; and she hoped that, by God's assistance and her Council's, all might be so provided that he should be most welcome : she referred us for further details to her Council, employing such kind and gracious words that it would be injustice to ask for any other proof of her great affection to your Majesty and his Highness. From this we passed with her Majesty to the discussion of the entertainment to be given to such as she deemed most worthy of trust : observing, [I stated] that your Majesty, to gain them to his Highness, had charged us to use some liberality towards such as she thought best ; I took, moreover, her judgment as to those who should be pensioned, and of such as she and the Council might select for the household and service of his Highness.

" Mary answered that your Majesty did far

---

pour asseurer la personne de son Altese, qu'elle espere avec l'ayde de Dieu et de son Conseil y pourveior de sorte qu'il sera le tres bien venu, selon que nous le pourrions plus amplement entendre de son Conseil ; et usa de telz propos, si gracieux et constans, que si l'on requeroit autre tesmoignage de sa grande affection et amitié envers vostre Majesté et son Altese l'on auroit tort. Et passames avec elle plusieurs propoz de l'entretient qu'elle pourroit faire à ceulx qui luy semble plus confidens et qu'ilz ont pouvoir et credit pour les gaigner, que vostre Majesté de sa part nous avoit echargé user de quelque liberalité envers ceulx qui luy sembleroit convenir, pour les attirer à la devotion de son Altese par son advis, et aussi à cuy l'on pourroit donner quelque pension, outre ceulx qui pourrount par elle et son Conseil estre choissy pour la maison et service de son Altese, selon que le traicté de mariage le porte.

" Surquoy elle nous a dit que vostre Majesté faisoit trop

more for her, her kingdom and her subjects, than
they deserved; nevertheless your Majesty's proposals, she said, were well judged, and should be communicated to her Council for their advice, and the
decision of what officers should be chosen.

" On Monday we visited the Chancellor, Arundel, the Comptroller, Pembroke, Privy Seal,
Paget, and the Admiral.    To each, separately,
we gave your Majesty's letters, and informed
them of your intentions according to our instructions; Count Egmont, in particular, spoke
to the Admiral as a person  whose services it
would be proper to secure for the present and the
future.    He even pressed him to take a pension
from his Highness, and to make himself useful in
his service, assuring him of its grateful acceptance:
this the Admiral accepted, with consent of the
Queen.    *        *        *

" Paget, having consulted with his mistress on the

---

plus pour elle, pour le royaulme et ses subjectz, qu'ilz ne meritoient; neanmoins que l'opinion de vostre Majesté estoit bonne,
et qu'elle communiqueroit à d'aucuns de son Conseil pour y adviser, et sur les officiers qui se sont apropos.

" Le Lundy nous fumes devers le Chancellier, Arondel,
Comptrolleur, Pembroch, Privesel, Paget et Admiral, auquel separement nous delivrames les lettres de vostre Majesté, et leurs
fismes entendre son intention selon l'instruction ; et plus particulierement le dit Sieur D'Egmont parla au dit Admiral pour
estre personnaige qu'il convient entretenir pour le present et
advenir, et mesme le pria accepter pension de son Alteze, et
s'accomoder à son service, l'asseurant de reconnoissance, ce qu'il
a accepté par le consentement de la dite dame. *    *    *

above points, sent us the enclosed note, with the names of such as should have pensions and chains. Without, however, at once embracing his opinion, we, to give satisfaction to the other Councillors, have communicated with the Chancellor and Comptroller, who have also furnished us with a list of names, adding to them the proper sums; according to which, the Lieutenant Damont has paid out four thousand crowns for chains, and the other thousand to be defrayed in money, as may be found best; and the Councillors have given us so favourable an answer, that, if the event corresponds to their speeches, we have little doubt that his Highness may come into the kingdom with security.

" On Sunday, the Chancellor, Arundel, the Admiral, Paget, Petre, and the Comptroller came to us at our lodging. They told us, that having well

---

" Paget, ayant communiqué à la dite dame sur ce que dessus, nous envoya le billet cy-joinct, où sont nommez ceulx à qui l'on pourroit donner quelque pension, et eslargir quelques chaines; et sans nous arrester à l'advis du dit Paget, pour donner satisfaction aux aultres, nous en avons communiqué avec le Chancellier et Comptrolleur qu'ilz nous ont aussi donnez par escript les noms d'iceulx et adjousté les sommes; suyvant quoy, le dit Lieutenant a fait fondre quatre mil escuz pour chainés, et les autres mil se repartiront en argent, comme l'on trouvera mieulx convenir; et nous ont fait les conseillers si bonne responce, que, si l'effect s'ensuyt conforme aux parolles, nous ne doubtons que la seurté sera pour l'avenue de son Altese en ce royaulme.

" Le jour de Dimanche les dits Chancellier, Arondel, Admiral, Paget, Petre, et Comptrolleur nous vinrent trouver en nostre logis, et nous dirent avoir pesé ce que nous leurs avons dit

weighed all that had been said the day before, as to
his Highness' safety, and after fully ascertaining the
intentions and wishes of each and all of them, they
could see no difficulty as to his Highness' coming ;
they hoped to take such order, that he would be as
safe as in his own land ; twenty ships should be com-
missioned, to be ready by the end of April ; five
were already at sea, and in four or five days seven
or eight others would be equipped. Such as were
ready, they said, would serve for the passage of
the Lord Privy Seal, Mason, and the other ambassadors into Spain. *  *  And for the affairs of the
realm, they were in good case, since it had pleased
God to lay open in a miraculous manner the practices of the unhappy rebels. *   *   *

" On the following Tuesday at three o'clock, the
Earl of Pembroke and the Admiral came to bring

---

le jour precedent de la seurté de la personne de son Altese, et
que apres avoir entendu et coigneu l'intention et volunté d'ung
chacun d'eulx, ilz ne trouvoient difficulté quelconque sur la venue de son Altese, et qu'ilz esperoient y donner tel ordre qu'il
seroit aussi seur qu'en ses propres pays, comme il estoit requis
pour le bien et reputation de toutes parties ; qu'ilz faisoient ar-
mer vingt navires que pourroient estre prestes pour la fin d'Avril ; qu'ilz en avoient cinq de prestes, et devant quatre ou cinq
jours ilz en auroient sept ou huict autres equippez. Que celles
qui sont equippez serviront pour la conduyte des Sieurs Privesel, Masson, et ceulx qui seront envoyez pour ambassadeurs en
Espaigne ; * * que les affaires de royaume sont en bons termes
puis qu'il a pleu à Dieu miraculeusement descouvrir les practiques des malheureux rebelles. *  *  *

" Le Mardy suyvant, à trois heures apres midy, les Sieurs
Conte de Pembroch et Admiral nous vindrent querir pour nous

us to the Queen and her Council; here, in a chamber where was the blessed Host, the ratifications of
her Majesty and his Highness were delivered, and
the oaths taken by both the one party and the
other: but, before this, the Queen fell on her knees,
and called God to witness that this marriage was
not in her the result of any carnal affection; that it
did not originate in ambition, or any motive except
the good of her kingdom, and the repose and tranquillity of her subjects; that, in truth, her single
intention in all she did was to prove faithful to the
marriage and oath which she had already made to
the crown; expressing this with so much grace,
that those who stood round were in tears.　＊　　　＊
After this, her Majesty, as she had already done,
dropped upon her knees, and requested us to join
our prayers with hers, that God would be pleased to
give her his grace to fulfil the treaty to which she

conduyre devers la dite dame et son Conseil. Et en une
chambre, où estoit le Sainct Sacrement, les ratifications de
la dite dame et de son Altese se delivrarent, et furent preste
les serment requis d'une part et d'autre; mais, avant ce, la
dite dame se met à genoux, et dit qu'elle appelloit Dieu à
tesmoing si le mariage par elle consentu a esté pour affection
charnelle, pour cupidité ou autre respect, sinon pour l'honneur,
bien, et proffit du royaulme, repos et tranquillité des subjetz, et
si elle a eu autre intention sinon de garder le mariage et serment qu'elle a fait à la Couronne; disant ce que dessus avec
telle grace que les larmes estoient aux yeux des assistans.
＊　＊　＊　＊　Puis la dite dame se mit autrefois à deux genoux
et dit aux assistans qu'ils voulissent prier Dieu avec elle qu'il
luy plaise luy donner sa grace d'accomplir le traité juré par
elle, et fortuner le dit mariage: oultre ce, le dit Sr d'Egmont luy

had sworn, and that He would make the marriage fortunate. Upon which, the Count Egmont presented to her the ring which your Majesty has sent, and which she showed to all the company, (and assuredly, Sire, the jewel is a precious one, and well worth looking at.) After this we took our leave, first enquiring whether her Majesty had any commands for his Highness; to whom she begged to send her most affectionate regards, begging us to assure him that for her part, as long as she lived, she would by all dutiful obedience endeavour to vie with him in mutual love and good offices: she added, that, as his Highness had not yet written to her, she deferred writing to him till he began the correspondence."

The same letter informs us that the Venetian ambassador was aware of the intended conspiracy of Wyatt, and knew the names of the conspirators " two months before it broke out." It appears also, by the following passage, that the ladies of the bedchamber, important personages when a marriage is in the wind, were not forgotten. " Your Majesty understands," says Renard, " that, at the

---

presenta la bague que vostre Majesté luy a envoyé, qu'elle monstra à toute la compagnie; et certes, Sire, la piece est telle qu'il merite estre veue. Et print congé, la requerant si elle vouloit commander aucune chose devers son Alteze; la quelle luy enjoignit de faire ses tres affectueuses recommendations à sa bonne grace, et luy dire que de sa part elle luy correspondra tant qu'elle vivra en tous offices deuz; et que, comme son Alteze ne luy a encores escript, elle differoit luy escripre jusques à ce qu'il eust commencé.   *      *      *      *

coming of his Highness, some little presents of
rings, or such like small gear, must be made to the
Queen's ladies : three are to be noted as chief in her
Majesty's confidence, and who have always spoken
a good word for the marriage,—Mistresses Cla-
rence, Shirley, and Russell."

In the following sentence of the same letter, the
state of the country, and the character of the English people at this period, are touched with a keen
though too severe a pencil.

" From time to time the ambassador will conduct
his researches as carefully and minute¹y as possible,
with an eye to discover the state of public feeling,
and to ascertain what new practices or conspiracies
are in hand, that your Majesty may be informed of
them ; it being not only difficult, but well nigh impossible, to foresee what the English may do, whose
natural character is inconstant, faithless, and treasonable ; a character which they have always exhibited, and which the whole course of their actions
and of their history has proved to be just.   *   *
To-morrow, Count Egmont sets out on his voyage
to Spain.   *   *   *   Cardinal Pole has replied to
the Queen's letters, and has sent her a copy of the
commission, by which she is authorised to proceed
to choose the twelve bishops to supply the vacant
sees.   *   *   *   London, 8th March 1553.

"  LAMORAL D'EGMONT.       S. RENARD."


The Spanish ambassador had addressed a letter
to the Emperor on the 1st of March, another on the

9th of the same month; the first written during the
examinations of the prisoners suspected of a concur-
rence with Wyatt's rebellion; the second, on the
very day on which Lord Thomas Grey, the brother
of the Duke of Suffolk, received sentence of death.
He observes, in his letter of the 1st of March, that
Croff, (he means Sir James Croft,) who was accused as an accessary with Courtenay and Elizabeth to the conspiracy of Wyatt, had " confessed
the truth, written his deposition, and admitted in
plain terms the intrigues of the French ambassador
with the heretics and rebels." *  He then alludes to
the declaration of William Thomas, regarding the
plot to assassinate the Queen, for which he suffered.   Thomas was Clerk to the Council under Somerset's Protectorate, and is the same person whom
we meet with in Sir Henry Ellis' Letters in the
character of a kind of political tutor to Edward
the Sixth†.  Renard also observes, " that William
Courtenay, the cousin of the Earl of Devonshire,
who had fled to France, was to receive pardon,
on condition of his revealing the particulars of
the conspiracy, and acting as a spy upon the
French government."   In his letter of the 9th,
the following passage is curious : " Some three
hundred children assembled in a meadow, and
divided into two bands to play at the game of

* The only deposition of Croft's which I have found, makes
no such admissions.

† Lingard, vol. vii. p. 165. Fourth edition.—Ellis' Letters,
Second Series, vol. ii. p. 187.

the Queen against Wyatt, in which several have
been wounded on both sides. To-day they have
taken the Bishops of Canterbury, Salisbury, and
Worcester to Oxford, to hear what reasons they
have to give for their obstinacy in religion; and, if
they do not recant, to burn them in the said place.
An alderman of London has made so able, vehe-
ment, and convincing a speech in the Guildhall,
persuading men to obedience to God, to religion,
to the Queen, and to justice, that several persons
who had strayed from the right way have been recovered from their errors and heresies." In his allusion to the childrens' games, Renard has deli-
cately omitted the catastrophe which befel one of
the little fellows who acted the part of Philip. We
learn from Noailles, that the Prince of Spain
was nearly hanged outright by his companions,
being cut down only in time to save his life. Mary
very properly had the urchins whipped and shut
up; but the French ambassador ridiculously adds,
that he was told the Queen wished to sacrifice one
of them for the people.*

In a later despatch from Renard to the Emperor,
written on the 24th of March, the ambassador en-
closes the following letter, which he had addressed
to the Prince of Spain. The idea that the English
are particularly turbulent *in the summer*, that " les
humeurs des Anglois boulissent plus en l'esté,"
alludes, perhaps, to the May-day riots of the London apprentices.

* Noailles, vol. iii. p. 130.

## SIMON RENARD TO PHILIP PRINCE OF SPAIN.
### 13th March 1553-4.

" MONSEIGNEUR. — The Earls of Bedford and Viscount Fealter [Fitz-Water] are about to be despatched to your Highness by the Queen of England, that they may in person receive ratification of the treaties and promises of marriage *per verba de præsenti;* but their principal charge is to conduct your Highness into this kingdom, and to give instructions and advice upon the points necessary to be known. With the same noblemen, the Earls of Dorset, [Garet,] the Lords Howard, Kempt, Schelt, Dudley, Drury, and several other noblemen,* pass into Spain by the order of the Queen; to whom your Highness will be pleased to give all proper entertainment, as well to gain

---

## SIMON RENARD TO PHILIP.
*Transcript from Orig. at Brussells.*    13th March 1553-4.

" MONSEIGNEUR.—Les Conte de Bedfort et Visconte Fealter s'envoient devers vostre Altese par la Royne d'Angleterre pour prandre ratifications personelles des traictez et promesses de marriage faictes par motz de present, et principalement pour conduire et amener vostre Alteze en ce royaulme, et l'instruire et pre-adviser de ce qu'est necessaire sçavoir ; avec lesquelz les Sieurs Contes d'Orceste, Garet, les Sieurs Havard, Kempt, Schelt, Dudely, Druty, et plusieurs aultres gentilhommes passent en Espaigne par le conger de la dite dame ; auquelx il plaira à vostre Alteze commander faire le traictement qui semblera convenir, tant pour les attirer à sa devotion, que pour par

---

* The ambassador mispells his names so, that sometimes I cannot make them out.

their minds to your devotion, as to cause them to give to others in this country a favourable account of the treatment which they have received. Specially, the above-mentioned Schelt who takes his journey with them as their ' interpreter,' being the only one amongst them who can speak Spanish. Besides this, Sir, I await the decision of his Majesty as to the pensions of which I have written; the object of which is to gain the hearts of the leading men here, and to have security for the safety of your Highness in your entry into this realm, which is a hazardous matter, as the hearts of the people here are inconstant, double, and very variable, of which we had ample proof in the last rebellion.

" Some are of opinion that there will be more security in your Highness passing into Flanders previous to your coming here, that there your train may be formed; and that you should not come before the month of September next, because the

---

eulx faire relation aulx aultres du pay du dit traictement; et specialment le dit Schelt va avec eulx pour estre truchement, et estre seul entre eulx qui saiche parler Espaignol. — Au surplus, Monseigneur, j'attend la resolution de sa Majesté sur les pensions dont je luy ay escript pour gaigner les coeurs des principaulx; pour asseurer son entré en ce royaulme, qu'est chose fort hazardeuse, pour estre ceulx de pardeça inconstans, doubles de pensée, et fort variables, dont le tesmoignaige s'est demonstré en la derniere rebellion. Plusieurs sont d'advis que seroit plus seur vostre Alteze passa en Flandres premier que venir pardeça, pour illic former son trahin, et ne passer en ce royaulme avant le mois de Septembre prouchain,

bad humours of the English, boil up more fiercely
in the summer, than at any other time.    Nevertheless, the Queen and her Council inform me
there is no danger, since all those who might
be willing to rebel are prisoners, and already some
of them punished; since Courtenay and Elizabeth, who would be likely to be the principal
promoters of the rising, are also prisoners, and an
inquiry instituted against them, so that, if they deserve it, they are to be corrected and chastised.
They add, that the whole force of the kingdom is in
the Queen's hands; that in the parliament, which is
fixed for the month of April next, more certain re-
solutions will be brought forward, and the articles
of the marriage treaty ratified; that, having once
gained the principals by pensions and gifts, we
need have no fear of the people.    Consequently,
their opinion is, that there is no danger in your

---

pour ce que ordinairement les humeurs des Anglois boulissent
plus en l'esté que en aultre temps.    Neanmoins la dite dame et
son Conseil m'asseurent que n'y a danger, pour ce que ceulx
quilz pouvoient rebeller sont prisonniers, et ja aulcuns d'eulx
puniz; que Cortenay et Madame Elisabeth, qui pouvoient estre
promoteurs et chiefz, sont ausi arrestez, et le proces d'iceulx se
faict, pour, s'ilz ont meritez, les corriger et chastier; que la
force demeure es mains de la dite dame; que par le parlement
assigné au mois d'Avril prouchain l'on y prandra resolution plus
certain, et fera l'on appreuver les articles du traicté par icelluy; que, gaignant et s'asseurant des principaulx par pensions
et liberalitez, l'on n'aura occasion de craindre le peuple; et
consequement ils sont d'adviz qu'il n'y aura danger en sa ve-

Highness coming; that you will be received with perfect safety; that all that is necessary will be for the Spaniards in your Highness' train to accommodate themselves to the manners of the English, and be modest; trusting that your Highness will conciliate them by your accustomed courtesy. But, Sir, as this 'Assurance' is so important, so necessary, and of such high regard, I dare not be arbiter upon these opinions, till I see what resolution is adopted in the proceedings against Elizabeth and Courtenay, and till the parliament is closed; especially since I am informed that the King of France practises all he can to raise new tumults by means of the heretics, and to set on foot enterprises against this kingdom, in which he spares neither money nor pains."     *     *     *

---

nue, et qu'elle sera receue seurement, et que seullement sera requis que les Espaignolz qui suyvront vostre Alteze comportent les façons de faire des Angloys, et soient modestes, confians que vostre Alteze les aicarassera† par son humanité costumiere.    Mais, Monseigneur, comme ceste asseurance est tant importante, tant necessaire, et de tel respect, je n'oserois estre arbitre entre ses opinions jusques à ce que je voie quelle resolution l'on prandra sur le proces de Cortenay et Elisabeth, et que le parlement soit achevé, signamment pour ce que je sceit [sais] le Roy de France practique tout ce qu'il peult tenter nouveau tumulte par les heretiques, et pour faire emprinses contre ce royaulme, en quoy il n'epargne argent et diligence."    *     *

---

† So in the original.   I have considered it an error for agaçera.

## SIMON RENARD TO THE EMPEROR.

### 14th March 1553-4.

" SIRE.—When I consider the state of things here, the condition of the Queen and this kingdom, the confusions in religion, the different parties amongst the Privy Councillors, the intestine hatred between the nobility and the people, the character of the English,—who are given so much to change, treason, and infidelity,—the natural enmity they bear to strangers, and all that from one time to another they have done against them,—which, too, is increased, especially against Spaniards, by the French intrigues and the evil reports spread by your Majesty's own subjects; and when, on the other side, I call to mind of what consequence it is that his Highness should not be thrown into any peril, on whose safety so many kingdoms, and countries, and

## SIMON RENARD TO THE EMPEROR.

*Transcript from Orig. at Brussells.* 14th March 1553-4.

" SIRE.—Quant je considere l'estat des affaires de la Royne et de ce royaulme, la confusion qu'est en la religion, la partialité qu'est entre les propres conseillers de la dite dame, la hayne intestine qu'est entre la noblesse et le peuple, le naturel des Anglois qu'est tant adonné à la mutacion, trahison, et infidelité, l'inimitié naturelle qu'ilz portent aux etrangiers, et ce que de temps à autre ilz ont fait contre eulx, qu'est accreue contre les Espaignolz par les persuasions Françoises, et malvaise relation que les propres subjetz de vostre Majesté en ont fait ; et, d'autre part, quant je considere combien il emporte que son Altese ne tumbe en danger ou hazard de sa personne, en la-

so many people depend and are supported; and moreover, when I look to the difficulty there is to get any pledges from the English on which we may rely;—having all this before me, I feel the burden of this charge so heavy, its importance so great, and my mind so troubled, that I know not in what way to satisfy or be conformable to the commands your Majesty has sent me by your last letters, of the 7th of this month.

"The reason is, that I feel it would be rash and perilous to give a perfect assurance; and yet things are too far past now to draw back or retard the marriage, or to put them in doubt or consultation again with your Majesty. It seems to me more proper that I should inform your Majesty that, since the victory which God has been pleased to give this Queen over her enemies, they have shown a negligence more than suspicious in not pressing

---

plus negligemment et suspectement à la fulmination du proces quelle reposent et s'appuyent tant de royaulmes, pays, et subjectz; et la difficulté qu'il a d'entrer en caution envers le peuple Anglois; je sentz le fardeau de ceste charge si pesant, de telle importance et consequence, et mon esprit si troublé, que je ne sçay par quel moyen je puisse correspondre ny satisfaire à ce que vostre Majesté me commande par ses lettres dernieres du vii$^e$ de ce mois. Pour ce que d'asseurer il seroit trop temeraire et perilleux de reculer et retarder le mariage, les choses sont trop avant de les mectre en doubte et consultation à vostre Majesté. Il me semble plus convenable à luy presenter, que puis la victoire qu'il a pleu à Dieu donner à la dite dame contre ses rebelles, l'on a procedé

forward the trial of Courtenay and Madame Elizabeth.   This delay, as it appears to me, is merely to
see what things may turn out which may give an
opportunity of saving them; and, even granting
that this were against the wishes of the Queen,
still she could not remedy it, because the Chancellor manages the whole matter, and has put Southwell into the Tower, as the examiner and the
guard over Elizabeth, a man who has always been
the principal promoter of the marriage of Courtenay with this lady,—not to mention that he is
one of the most ignorant persons in the kingdom,
the most venal and the most prejudiced; with
him is joined the Secretary Bourne, who is also
attached to the faction of Courtenay.   By this
means he is advised of all that is done or deposed
against him; and already they have allowed him
to be removed from his first prison to place him in
a larger room, without any order from the Council.

---

de Cortenay et de Madame Elizabeth que je n'eusse pensé,
tellement qu'il semble que l'on delaye tout apropos pour
attendre occasion pour les saulfver ; et, jaçoit que ce soit contre la volunté de la dite dame si est ce, elle n'y peult remedier
pour ce que le Chancellier manye le tout, qui a mis en la Tour,
pour examinateur et garde, Sudvel, qui a esté toujours le principal promoteur du mariage de Cortenay avec la dite dame,
qui est ung des plus ignorans du royaulme, le plus corruptible
et plus appassionné, et avec luy le Secretaire Bourgne, qui est
aussi de la partie du dit Cortenay ; que tout ce que se fait et
depose contre luy, il en est adverty, et l'avoit l'on eslargy de
la prison premiere pour le mectre plus au large, sans ordon-
nance de Conseil.

" Besides this, the Chancellor, without consulting the other Councillors, (except one or two,) has
fixed the Parliament to be held at Oxford,—actuated by a wish to impoverish the Londoners, and
without any consideration whether the measure is
expedient or not.   In addition to all this, he had
promised the Queen that all the criminal prosecutions should have been finished eight days ago, and
the third was not completed till the day was fixed
for the Queen's departure to Windsor, the 12th of
this month ; and still he persists that her Majesty
shall go to Windsor, altho' these prosecutions are
still unconcluded."

It appears from this, and on the best evidence,
that Elizabeth, as far as we have yet seen, owed
her safety, and the caution and delay with which
the case of her accession to Wyatt's plot was in-
vestigated, to Bishop Gardiner, a prelate who has
commonly been represented as her greatest enemy.
The whole letter shows that Gardiner was

---

" Item, le Chancelier sans communication d'autres conseillers, sinon d'un ou deux, assigna le parlement à Oxfort, soubz
pretexte que l'on appovriroit ceulx de Londres par l'absence de
la Court, procedant en ce principalement sans considerer s'il
estoit expedient ou non.   Item, il avoit promis à la dite dame
que tous les proces criminels seroient achevez il y a passé viii.
jours, et le tiers n'est fait jusques à avoir prins jour pour le
partement de la dite dame pour Windsor, au xii^e de ce mois ;
et persistoit toujours que la dite dame alloit au Winsor, jaçoit
les proces soient imparfaits."

held in great suspicion by the Emperor and his
friends, as being favourable to Elizabeth and
against the Spanish match.  It concludes by the
following allusion to the singular Protestant impos-
ture, " The voice in the wall," of which an account
has been given by Strype. *

" Whilst closing these letters, I have heard that
the heretics here have, for the purpose of raising a
mutiny amongst the people, placed a man and
woman in one of the houses in London, bidding
them give out that they heard a voice in a wall,
which they knew was the voice of an angel.
When they said to it, ' God save Queen Mary!' it
answered nothing.  When they said ' God save the
Lady Elizabeth!' it replied, ' So be it.'  If they
asked it ' What is the mass ?' it replied ' Idolatry.'
And such was the effect of this trick, that, at eleven
o'clock in the morning, more than seventeen thousand people were collected round the house.  The

" Achevant les presentes, j'ay sceu comme les heretiques
de ce lieu ont apposté en une maison de Londres une femme
et un homme pour mutiner le peuple, leur aiant fait dire que
l'on ouioit une voix contre une paroy, qu'estoit voix angelique ;
et que quand on luy disoit ' Dieu garde et saulve la Royne
Marie!' l'autre ne repondoit ; et que quand il disoit ' Dieu garde
Madame Elisabeth !' l'autre respondoit ' Ainsi soit il.'  Puis
luy interroguoit ' Que c'estoit de la messe ?' l'autre respondoit
que c'estoit idolatrie ; et sur cet invention ce sont assemblez

* Strype, Memor. vol. iii. pt. 1, p. 153.

Council sent thither the Admiral and Paget with the Captain of the Guard, and they have seized the man and woman that they may find out the author of the trick, which every one (even Elizabeth herself, who is stayed at court,) believes to have been got up in favour of the prisoners, with the hope of exciting the people against the Queen, raising the heretics, and troubling the kingdom."

In Renard's letter of the 22nd March 1553-4, the difficulties of Mary's situation, and the divisions in the Council on the subject of the Lady Elizabeth's accession to the conspiracy of Wyatt, are strikingly described. The famous letter written by the royal captive to Mary, at this most trying crisis, will be in the recollection of the reader.*

---

plus de 17ᵐ hommes alentour de la maison à unze heures du matin, où le Conseil a envoyé l'Amiral et Paget avec le Capitaine de la Garde, et a l'on prins l'homme et la femme, pour entendre d'où venoit ceste invention, que chacun juge avoir esté aposté pour favoriser les prisonniers, mesme la dite Elisabeth qu'est arrestée à la cour, eslever le peuple contre la Royne, conciter les heretiques, et troubler le royaume.

"14 Mars 1553."                    "SIMON RENARD."

* Ellis's Letters, vol. ii. Second Series, p. 254.

" It was only," says he, " because no one could be found upon whom to impose the task of guarding the Lady Elizabeth, that they resolved she should be sent to the Tower on Saturday last, by the Thames, and not through the streets. This, however, did not take place on that day ; and the reason was, that, at the hour when the tide served, she besought an interview with the Queen, affirming that this [her being sent to the Tower] was not done with her knowledge, but solely by the anger of the Chancellor. If she was denied to see the Queen, she wished to be permitted to write a letter to her : this was allowed ; and when she was writing, the hour of the tide, which alone would have served for her passage below the bridge, elapsed, and they were obliged to wait till yesterday.

" The Queen was much incensed with her

### SIMON RENARD TO THE EMPEROR.

*Trans. from Orig.   Brussels.   22nd March 1553.*

" Et seulement pour ce que personne ne voulut prendre charge de la garde de la dite Elisabeth, l'on resolut qu'elle seroit mesnée en la Tour Samedy dernier, par la Thamise, non par la rue ; que ne fut le mesme jour, pour ce que, à l'heure de le marée, elle pria pouvoir parler à la dite dame, disant que ce n'estoit de son sceu, que c'estoit seulement par la passion du Chancelier ; ou, si elle ne pouvoit parler, qu'elle peust escripre une lettre à la dite dame, que luy fut permis ; et, pendant qu'elleescrivoit, l'heure de la marée, et passage par dessoubz le pont de Londres quant la mere est haulte, se passa, et fut l'on contraint attendre au lendemain. Dont la dite dame fut fort alterée contre son Conseil, et leur dit plainement qu'ilz ne

Council for this, and told them plainly that they were not travelling on the right path; that they dared not have done such a thing in her father's lifetime, and she wished he were alive again were it but for a month. Since this occurred, no meeting of the Council has been held; nor does the Chancellor show any inclination to be there, although he has been expressly desired to attend. * * *

" On Sunday last the Councillors (moved by the premeditated intrigues of the heretics) came to a resolution that, as it was a day of devotion, the Queen should be entreated to exercise clemency, and not to shed the noble blood of England; that already the justice inflicted on the rebels amounted to cruelty; that the people ought to be forgiven; and that she ought not to follow the opinion of bloody men, meaning the Chancellor. On the instant they determined to set off to find her Majesty

---

suyvoient le bon chemin, qu'ilz n'ussent osoient faire telle chose de vivant de son pere, qu'elle desiroit il fut vivant pour ung mois; et des lors l'on n'a tenu forme de Conseil, ny le Chancellier s'y est voulu trouver, sinon qu'il soit esté mandé expressement. L'autre et seconde acte est que Dimanche dernier les dit . . . . du Conseil en absence du dit Chancellier, par pratique et meme deliberée les [des] dits heretiques, proposarent entre ceulx que, comme le jour estoit de devotion, il falloit inciter la dite dame à clemence pour non repandre le sang noble d'Angleterre; que ja l'on avoit fait cruel justice de rebelles; qu'il convenoit pardonner à la multitude, et non suyvre l'opinion des sanguinaires, entendant le Chancelier; et en cet instant conclurent qu'ils iroient trouver la dite dame pour luy remonstrer ce que dessus, et feirent que Paget, qu'est bandé

and remonstrate on this subject; and they employed Paget, who is banded with them (as much I believe from hatred to the Chancellor as for his religious opinions, which are suspected to be heretical,)
to carry the request to the Queen.    From this, neither Petre nor the Comptroller † dared to dissent.
They found the Queen in her oratory after vespers;
and not only took her by surprise, having given
her no warning, but talked in such a way, that,
against her wishes and goodwill, she pardoned six
gentlemen who had been sent to Kent for execution, and who had sided with Wyatt in his rebellion.
The worst is, that Paget told the Queen that they
had already squandered the blood of the house of
Suffolk, that he might work on her fears, and induce
her to be merciful to the brothers of the Duke, who
had been condemned."

In the same letter, Paget's jealousy of Gardiner
is strongly marked by an expression of his, which
the Spanish ambassador reports.

---

avec ceulx, tant pour la malveillance qu'il porte au dit Chancellier, que pour religion dont l'on le suspecte, porteroit le propos, à quoy ne osarent dissentir Petre ny le Controller ; qui sy
trouvarent et surprindrent la dite dame en son oratoire apres le
vespres sans la pre-advertir, et usarent de telz propoz, que,
contre son vouloir et bon gre, elle pardonna à six gentilshommes
que l'on avoit envoyé à Kempt [Kent] pour les executer,
et qu'avoient accompagné Houjet en la dit rebellion.   Le pir
fut que le dit Paget dit que l'on avoit espanché le sang de la
maison de Suffocq, pour, par craint, preparer la dite dame à
clemence envers ses freres qui sont condemnez." * * *

---

† Sir Robert Rochester.

" He [Paget] said that the nobility were not anxious again to have the Duke of Northumberland over them ; meaning, by this, the Chancellor." The tyranny of Northumberland over the Council was proverbial.

We have still to listen to what Mons. Renard calls his third act. The reader will smile at the ambassador presenting Thucydides to the Queen as the highest authority on the punishment of treason. He proceeds thus :

" We may now give the third act. On last Wednesday, the Chancellor intending to be at the Council for the purpose of communicating on the subjects to be brought before parliament, Pembroke and Paget, without leave, retired to their houses, because, as we presume, they would not consent to the points which touched upon religion, and afterwards contradict the Chancellor's intentions. Things are in such disorder that one knows not who is well-disposed or ill-disposed, con-

---

" Il [Paget] dit que la noblesse ne vouloit plus avoir le Duc de Northamberlant, entendant le Chancellier.

\*　　　\*　　　\*

" L'on pourroit adjouster pour le iiie acte, que Mercredy dernier le Chancellier se doigeant trouver au Conseil pour communiquer les poinctz que l'on pourra traicter au parlement, les dits Pembroch et Paget s'en allarent en leurs maisons sans congé, pour, comme l'on presume, ne consentir es poinctz qui toucheroient la dite religion, et apres contredire l'intention du dit Chancellier ; et est tel le desordre que l'on ne sçait qui est bon ou maulvais, qui est constant ou inconstant, qui est loyal ou

stant or inconstant, loyal or traitorous.   One thing is certain, that the Chancellor has been extremely remiss in proceeding against the criminals, and most ardent and hot-headed in the affairs of religion; being so hated in this kingdom, that I have my doubts whether the detestation against him will not recoil upon the Queen.   Assuredly, Sire, I have never ceased to admonish her Majesty as to the necessity of a prompt punishment of the prisoners.   I have given her Thucydides translated into French, that she may understand what advice he gives, and what kind of punishment ought to be inflicted on rebels."   *   *   *   *

Renard proceeds to observe in the same letter, that the great cause of all this confusion was to be ascribed to the multitude of Councillors; and that he saw no remedy for this but the formation of a new Council, to be limited to five or six members.   " Upon this project," he states that " Paget, Petre, and himself had conferred together at the Queen's request.   The other councillors and nobles, the Admiral, Pembroke, Derby, Shrews-

---

traistre; mais il est certain que le Chancelier a esté fort negligent à la procedure des criminelz, et fort ardant et chaloureulx es choses de la religion, estant tant hai en ce royaulme que je doubte l'hayne l'on a contre luy ne redonde à la dite dame; et certes, Sire, j'ay continuellement admonesté la dite dame pour le prompt chastoy des prisonniers, et donné Thucydide translaté en François pour veoir le conseil qu'il donne, et punitions que l'on doibct faire des rebelles." * * *

bury, Sussex, and the rest, were to be allowed to attend when they were at court, but not after the close of parliament. They were to be employed in distant parts of the realm ; whilst the Chancellor, Arundel, the Bishop of Norwich, Paget, the Comptroller, and Petre were to be entrusted with the affairs of the state. A reconciliation was to be made between Arundel, Paget, and the Chancellor; and they were to bind themselves by oath to fraternity, loyalty, duty, and diligence." If this scheme did not succeed, Renard declared that he sees no way of preventing a second rebellion, involving greater hazard than the first ; so that the coming of Philip would be attended with danger. He stated, at the same time, that Gardiner's party was the weaker, and unable to make a stand against his opponents.

### RENARD TO THE EMPEROR.
#### 27th March 1554.

" SIRE. — The Queen of England sent for me last Sunday, and informed me that by the persuasions of the Comptroller, Southwell, Petre, and those who had examined the prisoners, she had given

---

### SIMON RENARD TO THE EMPEROR.
*Trans. from Orig. Brussels.*  27th March 1554.

" SIRE.—La Royne d'Angleterre me manda querir Sambdi dernier, et me dit que à la persuasion des Comptroleur, Sudwel, Pieter, et examinateurs des prisoniers, elle avoit

their liberty to eight prisoners, having found no
ground for suspecting or accusing them of treason
in the late rebellion; amongst others, naming the
Marquis of Northampton, affirming that he had returned to the old religion; also Cobham and his
eldest son, Danet,* and four others whom she did
not name.  She added, that it has been from time
immemorial the practice for the kings of England,
on Good Friday, to extend their mercy to some
prisoners.  To all this I replied, that, since it was
her pleasure to use clemency, I could not and
ought not to find this anything but good, especially as she had done it by the advice of her Councillors: yet I presumed to think her Majesty might
have postponed the pardon till it had been ascertained, by the conclusion of the legal proceedings
against the prisoners, whether they were implicated
or not; for, if they were, she had only thus in-

mis en liberté huict prisonniers, pour non les avoir treuvé
suspectz ny accusez de trahison et derniere rebellion; entre
autres le Marquis Northampton, affermans qu'il se reduict
à la vielle religion, Cobham, et son filz aisnée Danet, et
quatre autres, qu'elle ne me sceut nommer; et que la cous-
tume a esté de tous temps, que, au bon jour de Vendredi
Sainct, les Roys d'Angleterre donnent graces et pardons à
aulcuns prisonniers.  A la quelle je dis, que puis il luy avoit
pleu user de grace et clemence, je ne pouvois ne debvois treu-
ver sinon bon ce qu'elle en avoit fait, puisque l'advis de ses
Conseillers y estoit entreveneu; mais qu'elle eust peu differer
la dite grace jusque à ce que par les procedures l'on eust cog-

---

* This name is misspelt, he means Daniel.

creased the number of her enemies by so many persons, besides giving countenance and strength to
the party of Elizabeth.

" Mary met my remark by observing that the
Chancellor had taken pledges and surety from
them ; and as for the Marquis, he had nothing left
him, she said, but what he carried on his person,
his whole property being confiscated, and she was
certain of his loyalty to his Highness [Philip] and
to herself.

" I took advantage of this to express the doubts
I entertained regarding the coming of his Highness
into her kingdom, and repeated article by article
the substance of my letters sent to your Majesty by
Sarron, how dangerous were the divisions in the
Council, and I added that it would become her
well to consider it, since all the sureties must come
from her side, and the Prince could not come in
arms ; that, if any thing befell him, it would be a

---

neu s'ilz sont esté de la partie, ou non ; et que s'ilz en sont esté,
elle a accreu le nombre de ses ennemis d'aultant de personnes
qu'elle a licentié et fortifié à la partie de Madame Elisabeth.
" A ce elle me repondit, que le Chancelier avoit prins caution et seureté d'eulx ; et que, quant au Marquis, il n'a que ce
qu'il porte sur son corps, et sont les biens confisqués, et se confie entierement qu'il sera leal à son Altese, et à elle.—Surquoy
j'ay prins argument pour luy dire la doubte je faisois de la
venue de son Alteze en ce royaulme, et repeté de point en
point le substantial de mes lettres envoiés à vostre Majesté par
Sarron.  La partialité des Conseilliers estre dangereuse, qu'il
emportoit grandement elle y pensa, puisque la seureté doibt
venir de son coustel, et que son Alteze ne peult venir en

scandal most disastrous and lamentable, and that
not only the person of his Highness would suffer,
but the lords and gentlemen who accompanied him;
and that I could not help bringing before her the
doubts I felt as to their having taken every necessary precaution.

" To this she answered, with tears in her eyes,
that she had rather never have been born than that
any outrage should happen to the Prince; that she
fervently hoped and trusted in God no such thing
would occur; that every person in her Council
would fulfil their duty in his reception, and would
put themselves to great expense; that her Council would be reformed and reduced to the number of six persons, which Paget and Petre had
advised; that she herself would make every effort
to conciliate the inclinations of her subjects; that
the people were anxious for the coming of his

---

armes; que s'il en mesadvenoit, se seroit ung scandale et inconvenient par trop lamentable, et non seullement la persone
de son Alteze souffriroit, ains les sieurs et gentilhommes qui
l'accompaignent; que je ne pouvois laisser de luy representer
les doubtes, à ce qu'il luy pleust pourvoir à ce qu'est necessaire.
" A ce elle me dit avec les larmes en l'œil, qu'elle aimeroit
mieulx n'avoir jamais esté née que l'on fit outraige à son
Alteze; qu'elle espere, et se confie en Dieu, telle chose ne ad-
viendra. Que tous ceulx de son Conseil se mectent en debvoir
pour recepvoir son Alteze, et font grande despence; que son
Conseil sera reformé et le nombre reduict aux six personnaiges,
que Paget et Pieter ont advisé. Qu'elle fera tout son mieulx pour
disposer les voluntez des subjectz; que le peuple desire la venue
de son Altese; qu'elle tiendra la bonne main pour, avant que

Highness; that she would exert every effort to have the proceedings against Courtenay and Elizabeth brought to a conclusion before his arrival." * *

Renard goes on to remark that the King of France was still suspected of plotting with Sir Peter Carew and John Courtenay. * * He protests, in conclusion, against the Spanish grandees being allowed to bring their wives into England.

" It is written me from Spain," says he, " that several noblemen have thoughts of bringing their wives with them here. If so, your Majesty would do well to provide against the occurrence of great disorder in this court. I am afraid that the people here will not suffer the Alcaldé to have any jurisdiction in this kingdom; and this not only because it is against the treaties, but for the consequences it may draw after it. I trust next Wednesday to have a final settlement upon every thing that I have recommended for the security of his Highness, (for which purpose the offer of the pensions will do good service,) and to write conclusively to your Majesty my opinion on the subject.

" London, 27 March 1554."    " SIMON RENARD."

---

son Alteze vienne, conclure les proces de Cortenay et de la dite Elisabeth.   * *

" L'on a escript d'Espaigne que plusieurs sieurs deliberoient amener leurs femmes avec eulx pardeça. Si ainsi est, vostre Majesté pourra preveoir ung grand desordre en ceste court. Je crains que ceulx de pardeça ne souffriront que le Sieur Alcaldé use de jurisdiction en ce royaulme, tant pour estre actes contraires aux traictez que pour la consequence, et ne trouve l'on bon qu'il vienne comme Alcaldé."   * *

We must now leave the Spanish ambassador for a brief space, to attend to the following letter of Wotton to his royal mistress. The details of the conversation between this minister and the Constable Montmorency are of much interest and importance in the light which they throw upon the relative positions of France and England.

### DR. WOTTON TO THE QUEEN.

*Orig.* St. P. Off. *France.* 31st March 1554.

" Pleaseth your Highness to understand, that the 20th of this present I received your Highness' letters of the 16th of the same; and the 22nd of that month I was at the court, and spake with the Constable, thinking it enough to declare mine instructions unto him, seeing they were but answers to the complaints which the Constable himself had made unto me the last time I had spoken with him. And having declared unto him the answers which the Lords of your Highness' most honourable Council made unto the French ambassadors, complaining unto them of the very self matters whereof the Constable had complained unto me, I afterwards also showed him that their ambassador had used a greater vehemency in setting forth and amplifying these his complaints, than he had used to do at all other times before ; and what, by occasion thereof, was said unto him by the Lords of your Highness' Council. And, finally, I required to know what was done for the ships of your Highness' subjects,

spoiled by the French at Brest, and for the apprehension of Peter Carew, of both which points I had
moved him the last time I had spoken with him.

" His answer was, that they had as yet received
no letters from their ambassador concerning this
last talk had betwixt him and the Lords of your
Highness' most honourable Council; but, to answer
as he had been informed already, he said that
your Highness' subjects of Margate did not only
not defend the Frenchmen, but took part with the
Flemings against them; which being so, said he,
was not done friendly, nor like good neighbours. As
for Wm. le Gras' matter, he said he remembered no
such clause in the treaty, that they who had been
wrongfully spoiled might not sue for restitution;
howbeit that, he said, might be looked for and
seen.

" As for new impositions, the Constable said it
was manifest; for they were fain to pay for divers
things, as caps, lead, and other, more than they
used to do, as the ambassador could well declare.

" As for the packets and letters, the Constable
made a very great matter of it himself, saying
that it was not one packet alone, but divers packets
that had been taken after that sort; and called a
servant of Noailles, who was come with letters
from his master about a fortnight before, to the
communication, who was as earnest in his talk as
his master was with the Lords of your Highness'
Council; for he not only affirmed that divers

packets of his master's had been so taken, but also
that the messengers had their money taken from
them, and not by the rebels, but by those which are
officers of your Highness, and of your Council,
and named Mr. Vice-Chamberlain ;* and that, altho'
he had commanded part of the money to be re-
delivered to the courier again, yet was there a good
sum behind, which the courier can by no means
recover, for any suit that the ambassador can make
of it.

"He said also, that the Emperor's ambassador,
sitting at his table, had openly declared certain
things which were written in cipher in his master's
packets ; whereby, he said, might appear whether
his master's packets had been showed to the Emperor's ambassador or not.

"He said that men had been appointed to
watch his master's door, to know who went out and
in ; and that certain Englishmen had been shent, †
for that they resorted unto his master : so that now
not one, neither English nor other, durst resort to
him, or company with his men ; no, not they to
whom his master oweth money dare not come to
ask it of him.    And where his master was wont to
send divers times packets of letters to Boulogne by
certain Englishmen, the Englishmen had been in
danger for it, so that his master could get never an
Englishman to carry any letter for him, for no
money.    He said also, that, for these two months

* Sir Harry Jerningham.              † Reproved.

past, there was never a Frenchman who could be
heard in any suit he had in England : and said,
that if it were as I had said, (which he could not
believe, having been well informed of the contrary,)
that they of Margate had defended the French the
best they could, yet were it your Highness' part to
keep your coast and havens free and safe from
danger of the Flemings, seeing that you require
that Frenchmen shall make restitution of any thing
taken or done in your Highness' ports; as, he said,
one of Dieppe had of late been fain to do.    These
things, with other like, the said servant declared
there before us.

"Lo! quoth the Constable, you may see whether our ambassador have cause to complain or
not; and therewith entered into a marvellous long
discourse, the effect whereof consisted principally
in these points.    That, betwixt two such great
realms as France and England, it could not be
but divers things should chance on both sides
whereby occasion of complaint should be given.
That, when such things happen, there is no better
way for the conservation of amity than that the
griefs be declared on both sides, whereby reformation of faults may ensue of it; for else, for every
wrong princes must fall out.    That, indeed, the
things being as the ambassador's man had declared,
his master was not well handled : and made a great
matter of that, that no man durst come at him;
and of the keeping his letters from him, for as for

staying of them in such a time, he never complained greatly of it. He said that these things were such, that it was not to be wondered though their ambassador, finding himself grieved with them, did earnestly speak in it; and that he thought my Lords of your Highness' most honourable Council ought not to take it in ill part, though in such a case the ambassador spake earnestly to them. And here he told me of one of our merchantmen who here at the court, before all the world, had used very hot words unto him; and yet for all that, 'quoth the Constable,' considering that the man had sustained loss, and did sue for justice, I said unto them that were about me, who were offended with him, that it was no marvel though he spake earnestly, for as much as the matter was of importance unto him.

" He said also, that Noailles was of his own bringing up, and had had the oversight and ordering of his eldest son, and that he had ever found him honest and gentle; and, intending to send a man into England meet for the entertainment and conservation of the amity, he had picked out and chosen him as one of the meetest for that purpose that he knew; and so, quoth the Constable to me, would you say that he were, if you did see the letters that he writeth; and so I earnestly willed him to do when he went hence.* And

* As to this, see Lingard, vol. vii. p. 152. Noailles' intrigues with the discontented noblemen, for the purpose of

therefore, quoth the Constable, like as I trust he will so use himself therein as there shall be no just cause to complain of him, so, if I knew indeed that he did use himself otherwise, he should be straight revoked, and should have as little thanks for his labour as he had deserved.

" In this discourse he was also very earnest to excuse D'Oysell, and whatsoever had been reported to your Highness of his practices in England ; he said, he thought it could not be true indeed as was reported, for that he had no such commission to do, and that he took him to be a man of too much knowledge and discretion to attempt any such thing; for, quoth the Constable, you must think us very simple, whereas the Queen your mistress is content to live in rest and peace with us, if we would seek occasions to fall out with her, being already enough occupied against such a great and mighty prince as the Emperor is; and said, he could not think that D'Oysell was so simple to put himself in such danger, for fear lest some of them with whom he should have entered in any such practice should have disclosed it, whereby he might have been troubled in his journey, specially having his wife in his company.

" And to the complaint that I made of our ships spoiled by Brest, he said, that the King had sent into Britain to Monsieur de Gye, and other his

raising a rebellion against Mary's government, were incessant ; so little sincerity was there in the asseverations of the Constable.

officers there, to enquire thereof, and that as yet they had learned nothing of it.

"As for Peter Carew, he said that the King had sent again for his apprehension; but that he was departed from Hable Neuf, and gone secretly his ways, so that it was not known where he might be found out: and that the King had given him no succour, whatsoever had been reported to your Highness; but the King doth intend to keep the peace and amity with your Highness, as he hath ever said he would do; yea, and would have been contented to have entered into a new treaty, if you had thought it so good, to make it the stronger.

"This was the principal effect of his large discourse. * * * † And as for Monsieur D'Oysell, I said that your Highness would not have so written unto me, unless the matter were true indeed, and that you were certainly informed of it. Why, quoth the Constable, if any man have so said by Monsieur D'Oysell, would you think he were to be believed in it if Monsieur D'Oysell deny it? or if any man here would lay any thing to your charge, would you think you were well handled if his word were believed before yours?—I think not, quoth I, that every man's word ought to be believed before Monsieur D'Oysell or me; but yet such might the persons be, and so many, that they should and ought to be believed against either of us, if we

† What follows, containing Dr. Wotton's reply to some points of the Constable's "large discourse," is unimportant.

would deny that which they said. But the Constable will not be persuaded that D'Oysell hath done any such thing; for that D'Oysell knoweth that, if he had so done, the King would be much discontented with him for it, as he saith.

"I have been in hand with him again for the apprehension of Peter Carew; and, besides that, have required that Sir Wm. Pickeryng, Stanton, and the two Percivals may likewise be apprehended for the like cause: and I took him a remembrance of it, praying him it might be delivered to the King, which he promised to do; and said again that Peter Carew should be sought for and apprehended if he could be found.

"In all this talk, although the Constable did excuse Noailles as much as he could, and defended the causes of his complaints to be just and great, yet seemed he nothing to take the matter so hot as Noailles did; but used still very gentle words and a good countenance to me, and at my departure presented me with venison and other dainties.

"The Legate, Cardinal Poole, lay still about a fortnight at St. Denis; and for because it was commonly spoken that he should not come to the King to Fontainbleau, but that the King would shortly after Easter go to Paris and there receive him, I thought I should have a good time to see him at St. Denis ere the King came to Paris, and for that purpose I departed from Melun upon Easter Monday to go to Paris, and so to take a convenient

time to see him at St. Denis.    But it chanced that
the King had sent for him ; and that self day that I
came to Paris he departed from St. Denis to go to
the court, and so was my journey frustrated.    And
for because he is lodged in the court, as I hear say,
therefore I suppose I shall have no convenient time
to see him till the King come to Paris, which is
thought will be within this se'enight or little more.

" That afternoon that the said Legate departed
from St. Denis, the Cardinal Chastillon came to
Paris, thinking to have met him there, as the said
Legate should have passed through Paris, but the
Legate took another way;  and so the Cardinal
Chastillon overtook him the next day at Corbeil,
and from thence accompanied him to the court.
It was Thursday or the Legate came to the court;
and, ere he came there by about a mile and a half,
met him Mons. d'Enghien, the Duke of Nemours,
the young Duke of Banieres (as they call him), the
Great Prior of France, and his brother the Marquis
d'Alboeuf, with their trains.    And so when they
were entered into the outer court of the Court,
there came to meet him the Dauphin, and the
Duke of Loraine ; wherewith the Legate, seeing the
Dauphin afoot, lighted, and the Dauphin brought
him in, giving him the upper hand ; and so passing
through the other court, the King, the Constable,
the Duke of Guise, and other of the Council received him beneath, even at the stair-foot ; and so
went up to the King's chamber, where the King
proffered him to enter before, but he refused it ;

and there were they together half an hour, and
from thence went to the Queen ; and, having done
there, the Cardinal Chastillon brought him to his
lodgings in the court.  That night, about six of
the clock in the evening, the Constable went to
him, and was two hours or more with him.

" I cannot learn that Peter Carew is gone to
the sea ; but, as I hear, is in some of the towns
upon the sea-coast, and, as it is thought, he is often
at Caen.  It may be that the King, upon the complaints I made to him, would not suffer him to go to
the sea with the Killigrews and other Englishmen,
lest, in so doing, he should show too openly that
he helpeth and succoureth him.

" I understand, by one of our merchantmen who
came yesterday hither from Roan, that on Monday
last he heard it spoken at Roan that there was a
commission come thither to apprehend Sir Wm.
Pickering and certain other Englishmen; but they
had friends, and found means to convey themselves
away.

" Wednesday in the Easter week arrived here,
as I understand, Sir Robert Stafford, a brother of
his, and another Stafford, who nameth himself servant to the Cardinal Poole, with certain other in
their company, who, as I hear, came together out
of England and landed at Boulogne.  I hear say
that their talk is very seditious, that no true
Englishman would abide in England to see the
realm brought under strangers, with other of like
sort ; wherein the Cardinal's man (who said he car-

ried letters from his master to your Highness) is as busy as the other. I understand by merchantmen that there come divers others daily over out of England by one way or other. The Constable showed me that the King was informed that the third part of England was agreed upon this conspiracy * against the Prince of Spain, as he calleth it.

" The French galleys are returned to Marseilles. The Italians say the Turk armeth again sixty galleys; and, for because they cannot perceive for what other purpose it should be, they take it to be to succour these men.

" It is spoken of here that the Prior of Capua, brother to Petro Strozzi,† returneth to the French King's service with five galleys of his own. And thus, having no other news to advertise your Highness of at this time, I beseech Jesu long to preserve your Majesty in health, honour, and much felicity.

" Written at Paris, the last of March 1554.

" N. WOTTON.

" POSTSCRIPT.—Even now came one of the Cardinal Poole's men, sent from him in post with a letter to me. The letter contained that he trusted well to have found me at the Court, and to have learned of me more certain advice of your Highness' prosperous estate, like as it was to his great comfort when both your Highness' ambassadors, by your commission (as he saith), did receive him

---

* Wyatt's plot.     † Leo Strozzi.

at the Emperor's court ; and, finding me not there,
had sent his man unto me, to learn by him somewhat of me thereof, for his more satisfaction of the
·due observancy he oweth your Highness, and also
to declare unto me certain things which he thought
meet for me to know.   The which, by his servant's
declaration, was, that my Lord Stafford's son,
named Thomas, as I remember, who brought letters to your Highness not long ago out of Poole
[Poland], is come over hither, and came to the
Cardinal Poole, his uncle, to the court.    And the
Cardinal, wondering much to see him there, asked
him whether he had any letters from your Highness ; which he denied : then asked him whether
he had leave to come away, which he likewise denied.   Why, quoth the Cardinal, how are you
come over then ?   The young man answered, for
because your Highness went about to do a thing
which he thought was not for the benefit and com-
·modity of the realm,—that is to say, to bring the
realm under the rule and government of Spaniards,
—he could not find in his heart to abide there to see
it.   The Cardinal hearing this, as his servant saith,
was sore offended with him ;  and having declared
his folly and misbehaviour towards your Highness
unto him, and rebuked him sharply therefore, commanded him that he should straight depart out of
his house, and come no more in his sight : and the
next day, hearing that he was yet in the court, the
Cardinal sent him word that he should depart out
of the court ; but the other made answer that he

might command him out of his house, wherein he would obey him, but not out of the court.

" This matter troubleth the Cardinal very sore, as his servant saith: specially for that the Cardinal was informed that your Highness bare your favour and goodwill to his said nephew, which he taketh that he hath now worthily lost again, having played such unkind and unnatural part towards your Highness. Hereof his servant said the Cardinal thought necessary to advertise me, to do in it as I should think it good; and that I should be assured that no man should be welcome to him that should not be faithful and true to your Highness, though it were his own brother. This is the effect of the errand done to me by his said servant.

" By his letter, and his servant's talk, it seemeth that he looked that I should have met him, like as, he saith, both your Highness' ambassadors did at Brussels, by your commandment; whereas, indeed, I have no such commission from your Highness, but thought to have seen him at St. Denis, as secretly as I might conveniently have done: so that it seemeth he thinketh it somewhat strange that I have not done to him as other your Highness' ambassadors did.

" His servant saith, that, because the King hunted yesterday, the Cardinal as yet had no audience of the King concerning his principal matter for the which he cometh. These things being come to me now, as I was closing up this letter, I thought it not amiss to add hereunto."

To return to the Spanish ambassador, his next letter to the Emperor, which is dated 3rd April, is a most interesting one. It regards the prosecution of the inquiry into the conduct of Courtenay and Elizabeth. Renard describes an interview which he had with Mary and some of her Council, and gives the particulars of two successive meetings, one with Bishop Gardiner the Chancellor, and the other with Paget. The subject discussed was, the security necessary to be had before Philip trusted himself in England. Hitherto, Gardiner had shown himself favourable to Elizabeth, but now, apprehending a popular tumult, he seems to have abandoned her cause, and made up his mind that she must be sacrificed. Renard observed to Mary, " that it was of the utmost consequence the trials and execution of the criminals, especially of Courtenay and of the Lady Elizabeth, should be concluded before the arrival of his Highness." To this the Queen replied, " that she had neither rest nor sleep for the anxiety she took for the security of his Highness at his coming." Gardiner then remarked, that, as long as Elizabeth was alive, there was no hope that the kingdom could be tranquil; * * and that, if everybody went as roundly to work in providing the necessary remedies as he did, things would go on better." Paget confessed that he himself and others had been much irritated against the Chancellor; but added, that he would rather die than harbour a thought prejudicial to the service of the Queen. Speaking of religion, he observed that he had formerly been in error upon the subject of transubstantiation, by the persuasions of one of the bishops here; but long since he had seen his error and renounced it, and had become of opinion that it was vain to think of remedying the affairs of the kingdom without the re-establishment of religion; this, however, he said, would be difficult if one were to follow the opinion of the Chancellor, who was anxious to carry through the matter by fire and blood. † * *

" As for the prisoners," observed Renard in the same letter, " they have sent new commissioners for their examination. Paget has promised me to use all necessary diligence; and it is resolved that Wyatt shall be executed this week. He has given great scandal to the Queen, for having, by the inadvertence of the Lieutenant of the Tower, communicated, at Easter, along with other prisoners, without having been first confessed, and for having uttered some strange speeches regarding religion and the sacrament. As touching Courtenay, there is matter sufficient against him to make his punishment certain; but for Elizabeth, they have not yet been able to fall upon matter sufficiently penal according to the laws of England, because those persons with whom she was in communication have fled. Nevertheless," continued Renard, "her Majesty tells me that from day to day they are finding new

† Qui vouldroit que par feug et sang l'on y proceda.

proofs against her. That, especially, they had several witnesses who deposed as to the preparations of arms and provisions which she made for the purpose of rebelling with the others, and of maintaining herself in strength in a house of that kingdom to which she sent the supplies.

" After having communicated at great length with Paget on the subject of the said Elizabeth, he told me that if they could not find proof enough to bring her to death, that he saw no surer expedient to secure her than to send her out of the kingdom to be married to a stranger; and, if they could find means to bring about her marriage to the Prince of Piedmont with ease, the parliament and the council would consent that the right of succession, which was in her, should go to him, in the event of the Queen having no children, for he could see no way by which at present she could be excluded or deprived of the right which she has by this parliament. And, if this took place, both the nobility and the people, it was said, would agree to the marriage of his Highness without difficulty; besides, it would be an alliance which might as much aid the Duke in the recovery of his country as any that could be thought of, because the kingdom would willingly contribute and give him assistance." * * * Of the parliament the Ambassador thus spoke :

" As to the parliament, it began yesterday, and the Queen was conducted thither with great solem-

nity, and made the communication [of her intended marriage] by the Chancellor; who, as I have
heard from those present, delivered a very good
speech; observing, that although the Queen was
in no way bound to inform her subjects upon
this measure, still, animated by her wish to confirm the affection which she felt for her kingdom,
and the tranquillity of it and of her subjects,
she wished them to consider with their best attention the ' articles' [of the marriage], which
were quite the reverse of those made public by the
conspirators; for, instead of his Highness making
an acquisition of England, England would make
an acquisition of your Majesty, his Highness,
with his kingdoms and provinces. *   *

" From what I hear," continued Renard, " on good
authority, there will be more controversy on the
subject of religion than on the point of the marriage. * * *   As the parliament proceeds, we shall
have an opportunity of discovering the various
humours and dispositions of the people, I should
think, in five or six days; the Queen having informed me that the parliament may terminate in
ten or twelve days; and she adds, that she will
do her best to make sure of the bad as well as the
good.   Her Majesty told me that in the church of
Westminster, before the usual mass of the Holy
Ghost began, which is generally said before the
assembly of the parliament, seeing Pembroke, who
had returned from his house where he had been

to keep his Easter, she made much of him, and bade him welcome, and his wife also; and she trusts that things will go on well. This is all I am able to say on the parliament for the present. And, assuredly, Sire, if the pensions had been given before this, and previous to the arrival of his Highness, it would have been the way to bring them over to our wishes, being a people over whom one should obtain influence by liberality and gifts." * * *

As to Mason, the Spanish Ambassador remarks that he had shown his dissimulation and feeling to be contrary to his professions regarding the marriage, in making a pretence of sickness that he might be excused from going into Spain with the Privy Seal. Two of his brothers-in-law, he remarks, had suffered for this rebellion; and he counsels the Emperor to look well to him on his return, as it was certain that both in the business of the marriage and on the point of religion he had shown himself very strongly biassed.

In the letter of the 7th of April we find that other practices had been discovered in favour of Elizabeth. The ambassador informed the Emperor there had been found, dropt in the streets, a letter in her favour as seditious as could possibly be conceived, upon which the Admiral had expressed himself passionately against the Grand Chamberlain,* who had the charge of this Princess; and

* Sir John Gage, Knight of the Garter.

told him that she would be the cause of the cut-
ting off of so many heads, that both he and others
will repent of it. He added, that the heretics, assisted by the French intrigues, did everything they
could to incite the people to take arms and break
into a new rebellion; that Sir Richard Morison and
some others of that party had applied for leave to
go abroad; and that, from what people said, it was
supposed they had forged some new scheme of revolt, and went away to watch its issue. The following letter from Wotton, relative to the English
refugees in France, confirms these suspicions.

### DR. WOTTON TO SIR W. PETRE.

*Orig.* *Mostly in cipher.* 17th April 1554.

" SIR.—For because Master Pickering hath had
long in his custody the ciphers which I occupy,
and is now here, I pray you to consider whether
there is any danger therein or no; and, in case there
is, to provide for it as ye shall think good. Sir,
seeing these rebels here will not be delivered, but
be employed here in service, which will by likelihood much increase their number here, in my
simple mind it were not amiss to seek some other
means to get them home. And in case there be
no other, rather than to suffer the number to increase, I cannot tell whether it were amiss that the
Queen's Highness did put them in hope of pardon,
if they returned home, and required it; whereupon
I believe that many of them would return home

with their hearts. \* \* \* Sir William Pickering told a servant of mine, that, of a letter which he wrote into England to the Queen's Highness, the copy was sent shortly after to the French King; and a scholar here told me that he heard say that the like was done to a letter which I wrote to the Queen's Highness; which thing though I cannot well believe, yet I thought it not amiss to advertise thereof that I hear. \* \* \*

" N. Wotton."

" Paris, 17th April 1554."

## RENARD TO THE EMPEROR.

### 22nd April 1554.

" Sire.—Since my last letters, the party squabbles, jealousies, and ill feeling of the Councillors have so increased and become public, that, at this moment, some from animosity against others will not attend the Council; what one does, another undoes; what one counsels, another contradicts; one advises to save Courtenay, another Elizabeth; and all at last

---

## RENARD TO THE EMPEROR.

*Trans. from Orig. Brussels.* April 22nd, 1554.

" Sire.—Puis mes dernieres lettres, les partialitez, envies, et malveullances des Conseillers se sont tant accreues et descouvertes, que presentiment les ungs pour despit des autres ne se treuvent au Conseil ; ce que l'ung fait, l'autre deffait ; ce que l'ung conseille, l'autre le desconseille ; l'ung parle pour saulfer Cortenay, et l'autre Elisabeth ; et y a telle confusion que

has got into such confusion, that we only wait to see the quarrel end in arms and tumult.   Thus is the Queen of England treated by those who ought to be her most intimate and devoted servants.

" The Chancellor,* the Comptroller,† Walgrave, Ingelfield, Southwell, the Chamberlain, Vice-Chamberlain, and the Secretary Bourne form one party; the Earls of Arundel, Pembroke, Sussex, the Master of the Horse, Paget, Petre, Cornwallis, and the Admiral make another : and whereas it was thought that the last reduction and reform in the Council of State to six, ought to be continued and become permanent, the Comptroller and his friends have murmured against it; they assert that they were the agents in maintaining the Queen in her royal right, and merited as well to belong to the Council of State as the others ; that they were Catholics, and the others for the most part heretics ;

---

l'on n'attend synon que le querelle se demesle par les armes et tumulte.   Ainsi est traictée la Royne d'Angleterre par ceulx qui luy devroient estre plus confidens et entiers.   Le Chancellier, le Comptrolleur, Walgrave, Ingelfield, Sutwell, le Chamberlain, Vice Chamberlain, et le Secretaire Bourgne tiennent une partie ; les Contes d'Arondel, Pembrock, Sussex, le Grand Ecuyer, Paget, Pietre, Cornwaille et l'Admiral tiennent l'aultre. Et comme l'on pensoit que la derniere reduction et reformacion du Conseil d'Estat en six debvroit continuer et estre permanente, le dit Comptrolleur et ses consors ont murmuré, disant qu'ilz avoient esté cause de maintenir la Royne en son droit royal, qu'ilz meritoient aussi bien d'estre du Conseil d'Estat que les autres, qu'ilz estoient Catholicques, et les

---

* Bishop Gardiner.       † Sir R. Rochester.

and they have so overwhelmed her Majesty, that she is disgusted with Paget and Petre.    \*    \*    \*

" The Chancellor has proposed in the parliament the restitution of the usurped property of the Bishop of Durham, and has carried the passing of the act by a majority of voices, against the will of the heretics, who raise such a murmur and noise about it that I look for much disorder, to the prejudice, loss of popularity, and danger of the Queen.   So much so, that the Chancellor had formerly resolved with her to propose only two acts ; the one concerning the marriage, the other touching the suspension of the title of Supreme Head of the Church ; as a means to which it was to be granted, that they who possessed church lands should continue to hold them, the consent of the Pope intervening ; and this, in order that they might arrive at a better reformation of religion.

" It is six days since the trial of a rebel named

---

autres pour la pluspart hereticques, et ont tellement abreuvée la dite dame, qu'elle s'est degoustée de Paget et Pieter. \* \* \*

" Le Chancellier a fait proposer la restitucion des biens usurpez de l'Evesque Durand, et à pluralité de voix a fait paser l'acte contre le vouloir des heretiques, dont il y a tel bruict et murmure, que je n'attend synon ung grand desordre, au prejudice, desreputation, et danger de la dite dame ; combien que le Chancellier eust auparavant resolu avec elle de non proposer que deux actes, l'ung concernant le mariage, et la suspense du tiltre du supreme chief de l'Eglise, moiennant quoy l'on accorderoit que ceulx qui possedent les biens de l'eglise les possederoient, entrevenant le consentement de Pape, pour parvenir à meilleure reformacion de la religion.   Il y a environ six jours que

Throkmorton.* He was acquitted by the twelve jurymen who had been chosen and impannelled, and who were all heretics; there being no doubt that in spite of the verdict he deserved to be condemned. And when they carried him back to the Tower (after his acquittal), the people with great joy raised shouts, and threw their caps in the air; which has so displeased the Queen, that she has been ill for three days, and has not yet got quite the better of it. People are disposed to have the jury punished; but for this she will not have authority or power enough with her Council, owing to the renewal of the feuds and parties in it. On the same day some one took away the head of Wyatt, which had been fixed on a gibbet; which is reckoned a great and scandalous crime in England.

---

l'on mena au jugement ung rebelle nommé Tragmarten, qui fut absoult par les xii enquesteurs que l'on avoit choisyz et appostez, qui sont tous hereticques, en non obstant qu'il merita condempnation; et comme l'on ramenoit en la Tour absoult, le peuple avec grand esjouyssement gectoient cryx, et bonnetz en l'air; que tant alteré la dite dame qu'elle a esté trois jours malade, et n'est encore bien d'elle : et est l'on apres pour punir les juges, mais elle n'aura auctorité, ny avoir entre son Conseil pour la division et partialité renouvellé. Le meme jour on ota la teste de Wyatt, qu'avoit esté planté dessus ung gibet, qu'est en Angleterre grand crime et schandale.

---

* The celebrated Sir Nicholas Throkmorton, for whose trial I refer my readers to Mr. Jardine's interesting volume of Criminal Trials, pp. 62—120, inclusive.

" Her Majesty has not yet come to a resolution
what is to be done with Courtenay and with Madame Elizabeth.  As to Courtenay, I see that she
is inclined in his favour, and persuaded to give him
his liberty by the intercession of the Comptroller*
and his friends, who have formed a close compact for
his marriage with Elizabeth.  And then as regards
Elizabeth herself, the judges can find no matter for
her condemnation.  Already she has liberty to walk
in the garden of the Tower ; and even if they had
proof, they would not dare to proceed against her,
for the love of the Admiral, her relative, who es-
pouses her quarrel, and has at present all the force
of the kingdom in his power; yet (on the other
hand) if they let her go, it seems evident that the
heretics will proclaim her queen; whilst, if they

---

" La dite dame est apres pour conclure ce que l'on fera de
Cortenay et de Madame Elisabeth.  Et quant au dit Cortenay, je la vois inclinée et persuadée pour luy donner liberté,
par les persuasions des dits Comptrolleur et ses compagnons,
qui ont tenu la main pour le mariage de luy avec la dite
dame.

"Quant à la dite Elisabeth, les gens de loix ne treuvent matiere pour la condamner, et a ja liberté de se promener par le
jardin de la Tour.  Et quant il y avoit matiere, l'on ne oseroit
proceder contre elle, pour l'amour de l'Admiral son parent,
qui porte sa querelle, qui a presentement toute la force
d'Angleterre en son pouvoir; et, la relaxant, il est apparent
que les hereticques la publieront pour Royne ; mectant en

---

* The Comptroller of the Household was Sir Robert
Rochester.

set Courtenay at liberty, his Highness cannot be
secure, for he will practise with the French, as he
has already begun to do.    \*    \*    \*

" In a conversation which I had with the Queen
upon the letters of Wotton, I have remonstrated as
far as I could possibly do ; begging her to take
special care, and look into and assure herself of
her affairs, and set things to rights in good season.
I stated that I saw the danger she might fall into ;
that she should heal the divisions amongst her
Councillors, and not allow herself to be abused or
trepanned ; and that I perceived the entry of his
Highness could not but be hazardous.    To this, she
answered, that they had written to all parts for
soldiers ; that Clinton would remain Lieutenant in
London ; that she did her best; that all the Lords
assured her his Highness should come safely, and

---

liberté Cortenay, son Altese ne sera asseurée, car il practi-
quera avec les François, comme il a ja commencée. \* \* \*
" Et communiquant avec la Royne sur les lettres du dit
Wotton, luy ay remonstré tout ce qui m'a esté possible
pour se donner garde, et pourveoir à ses affaires, les asseurer et remedier de bonne heure, autrement que je vois le
danger où elle tumberoit ; qu'elle remedia la partialité de ses
Conseilliers, et ne se laissa abuser ou prevenir; que je pre-
vois l'entrée de son Altese ne pouvoir estre synon hazardeuse.    Surquoy elle m'a dit que l'on a escript ça et là pour
avoir gens de guerre ; que Clynton demeure Lieutenant en ce
lieu de Londres; qu'elle fait le mieulx qu'elle peult; que
tous les Sieurs l'asseurent que son Altese viendra seurement,
et qu'ils mourront tous à ses pieds si l'occasion s'adonne;

that they would all die at his feet if any thing occurred; that the whole danger lay in London and the parts around it,—as in Essex, where they had within these few days burnt a church, and would not have the mass back again; that every one thought, if his Highness were once come, all would be quiet: she then showed me a bill which had been thrown on her kitchen table—the most seditious thing in the world—full of threats against herself, against the Chancellor, against the High Treasurer, and others; and in which there are strange things said about his Highness and the Spaniards, openly declaring that his Highness must take his chance at his coming. I have spoken to the Chancellor, the Comptroller, Paget, and Petre separately; and Paget has promised me to accommodate himself to my wishes, to suffer all things rather than throw any obstacles in the way of the Prince's coming, and that he will do his best to

---

que tout le danger est à Londres et aux lieux à l'environ, comme à Essex où l'on a bruslé une eglise ces jours passez, et ne veulent revoir la messe; que chacun est de ceste opinion, que si son Altese vient, que tout sera appaisé; me moustrant ung billet que l'on avoit gecté sur la table de sa cuysine, le plus seditieulx du monde, plain de menasses contre elle, contre le Chancellier, le Grand Tresorier, et autres, et auquel y a choses estranges de son Altese et Espaignolz, ouvertement declairant que son Altese courra fortune à sa venue. J'ay parlé au Chancellier, Comptrolleur, Paiget, et Pieter separement; et m'a promis le dit Paiget de s'accommoder et souffrir toutes choses pour non troubler la dite venue,

compose the troubles; the Chancellor says that he will speedily bring the parliament to a close. * * *

" The Queen has commanded me to write to his Highness, to see if it is his pleasure to accept the Order of England, which will be presented to him by a chapter of the Knights of the Garter. * * 22nd April 1554.

" And so, Sire, &c.

" SIMON RENARD.

" A report has been spread here that the Cardinal Pole calls himself Duke of York, and pretends a right to the crown."

RENARD TO THE EMPEROR.

28th April 1554.

" SIRE.—The Queen has more maturely weighed what I represented to her within these few days, (as contained in my last letters to your Majesty,)

---

et qu'il fera son mieulx pour remedier les troubles.  Le Chancellier dit qu'il fera finir le parlement de brief. * * *

" La Royne m'a commandé à escripre à son Altese, si luy plaira accepter l'ordre d'Angleterre, que luy sera presentée par le Colliege des Chevaliers de la Jarretiere demain.

" L'on a fait courir ung bruict pardeça, que le Cardinal Polo se soit appellé Duc de Jourch, et qu'il pretend droit à la corone."

RENARD A L'EMPEREUR.

*Trans. from Orig.*   *Brussels.*   28th April 1554.

" SIRE.—La Royne aiant, de plus pres, pesé ce que luy ay remonstré les jours passez, contenu en mes dernieres lettres à

the troubles, namely, which might arise from the divisions in her Council ; of what great consequence it was to bring the parliament to a close, and to proceed gently in the reformation of religion, to avoid giving the people any ground for a new rebellion, and to provide a strong force for the safe passage and entry of his Highness into the kingdom.   Her Majesty, having thought over all this, has consulted with her Council, and is resolved to prorogue the parliament till a more convenient time, to despatch her noblemen and captains to enlist soldiers, and to assign to different persons of trust the charge of the counties, and the task of keeping the people quiet.     *     *     *

" They have imprisoned the twelve jurymen who gave their verdict in favour of Throkmorton, having found proofs of collusion and ill-affection ; and, if they go on in the road they have now taken, there is an appearance of things getting better.

---

vostre Majesté,—l'inconvenient où elle pourroit tumber par la partialité de son Conseil, combien il emportoit de finir le parlement, de temperer la reformation de la religion, d'eviter occasion à ce que le peuple ne se rebelle de nouveau, prevenir par la force et asseurer le passaige et entrée de son Altese pardeca,—elle a parlé à son Conseil, et resolu de proroguer le parlement jusques à autre temps plus convenable, et depescher ça et là gentilzhommes et capitaines pour faire gens de guerre, et distribuer à plusieurs personnaiges de credit, charge es provinces pour contenir le peuple.     *     *     *

" L'on a emprisonné les xii hommes de la loy qui avoient sentencié en faveur de Tragmarten, pour ce que l'on a trouvé de la collusion et mechanceté ; et si l'on suyt le chemin que

Already the Chancellor and Paget seem half reconciled, and consult together.  It is resolved that the
city and  the Queen's guards shall be  in arms on
the 1st of May, lest the apprentices raise any commotion.*   The Admiral is at sea, and draws near
Portsmouth ; but from his letters, which I have
seen, he is little pleased with the armament which
your Majesty has sent, saying there are but three
or four ships which are above one hundred tons.

" The  preparations  for  the  reception  of his
Highness continue ; and  her Majesty  has  been
advised not to leave this place till some news of
the Prince arrive.  Some of the Council express
their astonishment that he has never written to the
Queen, or sent any person to pay her a visit, seeing

---

l'on prent, il y a apparence que les choses se remedieront.
Et ja le Chancellier et Paget communiquent par ensemble
comme à demy reconciliés, et ont deliberé que le premier jour
de May prochain la ville de Londres sera en armes, et les gens
de la Royne, à ce que les apretis ne facent quelque trouble.
L'Admiral est en mer, et tire contre Portmoun; mais, selon
que j'ay veu par les lettres qu'il a escript, il n'est content de
l'armée que vostre Majesté a envoié, disant qu'il n'y a que
trois ou quatre navires qui passent cents tonneaulx.   L'on continue les appretz pour recevoir son Altese, et est conseillé la
dite dame de non partir de ce lieu (avant) que l'on n'ayt nouvelles de son Altese; et s'esmerveillent plusieurs du Conseil
comm il n'a escript à la Royne, ou envoyé quelque personnaige

---

* The  1st of May (May-day) being  devoted to popular
amusement and licence, it was, perhaps, dreaded that the Spanish match might be ridiculed in their pageants or mummings.

the marriage is so far advanced; which I excuse as well as I can. *   *   *

" The act for the punishment of heretics with death has passed in the Lower House, but I learn that the Peers will not consent that there should be in it any capital clause. *   * They have not yet come to any resolution what is to be done with Elizabeth and Courtenay. * * *

" SIMON RENARD."

" To the Emperor."

In the above letter of Renard to the Emperor, dated 28th April 1554, he incloses two letters of Paget's, dated in April, but without the day of the month added; one of them is important and characteristic. I do not here add the French, as it is itself a translation.

PAGET TO RENARD.

April 1554.

" SIR.—As I know the entire affection which you bear to her Majesty the Queen and her crown, I cannot restrain myself; I must trouble you with the griefs I endure for her Majesty and my country.

---

pour la visiter, puisque l'alliance est si avancée, ce que j'excuse le plus qu'il m'est possible. *   *   *

" L'acte que l'on a proposé au parlement pour punir les hereticques de peine de mort, est passé en la chambre basse du dit parlement; mais j'entens que les nobles ne veullent consentir qu'il y ayt peine de mort. *   *   * L'on n'a encores prins resolucion que l'on fera de Madame Elisabeth et de Cortenay." *   *   *

Behold he whom you wot of,* comes to me since dinner with a sudden and strange proposal; saying that, since matters against Madame Elizabeth do not take the turn which was wished, there should be an act brought into parliament to disinherit her. I replied that I would give no consent to such a scheme for many reasons.

" Sir,—For the love of God persuade the Queen to dissolve the parliament instantly, and to send those who have been chosen for the government of the counties into their districts; for the times begin to be hot, men's humours are getting inflamed, warmed, fevered; and I see that this person, for his own private respects and affection, has resolved to hurry forward such measures as will create too much heat, with no regard to the circumstances in which we are placed, and to the coming of his Highness, and with no forecast of the danger which may ensue.

" You know, when the parliament began, we resolved, with consent of her Majesty, that only two acts should be brought forward; the one, concerning the marriage; the other, to confirm every man in his possessions; reserving to her Majesty to take what steps she pleased regarding her title and style. By God, Sir, I am at my wits' end, and know not what to do except to pray God to send us hither his Highness with all speed, for then all will go well; and, till then, things will take the course you see them running now.

* Probably Bishop Gardiner.

" Urge his voyage into England, and that with all diligence; and thus will you do the greatest service that ever was done to the Emperor, to the Prince, to the Queen, and to the kingdom; as knoweth God, whom I pray to give you ever his grace, and to keep me in yours.

" Yours, in all readiness to command,

" WM. PAGET."

SIMON RENARD TO THE EMPEROR.

1st May 1554.

" SIRE.—The Queen having understood that the French ambassador had made a complaint, and demanded the restoration of two of his packets, which he said were seized and detained in England, (he being only able to speak of the one of which your Majesty has a copy,) her Majesty, I say, has applied to the Chancellor to tell her what has become of the other. He has confessed to his having had it and read it; but says he knows not what he has done with it, or where he has put it. After search-

S. RENARD A L'EMPEREUR.

*Trans. from Orig. Brussels.* 1st May 1554.

" SIRE.—La Royne aiant entendu que l'ambassadeur de France faisoit doleance, et repetoit deux ses pacquetz qu'ilz disoit avoir esté detenuz et detrousez en Angleterre, n'aiant sceu à parler synon de l'ung dont vostre Majesté a eu copie, a fait instance devers le Chancellier pour sçavoir qu'estoit devenu l'autre; qui a confessé l'avoir leu et receu, mais il ne sçavoit où il l'avoit mis, ny qu'il en avoit fait apres l'avoir.

ing for it, his secretary recollects having made an extract from it, which bears in substance that Courtenay is to marry Madame Elizabeth; that the Queen must lose her kingdom and crown; and that the hired troops will turn against her because they are three years in arrear. The letter discovers the practices of Wyatt: it would have been of much consequence to recover the original, as a proof against Courtenay and Elizabeth; and the Queen is at a loss what to think of its having fallen aside, unless the Chancellor wished thus to save Courtenay. Already he had caused his name to be omitted in the decipher. Nevertheless, her Majesty yesterday sent for the men of the law, and those Lords of the Council who were to be judges, to hear their report upon the criminal process against Courtenay, and to understand the resolution they

---

Son secretaire s'est souvenu avoir fait extrait du contenu en icelluy, que porte en substance que Cortenay devoit epouser Madame Elisabeth, que la dite Royne perdroit son royaulme et couronne, que les pensionaires luy seroient contraires pour n'avoir esté payez de leurs pensions de trois ans en arriere, decouvrant la practique de Wyatt; et fut esté tres apropos que l'original se fut retrouvé, pour servir de justification contre le dit Cortenay et Elisabeth; et ne sçait la dite dame que presumer de la perdition d'icelles, synon que le Chancellier ait heu desir de saulfver Cortenay; et ja avoit il fait laisser le mot de son nom au premier dechiffrement.

" Neanmoins la dite dame feit hier assembler ceulx de la loy, et les principaulx Sieurs de son Conseil, qui doivent estre les juges, pour ouyr le rapport du proces criminel du dit Cortenay, et sçavoir quelle resolution l'on y prendroit; et enfin ilz

had come to.   The men of the law have unanimously given their judgment that he deserves
death, and he will be sentenced accordingly.   If
it be so decided, I shall urge instant execution.   It
is asserted that Courtenay has sent his regards to
the Lady Elizabeth by a child of five years old,
who is in the Tower,—the son of one of the soldiers
there.

   "As to Elizabeth herself, no resolution is yet
taken.

   " The Queen holds Paget in great suspicion for
two reasons, which she gave me.   The first, that
when it was proposed in the parliament to make it
high treason for any one to take arms against his
Highness, Paget spoke more violently against it
than any one ; although, before this, to the Queen
herself he had declared it quite right : the other,
that when a bill was brought in for the punishment
of heretics, he used all his influence with the

---

sont esté tous d'accord avec les ditz de la loy qu'il merite
la mort, et sera sentencié selon ce ; et sy ainsy advient, je so-
liceteray main soubz l'execution.   Et s'est adveré que le dit
Cortenay ait fait faire ses recommendations à la dite Elisabeth
par ung enfant eaigé de cinq ans, qu'est en la Tour, filz de
l'ung de souldars d'icelle.   Quant à la dite Elisabeth, l'on n'y
a encores prins conclusion.

   " La dite dame tient grandement à suspect Paget pour deux
actes qu'elle m'a recité.   L'ung, que quant l'on a parlé au parlement d'establir peine de rebellion contre ceulx qui prendroient les armes contre son Altese, le dit Paget y a plus
relucté que personne ; combien qu'il eust dit auparavant à la
dite dame que c'estoit chose raisonnable, et que se feroit :

Lords to oppose it, and to give no room for the punishment of death.    She added many little traits to show that he is flighty and variable.    *    *    It is true that I have observed Paget to hold constant intercourse with heretics ; and that he uses the advice of Mr. Hobby, one of the most malicious heretics in England, who in a few days is about to set out for the baths of Italy, and to follow Morison, and wishes to have letters to your Majesty that he may kiss hands on his way.    *    *    *

" SIMON RENARD."

" Sire.—Since writing my letters, I have learnt that the House of Peers have resolutely thrown out the act for the punishment of heretics ; so that the Council and all state affairs here are much embarrassed, the heretics encouraged, and the catholics

---

l'aultre, que quant l'on a parlé de la peyne des hereticques, il a sollicité les Sieurs pour non y consentir, ny donner lieu à peyne de mort : m'aiant recité plusieurs particularitez de ses actions du passée, par lesquelles elle le jugeoit inconstant et variable.    *    *    *    Vrai est que je me suis apperceu le dit Paget converse continuellement avec ceulx qui sont hereticques, et use le conseil de Mr. Oby, qu'est ung des malicieux hereticques que soit en Angleterre, qui s'en doit de brief aller aux bains d'Italye, comm il m'a dit, et suyvre Morison, et desire avoir lettres de faveur à vostre Majesté pour luy baiser les mains en son passaige."    *    *    *

" Sire.—Mes lettres escriptes, j'ay entendu que la Chambre des Nobles du parlement a rejeté absolument le statut de la punition des hereticques, tellement que le Conseil et les affaires de royaulme sont grandement troublez, les hereticques acoraigez, et les catholicques reduictz en crainte, dont l'ont ne

thrown into alarm. Indeed, we can look for little else than alteration and inconvenience. When I understand the particulars of the dispute, I hope to be able to touch on the point more fully."

### MASON TO THE QUEEN.

*Orig.* St. P. Off.   5th May 1554.

" Pleaseth your Grace, having at this present no kind of matter to write, other than may be declared to your Highness by my Lord of Norwich, I will not trouble your Grace with many words.

" My said Lord of Norwich is departed from hence, having left behind him a great contentation of his dealing in the whole court. * *  By him shall your Grace understand the state of the Emperor's person and all other occurrents here ; by whose declaration your Highness shall also perceive what talk we have had with Cardinal Poole, whose zeal to the good of our estate I find to be such as I think, surely, there is not a better English heart within the realm, neither that more heartily prayeth daily for the good success of all things in the same.

" For some declaration whereof he told us, among other things, that where he was utterly determined to have tarried in the court of France a

---

espere sinon grand inconvenient et alteration, comme j'espere, par le premier, toucher plus particulierement quant j'entendrez la dispute et particularité."

good while longer than he did, and, at the least, so
long as he might have certified the Emperor what
he had done there, and have received an answer,
perceiving the continual resort thither of a number
of rebels, and the King not to be minded to avoid
them out of his realm, (wherein, nevertheless, he
travailed with him very earnestly,) he could find
in his heart no longer to continue there, so much
was that sight grievous unto him.   If things were
as he wisheth, your Grace would govern in a
blessed estate.   In confirmation whereof he always
praiseth ripe, temperate, and modest proceedings.
I would to God the whole realm knew him as my
Lord and I do, and had that opinion of him as in
effect all estates of Christendom have.

" Your Highness is like very shortly to have a
great resort as well of personages of much nobility,
as of ambassadors from many great estates. * * *

" JOHN MASON."

"5th May 1554."

SIMON RENARD TO THE EMPEROR.

6th May 1554.   London.

* * * " THIS morning the Queen sent me word
by Basset, that the Parliament finished yesterday,
much to the contentment of the estates, the reputa-

---

RENARD A L'EMPEREUR.

Trans. from Orig. at Brussels.   6th May 1554.

* * * " CE matin la dite dame m'a envoié Basset pour
m'advertir que le parlement fut hier finy, au contentement des

tion of her Majesty, and the satisfaction of all; that
the ancient penalties against heretics were assented
to by all the peers ; that it was reported publicly
and expressly that they considered heresy as having
been extirpated as well as punished : the same Basset adding, on his own part, that never did parliament end with a better grace ; that, when the
Queen made her speech, she was interrupted five
or six times by cries of God save the Queen ! and
that the most part wept at the eloquence and goodness of her Highness ; that she has every hope
that God will restore matters to tranquillity ; that
the peers, especially, have spoken with her, and
promised all obedience ; and that I ought to dismiss
all fear and suspicion from my mind. * * Paget
[the Queen added in her message] had repented of
having behaved himself so ill in her service ; but
that it was impossible she could ever rely on

---

estatz, à la reputation de sa Majesté, et satisfaction d'ung
chacun ; que la peyne anchienne contre les hereticques fut
agreé par toute la Noblesse, et qu'ilz feirent dire expressement et publiquement qu'ilz entendoient l'heresie estre extir-
pée et punie ; adjoustant le dit Basset de soy mesmes que
jamais l'on n'a veu finir parlement de si bonne grace.  Que
quant la dite dame fit son propoz, il fut interrompu cinq ou
six fois par l'exclamation publique des y assistans, criant Dieu
saulve la Royne ; et que la pluspart d'eux pleuroient de l'eloquence et vertu que representait la dite dame ; qu'elle n'a espoir sinon que Dieu rengera les choses à tranquillité, que les
nobles en particulier luy ont parlé et promis toute obeissance,
et que je deusse oter toute crainte et suspition. * * * Paget
se repentoit d'avoir si mal versé en son service, qu'il n'estoit

him, or resume her good opinion of his constancy. * * *

"I send your Majesty a genealogy, which has been published in this kingdom to show that his Highness† is allied to the House of Lancaster; and, as Paget knows that this invention proceeds from the Chancellor, he has given out that he did it to confer upon the Prince a right to the crown, as the Chancellor himself has told me.

"I have the greatest possible trouble to know how to conduct myself between these two, for I cannot forget the part Paget has taken against the alliance,‡ and the earnest wishes of the Queen. I cannot excuse his intrigues against her Majesty's service; and still less can I bear to give suspicion to the Chancellor, considering his influence, his rank, and the place he holds; but, most of all, because I

---

possible elle le peut jamais qualiffier de constance, ne se fyer en lui. * * *

"J'envois à vostre Majesté une genealogie que l'on a publié en ce royaulme pour demonstrer que son Altese n'est etrangier, ains de la maison de Lancaster; et comme Paget a sceu que l'invention venoit du Chancellier, il a dit qu'il le faisoit pour donner droit à son Altese à la coronne, selon que le propre Chancellier m'a dit; et entre ces deux j'ay la plus grande peine du monde de me conduire, car je ne puis oublier l'office que le dit Paiget a fait pour l'alliance et contre l'affection de la Royne, et practiques contraires à son service, je ne le puis excuser, et moins penser de donner suspicion au dit

---

† Prince Philip.          ‡ The marriage.

shape all my actions with a reference to the great
end we have in view, his Highness' safe arrival
here.   Indeed, if Paget perseveres in asking leave
to go to the baths, it is my belief the Queen will
grant it him, but in such terms as will not only fill
him with remorse for his ingratitude and forgetful-
ness, but will expose him to the imminent danger
of losing honour, life, and property.   Such is the
inconstancy of the people here, that most of the
churches are in ruins. * * *

" Gresham,† factor to the Queen, who is the
bearer of these letters, goes to your Majesty to get
a passport permitting him to procure the powder,
saltpetre, and harquebuses mentioned in the enclosed memorial for the service of the Queen; and,
having begged me to give a licence for this, I could
not refuse, for reasons of which your Majesty is
aware." * * *

---

Chancellier, pour la consequence, et pour l'estat et office qu'il
administre, et signamment pource que je enchimine toutes les
actions au but tant recommandé, pour s'asseurer la venue de
son Altese; et s'il (Paiget) persevere à demander congé pour
aller aux bains, je tiens que la dite dame luy donnera, avec
termes que luy debvront donner remord d'ingratitude, et me-
congnoisance, et se mectra en grand danger de perdre l'honneur, vie, et biens.—Que sont la pluspart des eglises ruynées,
telle est l'inconstance pardeça."      *      *

---

† The celebrated Sir Thomas Gresham, the great financial
adviser and agent for the Queen.

## RENARD TO THE EMPEROR.
### 13th May 1554.

" SIRE.—Paget, stung with remorse, has lately presented himself to the Queen after her mass, and asked her mercy for his intrigues in the late parliament against the act for the punishment of heretics, and the statute which made it capital to take arms against his Highness.    As to the first, his excuse was, that Lord Rich had persuaded him the object of the statute was to wrest the church lands out of the hands which now held them ; and, for the second, he pleaded ignorance and inadvertence, protesting that for the future he would serve her Majesty with faith and loyalty.

" After some remonstrances the Queen pardoned him, recommending him to behave better in time to

---

## RENARD A L'EMPEREUR.
### *Trans. from Orig. at Brussels.*    13th May 1554.

" SIRE.—Paget, par remord de conscience, s'est representé devant la Royne à l'issue de sa messe, et luy a cryé mercy de ce qu'il a practiqué au dernier parlement pour empescher que le statut de la punition des hereticques ne se feit, et que peyne de rebellion ne fut apposée contre ceulx qui prendroient les armes en main contre son Altese.    Que, quant au premier, Millord Rich luy avoit persuadée qu'il se proposoit pour faire perdre les biens de l'eglise à ceulx qui les tiennent.    Quant au second, qu'il l'avoit fait par ignorance et inadvertance : qu'il la serviroit à l'avenir fidelement et loyaulment.    Et apres plusieurs remonstrances que la dite dame luy fait, elle luy pardonna, l'admonestant de faire mieulx cy apres.    Et comme le

come. As soon as the Chancellor and his party were
aware of such a mode of proceeding, they began to
suspect that some plot was in hand against the
Queen between Paget, Arundel, Pembroke, Cobham, and other noble heretics; and that, to
conceal it the better, Paget had adopted this course.
The fact has been brought to light by a gentleman, a friend of the Chancellor, whom Paget
forcibly detained in his house for two days, and
caused him to be examined as if he had been a spy
of the Chancellor's; his object being to discover
whether Gardiner had any ill designs against him.
By such conduct Paget has brought himself within
the pains of felony, abusing his office of a Privy
Councillor, turning his house into a private prison,
and showing openly that he bids defiance to the
Chancellor, and has conspired against him with the
heretics above mentioned.

Chancellier et autres de sa partye ont entendu ceste façon de
faire, ilz sont entrez en suspicion qu'il y avoit quelque conspiration sur mains contre la dite dame, entre le dit Paget, Arundel, Pembroch, Cobham, et autres nobles hereticques, et que,
pour la mieulx dissimuler, Paget avoit fait le dit acte ; ce que
l'on a decouvert par ung gentilhomme, amy du Chancellier,
que le dit Paget a tenu par force en sa maison l'espace de
deux jours, et le interrogué comme s'il fut esté espie du dit
Chancellier, pour sçavoir si le dit Chancellier avoit quelque
malvaise intencion contre luy ; commectant, par ce, crime de
fellonie par les loix d'Angleterre, faisant prison privée, et
abusant de son office de Conseillier ; donnant à cognoistre qu'il
se diffe du dit Chancellier, et qu'il a conjuré contre luy avec le
dits hereticques ; de sort que le dit Chancellier tient que les

" From all this, Gardiner has become convinced that there is really a plot of the heretics against him; their design, he thinks, is to seize him and clap him up in the Tower, and then compel the Queen to submit to their wishes, as was done before in the time of King Edward the Sixth.

" To counteract this, the Queen has been advised to imprison Paget, Arundel, and Pembroke; and there are twelve noblemen and gentlemen who have undertaken to defend her if she will give her consent. Upon this proposal she has held a consultation with the Chancellor, the Grand Treasurer,* and the Comptroller;† and after having fully discoursed together on the state of the kingdom, the designs of the French King, and his anxiety to invade this realm and throw impediments in the way of his Highness' arrival, the danger of rousing the

---

dits hereticques sont apres pour le prendre et mectre en la Tour, et gouverner à leur volonté la dite dame, commil il a autrefois esté fait en ce royaulme du vivant d'ung Roy Edouard; et, pour prevenir, l'on instigue la dite dame pour faire imprisonner le dit Paget, et sont douze qui entreprennent de garder la dite dame si elle veult consentir le dit emprisonnement, et des dits Arondel et Pembroch. Et sur ce la dite dame a consulté avec le dit Chancellier, Grand Tresorier, et Comptrolleur. Et apres avoir discouru l'estat des affaires du royaulme, la volunté et desseins que le Roy de France a de l'envahir et troubler la venue de son Altese, le danger où se mectra la dite dame de conciter les hereticques à prendre les

---

* William Paulet Marquis of Westminster.
† Sir Robert Rochester.

heretics anew, to take arms against her, giving the
French in this way a better opportunity of carrying forward their designs ; considering also that
this might restore Elizabeth's affairs, cause the
Admiral to join them and turn the naval force
against Mary ; having [as I said] weighed all
these probable inconveniences, and taking into
view also that there is nothing more than a mere
suspicion of a conspiracy, they have resolved for
the present to dissemble with Arundel, Paget,
and their friends ; to look narrowly into all they
do, and to strengthen the Queen's hands so that
she will be able to make head against them if
any thing is attempted. Besides this, it has been
ordered that no gentlemen shall bring to court more
than two servants, that the Earl of Sussex shall
be sent into Sussex, the Earl of Huntingdon into
his country, the Earl of Shrewsbury to the north,

---

armes en main contre elle, et que cependant les François auroient meilleure occasion d'executer leur deliberation, que ce
seroit le chemin pour redresser les affaires de Madame Elisabeth, que l'Admiral, s'en sentant avec eulx, pourroit convertir
la force de mere contre la dite dame; aians pesé les inconveniens qu'en pourroient proceder, et meme qu'il n'y a synon pure
suspicion, l'on a prins resolution que l'on dissimulera avec les
dits Arondel, Paget, et autres de leur ligue ; que l'on remarchera
leurs actions de plus pres ; que la dite dame se fortiffiera de
sorte que, quant ilz vouldroient entreprendre, elle sera forte
pour attendre secours ; que nul gentilhomme pourra amener à
la court plus de deux serviteurs ; que l'on envoiera les Conte
Susseix en Susseix, le Conte de Odmeton en son pays, le
Conte de Strosberry au Nort, le Conte Derby en son pays, les

the Earl of Derby to his country ; and, in short, all
who might have been tampered with are to be dispersed hither and thither under pretence of some em-
ployment ; it having been found that, when together,
they have greater facilities to plot and lay their
schemes.   Elizabeth is to be sent to a castle in the
north called Dhombreck,* to be guarded there;
the Admiral and his fleet are to be kept in the Chan-
nel to defend the kingdom from the attack of the
French, who, we hear, have certainly embarked
six companies of Gascon soldiers at Rouen, with
the purpose of making a descent on the Isle of
Wight and Portsmouth.   As for the defence of the
passage between Calais and Dover, six large ships
and three pinnaces are to be left for this service.
It is finally resolved that, in one way or other, the
prisoners shall be got rid of, either by pardon or
by execution ; and that the Queen shall not depart
hence till she have certain intelligence of the coming
of his Highness.

autres qui peuvent estre de la practique ça et là avec occasion
de quelque charge, pour ce que, quant ilz sont par ensemble,
ilz ont plus de moien de machiner et conjurer; que l'on envoiera la dite Elisabeth en ung chasteau qu'est au Nord, appellé d'Hombreck, pour y estre gardée ; que l'Admiral, avec les
navires de vostre Majesté, ne passera le Canal et costé d'Angleterre, ains gardera le royaulme contre l'enterprinse des
François, lesquels pour verité sont embarquez six enseignes de
Gascons à Rouen pour surprendre l'Isle de Wych et Portsmue ;
et que, pour assurer le paissage de Calaix, l'Admiral laissera en
Douvres sept grosses navires et trois pinnasses ; que l'on fera
fin des prisonniers, soit par execution ou grace ; et que la dite

* Pomfret.

" As to Courtenay, it is quite apparent to me that the Chancellor and his party wish earnestly to save him ; for, although his condemnation had been determined on, still, after all, they have managed to make the Queen change her opinion and confine him to the Tower. From this resolution I expect nothing less than new errors and new tumults; nothing in fact is settled here : if the information I receive from day to day be true, there are dangerous and underhand practices amongst the nobility; and I am confirmed in this opinion by the communication which I have had with both parties. All this I have imparted to the Queen and the Chancellor. * * *

" The Cardinal Pole has sent his chamberlain to the Queen to inform her of the little hope he entertains of negotiating a peace, * and of your

---

dame ne partira jusques elle ait nouvelles de la venue de son Altese.

" Et quant à Cortenay, me suis toujours bien aperceu que le Chancellier et ceulx de la ligue avoient envie de la saulfver, car combien qu'il fut esté conclud qu'il seroit condamné, neantmoins l'on a fait changer d'opinion la dite dame, et sera gardé en la Tour, dont je n'espere synon nouveau erreur et tumulte ; et n'y a rien asseuré par deça, ains, si les advis que je reçois de jour à autre sont veritables, il y a des dangereuses practiques et mesnées entre les Sieurs, et m'en suis apperceu par plusieurs communications que j'aye eues avec l'un et l'autre, comme je l'ay fait entendre à la Royne et Chancellier.   *   *

" Le Cardinal Polo a envoyé son chambrier à la Royne, pour

---

* Between France and the Emperor.

Majesty's desire that he should return to Rome. To this he objects, and would rather proceed to Louvain, where he might await the success of this marriage. * * They have printed a book here in praise of those noblemen who would not consent to the act for the capital punishment of heretics. * *

" And thus, Sire,

" To the Emperor."              " Simon Renard."

In the next letter, the Spanish Ambassadors presents a striking picture of the disturbed state of the country.

MONTMORENCY AND RENARD TO THE EMPEROR.

25th May 1554.  London.

* * * " The parties which divide the Council are so many, and their disputes so public, they are so banded the one against the other, that they forget the service of the Queen to think of their pri-

___

luy faire entendre le peu d'espoir qu'il a à la paix, et que vostre Majesté desiroit il retourna à Rome ; ce qu'il ne desiroit, ains plustot aller à Louvain, actendant là le succes de ce mariage. * * L'on a imprimé ung livre en la louange de Sieurs, qu'ilz n'ont consentez que peine de mort fut introduicte contre les hereticques." * * *

" Simon Renard."

MONTMORENCY AND S. RENARD TO THE<br>EMPEROR.

Trans. from Orig. Brussels.  25th May 1554.

* * " La partialité du dit Conseil est si tres grande, si descouverte, et si bandez les ungs contre les autres, qu'ilz oublient le service de la Royne pour penser à leurs vindications

vate passions and quarrels.  Nothing is done but
what the Queen expressly orders : Paget, with the
heretics, is leagued against the Chancellor and the
Catholics ; the Queen has information that he and
his party are arming themselves, and, if they could
be beforehand, that they would make the Chancellor prisoner, who, with the knowledge of her Majesty, is also arming with his adherents : Gardiner,
meanwhile, counsels the Queen to leave this city
with all speed, and to clap the Earl of Arundel and
Paget in the Tower, as they have private information that he is fortifying a castle of his near the sea-
shore.  They hear also that he is raising horse without the leave of the Queen ; and that, from day to
day, soldiers by four and five at a time come into
London, whilst Paget does all he can to estrange
several noblemen from their affection to the Queen.

" I learn, moreover, that strange words are uttered about the coming of the Alcaldé, and we

---

et passions particulieres ; tellement que l'on ne fait rien, si la
dite dame ne les commande expressement.  Paget avec les hereticques contre le Chancellier et catholicques ; aiant advis la
dite dame que le dit Paget et ceulx de sa partie s'arment, et
que, si ilz peuvent prevenir, ilz prendont prisonnier le dit
Chancellier, qui avec ses adherens, par le sceu de la dite
dame, la conseillant de partir le plustot qu'il pourra de ceste
ville, et de mectre en la Tour le Conte d'Arondel et Paget,
pour ce l'on entend que le dit Conte fortiffie ung chasteau qu'il
a aupres de la marine, et fait plusieurs gens de chevals, sans le
congé de la dite dame ; et que de jour à l'autre il y vient plusieurs souldars en ce lieu de Londres par quatre et cinq, et
que Paget practique plusieurs gentilshommes pour les divertir

have information by our spies, that a great revolt is brewing ; so that, Sire, it is impossible that these parties can be appeased without great trouble ; and, if such is the case, it is better that we should have it before the coming of his Highness than after.

" The inconstancy of the people here is incredible, and equally so their power of inspiring confidence when they wish to deceive you. It is the subject of religion debated in the last parliament which is the cause of these troubles ; and the Queen is reduced to such a state of perplexity that she knows not what advice to adopt, understanding well that all is done in favour of the Lady Elizabeth. They have removed Courtenay from the Tower, and taken him to a castle in the north. Your Majesty may well believe in what danger the Queen is so long as both are alive ; and when Paget,

---

de l'affection de la dite dame.  Oultre j'entens que l'on dit choses etranges contre la venue de l'Alcaldé, et a l'on advis par particuliers espies qu'il se brasse une grande revolte, tellement, Sire, que ceste partialité ne se peult appaiser sans grand trouble ; et, si ainsi est, il est plus expedient qu'il se soit avant la venue de son Altese que apres ; et n'est croyable l'inconstance de ceulx par deça, ny la confidence qu'ilz donnent quand ilz veullent tromper.

" Le point de la religion qui fut debattu au dernier parlement est cause de ce trouble ; et est la dite dame si perplex qu'elle ne sçait quelle conseil prendre,  car elle entend bien que le tout se fait en faveur de MADAME ELISABETH.  L'on a distrait Cortenay hors de la Tour, et mesné en une chasteau de Noirt ; et, vivant les deux, vostre Majesté peult entendre le danger où est la dite dame ; et que Paget, en cuy elle se con-

in whom she has so much confided, has so far forgot himself, and proceeded to such an extreme, that, to revenge himself of the Chancellor, he professes himself a heretic, and neglects the service of her Highness.

" Yesterday they had letters from the ambassadors of the Queen who have been sent to Spain, intimating that they had disembarked at Corunna. Here they were received by the Bishop of Betanze and the Governor of Corunna, who conducted them to the said Betanze, where they were met by the Alcaldé of Galicia and Raymond de Taxis, whom his Highness sent to bid them wait for his arrival there. This the Prince expected would be about the end of this month. He was then, he said, setting out by post to bid adieu to the Queen of Spain his grandmother; and to meet on the way, that he might save time, the Princess Dowager of Portu-

---

fiée, se soit tant oblyé et desmesurée, que, pour se vanger du Chancellier, il face profession d'heresie, et neglige le service de la dite dame.

" L'on receu hier lettres des ambassadeurs de la dite dame qui sont allez en Espagne, par lesquelles l'on entend qu'ilz desembarcarent à la Corunna, où ilz furent receuz par l'Evesque de Velence et la Capitaine de la Coronna, et conduictz au dit Velence, où survint l'Alcaldé de Galice, et Remondo de Taxis que son Altese envoya devers eulx pour les contremander à ce qu'ilz attendent celle part sa venue, que debvroit estre à la fin de ce mois; et qu'il se partoit par la poste pour aller prendre congé de la Royne d'Espaigne, Madame sa grande mere, et pour rencontrer de chemin la Princesse Douaigiere de Portugal,

gal, his sister, to commit to her the administration of affairs in Spain.

" The same letters speak of their honourable reception; and the English who came over with the Count D'Egmont, have written from Valladolid, the 13th of this month, an account of their kind reception by his Highness, especially of the banquets given them: they mention, also, that the Marquis de Las Naves is at Laredo, from whence he means to sail to England with four ships to visit the Queen, and give orders for the disembarkation of his Highness. All here are happy to have received news from Spain, by which they may regulate their own preparations; and we hear besides that their honours the Duke of Alva, Gotieres Lopez, Don Diego D'Azaviedo, a nobleman named Benavides, and one of the House of Corunna, bring their wives with them.

---

Madame sa seur, pour gaigner le temps, et luy recommander l'administration des affaires d'Espaigne; et qu'ilz sont esté fort honorablement recueilliz.   Aussi y a il lettres de Valladolid du xiie du present, par lesquelles les Anglois qui passarent avec le Sieur d'Egmont tesmoignent le bon accueil que son Altese leur a fait, particularizant les banquetz que leur sont esté faiz; et que le Marquis de las Naves est à Larede pour passer devers la dite dame, avec quatre navires, pour la visiter, et donner ordre pour le desembarquement de son Altese; et sont esté joyeulx ceulx de pardeça d'avoir nouvelles d'Espaigne pour se riegler selon icelles; et escript l'on que les Sieurs Duc d'Alva Gotieres Lopez, Don Diego d'Azaviedo, ung nommé Benairdes, et ung de la maison de la Coronna, ameinent leurs femmes avec eulx.

" The Sieur de Courieres and the Alcaldé set
out on Monday for Southampton, and they have
drawn up the commission of the Alcaldé, as your
Majesty will see by the copy here inclosed, about
which there has been a great dispute : most of the
Council did not wish it to be translated into Latin
as well as English ; and, unless the Chancellor had
taken this trouble himself, the Secretary would not
have sent it. * * *

" The Venetian ambassador of the House of
Michaeli has arrived here; and the old ambassador sets out on his return in eight days hence,
meaning to take his route by France, although he
had proposed to pass by Germany.

" The Duke of Savoy has written letters to the
Queen, in which he tells her that he will open himself more fully when they meet. He has written
also to Paget. I have been considering whether

---

" Les Sieurs de Courrieres et Alcaldé partiront Lundy pour
Hampton ; et a l'on riegler la commission du dit Alcaldé selon
que vostre Majesté verra par la copie cy-joincte ; pour l'expedi-
cion de laquelle il y a eu grande dispute, pour ce que la pluspart de ceulx du Conseil ne vouloient qu'on la mect en Latin
ains en Anglois, et, sans que le Chancellier print ceste peine
le Secretaire ne l'eust depeschée. * *
" L'ambassadeur de Venize de la maison de Michaeli est
arrivé en ce lieu ; et doit partir le vieux ambassadeur deans
huict jours pour son retour, doigeant prendre son chemin par
France, combien il eust proposé passer en Allemaigne.
" Le Duc de Savoye a escript lettres à la Royne, par lesquelles il dit qu'il luy dira le surplus de bouche ; et a escript
lettres à Paget ; et ay pensé, s'il y auroit quelque practique sur

there might not be some practice in hand which Mason has been brewing. We submit ourselves on this point to what your Majesty may be able to discover and more fully to understand.

" And thus, Sire, we pray God to give your Majesty the accomplishment of your high and noble wishes.

" From London, the 25th May 1554.

" J. De Montmorency.<br>" Simon Renard."

" To the Emperor."

The next letter of the Spanish ambassadors is dated from Richmond. After informing the Emperor that Mary had come there last Tuesday, accompanied by the Earl of Arundel, Paget, Secretary Petre, the Comptroller, the Chamberlain and Vice Chamberlain, they proceed in the following passage to mention some interesting particulars regarding Paget and Courtenay.

---

main, que Masson est brassée, nous remectant à ce que vostre Majesté en peult discourir et mieulx comprendre.

" A tant, Sire, nous prions le Createur de donner à vostre Majesté l'accomplissement de ses treshautz et tres nobles desirs. De Londres, ce xxv de May 1554.

"De vostre Majesté, &c.<br>" J. de Montmorency.

" A l'Empereur."                        " Simon Renard."

## MONTMORENCY AND RENARD TO THE EMPEROR.

### 4th June 1554. *Richmond.*

\* \* \* " PAGET is always preaching on his wrongs, yet he says he would sacrifice both life and estate for the service of your Majesty and his Highness; and Courtenay has confessed to one named (Sellier), who conducted him to the castle where he now is, that Paget has importunately pressed him to marry the Lady Elizabeth; adding, that if he did not listen to this, the son of the Earl of Arundel would marry her; that Hoby and Morison, instigated by Paget, have practised with him touching the same marriage; and that the Chancellor had been displeased, because in his absence they had recommended the same Hoby to your Majesty, although he is one of the

---

### MONTMORENCY AND RENARD TO THE EMPEROR.

*Trans. from Orig. at Brussels.* 4th June 1554.

" PAIGET presche toujours ses resentemens, et neantmoins il dit vouloir faire sacrifice de corps et biens pour la service de vostre Majesté et de son Altese ; et s'est decouvert Cortenay à ung nommé Sellier, qui le conduisoit au chasteau où il est, que Paiget l'a importunement sollicité pour se marier avec Madame Elisabeth, luy disant que, s'il n'y entendoit, le filz du Conte d'Arondel l'epouseroit ; et que Oby et Morison, par instigation du dit Paiget, ont practiqué devers luy le dit mariage. Et a esté deplaisant le Chancellier de ce que en son absence l'on a recommandé le dit Oby à vostre Majesté, pour estre le

most obstinate and worst heretics among her
Highness' subjects, and who they suspect, when he
is away from this country, will continue all his bad
offices, as there is a shrewd guess Cheek and Morison
have done.    It is to them that report gives the enclosed ballad against his Highness and the Queen.*
It was found thrown about in the streets, and is said
to be the most scandalous and seditious piece yet
seen; the Council were of opinion that it ought
to be sent to your Majesty, in case it may be possible in Germany, where Cheek and Morison have
gone, to recognise the hand-writing.

" The day before the Queen left London, the
French ambassador requested an audience, having no
other purpose than to discover whether she was well
or ill disposed to him.    When he spoke of the King

---

plus obstiné heretique et plus maulvais suject de la dite dame,
et duquel l'on prend grande suspition qu'il doige continuer tous
maulvais offices quant il sera pardela, comme l'on suspitionne
avoir esté fait par Shich et Morison, que l'on presume avoir
composé et fait imprimer la balade cy inserée contre son
Alteze et la dite dame, qu'a esté treuvée par les rues, qu'est ung
dicté le plus scandaleuz et seditieux qui soit esté veu; et a esté
d'advis le dit Conseil que la deussions envoyer à vostre Majesté,
pour sçavoir si les caracteres pourroient estre cogneuz es
lieux de la Germanie où les dits Shich et Morison sont
passez.

" Le jour devant que la dite dame partit de Londres, l'ambassadeur de la France demanda audience, sans occasion, sinon
pour voir si elle estoit bien disposée ou non ; et comme il parlit

---

* Unfortunately this satirical ballad is not to be found.

his master's anxiety for the continuance of the peace, and lamented that her Majesty had not shown a similar desire, the Queen replied drily, that the King and his ministers had shown by their past conduct little inclination for peace, and that, for all the kingdoms in the world, she would not have on her conscience the weight of what his master had done. This speech the ambassador took in such ill part, and flew into such a rage, that the Chancellor was forced to tell him his office was not to make trouble; and that, if the King knew his manner of comporting himself, he would not suffer it. In consequence of this he has written to the King of France, requesting his revocation ; and has sent the enclosed note to the Lieutenant D'Aumont, asking a safe-conduct on his return, regarding which your Majesty will be pleased to let us know your pleasure. There is the greatest probability that this

---

que le Roy son maistre desiroit continuer la paix,   quoy l'on ne correspondoit de la part de la dite dame, elle luy respondoit seichement,   que le Roy et ses ministres, par le passé, avoient tesmoigné peu d'affection et inclination à la paix, et qu'elle ne vouldroit avoir fait les actions dont elle s'est apperçue pour tous les royaulmes du monde, pour le bien de sa conscience ; ce que l'ambassadeur print de si malvaise part, et se mit en telle colere, qu'il forcea, par apres, le Chancellier à luy dire ses offices ne tendre sinon à trouble, et que, si le Roy entendoit ses façons de faire, il ne le comporteroit ; dont il a adverty le Roy pour estre revocqué, ayant envoyé le billet cy-joinct au Lieutenant Daumont, pour impetrer en sa faveur ung saulfconduict pour son passaige et retour, sur lequel il plaira à vostre Majesté ordonner son bon plaisir; et y a grande

kingdom will go to war with France for the causes
of quarrel which have been afforded by the King
and his ministers.  &ast;  &ast;  &ast;

  " Paget has informed the Lieutenant that the
ships of England and Spain have chased some
French ships into the ports of Normandy. &ast; &ast; &ast;

  " Richmond, 4th June 1554.

" And thus, Sire, &c.

" DE MONTMORENCY.

" SIMON RENARD."

" To the Emperor."

## BEDFORD AND FITZWATERS TO THE COUNCIL.

*Orig.*   ST. P. OFF.   *St. Jago.*   June 5th, 1554.

  " AFTER our very hearty commendations unto
your good Lordships.   The same shall understand
that, since our last letters writ unto your Lordships,
we have received one other letter from the Prince,
whereof we send a copy unto your Lordships here
inclosed.   The Marquis of Sara, who brought the
letter, arrived at Betanze, where we then lay, the
20th of May; and the occasion why he was so long
in his journey thither, was by reason of a fall of his

---

apparence que ce royaulme entrera en guerre avec les dits
François pour les occasions qu'en a donné le Roy et ses ministres. &ast; &ast; &ast;

  " Paiget a dit au dit Lieutenant que les navires d'Angleterre
et celles de vostre Majesté ont donné la chasse à aucuns
navires de France jusques aux ports de Normandie.

" A tant, Sire, &c.

" DE MONTMORENCY.

" A l'Empereur."             " SIMON RENARD."

horse, whereby he hurt his leg.  But, at our being there, he entertained us very honourably, and made us great cheer.  And, to show us more pleasure, he requested us to go unto a house of his near Betanze, where he feasted and banqueted us, and showed us all the pastimes he could, as well in hunting as otherwise.  He is a man of great possessions in these parts of Gallicia, and had in much estimation.  He cometh over with the Prince into England, and from thence he shall go in embassage unto Rome from the Emperor.

" Your Lordships shall further be advertised that the 30th of May we came hither unto St. James', where, God willing, we intend to remain until the coming of the Prince, which shall be, as we can gather by conjecture of those advertisements we hear, about the 15th of this instant; for he took leave of his sister and departed from Salamanca the 28th day of this last month, and went from thence unto a house of the Duke of Alva called La Abbathia, and so unto Samora, at which two places the Prince is feasted and banqueted by the Duke of Alva, and remaineth there until the 6th day of this instant ; and that day he meaneth to arrive at Beneventa, where it is thought he will remain for a time, considering there is great preparation made by the Count of the same to feast him, and to show him sundry pleasures and pastimes.

" From Bonaventura the Prince departeth to Asturgo, being distant ten leagues, where it is thought he will tarry but one night.  From hence unto Ponteferado, being distant fifteen leagues, where his household tarrieth his coming. From thence unto Villa Franca, being distant five leagues, where he intends to lie one day, and to be feasted of the Marquis of the same. And from Villa Franca unto St. James', being distant forty leagues, with all the speed he can conveniently make, where he stayeth about two days. And so to the Groyne, being distant from St. James' ten leagues, where he will stay only for a good wind; and, as soon as that serveth, he will take his voyage towards England.

" Your Lordships shall understand farther, that all the Prince's ships that were looked for out of Andalusia are already at the Groyne and thereabouts; and also the greatest number of those that should come out of Biscay; so that there is here ready for the Prince, whenever he shall arrive, one hundred sail of tall ships, well furnished with men and ordnance. Your Lordships shall receive herein inclosed a schedule of the names of certain of the noblemen of Spain, which we are informed shall come with the Prince into England; and, besides these, we understand there shall a great number come, which be men of name and of good houses.

" And herewith we bid your Lordships most heartily farewell.

      " Your Lordships' assured,

         " J. BEDFORD.    T. FITZWAUTERS."

" POSTSCRIPTA.—Your Lordships understand that we are informed the Prince is wont to be very sick upon the sea, and these seas that he shall pass into England are much worse than the Levant seas where he hath been heretofore. Wherefore, doubting lest he and his nobility will be desirous to land at the next land they can come to in England, (as all men being in their cases will covet and desire the same,) your Lordships shall do very well to take order that some preparation be made at Plymouth, and so along the sea-coast for him, if peradventure he should land. Nevertheless, we will do all that lyeth in us to bring him to Southampton, where all things are prepared for him."

## SIMON RENARD TO THE EMPEROR.

### 7th June 1554. *Richmond.*

\* \* \* " SIRE.—The Council are debating whether the Queen's name shall stand before that of his Highness, in their public acts; and, the moment I knew this, I told the Chancellor that neither divine nor human law, nor honour nor good faith, would suffer his Highness to be named last, if the treaty of marriage and the acts of par-

## SIMON RENARD TO THE EMPEROR.

### *Trans. from Orig. at Brussels.* 7th June 1554.

" SIRE.--Le dit Conseil est en dispute si l'on nommera la Royne devant son Altese es depesches du royaulme; quoy entendant, j'ay dit au Chancellier que ny la loix divine ny l'humaine, ny la reputation et honesteté consent que l'on nomme son Alteze le dernier; attendu mesme que les traictez et actes du parle-

liament gave him the title of King of England. What they may determine is still uncertain.

" On Tuesday, one of Count D'Egmont's servants arrived at Southampton from Spain, to prepare apartments for his master.   \*    \* I am told that Hoby has left this country to practise with the Duke of Savoy, and that Morison is intriguing in Germany in the house of the Count Palatine. It will please your Majesty to cause them to be looked to ; and especially as it is found that Hoby gave his consent to this last rebellion. And thus, Sire, &c. Richmond, 7th June 1554.

" SIMON RENARD."

" To the Emperor."

---

ment attribuent tiltre de Roy d'Angleterre à son dit Alteze. Je ne sçay encoires ce qu'ilz y resouldront. Mardy l'un des serviteurs du Sieur d'Egmont arriva à Hampton, venant d'Espaigne pour prendre logis pour son maistre. \*   \*   \* J'entend que Oby est allé par dela pour practiquer avec le Duc de Savoye, et que Morison practique en Allemaigne en la maison de Conte Palatin ; et, pour ce, il plaira à vostre Majesté faire prendre garde sur eulx, et ce treuvé que le dit Oby a esté consentant de la rebellion derniere.

" A tant, Sire, &c.
" SIMON RENARD."

" A l'Empereur."

### SIMON RENARD TO THE EMPEROR.

9th June 1554. *Richmond.*

" SIRE.—The Count de la Chapelle has written me the enclosed letters, by which your Majesty will perceive that the ships of the fleet are only victualled for fifteen days. * * The gentleman who brought the letters tells me that the Count Chapelle begins to suspect the English Admiral of privately treating with the French, or of some ill intentions against his Highness ; because, without communicating with him, he despatched a vessel into France or Spain. He has communicated also with Killigrew, one of the governors of the forts at Falmouth, whose sons are in France.

" Besides this, he tells me when [his] the Count Chapelle's soldiers landed, the Admiral's soldiers

---

### SIMON RENARD A L'EMPEREUR.

*Trans. from Orig. at Brussels.* 9th June 1554.

" SIRE.—Le S<sup>r</sup> de la Chapelle m'a escript les lettres cy-joinctes, par lesquelles vostre Majesté cognoistra les navires de sa flotte n'estre envitaillez synon pour quinze jours. * * * Le gentilhomme qui apporta les lettres me dit que le Sieur de la Chapelle entroit en suspition contre l'Admiral d'Angle-terre qui traicta avec les François, ou qu'il eust maulvaise in-tencion contre son Alteze, pour ce qu'il a despeché ung navire en France ou Espagne à son insceu ; qu'il a communiqué avec l'ung des capitaines —— des chasteaux de Fallamue, nommé Guillegreuy [Killigrew], les filz duquel sont en France ; que les souldars du dit Admiral, quant les souldars du dit Sieur de la Chapelle sont descenduz en terre, les ont provoqué à debatz,

tried to fix a quarrel on them, thrusting and pushing them, that the Admiral himself holds the Count Chapelle very cheap; that they have not met, nor had any communication, except by messages, for a month; and that the English Admiral calls the ships of your Majesty's fleet *muscle-shells,* with many other particulars; to avoid occasions of quarrel, the Count Chapelle has not come into port, but remains still with his sails up, and has forbid his men to set foot on shore.   *   *   The Queen sets out towards Southampton on Wednesday, and trusts that his Highness will experience no inconvenience in his arrival there; yet, since there are several persons to whom this alliance is most unpalatable, I shall do my best to search out whatever practices may be in hand, and to provide a remedy.

" There has been a deliberation regarding sending the Lady Elizabeth to the court of the Queen

---

les cerrans et poulsans; que le dit Admiral ne fait grand compte du dit Sieur de la Chapelle; qu'ilz ne se sont entreveuz ny parlez puys ung moys, synon par messaiges; qu'il appelle les navires de la flotte de vostre Majesté coquilles de moules, et plusieurs semblables particularitez; que, pour fuyr toute occasions, le dit Sieur de la Chapelle n'a prins port, ains demeure toujours à voilles, et a defendu à ses souldars de mectre pied à terre. * * *

" La dite dame partira Mercredi pour approcher Hampton, et confye que la venue de son Altese sera sans inconveniens, combien qu'il y a plusieurs particuliers qu'ilz ne peuvent gouster ceste alliance; je feray le mieulx qu'il me sera possible pour enfoncer les practiques que l'on pourroit tenir, et d'y remedier en tout debvoir. L'on a mis en deliberation l'envoie de

of Hungary, if she will receive her; but as yet no
certain resolution is taken.    *    *    *

"Richmond, 9th June 1554.

"And thus, Sire, &c.

"SIMON RENARD."

"To the Emperor."

## SIMON RENARD TO THE EMPEROR.

14th June 1554.    *Richmond.*

"SIRE.—On Saturday last the Marquis de las
Naves disembarked at Plymouth, where he was honourably received by the Bishop of Lincoln and
other noblemen, besides the Admiral, who gave
him a salute, which lasted a long time.  Having
been much fatigued by his voyage, he has written
me that he will repose himself for two or three
days, and then proceed to meet the Queen and
fulfil his commission.

---

Madame Elisabeth en court de la Royne d'Hungrie, si luy
plaisoit l'accepter; mais l'on n'a encoires prins resolution. * * *

"A tant, Sire, &c.

"A l'Empereur."            "SIMON RENARD."

## SIMON RENARD A L'EMPEREUR.

*Trans. from Orig. at Brussels.*    14th June 1554.

"SIRE.—Samedy dernier le Marquis de las Naves desem-
barqua au port de Plemoue, où il fut receu honorablement par
l'Evesque de Lincolnshie et plusieurs gentilzhommes; où assista
l'Admiral d'Angleterre, qui fit faire une salve d'artillerie qui
dura longuement: et pour avoir esté tant travaillé de la mer,
il m'a escript qu'il repousera deux ou trois jours; puis se mectra

" By the advices which I have received, the Prince
cannot be here before the end of this month. *  *
His Highness understands that your Majesty has
given him permission to accept the Order of the
Garter, which the Queen and the Knights have
determined to give him.  The Queen has had a
Collar made, which cost seven or eight thousand
crowns, besides several rich dresses for his Highness ; but, except this, I see no great preparations by the nobility, or by the people, for his
reception.  Indeed, there are not a few who suspect
that there is a plot or conspiracy on hand, the great
object of which is to marry the Lady Elizabeth
to the son of the Earl of Arundel, and of which
Arundel, Pembroke, and Paget are the chiefs ; but
neither the Chancellor nor other of the Council
take much heed of this.

---

en chemin pour venir trouver la Royne, et complir ce qu'il a
de charge ; et, par les advis que j'ay, son Alteze ne peult estre
pardeça avant la fin de ce mois. * * *  Son Alteze entend
que vostre Majesté luy doige donner licence pour accepter
l'ordre de la Jaretiere, que la Royne et les Chevaliers nt
concludz luy donner ; et en a fait faire une la Royne, qu'est
estimée sept ou huict mil escuz, et joinctement fait faire plusieurs riches habillemens pour son Altese ; et, hormis l'apprest
qu'elle fait, je ne vois grand apprest de la noblesse, ny du peuple, pour sa reception : dont plusieurs presument qu'il y ait
conjuration et conspiration, de laquelle les Conte d'Arondel,
Pembroch, et Paget sont chiefz, à quoy le Chancellier ny autre de Conseil ne donnent grand ordre ; et tient l'on que le
tout se fait pour marier le filz aisné du dit Conte d'Arondel
avec Madame Elisabeth.

"The Lord Mayor and Aldermen of London have called together the different nations here, to know what was their design as to getting up some pageants to welcome his Highness. I understand the Venetians, Florentines, and Spaniards replied that they had no such intention; nor do I see any preparations for jousts or tourneys by the noblemen. Their excuse is, that they have no money; and the Earl of Derby has been so much wrought upon, that he seems in a fume of discontent, and completely alienated from the service of the Queen.

"No one would believe the inventions sought out by the factious to stir up the people to tumult. A Venetian mariner, named Escrivain, has given out that he had seen three hundred French sail at sea; others have reported that, the moment his Highness arrives, the Scots will declare war against England; others, that his High-

---

"Les Maire et Odremans de la ville de Londres ont assemblé les nations qui sont en ce lieu pour sçavoir s'ilz estoient d'intention de faire quelque nouvelleté pour la venue de son Alteze, à quoy les Venetiens, Florentins, et Espaignolz ont respondu n'avoir intention de faire aucuns fraiz; et ne voit l'on que les gentilzhommes dressent tournois ny joustes, s'excusans qu'ilz n'ont de quoy; et a l'on tant practiqué le Conte de Darby, que je le vois quasi esbranlé et aliené du service de la Royne, et n'est croiable l'invention dont usent les partiaulx pour esmovoir le peuple à tumulte. Ung marinier Venetien, que l'on appelle l'Escrivain, a publié avoir veu trois cens voiles Françoises en mer; autres ont semé que, incontinent que son Altese seroit arrivée, les Escossois feroient guerre au royaulme d'Angleterre; les autres que son Altese venoit pour occuper

ness is coming to seize the kingdom with an army which he brings with him.   On Sunday last a musket was discharged at a Catholic preacher in the middle of his sermon, and when nearly four thousand people were round him.   It is not yet discovered who fired it.   The French talk confidently of the high spirits of their army in Italy and France, and boast that your Majesty will have enough to do to make head against them.

" I am much displeased to see Paget so completely diverted from the straight road, and so forgetful of his duty to the Queen.   He goes on from worse to worse.   We hear that within these few days he has sold land to the value of a hundred pounds; so that if his enterprise fails, and he is himself arrested, this hundred pounds may be saved from confiscation and distress ; and there is certain information that he intrigues with Mason, who

---

le royaulme, avec gens de guerre qu'il amene avec luy.   L'on tira, Dimanche passé, un coup d'arquebouse contre un predicant Catholique, estant au milieu de sa predication, à laquelle assistoient plus de quatre mille personnes, et n'a l'on sceu qui avoit tiré le dit coup.   Et les François font entendre que les forces du Roy sont gaillardes en Italie, et en France, et que vostre Majesté aura à faire à les soubstenir.

" Il me deplait de veoir Paget desvoyé du droit chemin, et qu'il se soit tant oblyé à l'endroit de la Royne, et qu'il continue de pis en pis ; car l'on entend que, ces jours passez, il a fainct de vendre cent livres de terre, afin que si son entreprinse ne reuscit, ou qu'il soit arresté, les cent livres soient saulfves de la confiscation et distraictes ; et a l'on certain advis qu'il tient practique avec Masson lequel luy escript souvent et particuli-

writes to him frequently and very particularly. If your Majesty would wish to have this confirmed, it may be easily done, as he entrusts his letters to the couriers who come from these parts, as well those from the court as from Antwerp. To come to a clear discovery of this would be highly advantageous to the affairs of the Queen.

" It is reported that the ambassador of Ferrara is come with a commission from his master to see whether he cannot bring about a marriage between his eldest son and the Lady Elizabeth.

" London, 14th June 1554.

" And thus, Sire, &c.

" To the Emperor."          " SIMON RENARD."

### SIMON RENARD TO THE EMPEROR.

#### 15th June 1554.

\* \* \* " THE Queen will set out to-morrow and await the coming of the Marquis of las Naves at

---

erement; et s'il plaisoit à vostre Majesté avoir confirmation, elle la pourroit aisement avoir, pour ce qu'il quiert ses lettres aux courriers qui viennent par deça, tant de la court que d'Anvers, que seroit esclairer chose grandement prouffitable à l'estat de la dite dame. L'on entend que l'ambassadeur de Ferrare, qu'est venu pardeça, a charge du Sieur Duc son maistre pour assentir si l'on pourroit dresser le mariage de son filz aisné avec Madame Elisabeth.          " A tant, &c.     S. RENARD."

### SIMON RENARD A L'EMPEREUR.

#### 15th June 1554.

\* \* \* " SIRE.—La Royne se partira demain et attendra le Marquis de las Naves à Guilfort. L'ambassadeur de France a

2 E 2

Guildford.  The French ambassador has sent word
to the Chancellor that he has information that his
Highness will be here at the end of the month.

" I have sent to the Count de Courrieres three
thousand ducats, besides the thousand crowns of
the sun, which I have already disbursed to the
Count de Chapelle.

" The Council here have determined that his
Highness' name shall stand first in all the despatches from this kingdom, and that the seals shall
bear on them the arms of both kingdoms. † * * *

" Richmond, 15th June, 1554.

" And thus, Sire, &c.

" To the Emperor."                    " SIMON RENARD."

These letters of Renard tell their own story,
and follow each other at such brief intervals that
any comment is unnecessary.  If I do not overrate them, they add many new and important facts
to the history of this period, on which Noailles'

---

fait dire au Chancellier qu'il a nouvelles que son Altese sera à
la fin de ce mois en ce royaulme,  J'ay envoyé au Sieur de
Courrieres trois mil ducatz, oultre les mil escuz au soleil que
j'ay desja furny pour le Sieur de la Chapelle.

" Le Conseil a resolu que son Altese sera prenommé en tous
depesches qui se feront en ce royaulme, et que les seelz seront armoyez des déux.

" A tant, Sire, &c.

" SIMON RENARD."

" A l'Empereur."

† " Les seelz seront armoyez des deux.'

despatches have hitherto been the great authority ; a slight glance at them will convince the critical reader how differently the same facts appear in Noailles' pages and in Renard's narrative. Both ambassadors undoubtedly had their bias, the one for, the other against, Mary ; and, between the two, we are likely to arrive at something like the truth. As to one point, Elizabeth's connection with Wyatt's plot, I confess, Renard's letters leave on my mind little doubt of her knowledge of the designs of the conspirators in her favour. That she in any way directly encouraged them there is no direct proof; and, if Wyatt wrote to her, and the Lord Russell delivered his letter, she could not help it. It may be said, concealment was equivalent to indirect encouragement; but we can imagine her shrinking from becoming an informer, and yet disapproving of the enterprise. As to Mary, Renard's picture of the state of the country goes far to justify her measures. The intrigues of France, the danger on the side of Scotland, the boldness of the Protestants, the hatred of Spain, the terrors of the Roman Catholics, and the anxiety with which all who meditated a change in the government looked to Elizabeth as their principal hope and comfort, rendered it absolutely necessary that she should watch her narrowly and have her near her. And here I must say a word on Fox's celebrated narrative of Elizabeth's sufferings.

Mary has been attacked with severity by most of the Protestant historians for her conduct in imprisoning Elizabeth at the time of Wyatt's rebellion. Their opinion, as far as I can trace it, appears to be founded on a narrative in Fox,* which has been copied by all succeeding writers from Strype to Mr. Turner; and on the letters of Noailles, the French ambassador. Where Fox got the particulars of this story, he himself does not inform us; but it is highly coloured: some facts are stated in it which are completely disproved by the best evidence; and it is important to notice, that on these facts the charges of the undue severity and cruelty of Mary towards Elizabeth are mainly founded.

He affirms, for example, that on the day after Wyatt's rising, (that is, the 26th of January, for he rose on the 25th,) Mary sent three of her Council, Sir Richard Southwell, Sir Edward Hastings, and Sir Thomas Cornwaleys to Ashridge with a troop of horse, to bring the Lady Elizabeth to court, " *quick or dead.*" These knights, he tells us, arrived there late at night, and insisted at that unseasonable hour on seeing the Lady Elizabeth, who was then very ill in bed. Some delay having taken place, they refused to wait; burst rudely into her bedchamber, informed her that she must away with them to court, and next morning, by ten of the clock, carried her off, amid the tears and remonstrances of her servants. Fox's narrative is long and minute, but this is the sum of it; and,

* Fox, vol. iii. p. 792.

were it true, no one could acquit Mary of cruelty. I proceed to show that, although copied by our best historians, it is completely erroneous.

When Wyatt broke into open rebellion, and when it was found, as we have seen, by the intercepted letters of Noailles, and, by the confessions of some of the prisoners, that Elizabeth and Courtenay were the great cards to be played by the conspirators against Mary and the Spanish match ; that the Queen was to be dethroned, Elizabeth crowned in her stead, and Courtenay to be married to her ; that France and Scotland were involved in the plot, and meditated a simultaneous invasion ; — when all this came out, Mary, instead of instantly sending, as Fox affirms, a body of horse to bring her sister to court, " quick or dead," acted with kindness and forbearance.　She addressed a letter to her sister on the 26th January, in which she alluded to the unnatural rebellion of Wyatt, to the *untrue* rumours that had been spread through the kingdom, to the insecurity in which Elizabeth must remain if she continued at Ashridge, and she concluded by bidding her make her repair with all convenient speed to court, where she would be safe and heartily welcome.*　Who, considering the circumstances in which she was then placed, can blame Mary for taking such a precaution ? and what opinion are we to form of a writer so culpably careless as to omit all mention of this letter,

* Strype's Memorials, vol. iii. part i. p. 127.

and to substitute in its place an ideal commission given to three of the Council to repair to Ashridge, and bring Elizabeth to court, alive or dead ? *

To this letter of Mary, written on the 26th January, Elizabeth returned a verbal answer. She was too ill, she said, to come at that time to court, but she would repair thither as soon as she could travel with safety; and she requested the Queen's forbearance for a few days. Now it is worthy of notice, that although, as we have seen from the letters of the Spanish ambassador, every day was bringing some new presumption that Wyatt's rebellion had for its principal object to raise Elizabeth to the throne, Mary's forbearance, at this trying crisis, extended not only to a few days, but to more than two weeks.† She waited for her sister's coming, from January 26th to February the 10th; and it was not till Sir Thomas Wyatt himself directly accused Elizabeth and Courtenay of being accomplices in his conspiracy, and cognizant of the rebellion, that the Queen, on the 10th of February, despatched Lord William Howard, Sir Edward Hastings, and Sir Thomas Cornwaleys to bring her sister to court. And how was it that she sent for her ?   Was it with the bar-

---

* We have a still stronger proof of Fox's carelessness in the fact, that he is not only contradicted by contemporary documents, but contradicted by himself; for I have since found, that the account given of the mission to Ashridge, in the body of his work, is entirely different from that of the narrative, printed as a kind of Appendix to the third volume.

† Strype's Memorials, vol. iii. part i. pp. 127, 128.

barous injunction, as Fox has expressed it, to bring
her thither " quick or dead ?"    So far from it, that
the Queen ordered her own physicians, Dr. Owen
and Dr. Wendy, to accompany these noblemen,
that they might see whether she was in a fit state
to be moved without danger ; and sent her own
litter for her to travel in.

Fox has given us no proofs upon which he founds
his statement, and I have already shown it to be
erroneous.    I can support mine by the letter of
the nobleman and knights who were sent by Mary.
It is addressed from Ashridge to the Queen, and
fully explains the object of the mission, and the
judicious, nay, I may say the tender, manner,
in which it was executed.    It appears that this
nobleman, with Sir Edward Hastings and Sir
Thomas Cornwaleys, arrived at Ashridge on the
10th of February, and requested to see the Lady
Elizabeth ; but so far from using haste, rudeness,
or abruptness, previous to the interview, they sent
the Queen's physicians to see the sick Princess,
and, having ascertained from their report that she
was able to travel without any danger to her person, they then delivered their message.    (So at
least, I understand the letter.)    Elizabeth declared
her readiness to obey, but expressed her fears that
her life would be in danger, if she ventured to travel
in her present weak state.    This was the natural
apprehension of an invalid ; but the opinions of the
physicians, the advice of the Privy Councillors, and
" the persuasions of her own council and servants,"

overcame her fear and reluctance, and she resolved
to remove from Ashridge to the court.   Neither
was there any undue hurry.   The Councillors arrived on the 10th, they remained all the 11th at
Ashridge, and on the 12th, Elizabeth set out, travelling by slow journeys in the Queen's litter.*   But it
is time to give this important letter.

THE  LORD  ADMIRAL,  SIR  EDWARD  HASTINGS,
AND SIR THOMAS CORNWALEYS, TO THE QUEEN.

*Orig.*  St. P. Off.  *Domestic.*   11th Feb. 1553-4.

 " In our humble wise.  It may please your Highness to be advertised, that yesterday, immediately
upon our arrival at Ashridge, we required to have
access unto my Lady Elizabeth's Grace ; which obtained, we delivered unto her your Highness' letter ; and I, the Lord Admiral, declared the effect of
your  Highness' pleasure, according to the cre-
dence  given to us, being  before  advertised of
her estate by your  Highness' physicians, by whom
we  did  perceive  the  estate  of  her  body  to  be
such that, without danger of her person, we might
well proceed to require her in your Majesty's name
(all excuses set apart) to repair to your Highness
with  all  convenient  speed  and  diligence.

 " Whereunto we found her Grace very willing and
conformable ; save only that she much feared her
weakness to be so great that she should not be

---

* See the Rev. S. R. Maitland's learned and convincing
papers on Fox's Martyrology in the British Magazine.

able to travel and to endure the journey without peril of life, and therefore desired some longer respite until she had better recovered her strength; but in conclusion, upon the persuasion as well of us as of her own council and servants, whom, we assure your Highness, we have found very ready and forward to the accomplishment of your Highness' pleasure in this behalf, she is resolved to remove her hence to-morrow towards your Highness, with such journeys as, by a paper herein inclosed, your Highness shall perceive; further declaring to your Highness that her Grace much desireth, if it might stand with your Highness' pleasure, that she may have a lodging, at her coming to the court, somewhat further from the water than she had at her last being there; which your physicians, considering the state of her body, thinketh very meet, who have travailed very earnestly with her Grace, both before our coming and after, in this matter.

" And, after her first day's journey, one of us shall await upon your Highness to declare more at large the whole estate of our proceedings here. And, even so, we shall most humbly beseech Christ long to preserve your Highness in honour, health, and the contentation of your godly heart's desire.

" From Ashridge, the 11th of February, at four of the clock in the afternoon.

" Your Highness' most humble and bounden servants and subjects,

" W. HOWARD.     EDWARD HASTINGS.

" T. CORNWALEYS.

ENCLOSURE.

*Orig.* St. P. Off.

" The order of my Lady Elizabeth's Grace voyage to the court.

" Monday.—Imprimis, to Mr. Cooke's, vi miles.

" Tuesday.—Item, to Mr. Pope's, viii miles.

" Wednesday.—To Mr. Stamford's, vii miles.

" Thursday.—To Highgate, Mr. Cholmeley's house, vii miles.

" Friday.—To Westminster, v miles."

Such is the account given of this celebrated mission to Ashridge, by Lord William Howard, the principal nobleman to whom it was entrusted.   It is a simple unvarnished letter from an honourable English nobleman, and, as far as I can judge, carries truth upon every word of it.*   It is unnecessary to add, that it totally demolishes the inflated narrative of Fox, which, unfortunately, has without any examination been believed, copied, and argued on, by every Protestant writer from the days of Elizabeth till those of her amiable female biographer, who, if she has erred, has done so in the best historical company.   And here let me for a moment point out a mistake of Carte, which has been

* The high opinion of Lord William Howard, expressed by Elizabeth to the Count of Feria on Nov. 10th, 1558, just before Mary's death, proves that he never could have conducted himself as Fox describes.—See Memorias de la Real Academia, de la Historia, vol. vi. p. 255.—Madrid, 1832.

repeated and exaggerated by Hume, Warton, and Turner. " When she arrived in town," says this author,* " on Thursday, February 22nd, she was so extremely swelled all over her body and face, that nobody who saw her expected that she could live. Yet," he adds, " Monsieur de Noailles styles it a *'favourable illness*,' since it was likely to save her sister (who wished she might die of it) from the crime of putting her to death by violence." Noailles, the French ambassador, was a person of note living at the time and on the spot, and, had such a sentence proceeded from him, it would be entitled to weight, although he is a witness strongly prejudiced against Mary; but no such sentence was ever written by him. Carte has mistaken a note by the Abbé Vertot, the publisher of the Letters, a writer whose embellishing propensities are well known, for the letter itself, and the error has been echoed by succeeding writers, but, unlike the echo, frequency of repetition has increased, not diminished, its intensity.

Leaving this discussion, and having placed, I trust, Mary's conduct to Elizabeth on its right footing, I proceed to her marriage. The following account of this ceremony is somewhat more minute than that given by our own chroniclers. It is translated from a French manuscript preserved in the archives at Louvain.

* Carte, vol. iii. p. 306.

RELATION OF WHAT PASSED AT THE CELEBRA-
TION OF THE MARRIAGE OF OUR PRINCE WITH
THE MOST SERENE QUEEN OF ENGLAND.

*Transcript. from Orig. at Louvain.*   20th July 1554.

" OUR Prince disembarked at South-Hampton
on Friday, the 20th July 1554, at two o'clock.   He
was accompanied by the Earl of Arundel, the Treasurer, and many other English noblemen; and, the
evening before his landing, he had sent the Prince
of Gavze, and Count D'Egmont, to the Queen,
then at Winchester, to inform her of his arrival and
good health.   Having come ashore, he repaired to
the church at Southampton, where the Earl of
Arundel brought him the Order of England—the
Garter, which he received with great pleasure and
joy.   And in this town the Prince remained till
Monday, when he set out for Winchester.

" Being arrived there, he went on horseback and
nobly attended to the church, where there was held
a great musical fête, Te Deum being sung by all
the clergy.   He then returned to his lodging,
where he dined; and about nine in the evening the
Earl of Arundel, with the Great Chamberlain, paid
him a visit, and after some conversation, being
joined by the Count D'Egmont, conducted the
Prince to the Queen secretly.   This was the first
time that they had seen each other.   On the following day, which was Tuesday, the Prince came
in great triumph and nobly accompanied to the

Queen's lodging; and, entering the great hall, found the Queen there, who advanced to receive him, and thus, approaching each other, they embraced and saluted; upon which the Prince took her by the hand, and conducted her to the seat under a rich canopy, where, having taken their places, they conversed for nearly an hour.

" From this they went into the Queen's apartment, where they remained in conversation for nearly two hours. Here wine was brought, and the Queen drank to the Prince, which is the custom in England; and his Highness, having bid adieu to the Queen, not without much courtesy and ceremony, retired to his lodging.

" On St. James' day the Prince left his apartment. His breeches and doublet were white, the collar of the doublet exceeding rich, and over all a mantle of rich cloth of gold—a present from the Queen, who wore one of the same; this robe was ornamented with pearls and precious stones: and thus dressed, wearing the collar of the Garter, and attended by several noblemen in rich apparel, he proceeded to the church, where, on his entry, there struck up a joyous concert of trumpets, clarions, and other sorts of music.

" Here the Prince waited for the Queen a full half-hour, who came splendidly attended, as well by the nobles and ladies of England, as by many who had come over with the Prince. They were then betrothed; and entering farther into the

body of the church, surrounded by the nobility
and six bishops who were present, the Emperor's
representative, Figueroa, delivered to the Prince,
on the part of the Emperor, a parchment scroll,
making at the same time a speech: having
read it, the Prince presented it to the Queen,
who handed it to the Chancellor of England,
and he, after perusing it, publicly proclaimed
that the Emperor had made a present to his son,
the Prince of Spain, of the kingdom of Naples;
at the same moment they sent for a sword of
state, (there was none there except the Queen's
sword of state,) which being brought, it was delivered to the Earl of Pembroke, who carried
it before the Prince, whilst the Earl of Derby
bore the Queen's sword. Having thus arrived further up (into the body of the church), the Archbishop of Winchester married them with great
ceremony, as the case required; and a solemn mass
was sung, which lasted from twelve to three.
Coming then out of the church, they walked hand-
in-hand to the court. At the banquet, the Earl of
Arundel presented the ewer, the Marquis of Winchester the napkin; none being seated except the
King and Queen; but, as to the rest of the entertainment, it was more after the English than the
Spanish fashion. The dinner lasted till six in the
evening, after which there was store of music; and,
before nine, all had already retired.

## " NAMES OF THE SPANISH NOBLEMEN WHO CAME OVER WITH OUR PRINCE.

| | |
|---|---|
| " The Duke of Alva, | " The Count de Feria, |
| " The Duke of Medina Celi, | " The Count Chinchon, |
| | " The Count Olivares, |
| " The Admiral of Castile, | " The Count de Saldana, |
| " The Marquis Pescara, | " The Count de Modica, |
| " The Marquis de Farria, | " The Count de Fuensalda, |
| " The Marquis del Valle, | " The Count del Castelliar, |
| " The Marquis d'Aguillara, | " The Bishop of Cuença, |
| " The Marquis de las Naves, | and some others." * |

On Mary's return to London, the Lady Anne of Cleves, who, since her divorce by Henry the Eighth, had lived in profound retirement, intimated, in the following letter, her desire to visit the King and Queen.

### ANNE OF CLEVES TO THE QUEEN.

*Orig.* St. P. Off. *Domestic.* Hever, 4th August 1554.

" AFTER my humble commendations unto your Majesty, with thanks for your approved gentleness and loving favour showed unto me in my last suit, praying your Highness of your loving continuance. It may please your Highness to understand that I am informed of your Grace's return to London again, being desirous to do my duty to see your Majesty

---

* Relation de ce qu'est passé en la celebration du mariage de nostre Prince avec la Serenissime Royne d'Engleterre.— From the archives de la ville de Louvain, Registre, Cote G. folio 889.

and the King, if it may so stand with your Highness' pleasure, and that I may know when and where I shall wait upon your Majesty and his; wishing you both much joy and felicity, with increase of children to God's glory, and to the preservation of your prosperous estates, long to continue with honour in all godly virtue.

" From my poor house at Hever, the 4th of August.

" Your Highness' to command,

" ANNA, the Daughter of Cleves." *

Addressed.—" To the Queen's Majesty."
Endorsed.— " The Lady Anne of Cleves to
   the Queen's Majesty.   4th Aug. 1554."

We must now return to Sir William Cecil.   In his brief manuscript Diary, written in his own hand, and preserved in the Lansdowne Collection, he has this passage : " 6th Nov. 1554. 2 Mariæ.   I set out with the Lord Paget and Mr. Hastings to the court of the Emperor, for the purpose of bring-

---

* The Lady Anne of Cleves was married to Henry the Eighth on the 6th of January 1539-40, and was divorced by that monarch in the month of July following.   Her humble letter, in which she submits herself wholly to his Highness' goodness and pleasure, and begs that, as a sister, she may sometimes have the fruition of the noble presence of her sensual and capricious Lord, has been printed in the State Papers published by Government.†   She died in England on the 16th July 1557, and was interred at Westminster.

---

† State Papers, Henry the Eighth, p. 637.

ing back the Cardinal.  We came to Brussels on
the 11th November.  We returned to Westminster
on the 23rd November with Cardinal Pole."*

When we last parted with this eminent man, he
had escaped from a calamity which overwhelmed
some of his best friends and patrons.  He had made
his submission to Mary, and, if not again admitted
into confidence, had at least received assurance of
pardon.  We now find him despatched, together
with Lord Paget and Sir Edward Hastings, to
bring Cardinal Pole into England; the principal
object of whose mission, as is well known, was to
restore that country to the bosom of the Roman
Catholic Church.

Now, this was a singular excursion for one who
had been so determined a Protestant under Edward ; and the question naturally arises, " What
was Cecil's conduct as to religion under the reign
of Mary ?"  Should the reader look for an answer in
the common lives which have been written of him,
he will find that little is known, whilst even that
little is contradictory and obscure.  As the point is
an important one, I shall examine it with some care.

At this moment, amongst the subjects of Mary,
as regarded religion, there were only three classes
of men :  they who soon after her accession fled

* 6 Novembris 1554, 2 Mariæ.  Cœpi iter cum Domino
Paget et Magistro Hastings versus Cæsarem, pro reducendo
Cardinalem.  Venimus Bruxelles, 11 Novembris; redivimus 23
Nov. Westmonasterium cum Cardinale Polo.

to the continent, and preferred expatriation to
the sacrifice of their faith; they whose consciences would not permit them to fly from the
post of danger, but who remained at home, openly
professed themselves Protestants, and endured
persecution or death; and, lastly, they who also
remained at home, but for the time became Roman
Catholics, — to this last class it always appeared
to me that Sir William Cecil must have belonged.
But I was checked in the confidence of my
opinion by the obscure and contradictory accounts
given by the writers of his life.   The Roman Catholics positively affirm that he not only adopted
their faith, but showed an extreme zeal, deeply de-
ploring his errors under Edward.   In a rare pamphlet, published abroad during the reign of Elizabeth, and which is written with much bitterness
against Cecil, then Lord High Treasurer, it is
declared that many, then alive, will remember how
the Duke of Northumberland, having been beheaded and Queen Mary established, " the Lord Treasurer bestirred himself to get credit with the Catholics, frequented masses, said the litanies with the
priest, laboured a pair of great beads, which he
continually carried, preached to his parishioners in
Stamford, and asked pardon of his errors in King
Edward's time;—it states that many still recollect
what he said and protested to divers, and particularly to Sir Francis Englefield, then of the Council,
about his belief of all points of the Catholic Roman

faith; how he deceived Cardinal Poole, and persuaded Sir William Petre to resign up his office the Secretaryship unto him, if Queen Mary would have admitted the same, who never could be persuaded to believe him. And lastly, how Mr. Cecil, being rejected by Queen Mary, began to serve the Lady Elizabeth, and how he entered with her afterwards when he came to the crown to persuade her to the change of religion for his own interest against the opinion of the Councillors." * Such is the Roman Catholic account of Cecil's conduct in religious matters under Mary, but it is evidently written with a strong bias against him.

Turning from this to his Life by a Domestic, published by Collins, afterwards by Peck, with learned Notes, and since adopted by most of his Protestant biographers, we find a totally opposite story. It asserts that Mary on her accession offered to retain him in the high office of Secretary provided he would renounce his Protestant principles, and conform himself to the Roman Catholic faith; but that he declined the proposal, and declared that he must obey God and his conscience rather than the Queen. As it relates to a disputed point, it may be as well to quote the passage.

" When Queen Mary came in she granted Sir Wm. Cecil a general pardon; and in choosing her Councillors, she had so good liking of him, as if he

* British Museum, printed Cat. $\frac{608. c.}{\textit{3.}}$ pp. 15 and 16.

would change his religion he should be her Secretary and Councillor. And to that purpose, some wise men were underhand set to allure him and discover his disposition ; but like himself, he wisely and christianly answered, he was taught and bound to serve God first, and next the Queen: but if her service should put him out of God's service, he hoped her Majesty would give him leave to choose an everlasting rather than a momentary service. And, for the Queen, she had been his so gracious Lady, as he would ever serve and pray for her in his heart, and with his body and goods be as ready to serve in her defence as any of her loyal subjects, so she would please to grant him leave to use his conscience to himself." * * " Here," concludes this writer, " was no turncoat nor seller of his soul, nor renouncer of his faith for ambition of a councillor's place, as many would do upon so fair an offer." †

One would certainly think at first sight that these statements could not both be true, and yet it is possible that the passage in the Life edited by Collins, may relate solely to what took place in the first year of Mary, whilst the passage in the Roman Catholic account has a reference to his conduct after the persecutions for religion began. When perplexed by these contradictory accounts, and finding it stated by Burnet, who had given no au-

† Life of Burleigh, published by Collins, from a manuscript in the possession of the Marquis of Exeter, pp. 11 and 12.

thority, that Cecil had made compliances under
Mary, I came upon a letter in Strype's Life of
Sir John Cheek, which seemed to me to prove that
such compliances must have been carried much farther than was generally suspected. It is obscurely
expressed, and much too long to quote entire, but
although I did not venture to think that it decided
the question as to Cecil's becoming a Roman Catholic under Mary's reign, it appeared to me to go
very near to do so. Under what other supposition
will the following passages be intelligible ? †

" I was very glad to hear of your being in the
Parliament house, supposing to be left in you such
fruits of honesty as would and should serve for the
commonwealth. My looking was not utterly deceived in you, and was, and am, as glad to hear
tell of your well doing to your praise and other's
profit as I am sorry many times when I hear the
contrary. * * * Ye know in philosophy what difference is between ακρασια [intemperantia] and
ακολασια [petulantia], and that the wise philoso-
phers have disputed of the comparison of those
vices, and what a man in his own life may judge of
them. I had rather, for my part, have you cor-
rupted in the lower part of your mind than hear of

† Cecil, in a parliament held this year, had, it seems, taken
courage to speak against some abuses and intrusions of the
Pope upon the liberties of the English crown. This speech
made some noise amongst the exiles for religion abroad ;—and,
Cheek, on the 18th Feb. 1556, addressed the letter in question
to his old friend.

you that both your parts were utterly rotted away from that soundness that common opinion of just causes hath had of you. So long as a man hath sparks left in himself, he may be assured as in a fire well raked up to light a candle or make a fire in a convenient time. If because things be usually done in others, commonly, or else of a few, or of yourself, they should be taken to be good, it should follow that either use should make good or bad and not God's commandment, or else men's judgments should cause goodness or badness in things and not Scripture." * * * And again he says : " Thus much have I said for this end, that ye do not as divers others everywhere do, (whatsoever they do either in private matters or common causes,) to allow (justify) it when they have done it, and to stand to the same as good and lawful ; and therefore either convenient to be done or sufferable. Ye ask me what [fault] find I in you that I talk thus long. I answer, I desire to find none; nor had been no great examiner of other men's doings ; and you know that my wit is θεπκον in writing. * * * I mean my friends thus much good, that if they will corrupt their own doings (as I can say nothing of yours), yet where I fear that I knew, I was then avoiding that I fear, if they would keep their judgments sound and not so love their own doings,—that they make them the rule of their judgment. * * * But I must leave — my paper biddeth me so ; and thus I commend [myself] to you and to my lady, and you both to God.    Wishing you that stedfastness in the truth, and that choice of doing well that I do desire of God for myself.    Fare ye well, and bring up your son in the true fear of God.

    " From Strasbourgh, the 18th Feb. 1556,
        " Your assured brother,
                " JOAN. CHEEK."*

It appeared to me that this letter went far to show that there was some foundation for the account of the Roman Catholic writer; and there were several circumstances which confirmed me in this view. Cecil's continuance at court; his friendship and influence with Cardinal Pole, his being sent to bring this ecclesiastic into England; his continued influence with Paget, Petre, Mason, Gardiner, and most of Mary's ministers and councillors; and his prosperous condition, whilst his brother-in-law Sir John Cheek, his father-in-law Sir Anthony Cook, his friend the Duchess of Suffolk, and many others, were exiles for religion;— all appeared to afford a strong presumption of this fact.    On the other hand, the confident assertions of many of the writers of his life, that he remained a Protestant, and sacrificed the offer of service and high promotion to his conscience, naturally created hesitation in the absence of direct evidence to the contrary.    When thus perplexed, I found, on con-

* Life of Cheek, pp. 99 and 100.—Oxford, 1821.

sulting the work of Dr. Nares,* that this author, although he does not admit that Cecil ever became a Roman Catholic, gives a brief extract from a paper communicated to him by the late Mr. Lemon, and said to be preserved in the State Paper Office, from which he concludes, that to a certain extent he complied with the times. It appeared to me, that if the original of this paper could be found, it would set the question at rest, and to my great delight I discovered it after a search of nearly three days, amongst a loose collection of notes and memoranda which had been put up by themselves as illustrating the private life of Lord Burleigh. The papers in this bundle are of various dates, and of a multiform description : embracing account-books containing his various expenses, little note-books of rural work intended to be done or in progress at Burleigh, tailors' and carpenters' bills, memoranda of sums due by him, scrolls of letters, and lastly, tithe-books of his different church benefices, embracing a minute analysis in his own hand of the various quantities of eggs, butter, cheese, wool, pigs, geese, lambs, and other small gear, which were paid by his parishioners at Wimbledon, Stamford, and other places. Amongst these is the paper in question, endorsed in Sir William Cecil's hand.

* Life of Lord Burleigh, vol. i. pp. 674, 675.

## "EASTER BOOK. 1556.

" The namis of them that dwelleth in the pa-riche of Vembletoun, that was confessed, and resav-ed the sacrament of the altre. ·

" *My master Sir Wilyem Cecell and my lady Myldread his wyffe.*

" *Thomas Cecell*, ii$^d$.

" Raff Baulding, ii$^{d.}$

" Hary Stevenson, ii$^{d.}$

" Wilyem Kawart, ii$^{d.}$

" Quintyn Swentin, ii$^{d.}$

" Hary Hugenoe,

" John Fenton,

" Thomas Cowper and his wife,

" Peter Putler,

" Gilbard Torre,

" John Michelson,

" Elisabeth Cooke,

" Margaet Wyght,

" Elsabecht Bardyn,

" Margrat Brown,

" Nell Crackes," &c. &c.

It is needless to add the names of the remaining persons who attended mass, one hundred and twenty-six in number, or their offerings, which are also stated ; the sum total being calculated in Sir William's hand, and amounting to twenty-four shillings and twopence halfpenny : but it may be curious to give from the same paper the following small account, as it is connected with some entries in a note-book of Sir William Cecil's.

" Item for vi. quarts of wine  .   .   .  xviii$^{d.}$

" Item for bread  .   .   .   .   .  vi$^d$.

" Item for ii$^{lb.}$ of wax in tap$^s$  .   .   .  ii$^{s.}$

" Item for oil and creme .   .   .   .  viii$^{d.}$

" Item for his bootehyre [boat-hire] to London to fetche this, &c. — and again  .   ·   .   .   .  iiii$^{d.}$

v$^s$.

Totalis de claro * xix$^{s.}$ ii$^{d.}$"

* *i. e.* The net or *clear* proceeds after a sum has been deducted.

The first of these papers explains itself; the second is an account of the expenses of the altar at Easter, drawn up probably by the Priest.   Now I have found amongst the series of Sir William Cecil's papers and letters already described, a small book, written in his own hand, in which this same account is engrossed.   The book is endorsed by him,

### " THE BOOK OF WIMBLETON PARSONAGE.

" ACCOUNT OF THE RECTORY OF WYMBLETON, FOR THE
RECEIPT THEREOF.

" PUTNEIGH.—Imprimis, &c. Mr. Welbeck.

" MORTLAK.—Item de Joe Mont.

" WYMBLETON.—Item for oblations at Easter, as appeareth by the Vicar's book, *de claro* ult$^a$.

vi. qu$^{rts}$ of wyne xviii$^d$. ii. tap. ii$^s$.
Oleo and cream, viii$^d$. his boathyre iiii$^d$.    } xix$^{sh}$. ii$^d$.
In toto v$^s$.
Item crysas xl. quod donatur vicario.

I omit his minute accounts kept of tithe pigs, geese, lambs, wool, &c. and shall only give one other page.   It is entitled,

### CHARGES OF THE BENEFICE.

" Imprimis, the yearly rent of the parsonage, xlix$^l$.

" Item to Giles Smith for the rent of the Vicar's house, xx$^s$.

" Item, given to the Priest at Putney, in reward, x$^{sh}$.  }
" Item, given to the Priest at Morthlak    .    . x$^{sh}$.  } xx$^{sh}$.

" Item, paid for the holy loaf, i$^{ob}$.

" Item, for gathering of the tithes, to Wm. Cole, xxvi$^{sh}$. viii$^d$.

These  papers  could  never  have  been  consulted

by Dr. Nares; for they contradict his conclusions, establishing beyond a doubt that, during Mary's reign, Sir William Cecil became a Roman Catholic, and that the commonly received opinions regarding his consistent and conscientious adherence to the Protestant faith are erroneous. They prove that he retained his benefices, of the profits of which he kept a very strict account; he confessed, he attended mass with his wife Lady Cecil, and he brought up his son Thomas Cecil, afterwards Earl of Exeter, in the profession of the Roman Catholic faith. These truths are now established upon evidence which cannot be controverted.

We are not to be surprised therefore that he should have consented to accompany Paget and Hastings in their mission to bring Cardinal Pole into England. The following paper explains the nature of the service on which they went; but, as Cecil's name does not occur in the instructions, it is difficult to say what was his official capacity, nor indeed is there direct proof that he went in any.

THE MINUTES OF INSTRUCTIONS GIVEN TO THE LORD PAGET AND THE MASTER OF THE HORSE.

*Orig. Draft.* St. P. Off. *Germany.* 5th Nov. 1554.

" Whereas the most Reverend father in God, our right entirely beloved cousin, Cardinal Pole, being sent from the Pope's Holiness, not only to congratulate us on our marriage, and other great

benefits which Almighty God of his only goodness
hath abundantly poured upon us since our first
entry to the government of our realms, but also to
travail with us upon sundry other matters concerning the restitution of our realms of England and
Ireland to the true honouring of Almighty God
and unto the Catholic church; for which purpose
our said cousin having long travailed, and with all
patience tarried till such time as considering the
state of our subjects, we might think most meet for
the quiet performing of his godly purpose; for as
much as we be in good hope that by the help of
Almighty God the time so serveth, that at this
parliament, summoned against the 12th day of
this month, this godly matter" ——— I am sorry
to say the paper here breaks off abruptly. It
afterwards enjoins the ambassadors first to open
the matter to the Emperor, then to seek the
Cardinal, to whom they are to " declare how
that the greatest and almost only mean to procure the agreement of the noblemen and others
of our Council was our promise that the Pope's
Holiness would at our suit dispense with all pos-
sessors of any lands or goods of monasteries, col-
leges, or other ecclesiastical houses, to hold and
quietly enjoy their said lands and goods without
any trouble or scruple; without which promise it
had been impossible to have had this consent, and
shall be utterly impossible to have any fruit and
good concord ensue: for which purpose you shall

earnestly pray our said cousin to use all the possible diligence, and say that (if he have not already)
he may so receive authority from the See Apostolic
to dispense in this matter, as the same being now
in good towardness, may, this parliament, take the
desired effect; whereof we see no likelihood of,
except it may be therewithal provided for this matter of the lands and goods of the church."

Touching the order of his coming, Mary observes in the same paper, that "although she and
a great many others accept him as *Legate de
latere*, yet, at present, till he himself witnesses
the state of the country, she thinks it best he
only enters as a Cardinal and ambassador. * *
And, discoursing further unto him the state of
religion presently in this realm, our pleasure is
you shall give your attendance upon him till his
coming to our presence." *   *   *

About the time that Paget, Hastings, and Cecil,
were sent to Brussels to bring over the Cardinal,
the Lord Admiral Clinton was despatched with the
order of the Garter to the Duke of Savoy; an honour paid to this renowned captain in contemplation of a scheme which Philip had much at heart,—
a marriage between him and the Lady Elizabeth.
Clinton gives the following account of his embassy
and noble reception by the Duke, whom he found
in the midst of his army.

## LORD CLINTON TO SIR WILLIAM PETRE.

*Orig.*   St. P. Off.   *Germany.*   8th Nov. 1554.

" After my most hearty commendations.   It
may please you to understand that upon Sunday
last I arrived at Hedingfert, where I found the
Duke of Savoy; and, for that he thought there was
no meet place there to receive the Order in such
honourable sort as he desired, he deferred the receiving thereof for two days longer, to the end that
at his coming to Osyshatewe he might receive it :
and so upon Monday the camp marched thither ;
and upon Tuesday he received the Order and went
to the church, being a good distance from the
castle, accompanied with all the nobility and other
captains in the camp.

" I assure you it was so honourably used as
might be possible, and the greatest entertainment
and courtesy shown unto me and all other gentlemen in my company that ever I have known showed to any; not only at the Duke's hand, but of
the nobility, both Spaniards and Bourguignons; and
such a demonstration of favour borne unto us, coming from the King and Queen's Majesty, as I assure you I wish in my heart that all Englishmen
knew it.   I assure you I cannot write too much of
it as it deserves.   The Duke sent to me, I being at
Ayer, a gentleman of his, and divers of his own
horses, to bring me to the camp; and also sent conduct of men of arms for me ; and, within half a mile

of Heding, there met me a nobleman of Spain, called Don Anthony Suynça, accompanied with many
noblemen and gentlemen ; and, ere I came at the
camp, the Duke of Savoy accompanied very
honourably did meet me, and brought me to his
lodging. I was lodged near unto him, and all
that came with me, in his own stuff and at his
charges all the time of my being in the camp till
my return hither ; and every meal I was at his
own table, and all the gentlemen that were with me.

" The same day that he received the Order in the
afternoon, there happened a great skirmish between the French and them ; and the Duke took
his horse and went to it, and it endured three
hours : at which skirmish there were taken thirty
or forty Frenchmen, Scots, and Englishmen ; so at
his return he said, This good luck is happened
the day that I have received this noble Order.

" Upon Wednesday he marched from Osysshat-
tewe, with the whole camp, four leagues into
the country of France, and so (as I perceive) to
invade and burn the country ; and so do some
enterprise, as I judge, about Reive, where the
Rhinegrave lyeth, but I am not certain of it. I
assure you they have a strong army both of horsemen and footmen, and well appointed ; which army
he and the noblemen showed me, marching every
regiment severally, and caused them of purpose to
stay that I might see them at leisure.

" At my departure the Duke sent to the gentlemen in my company, which were eight in number, with Mr. Garter, to each of them a chain, worth, as I judge, forty or fifty pounds a-piece; and to me he sent a jennet, very fair, which he esteemed much, and was the horse for his own saddle well appointed. He sent me also armour and weapon for a man of war of divers kinds, very fair; which he sent me word was the present of one soldier to another, as it pleased him to term it. This I thought meet to advertise you, to the end that it may please you to declare the same to my Lords of the Counsel, that the King and the Queen's Majesties may be advertised of it; and this day I depart from Bytane towards the Emperor's Majesty, to present the King and the Queen's Highness' letters, and I shall then make my return into England with all diligence.

" The Duke sent hither with me two bands of horsemen of two hundred, to conduct me hither from the camp. I perceive by him that he intendeth upon his return to the Emperor from the camp, immediately after three or four days' tarrying there, to take his journey to see the King and the Queen's Majesty in England; which, as I perceive by him, will be within these twenty days.

" And thus I commit you to Almighty God, who ever have you in his blessed keeping!

" From Betwane, this 8th of Nov. 1554.

" Yours assured to command,

" E. CLYNTON."

The following letter of Sir John Mason contains an account of his interview, first with Pole, and afterwards with Charles the Fifth. It is minute and interesting.

SIR JOHN MASON TO THE KING AND THE QUEEN'S MOST EXCELLENT MAJESTIES.

*Orig.* St. P. Off. *Germany.* Nov. 9, 1554.

" PLEASETH your Majesties to be advertised, that on Thursday morning before day, being the 8th of this present, arrived here Francisco the courier, with your letters of the 5th of the same. Upon the receipt whereof, as soon as time served, I resorted to the Cardinal, to whom I declared your Graces' proceedings with your Council touching his coming into England, and your desires, for good respects, to have him to set himself toward that journey with as good speed as he might conveniently. I named also unto him such personages as, to conduct him to your presence, and to instruct him in the state of the realm, your Highnesses had appointed to repair to him.

He took this message very joyfully, and said that he perceived daily more and more the work of God in your Majesties' hearts; whom he doubted not but he had chosen for special instruments, not only for this matter, but for many other godly things that thereof would ensue. For himself, immediately upon the arrival of his chaplain, he said he had begun to put himself in order, and within a few days he trusted to be fully ready. Marry, quoth he, you know I am at this present as it were in another ward; I must depart when please the Emperor, who is not at all times to be spoken withal. And having already one sent to Mons. D'Arras, to be my mean to have access to his Majesty for the taking of my leave, &c. he sent me word that he would move his said Majesty for me: marry, the truth was that they had as yet heard nothing out of England of your Highnesses determination in this matter, whereby it should seem, quoth he, that they mind not to meddle with me till they have some word from thence.

" That shall they shortly have, quoth I, for I have commission both to show unto the Emperor the King and the Queen's proceeding in their Council in this behalf, and to pray him, for such consideration as I shall open unto him, to dismiss you as shortly as his Majesty shall think meet and convenient. And I have, quoth I, for my better credit, letters unto his Majesty from the King.—I am very glad, quoth he, thereof; then I trust my abode here shall be very short.

" This done, I sent to signify to the Emperor that, having letters from your Majesties for certain things to be communicated unto him, I was desirous, if it should not be incommodious, to speak with him.

" I had for answer, that I should not be out of the way in the afternoon, for that he intended to signify unto me his pleasure for answer to my request. About three o'clock it liked him to send me word that, if I would come immediately unto him, I should be welcome.

"At my coming into his presence, after your Majesties' most affectuous commendations, I declared to him at good length your Majesties' proceedings with your Council, and their conformity and unities of opinion touching the coming of Cardinal Poole into the realm, how desirous you were to have him there speedily, what personages you had appointed to conduct him to your presence, and your request that it might like his Majesty to license him to depart as shortly as might stand with his pleasure, and to give him also at his departing such good counsel and advice as might seem to his great wisdom fit and convenient. For the messengers appointed to attend upon him, I told him that, rather than any stay should be upon their coming to this court, I had commission to tell the Cardinal they should meet him by the way.

"This done, I delivered unto him your, the King's Majesty's letter, which after he had read, he said it did very much rejoice him to understand both by my tale and by the letter, which confirmed the same, those matters to be in so good a train, whereby must needs ensue the settled good of the realm, and the undoubted contentation of Almighty God. And, for my part, quoth he, I am as glad of it, and take as much pleasure to understand it, as ever I did of any thing in all my life; and I

could have been content that this ambassade had
been put in ere long since : but you may see the
work of our Saviour, by whose ordinance, out of
doubt, the thing hath been hitherto deferred,—
not the letting thereof, but for the riping, and so
for the furthering of the same ; for all things have
their time, and a good thing attempted before the
time loseth many times the whole good effect that
otherwise it might have produced. I will, quoth he,
dismiss my Lord Cardinal as soon as I can, and I
think by Sunday or Monday at the farthest to be
ready for him. Hereby I judge he meant the preparing of his present, which belike will not before that
time be ready. Nevertheless, I assure you, quoth
he, I would be sorry that such personages as be appointed to fetch him should enter into my country
without seeing of me. My Lord Paget, quoth he,
I would be glad to see for old acquaintance, whose
affection I have always found very good towards
my affairs, besides his service lately done for the
bringing of my son and daughter together ; the
other, for his loyalty showed unto the Queen, and
for the trust I perceive she hath therefore still in
him, I would be glad to know.—Sir, quoth I, they
make great haste, and possible it is they may be
here before the Cardinal shall be ready to depart.
Nevertheless you know the sea must be attended
upon ; and oftentimes men lie eight, nine, or ten
days waiting the pleasure thereof. In those cases
it were not convenient his departure were stayed.—

The wind, quoth he, as I take it, serveth very well, and therefore I hope they shall come time enough.

" Here pausing awhile, How goeth my daughter's belly forward? quoth he.— Sir, quoth I, I have from herself nothing to say therein, for she will not confess the matter till it be proved unto her face; but by others I understand, to my great joy and comfort, that her garments wax very strait. —I never doubted, quoth he, of the matter, but that God that for her had wrought so many miracles, would make the same perfect by assisting of nature to his good and most desired work. And I warrant it shall be, quoth he, a man child.—Be it man, quoth I, or be it woman, welcome shall it be; for by that shall we at the least come to some certainty to whom God shall appoint, by succession, the government of our estate;—being that thing yet so uncertain unto us as it maketh all good men to tremble to think the Queen's Highness must die; with whom, dying without fruit, the realm were as good also to die.—Doubt not, quoth he, God will provide both with fruit and otherwise; so as I trust to see, yet, that realm to return to a great piece of that surety and estimation that I have in my time seen it in.

" And here he discoursed what a flourishing realm he had known it, and by what means it was decayed; the principal occasion thereof was our forsaking of God, to whom he trusted we were already partly, and soon should be wholly, reconciled. He willed me, finally, to make his recommendations to both your Majesties, and so I took my leave of him; assuring your Graces that, these seven years, I never saw him in plight that better liked me. I found him sitting very cheerfully at a table. His face, that was wont to be somewhat more full than naturally it ought to be, is now come to the very natural; his colour much amended; his arms at commandment, notwithstanding the late fit which he hath had of his gout; and in all other gestures of his body, were it for the joy conceived of the message, whereof undoubtedly he was very glad, or else by reason of better disposition of his body than before he hath had, he was so lively as I have not of long time seen the like lustiness in him.

" From him I repaired eftsoons to the Cardinal, whom it pleased very much both to hear that his Majesty minded shortly to dismiss him, and to understand also his person to be in so good an estate as I declared to him it was. He will be ready to depart on Tuesday next, or on Wednesday at the farthest. Between this and Calais he must make at the least six days, and peradventure seven; the constitution of his body being so easy to be overthrown, as a little travel taken more than it be able to bear were enough to lay him up, and therefore he useth most to be carried in his journeys in a litter. But your Majesties may be sure that what labour his spare body is able to sustain, he will use it in making speed towards you. I think he may be there about the 24th or 26th of this month. In the mean time the parliament may be led forth and entertained with some by matters, as I have seen it at many other times used.

" He bringeth with him a train which, for learning, soberness, good life, and all other virtuous qualities, may be an example to the rest of the world.

" Thus, Almighty God have your Majesties in his most blessed keeping!

Nov. 9th, 1554. " JOHN MASONE."

We have already seen that Paget and Hastings, accompanied by Sir William Cecil and other gentlemen, were sent to Brussels to conduct Cardinal Pole to England. On the same day on which they arrived in that city, they were admitted to an audience of the Emperor. An account of the interview is given in the following letter.

## LORD PAGET AND SIR EDWARD HASTINGS
## TO THE QUEEN.

*Orig.* St. P. Off. *Germany.* 13th Nov. 1554.

" IT may please your most excellent Majesty to be advertised that, arriving here upon Sunday last in the forenoon, we had audience of the Emperor's Majesty in the afternoon, notwithstanding that the same had that day received the blessed Sacrament,

whereby we noted a great care in him for the expedition of us hence again.

" After due commendation made unto him by
us on your Majesty's behalf, and the causes of our
coming declared unto him, with such circumstances
as by the tenor of our instructions we had in
charge to open unto him, he rejoiced very much
to hear the same; and first giving unto you both
most hearty thanks for your commendations, and
then inquiring very diligently of your good pros-
perities and welfares, and specially, Madame, of
the state of your Majesty's person, he roused himself with a merry cheer, and said that, among many
great benefits for the which he thought himself much
bounden unto God, this was one of the greatest,
that it had pleased him to hold his blessed hand
over that realm ; and so, taking occasion to re-
hearse in what good estate and great reputation
he knew the realm of England had been in the
beginning, and afterward into what calamities the
same fell into, (much, he said, to his regret,) he gave
God thanks not only for the great miracles which
he had showered upon your Majesty, to make you
his apt minister for the restoring of that kingdom
again to the ancient dignity, wealth, and renown,
but also for that it hath pleased him to give you so
soon so certain a hope of succession, whereof like
as he had cause for his part, he said, to rejoice
and take great comfort, so hath all England greater
cause to think themselves most bounden unto God

to praise him, and to serve him for the same. These tidings, he said, of the state of your Majesty's person, Madame, with the report that we had made unto him of the great conformity and whole consent of the noblemen and others in their proceedings before your Majesty touching the receiving of my Lord Cardinal into England, and their earnest submissions to the obedience and union of the Catholic church, were so pleasant unto him, as, if he had been half dead, yet they should have been enough to have revived him again.

" These and many other such like words he used, to declare the joy and contentment of his mind for the good success of this matter; in the managing whereof if anything, he said, should fortune wherein his advice might be thought requisite, your Majesty should not only find the same ready, but also any other thing that lay in him which might serve to your honours and the benefit of the realm.

" To this, when we for our part had joined such talk as to this purpose seemed to our poor wits convenient,—declaring your godly dispositions in this matter, how much you reposed yourselves upon his great wisdom and experience, what confidence you had in his fatherly love and friendly affections towards your Majesties and the benefit of your realms,—we took our leaves of his Majesty, and repaired forthwith unto my Lord Cardinal, whose gladness of our coming we shall not need with

many words to declare unto your Majesties; nor
yet what speech he used to set forth how much he
was bounden unto your Majesties for your gracious
disposition towards him, and how much both you
and he were bounden to Almighty God for the
bending of your hearts this ways; for your Majesties
shall, marry, perceive the same more plainly by
himself at his coming unto your presence.

" This, under your Majesties' correction, we may
be bound to write unto you, that we believe verily
that, whensoever he shall be in England, the same
shall fare the better for him; for he is the man
of God, full of all godliness and virtue, ready to
humble himself to all fashions that may do good;
and therefore he is contented not only to come into
England in such sort as your Majesties have appointed, not as a Legate, but as a cardinal and ambassador to your Majesty, or in any other sort
whatsoever it be that your Majesties will appoint,
he assuring your Majesties that, touching the matter of possessions, all things shall come to pass on
the Pope's behalf in such sort that every man there
shall have cause to be contented.

" Yesternight he took his leave of the Emperor,
and so did we also. This day he repaireth onwards
his journey to an abbey two miles hence, whither
he has used much to resort the time of his abode
here; to-morrow at night to Dendermount; Thursday, to Gaunte; Friday, to Bruges; Saturday, to
Newport; Sunday, to Dunkirk; and, Monday to

Calais,—for his weak body can make no great journeys, and his estate also is to be considered.

" In this journey we shall not fail to do him all the honour and service we can, as well for that we take it to be our special charge, as for that also his great virtues have won us, and bind us to the same.

" We have written now, besides our speaking at our passing by, to the Lord Deputy of Calais for all things to be in a readiness for his transportation, so as we trust we shall not have occasion to tarry long there.   And thus we beseech Almighty God to preserve both your Majesties long, and long to live together to your own good contentments, and to the great comfort and benefit of us your poor subjects.

" From Brussels, the 13th of Nov. 1554.

" Your Majesties' most humble, faithful, and obedient servants,

" WILLIAM PAGET.   EDWARD HASTINGS."


Pole arrived in England on the 24th of Nov. when he was received by the King and Queen and the whole Court with the greatest distinction. Soon after, it was resolved unanimously, in the House of Lords, and with only two dissentient voices in the Commons, that a petition should be presented to the Legate, praying for a re-union with the Church of Rome.   On the 30th of Nov. the Queen took her seat on the throne, having the

King on her left and the Cardinal on her right
hand; the petition was then read, and Pole, after
a long speech, absolved the nation from the sin of
heresy, and restored it to the communion of Holy
Church. To this solemn ceremony, and the account of it which he gave to Charles the Fifth,
Mason alludes in the following letter.

SIR JOHN MASON TO THE COUNCIL.

*Orig.* St. P. Off. *Germany.* Dec. 25th, 1554.

" My humble duty remembered unto your good
Lordships. Your letter written unto me the 10th
of December came into my hands the 19th day of the
same; in the which it liked your Lordships, by order
of the King and Queen's most excellent Majesties,
to advertise me particularly of the great and ines-
timable grace of Almighty God poured upon the
realm, whereby it doth appear that, having suffered
his sheep for a time to stray, he hath not minded
to forsake them for ever. * * *

" Upon receipt whereof I sought incontinently
to have audience of the Emperor; * * and on Sunday, which was the 24th of this present, having
access to his Majesty, I told him I had brought
him comfortable matter, but no great news, for
that I knew he had particularly heard the same
before, which nevertheless the Queen's Majesty
thought she should not well acquit herself, if he
understood not also by her mean. * *

" And so, following the order of your Lordships'

letter, I told him in her name the particularities of
the same; that is to say, the order of the coming
of Cardinal Poole into the realm; the honour showed both by the way, and by the King and Queen's
Majesties' own persons at his arriving at the court;
his oration made at the parliament, wherein he
forgot not to declare the commodity meant unto
the realm by the most happy conjunction of the
Queen with his son; how much we were bound unto
him, that would, being so great a prince, enter into
so dangerous a journey, leaving behind him his
sword and kingly authority, for no interest or commodity of himself, but to serve the realm, and to
help to restore unto the same the fear and love of
Almighty God, for the which purpose, as a Solomon,
he was chosen to the building of the Temple; the
submission and supplication exhibited to the King
and Queen's highness; the absolution given thereupon, first in the court, and afterwards in the
church of St. Paul's; the great mercy of God
showed unto us by our entering again into the
flock of Christ, from the which we had been so
long separated and divided; and, finally, I showed
him that Almighty God, for a further declaration
of his minding to pour abundantly his mercy upon
us, had given unto the Queen's Highness assured
hope of the fruit of marriage, whereof order was
taken through the realm for thanks to be given to
the Author of all goodness, the people by fires and
sundry other kinds of outward signs having de-

clared the inward joy which they have great reason
to conceive of this so great and necessary a gift of
God. * * *

" He took the message in very good and most
joyful part ; and albeit he said he had been advised
before of all the particularities by me rehearsed, for
thanksgiving to God, wherefore he had taken order
throughout all his dominions in these Basse Countries, yet to understand the same again from such
an authority as was the Queen's Highness, it could
not but be very grateful unto him, to whom he
bare the affection not of a father-in-law, but of a
natural father.

" And touching the good train the realm was in
concerning God : never was there news whereof
he conceived more gladness ; for now, he said, was
it in estate to be cured thoroughly of all the sickness and diseases wherewith it had too long travailed, which before by no medicine nor good-will
of any helping hand could have been done.  Now
was it apt to receive all good kinds of curing, and
to feel ease and amendment by the same ; whereby
he trusted, before he died, to see again a great re-
presentation of such a state as a good piece of his
life he had beforetime seen it in.   He had with me
a great discourse how flourishing he had seen it ;
how desirous he had been ever to see the continuance thereof ; what had been the occasions from
the first to the last of the decay of the same,
whereof the principal was ingratitude towards God.

" Touching his son, he was glad to hear so good a report of him by the Queen's Highness; albeit, he said, lovers were scant indifferent judges. He trusted God had ordained him to do some good to the whole estate of Christendom, and [mainly] to that realm ; not doubting but he would order himself with such *douceur* and gentle demeanour as no good man should have occasion to mislike God's appointment of his coming into the realm.

" Here he entered into a great discourse of the difference between governing with rigour and severity and the governing in such sort as the prince and the subjects *se peuvent s'entre entendre et s'entre aimer;* which, for that it were too long to write, I do omit.

" Finally, it was no small joy to him to understand by the Queen's own confession that she was certainly with child ; for the bringing whereof into the world it was all good men's parts to pray, so much good hanging thereupon, particularly to these countries, and generally to the rest of the whole estate of Christendom. * * * And thus, requiring me to make his most affectuous commendations both to the King and to the Queen's Majesties, he dismissed me.

" I found him in right good estate, and in such disposition as, to be looked upon, he was not these ten years better to be liked. And in so good point found he himself, as he said he would do this

Christmas that he had not done a great while; and that was, that he would, by God's grace, be at matins on Christmas-day in the morning. * * * The King of Romans departed from Vienna the 10th of this present, to come to Augusta, where we say he keepeth his Christmas, of intent immediately after the feast to begin the Diet. * * *    And thus, &c.

"25 Dec, 1554, Bruxelles.

"JOHN MASONE."

On the 9th of April 1555, Marcello Cervino, Cardinal of St. Croix, was chosen Pope, in the room of Julius the Third, and took the name of Marcellus the Second.† The character given of him by Father Paul confirms the good opinion pronounced by Mason, but the Pontiff died within a week after the date of this letter. He was succeeded by Cardinal Caraffa, who took the name of Paul the Fourth, having been elected on the 25th of May.‡

MASON TO THE COUNCIL.

*Orig.* ST. P. OFF. *Germany.* 26th April 1555.

"IT may like your good Lordships to be advertised, that this day is come unto the Emperor the confirmation of the news of the Pope's election, which hath been so long looked for as we began to

† Paulo Sarpi, Histoire du Concile de Trente, vol. ii. p. 19, par Courayer.

‡ Id: vol. ii. p. 20.

suspect the first advertisement, and to take it for a matter grounded only upon some fond bruit ; but now it is out of all doubt, being the same made clear by letters from himself, as well to the Emperor's Majesty as to Cardinal Poole and sundry others.

" The man is much commended for his wisdom and all other good parts fit for the place, void of corruption, and not wont to be led by any partial affection ; and therefore, in the discourse made of the division of the Cardinals, between the one side and the other he was accounted neuter. He was brought up under Papa Paulo, whose secretary he was ; and therefore hath he in sundry things much (somewhat in times past) seemed to lean to the faction of Farnese, with whom he was sent to the wars of Almain as councillor and paymaster of the bands sent at that time by the Pope to the aid of the Emperor; and about the same time was he made Cardinal. Nevertheless, the conjecture that the world hath of him is, that he will without respect in this charge demean himself uprightly, and so as may best tend to the universal peace of Christendom.

" The Emperor kept this year the Feast of St. George very solemnly in his chamber of presence ; whereat, nevertheless, there was no great estate more than himself and the Duke of Savoy. Me it liked his Majesty to call thereunto, and none other ambassador ; with whom it pleased him much to talk touching the ancients of the order, and the long time that he had enjoyed the same; so as now, he said, he was the most ancient thereof, having been a knight thereof the space, at the least, of forty-three years.

" The occasion of this Feast made him somewhat to show himself, to the great comfort of many; who, since the late fit of his disease had not seen him. He is, thanks be to God! in very good plight; and with this seasonable weather, which till this time we have long lacked, he is like daily to grow to more perfection of health, and more.

" Sundry noblemen and noblewomen in this court are much desirous to have some cramp rings of this year's blessing. If it may like your Lordships to be suitors to the Queen's Highness to send unto me some little number of them to be divided amongst them, your Lordships shall do a great many much pleasure.

" The Duke of Alva arrived here yester-evening.

" And thus I commit your good Lordships to the tuition of Almighty God.

" From Brussels, the 25th April 1555.

" JOHN MASONE."

About this time the Queen's idea that she was about to give an heir to the throne, occupied much of the talk both of the court and the country.

In the State Paper Office are preserved some curious proofs of the extent to which preparations had been made in the idea of Mary's approaching delivery. Numerous letters had been prepared, signed by the King and Queen, informing the various continental sovereigns of her safe delivery; the word *fil* being left unfinished, so that by the after addition of *s* or of *le* it would serve for a boy or a girl: but one of these singular documents is still more decidedly worded. It is the letter prepared to be sent to Cardinal Pole, who was abroad, and informs him in express terms, " that God had been pleased, amongst his other benefits, to add *the gladding of us with the happy delivery of a Prince.*" In the concluding part of the following letter we see how deeply the hope was riveted in the mind of the Emperor, and how loath he was to give it up.

MASON TO SIR WM. PETRE.

*Orig.* St. P. Off. *Flanders.* 3rd May 1555.

" Sir.—You shall hereby receive the articles of accord between the Emperor and the Genoeses. The army remaineth yet entire, minding to attempt the recovery of the rest of the state of Genes, holden yet by the French, whereof the principal places are Port Hercole, Grossetto, and Mont Alcino.

The Duke of Savoy is departed, post, towards Italy, accompanied with one man only, and his guide, to pass the fairer through Almayne. The rest of his train to the number of twelve, in post, follow by this day, being expected to overtake him

at Augsbourg; reckoning that from thence he
may go safely forward to the rest of the journey,
without fear of Marquis Albert or any other.   His
departing that way is diversely discoursed; nevertheless, the truth is, that he goeth into Piedmont
with contentation both of the Emperor and of the
Queen, and hath promised to be here again the 20th
of this month.

"Yesterday came hither tidings which rejoiced
out of measure this whole court, the effect whereof was, that the Queen's Highness was delivered
of a Prince; whereupon the Emperor sent for me
this morning at four o'clock, and by five I was with
him at his bed-side.   He enquired of me what I
had heard of this matter.   I told him I had heard
from London that the news were true; marry from
the Court I had heard nothing, and therefore I
had the matter suspected.   Loath was he to bring
the thing to any doubt.   But by nine o'clock appeared a courier despatched to the Duke of Alva,
who brought advertisement of the bruit that was
through London, which, nevertheless, he wrote,
was without ground; being the thing otherwise,
and that yet this procrastination was not to be misliked.   We were merry for the time, and now are
we returned to our accustomed hope and expectation.   God send us shortly certain news! And thus,
most heartily fare you well.

"From Bruxelles, the 3rd of May 1555.

"JOHN MASONE."

The letters of Renard have already informed us how deeply Courtenay Earl of Devonshire was suspected of being implicated in the rebellion of Wyatt; and we have seen that the men of the law pronounced him worthy of death. It is therefore to the credit of Mary that, after all, he was not only pardoned, but treated with much kindness, and sent to travel for his improvement. The following letter has a reference to the preparations for the equipment of this young nobleman before he set out for the Low Countries, where he was introduced to the Emperor, to whom the King and Queen had warmly recommended him.

### MARTYN TO THE EARL OF DEVONSHIRE.

*Orig.* St. P. Off. *Domestic.* April 29th, 1555.

" AFTER my most hearty commendations unto your good Lordship, and to my very good Lady your Mother.—I did faithfully your Lordship's message to my Lord Cardinal, to my Lord Chancellor, and to Mr. Secretary Petre. Mr. Bassett had the Council's letter unto Mr. Mason to bring unto you. Your commission for carts and post-horses I have sent herewith by my servant, with one or two more than you speak of, for the better furnishing of the Spanish friar, whereat my Lord Chancellor and certain others of the Council did laugh most heartily.

" I have herewith sent a letter of commendation, for the better expedition and direction of your Lordship's doings among the merchants, unto my very good friend, and both a trusty and wise young man, named Thomas Aldersye, who was embrued with the new found faith, but since, he is reclaimed, and in good estimation with divers of the Council : and in lieu of a letter, for want of leisure, I have sent my commendations unto the Governor of the English merchants, and to Mr. Alderman Whyte, who I doubt not but will do you such service and pleasure as men of their calling may do unto a man of honour.   And thus, leisureless, I cease further to trouble your Lordship's business.

" From the Court, the 29th of April.

" Your Lordship's most assured to his dying day,
            " THOMAS MARTYN."

We find it stated in a letter from Mr. James Basset to the same young Earl, written soon after this (9th May 1555), that " the King's Highness hath specially sent to the Duke of Alva, that if his Lordship arrived there before his departure, the Duke himself should present him to the Emperor; and Philip had given express order that Courtenay should be as much honoured and made of there as may be." * * The same gentleman adds, " I have written at length to Mr. Bonvisi for your Lordship, and have declared fully unto him your estate, how freely you are delivered without any condition, and how greatly the King's Highness and those that be about him hath recommended you unto divers there." * *   In concluding his letter, he informs Courtenay that, "thanks be to God, both their Majesties are in good health; and as for her Highness, [says he,] I have not seen her these many years so healthful and look so [well] as she doth now."

### THE COUNTESS OF EXETER TO THE EARL OF DEVONSHIRE.

*Orig.* St. P. Off. *Domestic.* 16th April, 1555.

On the 16th of May, I find the following short but simple and affectionate letter from the Countess of Exeter, the mother of this young Earl, to her son.   The use in it of the word " natural," for " loving " or "affectionate," is singular.

" Son.—Your letter written to me the 8th of May, I received the 15th of May.   I thought long till I heard you were safe past the seas, the which I was glad to hear; assuring you I shall never be quiet till I see you well in England again; praying to our Lord to preserve you from all perils both in soul and body; desiring much to hear how you have your health in the country you be in.   And because my hand is so ill to read, I have written another letter, whereby you shall perceive, after your departing, what I did at Kew.   And this my most natural blessing I give you, committing you in the hands of Almighty God, to whom I will daily pray for you.

" Written the 16th of May, from Wallsanger, Master Coram's house.

" By your most natural Mother,
" GERTRUDE EXETER."

On the 20th of May, Courtenay addresses the following letter to the Queen, informing her of his kind and honourable reception by the Emperor.

### THE EARL OF DEVONSHIRE TO THE QUEEN.
*Orig.* ST. P. OFF.  20th May 1555.

" IT may please your most excellent Majesty to be advertised,

" On Sunday last, being the 19th of this month, the Duke of Alva brought me to the Emperor's Majesty's presence; unto the which I delivered your Majesty's letters, and therewithal offered my humble service. Of whose Majesty the same was received even accordingly to the honourable and good nature of his Highness, and as appertained to the letters of recommendation written from your Majesty. For the which benefit and goodness of your Grace, I think not myself less bounden to the same, albeit I have received both very many and most great; so that not only by service I am not able to acquit the same, but also I cannot by words express the due and humble thanks that I owe unto your Majesty : so that this only resteth in my power that I shall not cease to pray Almighty God to preserve not only to mine, but generally to the benefit of all Christendom, both your Majesty and the

Emperor's Majesty; whom, greatly to my comfort, I saw sitting up in his chair in such case as it appeared his Highness had both ease and convenient health of his person. Thus now I leave to trouble your Highness further, remaining most humbly at your Majesty's commandment. The 20th of May 1555. From Brussells.

"Your Majesty's most humble subject at commandment,

"EDWARDE DEVONSHER."

In Lord Burleigh's Precepts, addressed to his celebrated son Sir Robert Cecil, afterwards Earl of Salisbury, the aged statesman says, "Be sure to keep some great man thy friend, but trouble him not for trifles, compliment him often with many and small gifts, and if thou hast cause to bestow any great gratuity, let it be something which may be daily in sight, otherwise, in this ambitious age, thou shalt remain like a hop without a pole, live in obscurity, and be made a foot-ball for every insulting companion to spurn at."* We can trace the influence of this aphorism, which breathes so shrewd a spirit of worldly wisdom, in the early career of its author, first under the Protector Somerset, then in his attachment to Northumberland, and, lastly, when Mary came to the crown, in the assiduity with which he seems to have cultivated the friendship of Cardinal Pole, the great man of the day to whom she gave her chief confidence. It has been already shown that he

* Peck's Desiderata Curiosa, p. 47.

accompanied Paget and Hastings in their mission
to bring Pole to England, not in any official
capacity, but as a friend in their suite ; and we
find that, when the King and Queen sent the Cardinal and others of her Council to hold a conference
with the Constable Montmorency, on a peace between Henry the Second and the Emperor, Sir W.
Cecil again attended him, this we learn from the following entry in his MS. Diary, so often alluded to.

" 18th May 1555.—I passed the sea, and came to
Calais with the Cardinal Pole."

Again he writes,

" 25th May 1555.— At Antwerp."

We find him again at Calais, with his servant
Harry Stevenson ; and here it appears by the same
Diary that he remained till the 26th June, when
he returned to England.

Pole was accompanied in this public mission
by Gardiner the Chancellor, to whom were joined
the Earl of Arundel, and the Lord Paget.   The discussions between the English and French commissioners were extremely violent, as we learn from
the following letter of Thomas Martyn to the
Earl of Devonshire, and the pacific attempt of the
Cardinal and his colleagues completely failed.
Martyn's anticipations as to the probability of
Pole's election to the Popedom were singularly
unfortunate, for already when he wrote, the Cardinal
Caraffa, who took the title of Paul the Fourth,
had been chosen in the conclave.

THOMAS MARTYN TO THE EARL OF DEVONSHIRE.

*Orig.* St. P. Off. *Domestic.* 31st May 1555.    *Calais.*

" My duty premised unto your good Lordship, as it appertaineth.  I have of myself moved my Lord Chancellor to procure you licence to go unto some of the King's Majesty's countries, as Milan or Naples, whereby your Lordship should have less occasion to look homeward, and better means to advance yourself in farther knowledge, and therewithal do you more notable service at your return. He said that he thought your being at Brussels was but very dull, and I think no less ; but if he may perceive by your Lordship's letters your mind and will in this point, that immediately after his return, (which will be shortly,) he will procure the same.

" Hitherto the time hath been spent betwixt these honourable personages in embracing one the other, in reading their commissions, and in fruitful exhortations made by my Lord Legate and by my Lord Chancellor unto them both in the Parliament house, as likewise in putting up each part his griefs, with abuses now past of the same : and on Thursday last they fell so far at square, that my Lord Legate of his part, and our commissioners on their parts, had much work to take up the matter betwixt them.  At the last an agreement was made, so that they parted friends.  And to-day there came the Bishop of Orleans from the French, and Mon-

sieur Viglio from the Imperials, to the foresaid commissioners ; and to-morrow we shall have a great
aim whether we shall have peace or war; which
howsoever it shall fall out, my Lord mindeth to
haste hence as soon as he may possibly, for the evil
airs that be here, which must be purged, for fear
of further infection, or else it is like that many a
soul will perish.   There are four rumoured in the
likelihood  to  be  popes,  Pole,  Theatin,  Moroni,
and De Fano.   We have sundry letters from Rome
that the first is most like to speed.   If it be so, it
will be a good occasion for your Lordship to have
the conduct of your own kinsman to his see at
Rome; and I doubt not but it will come to pass.
Thus, upon hope to send you farther news within
these two days, I bid your Lordship most heartily
to fare well.

"From  Staples  Inn  at  Cales,  the  31st  of  this
month of May.        Your Lordship's assured,

"THOMAS MARTYN."


The most interesting part of the following letter
is that which relates to the person named Dee,
who is none other than the celebrated mathema-
tician, astrologer, and spirit-seer, Dr. John Dee.
He was accused not only of calculating the na-
tivities of Mary, Philip, and Elizabeth, a piece of
folly common in those days, but of practising by
enchantment against the Queen's life.[*]

* Smith, Vita Joannes Dee, p. 8, and Biog. Britt. art. Dee.

THOMAS MARTYN TO THE EARL OF DEVONSHIRE.

*Orig.* St. P. Off. *Domestic.* 8th June 1555. *Calais.*

" My duty premised unto your good Lordship, as it appertaineth.  This day, about four of the clock at afternoon, my Lord Chancellor taketh his journey towards England ; having rather made a mean to a peace to be hereafter condescended unto, than a peace at this time in any point determined.

" In England all is quiet.  Such as wrote traitorous letters unto Germany be apprehended, as likewise others that did calculate the King's and Queen's and my Lady Elizabeth's nativity ; whereof one Dee, and Cary, and Butler, and one other of my Lady Elizabeth's, are accused, and that they should have a familiar spirit ; which is the more suspected, for that Ferys, one of their accusers, had, immediately upon the accusation, both his children strucken, the one with present death, the other with blindness.

" Thus, trusting shortly to do you in another place better service, I bid your good Lordship most heartily farewell.

" Written from Calais, the 8th of June.

" Your Lordship's most assured,

" Tho. Martyn."

Endorsed, 8th June 1555.

The two next letters, from Sir Edward Carne to the Queen and the Council, give us some little insight into the depraved condition of the Roman Court.

### SIR EDWARD CARNE TO MARY.

*Orig.* St. P. Off. *Italian States.* 9th Sept. 1555. *Calais.*

" Pleaseth your most excellent Majesty to be advertised, that since my letters of the 2nd of this, addressed to the same, the occurrents here be no other, but the self-same persons that I wrote of then do remain yet in Castle Angell. The cause why the Cardinal de Sancto-flore is there was declared before all the Cardinals by the Pope's holiness to be that it should be for disobedience; but the rumour is, that there be other matters laid to his charge that should touch the Pope's own person, but I can hear no certainty thereof.

" As for Signor Camillo de Colonna, as I am credibly informed, there is laid to his charge the murder of a lady called Signora Livia, that his son should murder in her bed the last Shrovetide here, her daughter and heir being married to the same that slew her. The Count Michael Angell, and he that was treasurer to Pope July the III, be yet also in prison.

" This last week the Pope hath sent out of Castle Angelo divers great pieces of artillery, which went towards the state of the Colonnas. The saying is that the Pope will have no strongholds within the lands of the Church but his own. He himself looketh better now than he did when he was Cardinal, as they say that saw him then; but now he looketh stoutly, and better than he did at my first coming hither.

"He hath banished the Cardinal of Ferrara out of the lands of the Church, for because, as I hear, of the death of Pope Marcellus, whereof he should be suspected. I hear that the said Cardinal made great labour to come to his answer, but I cannot hear that the Pope will hear of it.

"There is proclamation made here that all the armour that any man hath here in the city should be brought to the Capitol, except sword and dagger; which is thought very strange here.

"Other occurrents here be none that I can hear of. And thus I beseech Almighty God to conserve your Majesty in long and prosperous life.

"From Rome, the 9th of Sept. 1555.

"Your Majesty's most humble servant and poor subject,

"EDWARD CARNE."

It has been observed by Sir James Macintosh, that Philip, when the prospect of having children by Mary became visionary, hastened to quit England, and afterwards "disregarded the affairs of a turbulent people, upon whom he had no hold but the slight thread of the life of a hypochondriacal woman.*" Here this eloquent writer has been

* History of England, vol. ii. p. 335.

led into error.  Although Philip quitted England, he constantly corresponded with the Privy
Council, received long despatches from them, and
replied to them at equal length.   No affair of
any public importance was determined without
his being consulted ; the minutes of the meetings
of the Privy Council were translated into Latin
and transmitted to him at Brussels: these he
seems to have read with much attention ; having
made his remarks, likewise in Latin, he sent
them back to the Council, and they still remain
in the State Paper Office, with the King's notes
on the margin.   Instead, therefore, of disregarding
the affairs of England, he continued, though absent, to take an active interest, and exercise a con-
trolling influence upon public matters.   The following brief extracts, translated from the original,
and selected from a larger mass of letters and state
papers, will amply justify this assertion, and may
lead the future historian of England to consult
authentic documents.

MATTERS DONE AND EXPEDITED IN THE COUN-
CIL OF THE KINGDOM OF ENGLAND FROM THE
TIME OF THE DEPARTURE OF OUR SERENE
AND POWERFUL KING.

*Orig.* St. P. Off.   Sept. 1555.

" Things expedited after the beginning of September.

PHILIP'S REMARKS.

" On Sunday in Sep-
tember the preacher at
St. Paul's Cross read
publicly the bull of con-
firmation of those rights
regarding the alienation
of church property, which
were granted in his in-
dulgence by the Reve-
rend Lord Legate in the
last parliament.

" It was ordered that
this bull be printed both
in Latin and English, so
that the people may be
admonished not to give
ear to such seditious ru-
mours as are scattered
here and there." * * *

" This seems to be
well done."

212

" Things proposed in Council, but not yet carried into effect.

" A discussion took place regarding the abrogation of the statute concerning first - fruits and perpetual tenths exigible by the clergy, concerning the confirmation of the grants of ecclesiastical benefices made by the crown, with the intent that they should be brought back to their original ecclesiastical uses."
\*    \*

" It appears to the King that all these matters ought to be treated by a Council of eight select Councillors ; and, when they have canvassed the matter, they should then inform the King's Majesty, who will communicate his decision to them.    And as his Majesty, for his earnest love to the kingdom of England, is anxious that all things which concern its welfare should conveniently be provided for, he desires also that nothing should be proposed in parliament without its having been first communicated to his Majesty, in order that he may signify his opinion, when the time fixed for the convocation of the parliament permits it."

## MINUTES OF COUNCIL TRANSMITTED TO PHILIP.

*Orig.* St. P. Off. *Domestic.* Sept. 1555.

PHILIP'S REMARKS.

" As it appears from the letters and the information of the captains of our ships that the greater ships, and even some of the smaller, are so shattered and damaged by the winds and tempests to which they have been exposed, that without imminent peril they can no longer be kept at sea; it is resolved that such ships as are so damaged shall be brought into the Thames and repaired with all speed, that to the crews of the other ships which are still seaworthy there should be added a sufficient number of the best mariners and soldiers selected from the whole fleet, and that the straits between Dover and Ca-

" As to the ships, the King agrees with what is stated in the first head. But as his Majesty understands that England's chief defence depends upon its navy being always in good order to serve for the defence of the kingdom against all invasion, it is right the ships should not only be fit for sea, but instantly available. And, as the passage out of the river Thames is not an easy one, the vessels ought to be stationed at Portsmouth, from which they can much more easily be brought into service.

" The King is the more inclined to this, because the Emperor has determined to sail for Spain about the end of October or the beginning of November, and has expressed a wish that twelve or fourteen English ships should accompany his fleet beyond Ushant.

lais should be guarded by these ships." This circumstance makes his Majesty the more anxious that these ships should be ready and in the best condition ; so that, besides other necessary uses, they may go upon this service, which will be especially grateful to his Highness."

### SIR EDWARD CARNE TO THE COUNCIL.

*Orig.* St. P. Off. *Italian States.* 30th Nov. 1555.

" Pleaseth your most honourable Lordships to be advertised that yesterday in the consistory the process made there against Mr. Cranmer, the late unworthy Archbishop of Canterbury, was referred by the most reverend Cardinal de Puteo, who showeth himself very ready to further the King and the Queen's most excellent Majesties' suit therein, and so declareth to be in all other ; and declared certain translations of the heresies comprised in the books sent hither, and acknowledged by the said Cranmer to be his own work and doing. The next consistory sentence shall be given ; the citations shall be observed in the contradicts the mean season.

" Upon Wednesday last in the consistory then holden, which dured long, and occupied with the French Cardinals, viz. Lorain and Tournon, first the Pope's Holiness made a long oration upon the overture of the French King, with commendation also of the Emperor's Majesty, and also of the King's Majesty, but of the Queen's Majesty above all. The effect thereof was the overture of all variance to be put in his Holiness' hands; and, for opening the French King's mind therein, referred him to the French Cardinals last come : whereupon the Cardinal Lorain made a solemn and eloquent oration, wherein he did not only commend his own master, but extolled both the Emperor and the King's Majesties, attributing unto them as much virtue as need be required in such mighty and noble princes, and the Queen's most excellent Majesty of all worldly queens most worthy. The effect was in the end to declare that readiness in the French King to abide his Holiness' order in all these points that I wrote to the Queen's most excellent Majesty the 25th of this; that is, to put war and peace in his Holiness' hands, and that he shall be sure of his aid in all his troubles, and to observe such order as he should think good to determine for reformation of the church.

" The Marquis de Marignian is departed to God, whose soul God pardon! Other occurrents here be none. * *

" Your most humble poor beadman,

" EDWARD CARNE."


We have seen that, during Mary's reign, Sir William Cecil held no official situation ; and, although he kept up his connection with court and

his powerful friends there, he devoted much of his
time to rural affairs and the improvement of his
estate.    The lands of Burghley belonged to his
mother; but, from her advanced age, she seems to
have committed the chief management of them to
her son.    He built an addition to the old house
there, and he possessed besides many church lands
which had been bestowed on him by Edward the
Sixth; to the cultivation of which we have seen, by
the minute accounts he has left, he paid the most
scrupulous attention.    He seems to have employed
the priests or vicars of his various benefices as his
land  stewards  and  superintendents  of  country
affairs.    The following letter from Sir John Abraham, one of these pluralists, is amusing, from
the rural scenes it brings before us, and the quaint
style in which they are described.    Sir John and
Mr. Alen's man selecting the ewes *alternis vicibus,*
— his eulogium on their plump appearance, — the
chestnuts and apple kernels sown in the place
which Cecil had himself chosen for them,—the care
taken of the swans,—the interest expressed for the
fawns, and the affectionate minuteness with which
he describes their life and conversation, sometimes
in the farm-court, sometimes in the orchard, sometimes following the maidens when they go to milk
in the fields,—are all pleasant traits; giving us a
glimpse into the rural life of England at this period, and bringing out one of the finest points in
the character of the great statesman to whom the

letter is addressed, — his relish for the simple and
rational pursuits of planting, farming, and garden-
ing. But perhaps the most amusing part of the
letter is Sir John Abraham's desponding reflections
on the inscrutable depths and changes of old Mrs.
Cecil's heart, which last year had been fixed on removing to Stamford, and now would be satisfied
with nothing but the oak-field at Burghley for herself and her four calves.

### SIR JOHN ABRAHAM TO SIR WILLIAM CECIL.

*Orig. Lansdowne.* 3. 56. 12th Dec. 1556.

" *Deus misereat nostri, et benedicat nobis !*— My
duty remembered, and most humbly premised, unto
your Worship.—Advertising your Worship, that
upon Thursday the 26th of Nov. I was with Mr.
Alen his men at Wywell, where I did draw three-
score ewes *alternis vicibus,* I one and his man another, which are fair, good, large, and young. I
would that I had so many like to them for xvi*li.*
xiii*s.* iiii*d.* ; what your price is I know not.

" I have received by Mr. Lacy's man seventeen
chestnuts, which were set the second day of this
month with those that Emley brought, and twenty-
eight that a stranger brought, in the place where
your Worship appointed. Kernels of apples and
of pears shall not be unsown as the s[ame] may
be gotten, and as the time may serve ; neither other
things undone that your Mastership requireth to
be done, as the time shall require, by God's help.

There are four swans in Ledyng, whereof two are but lately put in, ten days ago. * * * * *

" I cannot as yet, neither by myself, neither by any other, make any bargain for any grain but two semes of wheat that Lawrence hath bought. I trust it will be cheaper at our next Easter than now, or else many will die of hunger. Our Lord God be merciful to us, and make the hearts of the rich both pitiful and liberal unto the poor !

" Your fawns do well, and are sometimes in the court, sometimes on the back-side, and sometimes they go into the closes when the maidens go to milk, and sometimes in the orchard. When the snow shall be gone, I mean to put them with your calves in the horse pasture, that we may keep them there, for they are wild still. * * * *

" Your Mastership hath written to me to let you understand what cattle my Mistress your mother hath at Burghley, and what she meaneth to do with them at the next spring. Your Mastership shall understand that, besides four calves, she hath none but in her own close, neither will have any afore the spring time ; but then she saith that she trusteth that ye will be contented to let her have the oak close, a strange alteration of mind ; for at the first she was very desirous to go to Stamford, and to leave Burghley with the pertinents for a rent sufficient, and now anew to covet part which cannot be spared ! ' *O quam inscrutabile est cor humanum, veriùs fœmineum !*' Of this matter she hath written to your Mastership. I pray God that it be so that both your Mastership and she may be contented. God bring it to pass that it may be to your Mastership's worship, both now and here-after.

" Your Mastership's answer to my Mistress your mother, made in such sort as your wisdom can best devise, shall in few words finish this matter, whereof my fond brains make so many doubts whether it shall be to grant it or to deny it.

" Thus I will leave off to trouble your Mastership any longer, and will pray God long to pre-serve your Mastership and my good Lady in health, grace, and peace, with increase of much worship.

" At Burleigh, by your servant, the 12th of De-cember. ABRAHAM."

*This letter is endorsed by Cecil himself,*
" Sir John Abraham, 12th December 1556."
*It is addressed*
" To the Right Worshipful and my very good master Sir William Cecil, Knight, give these at Canon Row."

I have already explained that it was not my intention to add to the voluminous collections, regarding the religious history of this period, which have been accumulated by the labours of former writers ; and such is the dark and dreadful picture of persecution which it presents, that I gladly escape from the task. For two years, Mary's government had been comparatively lenient; but during the latter portion of her reign her policy was completely changed, and from the month of February 1555-6, till within four days of her death,* those flames were kindled in which nearly three hundred victims were consumed. To ascribe all this to the personal cruelty of the Queen would be unjust, as on other subjects her natural temper and disposition were neither harsh nor austere; but we are not to wonder, that these fires should have impressed upon the national mind an indelible hatred for the Government which could advise, and the Sovereign who could sanction, such proceedings.

In turning from the religious to the civil history of the country during the concluding years of Mary, or in casting our eye from this to the royal pair who presided over its destinies, we find little else than disaster and unhappiness. A marriage of devoted attachment on the part of the Queen was repaid by coldness and severity from her husband; and, notwithstanding a partial triumph experienced by England in the defeat of the French army at St. Quentin, the war ended ingloriously with the loss of Calais.

The following letter of the Earl of Bedford was written to Sir William Cecil immediately after the battle of St. Quentin.

* Turner, p. 284.—Wilkins, Concilia, vol. iv. p. 174.

### EARL OF BEDFORD TO SIR WILLIAM CECIL.

*Orig.* St. P. Off.   Sept. 3rd, 1557.

" RIGHT WORSHIPFUL.   After my very hearty commendations.—These are to signify unto you that there are no great news to write you at this time, but of the great victory the King's Majesty hath had in getting of the town, whereof ye are already thoroughly instructed; but, for my part, I have not seen the like in all my life.   The *sault* was soon won, and with the loss of no great number ; but the slaughter was in the town about the spoil.   The Swartzrotters, being masters of the King's whole army, used such force, as well to the Spaniards, Italians, and all other nations, as unto us, that there was none could enjoy nothing but themselves. They have now showed such cruelty, as the like hath not been seen for greediness : the town by them was set a-fire, and a great piece of it burnt; divers were brent in cellars, and were killed immediately ; women and children gave such pitiful cries, that it would grieve any Christian heart. Now, whether we shall to some other new siege, or tarry the fortifying of this that we have gotten, and so break up our camp, we do not as yet know.

" Thus, having nothing else but my hearty commendations to my Lady, I even bid you both most heartily farewell.

" From our camp beside St. Quentin, the 3rd of
Sept. 1557.
                    " Yours always to command,
                              " F. BEDFORD."


Let us turn, for a moment, from the flames and
din of war to honest Sir Philip Hoby and his preparations for a blazing hearth and a happy circle
at Christmas.

The following invitation to Sir W. Cecil, in
which we meet Lady Cecil and her little daughter
Anne, under the familiar and endearing name of
*Tannikin*, is a happy specimen of the easy episto-
lary style of the times.


### SIR PHILIP HOBY TO SIR WILLIAM CECIL.

*Orig.* ST. P. OFF. *Domestic.* Nov. 30, 1557.

" AFTER my hearty commendations. — I have
perceived by my brother that you will not be here
at Bysham this Christmas but as guest-wise, and
that my Lady will not then he here with you; all
which I know doth come of my Lady because she
cannot leave little *Tannikyn* her daughter. You
know how long it is since I did enjoy you ; and, if
you now deprive me and this good assembly of
your company at that time, I must think it so
great a sin as cannot be either forgotten now, or
forgiven hereafter ; and, in your so doing, you shall
be the occasion why I shall not have here him
whom I so much desire, and to whom I am so

much bound, namely, Mr. Mildemay and my Lady his wife; and yet for no such strange thing or great cheer that here is to be had, but because Mr. Mason and my Lady have promised to be with me, who will make us all merry.

" I pray you desire my Lady to come, and to bring *Tannikin* with her ; and I hope so to provide for her and her nurse, as all the house shall be merry, and she notwithstanding at her own ease and quiet.

" I look for no nay hereunto ; but, remembering how long it is since we last met, so long it must be ere we depart after our next meeting, to make amends for that that is past, and especially at this time of the year.   And till then I bid you both farewell.

" From Byssham, this last of Nov. 1557.

" Your own, as ye know,

" PHILIP HOBY."

" To the Right Worshipful and my very
   good friend Sir William Cecil, at Wimble-
   ton, or London, or elsewhere."
Endorsed in Cecil's hand,  " 30 Nov. 1557."

The unfortunate Queen, who had never enjoyed good health, was seized with a recurrence of her constitutional disease in October 1558; and, strange to say, misled by her desire for children, once more suffered herself to be deluded by the idea that she was about to have it gratified.   At this juncture, when all who knew any thing of Mary's real state

despaired of her recovery, Philip, who was in
Flanders with his army, despatched the Count de
Feria into England with secret instructions to
Mary, Cardinal Pole, and Don Juan de Figueroa,
Regent of the Council of Aragon, a nobleman
much in his confidence.   An interesting account of
this mission, drawn up from the original papers and
letters preserved at Simancas, has been given by
Gonzales in the Transactions of the Royal Historical Academy of Madrid.*   It appears that the
Count de Feria arrived in London on the 9th of November 1558.   He had been instructed by Philip to
congratulate Mary on her pregnancy, which the
King declared to be the best piece of news he had
received since his grief for the loss of Calais; but
the Count learnt on his arrival that the unfortunate
Queen was despaired of both by her English and
Spanish physicians.   He saw her, however, and she
seemed much pleased with his mission, but was unable to read the King's letter.   It has generally been
believed that Mary had never ceased to entertain
the strongest personal aversion for Elizabeth ; and
Carte, an author whose character of this Queen
has more in it of railing than history, asserts that
she hated this Princess, and would have excluded

* Memorias de la Real Academia de la Historia ; Madrid,
1832; tom. vii. p. 248.—I am indebted to the polite and kind
attention of Mr. Henry Howard of Corby, not only for an
opportunity of examining this work, which is rare, and for his
own abstracts, of which I have availed myself, but for the

her had it been practicable.*   We learn, however, from the indisputable evidence of a letter written by one of Philip's confidential councillors, who had visited Mary in her last illness, very shortly before her death, that, so far from showing hatred, she expressed herself much pleased † when he proposed that Elizabeth should be publicly declared her successor; only adding two requests to her parliament,—the first, that they would pay her debts; the second, that they would maintain the old religion.‡

Having paid his respects to his dying sovereign on the 9th, the Count de Feria aware that Mary was sinking fast, turned his gaze towards the rising sun, and in obedience to the instructions of Philip waited on the Princess Elizabeth.   His account of the interview, as it is abridged by Gonzales, is well worthy of notice.

He informs us that on the 10th of November he went thirteen miles from London, to where Elizabeth resided, in the house of a certain nobleman, whose name he omits.   She received him well, although not so warmly as on some other occasions. He supped with the Princess, and with the wife of

communication of other manuscript papers copied from originals, during his researches both in England and on the continent.   I regret that the advanced state of my printed sheets prevents me at present from giving any selections.

* Carte, Hist. of England, vol. iii. p. 353.
† *Muy Contenta.*
‡ Gonzales, p. 253.

the High-Admiral Lord Clinton, who was in company with her; and after supper opened his discourse, according to the private instructions which he had received in Philip's own hand. The Princess had then three ladies with her: she told the Count they understood nothing but English; to which he answered, that he would be well pleased if the whole world heard what he had got to say.

Elizabeth expressed herself much gratified by the Count's visit, and the message which he brought from Philip. She acknowledged the high obligations which she owed to him when she was in prison; but seemed to receive rather more dubiously the discourse of the Count when he endeavoured to persuade her that the declaration of her right to the crown was the work, neither of Mary nor the Council, but solely of his royal master. Having given these few particulars of the meeting, De Feria adds the opinion he had formed of the character of Elizabeth. " It appears to me," says he, addressing the King, " that she is a woman of extreme vanity, but acute. I would say that she must have great admiration for the King her father's mode of carrying on matters. I fear much that in religion she will not go right, as I perceive her inclined to govern by men who are held to be heretics; and they tell me that the ladies who are most about her are all so. Besides this, she shows herself highly indignant at the things done against her in the lifetime of the Queen. She is much attached to the people, and is very confident that they are all on her side (which is indeed true); indeed she gave me to understand that the people had placed her where she now is.  On this point she will acknowledge no obligations either to your Majesty or to her nobles, although she says they have one and all of them sent her their promise to remain faithful.  Indeed, there is not a heretic or traitor in all the country who has not started as if from the grave to seek her with expressions of the greatest pleasure." *

The Count de Feria proceeds to enumerate those Councillors who, as far as he could collect from Elizabeth's remarks, were most in her favour, as well as those who were not in her good graces. Amongst the first class, her favourites, he includes some of our old friends, whom we have seen in more coats than one during the course of these letters,—Paget, Petre, Wotton, and Sir John Mason. He adds : " I am told for certain that Cecil, who was Secretary to King Edward, will be her Secretary also.  He has the character of a prudent and virtuous man, although a heretic."†

From this visit to her who, although not yet a Queen, already acted as if she felt herself one, let us turn for a moment to the deathbed of Mary. On the 16th of November at midnight she received extreme unction, and early in the morning, mass was celebrated in her chamber.  She listened with that

* Gonzales, pp. 254, 255.         Ib. 256, 257.

deep devotion which had marked her whole life, —
appeared perfectly sensible, — and at six o'clock, a
few minutes before the conclusion of the service, she
expired.*   It was a remarkable circumstance that
Cardinal Pole, who had been confined with a fever
during the Queen's sickness, died only twenty-four
hours after the Queen.  Gardiner's death had taken
place in 1555; so that England, delivered from the
dominion of those who deemed persecution for religion a Christian duty, began to breathe anew, an-
ticipating rest and deliverance.   After what has
been already said, it is superfluous to add any reflections on the personal character of Mary.   Amid
the exaggerated praises of the Roman Catholic writers, and the high-wrought invectives of their Protestant opponents, the calm and unprejudiced decision of Bishop Godwin, himself a Protestant, is perhaps the nearest to the truth.  " She was a lady very
godly, merciful, chaste, and every way praisewor-
thy, if you regard not the errors of her religion."*

* Gonzales. p. 256.
† " Mulier sane pia, clemens, moribusque castissimis, si reli-
gionis errorem non spectes."   I have used the old translation,
London, 1630, p. 340.

## L'Envoy.

And now, to address thee after the old and kindly fashion,—

MOST GENTLE READER. —These ancient Letters, and with them the Author who hath endeavoured to demonstrate their value, must bid thee farewell. To him they have been pleasant companions; nay, instructive friends. May they be so to thee. May they inspire thee with that passion for the search of Truth amid the ruins and relics of days long gone by, than which, if thou wilt credit an old angler in these Lethean pools, there are few happier employments. Trust him when he tells thee, it is to wander with a pure object through a pleasant country. In the journey thou wilt be led on by the hope of discovery, and cheered by the feeling of progression; the difficulties thou meetest will be but so many little hills, on surmounting which, a sweeter and a sweeter valley, or forest glade, or ivy-covered castle, will open to thy ken; the search, too, will teach thee many a lesson of charity and self distrust; thou wilt become a lover of History, not from any lower motive, but for its own sake; and she—I mean the fair Muse, to whom historic truth is dear—will, like a generous mistress, repay thy devotion by meeting thee — not, in the saloons of the great, or the ambitious circles of the learned; but alone, in thine own library, the scholar's true palladium. There, whilst the fire burns brightly, and warms the pictured wall, and casts its ruddy glow on thy books, those dear mute friends, will she sit and teach thee her secrets; some of which, but ah! how far too few, she hath deigned to impart to him who now closes his imperfect labours.

" May she be yet more liberal to thee, my gentle Friend; may she make thee, shouldst thou be ever tempted to intrust thy researches to the envious world, independent of all the ills of authors, steel proof against the stings of critics, thy days untainted by the breath of envy, thy nights unvisited by dreams of invaded or expiring copyrights; thyself and thy works triumphant over that which hath been pronounced the worst disease which can seize the body bibliographic — " an impeded circulation."

# INDEX.

## A.

ABRAHAM, Sir John, his letter to Sir William Cecil, ii. 489.

Admiral Lord High, of England; see Seymour, Thomas.

Adrian, a favourite of the Emperor Charles V, notice of him, ii. 134, n.

Africa, or Mahadia, capture of the town of, i. 328.

Agricola, John, the composition of "The Interim" imputed to him, i. 85; see Interim.

Albert, Duke, Margrave of Brandenburgh, joins the Emperor of Germany in his war against the Protestant Princes, i. 8; his engagements with the Elector Maurice and the Protestant Princes, 265; defeated at Siverhausen, 266; his personal appearance, ii. 144; unites his army with the Emperor's, 145; defeated by the Elector Maurice at the battle of Siverhausen, 216; escapes to Hanover, 218.

Alford, Mr. Roger, his account of Secretary Cecil's signing the will reversing the succession, ii. 172; extract from his letter respecting Cecil, 202.

Anabaptists, number of, resort to England, i. 260; many of them taken in a wood at Ghent, 379.

Andelot, Seigneur d', (Francis Coligni,) account of him, i. 36, n.

Arran, Earl of, appointed Regent of Scotland during the minority of Mary Queen of Scots, i. 4; his attempts to retain the governorship of Scotland, in opposition to Mary of Guise, 354.

Arras, Granvelle Bishop of, account of his reception of Sir R. Morysine, ii. 133.

Arundel, Thomas Earl of, favour shown to, by the Duke of Somerset, ii. 29; imprisoned for his connection with the Duke's conspiracy, 37. 42; Crane's information against him, 38; his confession, 43; account of his taking leave of the Duke of Northumberland, ii. 200; of his arrest of the Duke, 208; reflections on his conduct, 209.

Ascham, Roger, his description of the Landgrave of Hesse, i. 61; of the Elector of Saxony, 62; his pun respecting Pope Julius III, 305, n.; extract from one of his Latin letters, 343; character and account of him, ii. 120; origin of his work "The Schoolmaster," 122; extracts from his Journal, 123; his description of the court of the Queen Dowager of France at Brussels, 125; of the appearance of Albert Margrave of Brandenburgh, 144; his narrative respecting Lady Jane Grey in his "Schoolmaster," 294.

Aubespine, Monsieur Claude de l', account of him, ii. 99, n.

Audley, John Lord, his letter to Sir W. Cecil, ii. 169.

Augsbourg, a Diet assembled at, to settle the religious contentions in Germany, i. 259, ii. 211; opening of, i. 311; liberty of conscience granted by the Diet to the Lutheran Protestants, ii. 213; confession of, see Confession.

Aumale, Duke d', his anxiety to have a portrait of King Edward VI, i. 330.

Austria, account of the rise of the house of, i. 4, 5; European powers jealous of, 6.

Aylmer, Bishop, his eulogium on the Princess Elizabeth of England, i. 69.

## D.

## E.

hailed as the harbinger of peace in
France, ii. 211; his embassy to
England on the accession of Queen
Mary, 237; his paper of instruction respecting Queen Mary's assumption of the title *Supreme Head
of the Church*, 243; the Emperor
Charles's jealousy of him, 300; his
suspicions of him respecting the
marriage between Philip II. and
Queen Mary, 245; his reception
in France, 360; his conversation
with Thomas Stafford, 363; with
Sir John Mason, 451; his arrival
and reception in England, 461;
absolves the nation from heresy,
restores it to Holy Church, 462;
his letter to the Earl of Warwick,
i. 165.

—— Jeffrey, brother to the Cardinal,
his conversation with Sir John Masone, i. 314.

Popes, see Paul III. Julius III.
Marcellus II. Paul IV.

Poynet, Bishop of Winchester, his
opinion of his predecessor, Bishop
Gardiner, i. 109.

Proclamation respecting the conspiracy against the Protector, i.
205.

Protestants, increased number of in
Germany, i. 6; the Emperor's project for their subjugation, 7; liberty
of conscience granted to the Lutheran Protestants by the Diet of
Augsbourg, ii. 213.

—————— religion, abolished in England on Queen Mary's accession,
ii. 244.

Prisoners, report of the prisoners in
the Tower in 1549, i. 268; list of
the persons imprisoned for the conspiracy of the Duke of Somerset, ii.
37.

Privy Council, letter from, to the
justices of the peace, ii. 33.

## R.

Rebellion in England, under the Protectorate, i. 176, 177; the Protector's answer to the insurgents,
178; rebellion on the projected
marriage between Queen Mary and
Philip II, ii. 278. 280. 282.

Renard, Simon, his embassy to England from the Emperor Charles V,

ii. 299; his jealousy of Bishop
Gardiner and Cardinal Pole, 300;
ambassador from the Emperor
Charles V. to Queen Mary, 365;
his account of the discussions respecting the Princess Elizabeth and
Courtenay, Earl of Devonshire,
365, 366. 375; of the Queen's
opening parliament, 367; his suspicions of Sir John Masone, 369;
his account of the divisions in the
Council, 372; of the trial of Sir N.
Throckmorton, 374; his conversation with the Queen respecting the
precautions necessary upon the
arrival of Philip II, 376; his account of the discovery of a packet
of the French ambassador relating
to Courtenay and the Princess
Elizabeth, 383; his letters to—the
Emperor Charles V, 302. 306.
313. 336. 371. 383. 388. 392. 398.
405. 411. 413. 415. 419; Philip
Prince of Spain, 332. 378; letters
to him from Sir W. Paget, 381.

Renty, castle of, besieged by the
French, ii. 212.

Rheims, Charles de Guise, Bishop of,
(Cardinal Lorraine,) character and
description of him, i. 44.

Rich, Lord Chancellor, his character, i. 199; letter to Sir W. Cecil, *ib*.

Ridley, Bishop of London, his cha-
racter, i. 428; kindness to Bishop
Bonner's mother, 429; his letter to
Cecil, 430.

Rochlitz, battle at between the Protestants and Catholics, i. 10.

Roman Catholic party in England,
triumph of, after the fall of the Protector, i. 255.

Russell, Lord, his communications
respecting Lord Thomas Seymour's
treason, i. 142, 143; defeats the
rebels at Exeter, 195; his defec-
tion from the Protector, 216; his
letter to him, 217; to the Council
at London, 231.

## S.

St. André, Monsieur le Marechal, his
embassy to England from Henry II.
of France, i. 409.

St. Quenten, defeat of the French army
at, ii. 492.

Thou, M. de, his account of Charles
V. at the battle of Mulhberg, i. 54;
of his interview with the Elector of
Saxony, 55; his account of the
battle of Siverhausen, ii. 217; of
the elector Maurice's death, 219.

Throckmorton, Sir N., his trial and
acquittal, ii. 374.

Thynne, Sir John, his letters to Sir
W. Cecil, i. 318.

Toleration in religion, absence of
during the reigns of Elizabeth and
Mary, ii. 210.

Tournon, Cardinal, character and account of him, i. 37, n.

Tower, report of the prisoners confined in, in 1549, i. 268.

Turner, Dr. William, a puritan minister, remarks on his " Dialogue
against the Mass," i. 332; on his
advice to Secretary Cecil, 333; on
his persecutions by his clerical
brethren, 372; his letter to Sir W.
Cecil, 333. 272.

Turkey, account of a domestic tragedy
in, ii. 275, n.

### V.

Vane, Sir Ralph, sent to the Tower
for his concern in Somerset's conspiracy, ii. 17.

Vega, John de, Viceroy of Sicily, one
of the commanders of the expedition
to the town of Africa, i. 328, n.

### W.

Warwick, John Dudley, Viscount
Lisle, Earl of, (afterwards Earl of
Northumberland,) account of him,
i. 26; notice of his intrigues for the
overthrow of the Protector Somerset, 175; appointed to command
the expedition against the rebels in
1549, 193; completely defeats them
at Dussindale, 195; conspirators
against the Protector assemble at
his residence, 204; he proclaims the
Protector Somerset a traitor, 211;
course of his intrigues against him,
235; plan to procure his arrest, 241;
presents himself to the King at
Windsor, 243; his proceedings
against the Protector, 246; his ambitious spirit, 255; embarrassment

in regard to France, 256; nego-
tiates with the French minister for
the delivering up Boulogne to
France, 257; account of the increase of his power, 261; notice of
his ambitious plans after the death
of King Edward, 267; appointed
Lord High Admiral, 273; his conspiracy to ruin the Duke of Somerset, ii. 2; remarks on his system
of secret information, 20; his conference with R. Whalley respecting
Somerset, 21; communications
with Cecil, 25; appointed to the
wardenship of the northern borders, 28; created Duke of Northumberland, 30; remarks on his
character, 103; on the friendship
between him and Cecil, 110; death
of his daughter, 114; the reformer
Knox's opinion of him, 147; his
acknowledgment of the Protestant
faith, 148; his plan regarding the
bishopric of Durham, 151; remarks on the hypocrisy of his
character, 154; procures the reversion of the succession in favour of Lady Jane Grey, 164;
attempts a reconciliation between
France and Germany, 177; his
proceedings on the death of Edward VI, 186; informs Lady
Jane Grey of her succession to the
throne, 188; proceeds against
Mary's army in person, 190; his
failure and arrest for treason, 191;
plots of Cecil and the Council
against him, 197. 201; his trust
in the Council, 199; account of his
arrest, 207; his trial in Westminster Hall, 223; his questions
to the Court, ib.; speech after his
sentence, 225; his execution, 226;
further particulars respecting him,
227. 229; his open confession to
the people on the scaffold, 230;
his letter to—Sir W. Paget, i. 28;
Sir W. Cecil, 193. 198. 428;
ii. 103, 104, 110, 111.115. 142.
148. 152. 154. 158; the Lord
Chamberlain, 108. 112. 115. 160;
letters to him from—the Bishop of
Winchester, i. 108; Cardinal Pole,
165.

Westminster, Dr. Thirlby, Bishop of,
ambassador to Germany, super-
seded by Sir P. Hoby, i. 98; his
interview with the Emperor Charles,

THE END.

LONDON :

PRINTED BY SAMUEL BENTLEY,
Dorset Street, Fleet Street.

13014129R00303

Printed in Poland
by Amazon Fulfillment
Poland Sp. z o.o., Wrocław